A Companion

to Local History

Research

A
Companion
to
Local History
Research

John Campbell-Kease

Alphabooks

A & C Black · London

© John Campbell-Kease 1989

First published 1989 by Alphabooks Ltd,
Sherborne, Dorset, a subsidiary
of A & C Black (Publishers) Ltd
35 Bedford Row, London WC1R 4JH

ISBN 0 7136 3145 7

A CIP catalogue record for this book
is available from the British Library.

*Title page illustration: The Court of the
King's Bench in the fifteenth century. The five
presiding judges sit at the top.*

Phototypesetting by L.P.& T.S. Typesetting, Langport, Somerset

Reproduced, printed and bound in Great Britain by
Hazell Watson & Viney Limited
Member of BPCC Limited
Aylesbury, Bucks, England

Contents

Introduction

This book identifies and describes the principal material available for the study of local history, indicates where it may be found, and sets it against the broader framework of national, as well as regional, events, for without an appreciation of the wider scene parochial research can lose much of its interest and, ultimately, its value. In addition, the book provides information on a range of related subjects such as archaeology, architecture, place and field names, and palaeography (the study of ancient scripts and writing).

Many local histories, especially those published privately, are not really histories at all. They are most frequently collections of fairly readily obtained information culled at random from across the centuries with insufficient effort made to weave them into an interesting and coherent story. Each is, in fact, material towards a local history rather than a history proper. Sometimes rather too much space is devoted to the last hundred years or so, and but superficial and sporadic attention paid to preceding ages. Frequently geographical, economic, cultural and political factors are ignored, and scant attention paid to agricultural and industrial evolution, or the impact of national events, legislation and forces on the local scene.

Works of the kind described are not to be denigrated, for they probably gave their authors much pleasure at all stages of creation, but many suffer from less than thorough research, and, equally important, impatience, for when setting out on the task the author may not have appreciated just how much work was going to be involved. The researching and writing of a good local history will take at least five years. It will mean buying or borrowing *dozens* of books, chasing down footnotes in obscure journals, making journeys some of which will be lengthy, arranging for pictures and copies of maps and documents, but it will be very rewarding; and the place to start is at the beginning, with the first traces of the works of man.

This book is divided into a number of sections. The first outlines, from the perspective of the local historian, events in English history from the earliest times to the present day. The second identifies the main sources of information. These are, at national level, available through published works such as those listed in volumes issued by HMSO (Her Majesty's Stationery Office) under the headings *British National Archives* and *The Publications of the Royal Commission on Historical Documents*. Also in this class are nine (of the projected twelve) volumes *English Historical Documents* put out at intervals between 1953 and 1975. An auxiliary work is *An Introduction to the Use of the Public Records* by V.H. Galbraith (Oxford 1934), an invaluable, if slightly dated, guide. In addition, *The Victoria History of the Counties of England* (insofar as it has emerged from the press — see Appendix II), the *Inventories* (where they exist) of the

Royal Commission on Historical Monuments, and the *Monasticon Anglicanum* are discussed as vital sources. At local, as distinct from national, level, materials available through the National Register of Archives, local authority record offices, and estate papers' repositories are dealt with. The third section of the book, comprising eleven chapters, uses the time divisions set by *English Historical Documents* and discusses many of the records (from the earliest surviving written texts to present-day documents) which the local researcher will find essential. This section also employs the interpretive *Oxford History of England* (currently occupying sixteen volumes covering the time from the coming of the Romans until the present day).

In the penultimate section sixteen chapters are devoted to specialized topics and include, in addition to those already listed, geology and geography, the evolution of towns and villages, material prosperity, social development, surname patterns, heraldry, chronology, vocabularies and orthography (spelling), personal reference libraries, and archives and collections. The book ends with a short 'history' of a fictitious place, but using 'real' data, as a demonstration of a number of themes which may be tackled.

Author's note and acknowledgements

This is the book I looked for many years ago when I started to take an interest in local history. I had a broad knowledge of English economic history, the usual smattering of military history, but could not at that time tell a *hōc* from a handsaw. A study of English literature from Saxon times onwards had given more than a nodding acquaintance with bygone language and customs, but of local history I knew nothing.

My interest had been kindled initially by a deeply felt sense of irritation. I had recently moved to a large village with no obvious centre — the church was a mile from the village hall, the post office a mile from both, the pub was near none of these, and there was no village green. Equally importantly, there was no one in the locality who had any real idea of the history of the place or why such a multi-focal layout had come into being. A folk tradition (which later proved to be an invention of the early twentieth century) talked of a dispersal following the Black Death, but there was little else. No one knew whether any of the scattered settlements which made up the village had been mentioned in Domesday, whether any court rolls existed, or the name of the current holder of the 'lordship'. I determined to research the history, perhaps even write it, and so started from scratch. Local history literature in the reference library of the county town was plentiful, indeed several of the books are recommended in the pages of the present work. In addition to these valuable publications were lots of others, but they leapt from the simplistic to the arcane. There were the usual twenty-page pamphlets along the lines of 'You too can write the history of your parish' (census returns, a pointer towards Domesday, and yarns told by the older inhabitants), and obscure expositions on 'Celtic fields' or the use of quantitative methods for the analysis of social data, but not a general book of the kind I needed. Over the years I read many volumes, attended many lectures, and in such free time as was available studied local history in earnest. The problem of the village without a nucleus was solved — it was the developed pattern of very early Saxon farm clusters — and I wrote its history.

Today there are many books on local history, some of which are excellent, some not, but none is the book I looked for years ago. So I have written it myself in the hope it will be of value to those seeking to research the story of their town, village, parish or county and to place it in the great and wonderful jigsaw of English history. So many people have helped me over the years they cannot be named, but the following have permitted illustrations and charts to be reproduced. To them and all the others I am most grateful. Special thanks also to Sarah Bridges and Hugh Jaques of the Dorset Record Office, for untiring and inspired help. The publishers have made every effort to ascertain copyright of the illustrations used in this book. If any infringement has occurred, sincere apologies are offered, and correction will be made during reprinting.

B T Batsford 134; Bodleian Library, Oxford 79 (MS Hatton 20, f.34), 227 (MS Junius 11, p. 81); Janet and Colin Bord 13 (left); City of Bristol Record Office, ref 01250(1) (photo Royal Academy of Arts) 27; British Library 21, 71, 95, 104, 108, 118 (left); By courtesy of the Trustees of the British Museum 12, 84, 307; Buckinghamshire Record Office 243; Cambridge University Committee for Aerial Photography 29, 128, 208, 213, 221, 311; Chertsey Museum 285; Chippenham Civic Society 46, 287; Peter Crawley 309, 313; Crown copyright material in the Public Record Office, reproduced by permission of the Controller of Her Majesty's Stationery Office 59 (E372/20 rot.1), 61 (E198/1/2 rot. 4), 86, 88 (E31/2, f.299), 93 (E198/1/3), 261 (MH 12/4864); Pamela Cunnington 239, 317: Courtesy J M Dent & Son 201 (from Villages in the Landscape, T Rowley), 206 (from Landscape of Towns, M Aston & J Bond); Courtesy Dorset County Record Office 42 (BG/CC:X4/5/1, Christchurch Poor Law Union), 44 (D.60/ Z6, Bloxworth Estate Archive), 50 (D.204/CH8, Sherborne Almshouse Archive), 55, 65 (PE/ HAZ:RE1/1, Hazelbury Bryan Parish Records), 70 (D.124, Fox-Strangway/Ilchester Archives), 130 (D.204/A110, Sherborne Almshouse Archive), 136 (PE/WM:CP2/1/132, Wimborne Minster Parish Records), 175 (BG/CC:X4/5/1, Christchurch Poor Law Union), 182 (QDE(L): 17/39/12, Dorset Quarter Sessions), 186 (LA 3/8/5/8, Lieutenancy Records), 255, 265 (D.1/ MO3, Dorset Natural History & Archaeological Society); Courtesy Rt Hon John Max, Baron Egremont, and Professor Gordon Batho, 233; David Flinn 295 (2 samples); Trustees of the Goodwood Collection 32; Reproduced by kind permission of the Harris Museum & Art Gallery, Preston, Lancs, 223; Hereford City Museum 314; History Today Archives 141; Hulton Picture Library 147, 170; Keele University Library 262; Mansell Collection, title page, 45, 96, 118 (rt), 121, 180; Richard Muir 68, 231; Courtesy of Hugh, tenth Duke of Northumberland 155, 253, 271; Norwich Castle Museum, Norfolk Museum Service 132; Nottinghamshire County Library Service 235; The Gerald Pitman Sherborne Pictorial Record Collection 192; Ann Ronan Picture Library 260; Courtesy Royal Commission on the Historical Monuments of England 115, 205, 245, 298; L. Sayers 210; Courtesy RIBA (from The Builder, 1854) 189; William Salt Library, Stafford (ref 48/49) 163; Mick Sharp 10; The Sutcliffe Gallery 237; Museum and Art Gallery, Bath Road, Swindon 236 (top); Dept of Transport (SWRO), Courtesy MRM Partnership 197; Master and Fellows of Trinity College, Cambridge 106, 256; Wiltshire County Council 236 (bottom); Dean & Chapter of Worcester 120; York Archaeological Trust Picture Library 217. Line drawings by Peter Haillay 13 (rt), 14 (after fig. 199, Atlas of Anglo-Saxon England, D Hill, Blackwells), 15, 22 (after The Black Death, P Ziegler, Penguin Books), 24 (left: after fig. 129 Age of Chivalry, Royal Academy of Arts, right: after fig. p. 49 Chaucer's England, D Taylor, Dobson Books Ltd), 35 (after fig 68, Tudor England, P Lane, B T Batsford Ltd), 67, 99, 150, 157, 158, 183, 194, 240, 359, 369 (Institute of Historical Research, University of London).

Section I
OUTLINE HISTORY AND SOURCES FOR THE LOCAL HISTORIAN

1 Earliest times to 1066

The seventeenth-century metaphysician John Donne tells us in one of his *Meditations*, 'No man is an island, entire of itself; every man is a piece of the continent, a part of the main; if a clod be washed away by the sea, Europe is the less, as well as if a promontory were, as well as if a manor . . .'. So with any village, parish, borough, county town or city which is to be the subject of a written history. There is nowhere that can be written about in isolation, for each place is bounded by other places and the boundaries themselves are but accidents of history. Everything that happens in a place, everything that lies within it, has been shaped by, and is related to, things which occurred beyond. It is, therefore, quite impossible to write a good local history without some broad knowledge and appreciation of much greater events and forces — for these are enshrined in the names of the local settlements, streets and fields, in the layout of the village or town, in the occupations and attitudes of its people, in the workings of its local council.

Since this book is to be a companion to research about places in England, although not necessarily carried out by English people, a most important point to be made is the need for a good general appreciation of British and, later, English history. It is, of course, a fact that many English settlements are of post-Conquest foundation, and the written records of the vast majority of those of earlier date began after the upheavals of the years AD1066-9, but the history of the kingdom began long before that and, indeed, many of the civil administrative and ecclesiastical systems which the Normans used existed well before the Conquest. But we need to go back much further than this if a total picture is to be revealed. There are few places in England that have not at some time or other been the site of archaeological discoveries of a deliberate or accidental kind. Prehistoric animal remains, stone tools, weapons, pottery, burial grounds, body ornaments, coin boards, cultivation traces and other evidence of previous inhabitants have been found, studied, interpreted and placed in context. A discovery in one place has been related to a discovery in another, and together the finds have contributed to an understanding of the way man and his predecessors have lived since before the sheet ice finally retreated and a climate developed in which our ancestors could more easily flourish.

Local history becomes interesting, it may be suggested, from around 8000-6000BC, just after the sea had finally severed the land connection with continental Europe, when the people the archaeologists term Mesolithic began to seek to change their environment, rather than merely taking what it had to offer. It is true that at that time

Interior of a Neolithic house c.1600-1400BC. Although situated in a village at Skara Brae in Orkney, the construction is typical of the mainland period, and includes a stone box-bed and 'sideboard'.

11

and for three or four thousand years more these folk, and their successors the Neolithic, were largely nomadic, but evidence has been accumulating of their short-lived occupancy sites, their cultivation techniques, their religious practices and, later, their more permanent settlements. Some knowledge of all this will be of value to the local historian should any Stone Age remains be found in his particular area. As to how the knowledge may be gained, this is dealt with later in this chapter, for what is true of these early times is equally true of later prehistoric ages.

Around 1700BC, and for many centuries thereafter, new people were migrating to Britain. These Bronze Age folk — Matthew Arnold's 'dark Iberians' — had sailed up the Atlantic coast from what is now Spain and Portugal, and made landfall on the south coast of Britain. The newcomers were an advanced people with a great megalithic culture — they constructed Stonehenge around 1600BC — they were artists and traders, craftsmen in metal, peaceful and hard-working. They set up small communities with circular huts and farm 'yards', they cultivated grain, domesticated animals, wove simple woollen clothes and buried their dead in cinerary urns as well as graves. Evidence of their presence, ways of life and death is found widely in Britain from Cornwall in the south to Yorkshire and beyond in the north. In their turn they were succeeded by other newcomers.

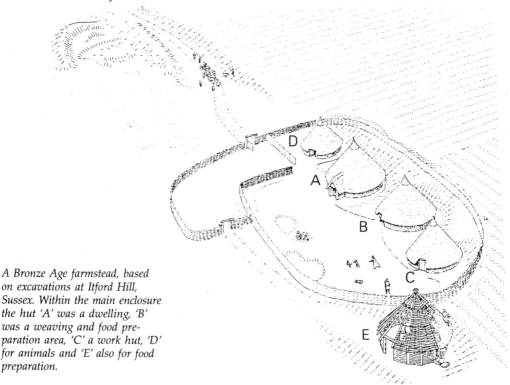

A Bronze Age farmstead, based on excavations at Itford Hill, Sussex. Within the main enclosure the hut 'A' was a dwelling, 'B' was a weaving and food preparation area, 'C' a work hut, 'D' for animals and 'E' also for food preparation.

In the first centuries before Christ, Celtic tribes, originally occupying northwestern Germany and the Netherlands, were moving across Europe and invading Britain in successive waves, subduing not only the Iberians but also any previous settlers of their own races. They were a tall, light-haired people, fiercely tied by bonds of kinship

LEFT *Burgh Castle, Norfolk, part of the Roman defences on the 'Saxon shore'.* ABOVE *The administrative divisions of Roman Britain based mainly on pre-Conquest tribal areas.*

under tribal chiefs. Justice was the justice of the clan; the aristocracy devoted itself to hunting and related pursuits, the lower orders carrying on such agriculture as was deemed necessary. But Celtic society was, at another level, diverse and included metal-workers, carpenters, herdsmen, fishermen and others who have left their traces throughout the land, for their widespread use of iron brought great prosperity of an enduring kind. The Celtic communities scattered wide, and Britain was settled, extensively cultivated and grazed, the people living wherever the land permitted (it must be remembered that much of Britain was still forest, marsh and swamp), establishing their circular-hutted hamlets, hill forts, burial mounds, mines, salt-workings, potteries and so on. Throughout their tenure they maintained powerful links with the Continent, trading with the Mediterranean and other areas. Petty kingdoms arose, and although these were belligerently independent of one another, Celtic Britain became a nuisance to Imperial Rome and at the same time a tempting prize, and, in AD43, the country was invaded by the legions of the Empire.

The Romans remained in their new province for almost four hundred years, to the time when *c.*AD410, the Emperor Honorius, plagued by heathen incursions, withdrew all support and left the *civitates* (Romano-British communities) to fend for themselves. During their period of dominion (which lasted the equivalent of the time between the coming of the Spanish Armada and the 1982 Falklands war) Britain was a part of the Imperium. Christianity came to Britain, the Romans built a road network, and established villa estates and towns (to all intents and purposes they founded London, even if its name *is* Celtic). True, they largely neglected Devon and Cornwall, and north of the Humber and Trent there were strong elements of Celto-Iberian tribalism. Wales was not much affected, but elsewhere stability was created and maintained. The valleys of the Trent and Thames were waterlogged, large areas of the Midlands were left to forest and fen, but governing towns such as Verulamium (on the west side of present-day St Albans in Hertfordshire), Colchester, Lincoln, Gloucester and York held jurisdiction over large rural areas. Today, archaeological exploration has revealed

13

a great deal about the Roman occupation — the run of the roads, the design and layout of their villas, farming methods, baths, temples, and town sites. The local historian should pay careful heed to any evidence of Roman habitation in his locality for it is very likely to have had a lasting impact on the way later settlements developed. And he may also find it useful to refer to the ancient classical Latin authors, a number of whose writings bear on the colonisation of Britain.

Starting about the year AD250, the presence of various Germanic races (broadly termed the 'Saxons') began to be felt, and over the next three hundred years they gradually gained footholds and then possession, the Romano-Celts retreating into the fastness of the Welsh mountains and other remote areas. There are no real chronicles of the Saxon conquest, the invaders had but a simple runic script which they used almost exclusively for ritualistic purposes. The world of the Britons was swept aside and from about AD350 to the coming of St Augustine in AD597 there are virtually no written records although, as will soon be described, there is a good deal of evidence of other kinds to be drawn on. The early Saxon period was one of great conflict, the rise of the petty kingdoms of the 'heptarchy' being followed by periods of supremacy of Mercia and then Wessex. From the middle of the seventh century, however, about the time of the overthrow of the militant heathen King Penda in AD654, an age of civilisation developed, an awareness of Latin and Greek grew, and organised learning was established by early missionaries. The age of King Inc, *c.*AD700, saw the codification of West Saxon law, and the reign of Alfred AD871-99, brought with it translations of the

LEFT *The major roads of the Anglo-Saxon period. The network linked the principal towns. The existence of a system of 'royal roads' (bold lines on the map) protected by royal prerogative no doubt enabled Harold to move quickly from Stamford Bridge to Hastings in October 1066. The fine dotted lines radiating from Droitwich represent the 'salt ways'.*

RIGHT *The kingdoms of England in the 8th century were in a state of flux and subject to conquest. By the end of the period only those names underlined seem to have maintained any degree of real autonomy.*

FAR RIGHT *The approximate boundaries of the dominion of Wessex, Mercia and the Danelaw. In broad terms, Wessex and Mercia were divided in to hundreds with sub-division of hides (sulungs in Kent), and the Danelaw into wapentakes with land units of carucates. There were, however, exceptions.*

books 'most necessary for all men to know'. A complex social order developed, and the countryside was divided up in accordance with it. By the tenth century scattered and nucleated settlements were clearly known by name and their boundaries were well established, as is plainly shown by the charters of the period. In Wessex the fundamental institutions of local government based on the geographical 'hundred' and the political and social folkmoot (*folcgemot*) had evolved, probably sometime prior to the reign of Edward the Elder (900-25). But we must go back a little.

From around the year AD800 the Vikings of the Scandinavian countries began raiding England, and over the next fifty or so years they achieved a position of such power that large portions of the eastern half of the country — from Buckingham, Middlesex, and Essex at the lower end to Yorkshire at the upper — fell totally under their sway and comprised the 'Danelaw'. It was only in the early tenth century that the kings of Wessex reconquered this territory to become the first rulers of the Anglo-Danish kingdom of all England. The local historian will be well advised to bear in mind the geographical position of the place being studied, for on this will depend not only the pre-Conquest administrative practices which prevailed, but the general social customs and the very language itself. The ways of, and terms used in, Wessex, Mercia and the Danelaw differed in important respects and the area covered by Northumberland, Lothian, Westmoreland and Cumberland lay outside all three.

In the late tenth century Wessex collapsed, and in 1016 the Scandinavian monarch Canute (Cnut), king of Denmark, Norway and the Hebrides accepted the English

throne, and the policies he adopted gradually reconciled the different races who were now at home in England. In 1042 the Saxon line was restored in King Edward the Confessor, whose parents were King Ethelred and Emma, daughter of Richard I of Normandy. During his reign tensions grew between his parents' nations and, finally, there was conflict. Then one evening in October in the year AD1066 the Franco-Viking cavalry under William the Bastard, Duke of Normandy, broke the shield-wall of Harold Godwinsson's Scando-Engelish infantry at a place called Hastings.

Sources

The year 1066 marks a convenient point at which to turn away from a purely narrative account of national history to consider some of the sources available to the local historian for the periods dealt with so far, and these sources are of three main kinds: discussions and correspondence with archaeologists, contacts with museums and learned bodies, and reference to manuscripts, printed works, maps and photographs.

Contacts with archaeologists

Unless the local historian is reasonably familiar with an outline of prehistory and the early recorded periods it is recommended that some of the books (see Printed Works, below) be studied before any approaches are made. Then, depending on needs, a meeting with the archaeologist employed by the local authority will prove of great value, particularly if the officer concerned has held his appointment for a number of years. Not only will he have a considerable academic background but he will be familiar with all past finds in the area of study, the location of sites of interest and, equally importantly, will almost certainly have methods of keeping in touch with reported discoveries as they occur. He will know of private collections of artifacts which may be available for inspection, and will be able to provide access to records and photographs not widely publicized.

An important and interesting recent development in one local government area has been the appointment, at parish and town level, of volunteer honorary ancient monument liaison officers (AMLOs) who, under the chairmanship of a properly appointed person, act as local correspondents on archaeological and related matters of importance. Local historians may well wish to become AMLOs for their particular areas, should the trend continue.

A second avenue to be explored is discussion (by actual visit, or correspondence) with the Archaeological Branch of the Ordnance Survey. This department has a large collection of maps and photographs, and an extensive card index from which information may be extracted. It maintains contact with the Air Surveyors' Branch and the Directorate of Aerial Photography at Cambridge University.

The Royal Commission on Historical Monuments employs a number of specialist investigators, some of whom are archaeologists of distinction. Correspondence (or meetings if geography and financial resources permit) with these officers can frequently be of mutual benefit, for they are able to take a wide view of a locality, region and, indeed, the country as a whole.

Several of the public utilities, such as British Gas, employ consultant archaeologists who may be contacted regarding any possible finds which may have been made during pipe-laying or similar operations.

Contacts with museums

The obvious place to start is the town, county or other well established museum. A simple visit is likely to be of little value. An appointment with the curator will provide the occasion for not only seeing the early material on display, but learning what is in the reserve collections — hence seldom, if ever, seen — and ascertaining what has been published in book or pamphlet form, or in the proceedings of any learned society. Arrangements can often be made to take photographs of relevant pieces the museum has in its custody.

Finally, contact should be made with the Department of Prehistoric and Roman Antiquities, and the Department of Medieval and Later Antiquities, both of the British Museum in London. An initial general enquiry regarding a particular region will elicit information of what the museum holds in its collections, and subsequent follow-up will be of inestimable value to the historian in building his knowledge of the period under review.

Manuscripts and printed works

The following pages list some of the more important works the local historian may wish to read in the acquisition of background knowledge. The bibliographies contained in many of the books cited will point to other avenues to be explored. Perhaps the best single-volume work is *A Shortened History of England* by G.M. Trevelyan (Pelican Books 1959). This book deals, in some 600 pages, with the country's history from earliest times up to the outbreak of the Second World War. In addition to seventeen maps (five of which refer to the period up to AD1066) there is a helpful chronological outline dating many hundreds of notable events, which is of considerable value as a quick and easy reference. Specifically for the early epochs, the following books and manuscripts will be found to contain valuable source material:

Prehistoric period *Prehistoric Britain* Hawkes, J. & C. (Penguin 1958); *Prehistoric Communities in the British Isles* Gordon Childe, V. (London 1940); *Introduction to British Prehistory* Megaw, J.V.S. and Simpson, D.D.A. (Leicester 1979); *Penguin Guide to Prehistoric England and Wales* Dyer, J. (London 1981); *Prehistoric and Roman Britain* Muir, R. and Welfare, H. (London 1983). This last volume is written in a highly readable style and is profusely illustrated. It will act as a good 'popular' introduction. It contains some useful maps and a bibliography.

The Ordnance Survey has published a number of what it is pleased to call 'maps', but which are very much more, for each contains a scholarly introduction, index and explanatory matter. The maps are of three types: General, dealing with specific periods or cultures; Thematic, showing the distribution and character of certain features; Individual Monuments. There is a map which deals with the prehistoric period: *Ancient Britain*, in the form of a large-scale record of the major *visible* antiquities of Great Britain older than AD1066. It contains a very useful bibliography and a comprehensive index. The periods covered are palaeolithic, mesolithic, neolithic, bronze and iron (plus the Roman and Saxon times). *Southern Britain in the Iron Age* is a publication which includes a sixteen-page introduction outlining terminology applied to the various iron age cultures, plus commentaries on hill forts, open settlements, lake villages, farms, fogues, shrines, burial grounds, dykes, hill figures and trackways. There is a section on Celtic coins and a pertinent series of small-scale maps, a twenty-three page index plus a tinted map to a scale of about 10 miles to the inch, showing the distribution of the monuments and sites of interest.

The National Monuments Record (formerly the National Buildings Record) was founded to be a systematic photographic record of English architecture, but its work was extended into the fields of archaeology and air photography. Its collections include two million photographs, measured drawings and written reports of archaeological sites and historic buildings in England, and 800,000 photographic negatives. In addition it maintains on microfiche the Ordnance Survey card index record, already referred to, of archaeological sites and excavations, currently amounting to some 400,-000 items.

Reference was made earlier to the work of the Royal Commission on Historical Monuments. This includes a series of printed volumes published (via HMSO) as *An Inventory of the Historical Monuments in the County of (county name)*, the monuments of each county taking up as many as ten individual books. Each volume contains sections on prehistoric earthworks and monuments, as well as descriptions of early items to which it has not been possible to assign dates. Wherever possible, monuments are listed under the names of the civil parishes in which they occur, but exceptions are made for such things as Celtic fields, which are dealt with on a larger geographical scale. Each volume contains a sectional preface which very usefully generalizes on matters of the wider archaeological interest in the area concerned. However, not every county is yet covered. A list appears in Appendix I, of these volumes and other RCHM publications.

Roman and early Saxon times Until 1981 the definitive book on these centuries was *Roman Britain and the English Settlements* by Collingwood and Myres. In fact two separate volumes in one cover, it lasted from its publication in 1936 to its last reprint in 1975. It is still worth looking at. In 1981, however, Oxford University Press published the work which replaced the first part of the earlier work, the 824-page *Roman Britain* by Peter Salway. The book starts with an outline of the Iron Age settlements and ends with the state of Britain at the collapse of the Empire. It has twenty-three pages of bibliographical references.

For the local historian who wishes for an account somewhere between Trevelyan and Salway, a useful book is *Roman Britain* by I.A. Richmond (Penguin 1955). This too contains a lengthy bibliography.

An Atlas of the Roman World by T. Cornell and J. Matthews (Phaidon 1982) not only has a chapter on Britain and relevant maps, but, being a general review of the Republic and the Empire, throws interesting light on social organisation, technology, agriculture and communications which suggest generalisations. The Ordnance Survey's *Map of Roman Britain* has gone through several revised editions since it first appeared in 1928. Its lengthy introduction deals with military sites, towns and other communal settlements, the countryside, monuments, industry and mining, roads, canals, aqueducts, lighthouses and theatres. There is a useful chronological table from 55-54BC to AD446, and a section on names of places and of tribes. Small-scale maps range from that of Britain according to Ptolemy (second century AD), to local definitions of a few selected areas. There is an exhaustive index. The map is drawn at 16 miles to the inch and includes the totality of known Roman sites and constructions, up to the time of the last revision.

For the local historian interested in urban development *The Towns of Roman Britain* by John Wacher (Batsford 1974) will be of value. It describes the different kinds of towns and their functions, contains splendid line drawings and photographs, and has a useful collection of notes. The collections of the National Monuments Record and the publications of the Royal Commission on Historical Monuments (as above) should also be referred to.

It is sensible to include in this section the period of history between AD446, when the final appeal for help by the British *civitates* went unheard in Rome, and, roughly, the accession of Alfred to the throne of Wessex in 871. These are the Dark Ages so beloved of poets and ballad makers. Mention has already been made of the contribution of J.N.L. Myres to the 1936 publication *Roman Britain and the English Settlements*. The appearance in 1981 of the new definitive work on the earlier period by Salway was followed in 1986 by a further new volume in the *Oxford History of England: The English Settlements*. This book was also by J.N.L. Myres who, fifty years after his previous contribution to our knowledge of the times, was able to compose a totally revised statement. The new book has a number of maps and a select bibliography.

Arthur's Britain by Leslie Alcock (Pelican Books 1973) covers the years AD367-634. Its title is a 'popular' one, and given our slight knowledge of Arthur is unfair to the book, which ranges widely over the period — as one might expect from a distinguished professor of archaeology. It has many useful maps, drawings and photographs, together with extensive references and a bibliography.

The Ordnance Survey map *Britain in the Dark Ages* is specific to the period 'approximately AD410 to AD870'. It starts with a twenty-seven page introduction covering progress in archaeological studies up to 1974 under the headings: towns, villages, royal residences, defensive structures, earthworks, pagan burials, shrines, monasteries, bishoprics, churches, symbol stones, evidence of settled life in northern Britain, fortresses in Celtic areas, the coming of the Northmen and some notes on names of various kinds.

Further works which may be of general value to historians working in what was an area of special Celtic influence or the Danelaw are *The Celts* by Nora Chadwick (Pelican 1970), *The Danes in England* by Sir Frank Stenton (British Academy 1927), and *The Vikings* by Johannes Brøndsted (Pelican 1965).

The later Saxon era The earliest authority on Old English history comprises a number of annalistic works referred to *in toto* as the *Anglo-Saxon Chronicles*, said to be the 'authentic voices of England from the time of Julius Caesar to the coronation of Henry II'. Seven chronicles survive, each somewhat different from the others. They have all been the subject of modern critical analysis, and the most useful edition for present purposes is probably that published in London in 1961 as *The Anglo-Saxon Chronicle: A Revised Translation* by Whitelock, Douglas and Tucker. A more recent volume is that prepared by Anne Savage, *The Anglo-Saxon Chronicles* (London 1982). This is a conflation of the four major manuscripts, and contains dozens of photographs. The local historian is recommended to these chronicles, for in addition to being a fascinating (if inaccurate) year by year story of the times, they also contain many hundreds of references to places of specifically local interest. The second early work which should be read with care is Bede's ecclesiastical history of the English people. This work, which dates from AD731, is available in Penguin Books as *A History of the English Church and People*. It relates the history 'of Britain, formerly known as Albion . . . an island in the ocean . . .', and concludes with a description of the 'state of the English nation and the rest of Britain' in AD725-731. As may be expected, the first few chapters are fantastical in nature (as indeed are parts of the Anglo-Saxon chronicles), but the whole is worthy of attention for the general background it gives, and Bede (or Baeda) mentions a number of places by easily recognised names.

The basic modern text book devoted to the period remains Sir Frank Stenton's *Anglo-Saxon England*. First published in 1943, it went into a third revised edition in 1971 and has not been superceded. It has a forty-three page bibliography in thirteen sections. It also contains a key to Anglo-Saxon place names which is valuable as a reference, before pursuing more detailed research. A useful, if slightly less demanding, book is *An Introduction to Anglo-Saxon England* by Peter Hunter Blair (Cambridge 1971). This work covers the foundations of England, Britain and the Vikings, the church, government, the economy and the growth of learning. The maps are informative and the well organised bibliography is particularly helpful.

The Ordnance Survey map *Britain before the Norman Conquest* deals with the years from AD871 (the accession of Alfred to the throne of Wessex) to AD1066 (the year of the Conquest itself). The map is made up of two sheets at a scale of about 10 miles to the inch. The south sheet is an important reference, for it shows the boundary of the Danelaw with some precision from the Thames estuary to a point near Shrewsbury. Textual matter includes a historical summary of the period, the Scandinavian settlements, towns, defences, and a history of the church (including the development of parishes). The document contains a summary index and a detailed index, and, although not relevant here, a map of the Welsh cantrefs at a scale of 20 miles to one inch.

One of the most valuable publications of recent years is *An Atlas of Anglo-Saxon England* by David Hill. First issued in 1981 it was reissued in paperback, with corrections, in 1984. It would be difficult to over-stress the usefulness of this volume to those local historians fortunate enough to be researching a place with a pre-Conquest history. In the course of 180 large pages with 260 maps, plus numerous diagrams, it covers all the major aspects of the late Anglo-Saxon culture and history that can be expressed in a graphical manner —settlement patterns, regnal lists, place names, invasions, military campaigns, itineraries, mints and coinage, landholding, towns, agriculture, trade, monasteries and the church.

There are, no doubt, other books which might have been mentioned here, and most are listed in one or other of the bibliographies indicated in the course of this chapter. To sum up: the principal sources outlined, both written and other, are sufficient to provide the local historian with an overview of British and English history from the earliest times to the Conquest, which is so necessary if the parochial record is eventually to be presented to the maximum effect.

A scene from an early metrical calendar, depicting the labours for the month of March.

2 The Conquest to 1485

The subjugation of England by the Normans was the final act in the series which created the English nation. The invaders of previous centuries had played their parts in its development, but there were still essentially two systems of local government, one founded on the Saxon practices of Wessex and the other on the Scandinavian customs of the Danelaw. Administration in the area which had been Wessex was grounded in the laws of Ine and his successors, and based on the shire and the hundred with an ealdorman and shirereeve representing the king and people. In the Danelaw, 'shires' had been created out of the old Viking military districts, each with a borough at its centre, wapentakes as its subdivisions, and a Danish earl (*jarl*) at its head, this nobleman being responsible solely to the English king. There was, therefore, a rich variety of laws and practices, sometimes based on the whim of the king and sometimes on local custom as interpreted by the hundred and wapentake courts.

The view taken by King William I was that all the land was his, and that his followers held their estates by his pleasure alone in return for specified services. A single unifying system was arbitrarily imposed and forcefully maintained. Gradually the great offices of central government and their local offshoots (many of which exist in mutated form today) were instituted: the treasury, the king's council, the office of sheriff, the judiciary — all assisted the creation of an instrument for centralised control.

The great survey of AD1086 (subsequently known as 'Domesday') provided the king and his officers with the raw data on which they could fashion their new procedures and governmental structure. The concept of the 'manor' as the basic tenurial unit was refined, its duties and responsibilities codified and the manorial court instituted.

Slowly, actual service in return for land (knights' service, serjeanty, frankalmoign and so on) gave way to money payments. The growth of towns continued; merchant gilds arose; the country's mineral wealth in coal, iron, tin and lead — sadly neglected by the Saxons — was developed; the wool and cloth industries thrived, and foreign trade was encouraged. The bitter and divisive years of the anarchy (1135-54) were followed by the forward-looking reign of the Angevin Henry II, whose composite realm stretched, by way of England, Normandy, Anjou, Maine, Touraine, Aquitaine, Poitou and Auvergne, from the Scottish borders to the Pyrenees.

A great period of legislation followed: in 1164 the Constitution of Clarendon defined relations between the church and state; the common law (that is, law common to the whole kingdom) was evolved and its administration placed in the hands of a bench of royal judges. The Grand Assize of 1179, which determined rightful ownership of property, stimulated the institution of trial by jury in the royal courts; two years later the Assize of Arms reorganised the military forces.

The coronation charter of Henry I (1100-35), followed by the 'unknown charter of liberties', led, in 1215, to the great charter *Magna Carta* (although this barely touched the common people). The baronial wars of the mid thirteenth century precipitated parliamentary reforms, burghers and knights of the shire representing local interests. The reign of Edward I ('the hammer of the Scots') saw the consolidation of parliament into the instrument of government which has evolved down to the present day. The courts of the king's bench and common pleas were made independent of one another, and a court of equity (the chancery court) was created to give redress when other measures failed. Conservators of the Peace (forerunners of the Justices of the Peace of the next century) were appointed. Inquests and statutes of lasting import, particularly affecting the rights of people and the holding and transfer of property, were instituted.

The mid fourteenth century saw great English victories on the field of battle — Sluys, Crécy, Poitiers; but the period was dominated by the ravages of the great plague called the Black Death, and what it brought in its train as social upheaval. In the course of the two years 1348 and 1349 this scourge swept the country from south, where it entered, to north. It came again in 1361 and in 1369, and it is estimated that the population was reduced by between a quarter and a third. As may be imagined, many manors and estates suffered through losses in the labour force and, to a lesser extent, the deaths of the lords. In 1351, following the first epidemic, the Statute of

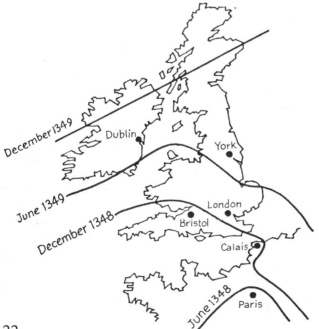

Map showing the progress of the Black Death through northern Europe and the British Isles in the years 1348 and 1349. Having reached southern France by December 1347, the plague entered England in June of the following year. The chronicle of the Great Friars at Lynn records, 'In this year 1348, in Melcombe in the county of Dorset, a little before the Feast of St John the Baptist, two ships, one of them from Bristol, came alongside. One of the sailors had brought with him from Gascony the seeds of a terrible pestilence and, through him, the men of that town of Melcombe were the first in England to be infected.'

Labourers fixed wages and the price of food. The loosening of the bonds which held the peasant to the soil was speeding up and rural society was shaping into the mould of freeholders, tenant farmers, and labourers with little or, more likely, no land, that was to hold for some four hundred years. The peasants' revolt of 1381 affected many areas — St Albans, Suffolk, Norfolk, Cambridge — and continued the process of freeing the country-dweller from archaic and oppressive restrictions.

In the towns, recession after the plague was marked, but trade grew again and towards the end of the century merchants were exporting coal, tin, metalwares, leather goods and dairy products to numerous overseas markets. But the *sovereigne march-andise* contributing to the country's prosperity was wool. The dictum of Kenilworth of 1326 established staples for the protection of the wool trade and was followed by a full-blown statute in 1354. The cloth trade grew and the wine trade flourished. Wealthy traders, craftsmen and artisans of low degree continued to organise them-selves into fraternities, gilds and misteries. A few of these bodies obtained royal charters as their authority, and while many did not, each flourished at its different level — from the simple parish gild with limited objectives, to the large and powerful merchant group in the great town.

From the point of view of this present volume a significant event occurred in 1362 when a statute ordained that henceforth pleadings in courts of law should be in English not French. It is surprising that this measure took so long, for as early as the reign of Henry III, a hundred years before, the barons —descendants of Norman invaders almost to a man — were saying *Nolumus leges Angliae mutari* ('we do not want the customs of old England changed'), indicating, perhaps, their recognition of nationhood.

England remained, in the late Middle Ages, an agricultural country, and in its most important parts an open field system of cultivation continued. In each village, land was divided into two, three or sometimes four great fields in which the peasants and occasionally the freeholders maintained their scattered strips. This is not to say that a uniform system prevailed over the whole country. The method of large open fields with crop rotation common to the midlands was different from that of the small open fields of the western shires, where intense cultivation was resorted to. Different again were the practices in the woodland pastures of Kent and the moors and heaths of Devon and Yorkshire.

Standards varied too. On the great estates of the major barons or richly endowed abbeys specialisation could be introduced — sheep rearing, dairy farming and horse breeding — but in remote areas or in single-village single-manor communities, self sufficiency through co-operation and diversification was forced on the inhabitants, the demesne acres being no different from the tenants' and common land.

The depression that followed the Black Death (aggravated by the burdens of the Hundred Years War) brought changes — the leasing of demesne land, sheep and even cattle became widespread — but the structure of rural society remained basically intact, although there were increasingly different standards of living between the poorer and more primitive north of England and the more advanced areas to the south. It was, however, a time when great social progress could be made. True, it was almost impossible to break into the circle of the great families, the heads of which were men like the earls of Northumberland and Westmoreland, but it was entirely

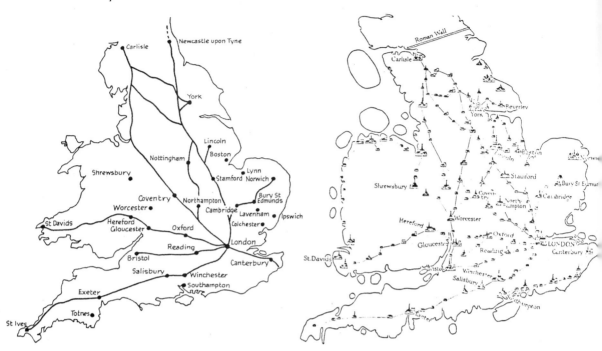

The principal roads of England in the 14th century. The map on the left is a modern one based on an interpretation RIGHT of a contemporary map by Gough.

feasible for the peasant to aspire to the station of a yeoman, and the yeoman to become a gentleman. The gentleman could seek or be granted knighthood, and progress beyond that degree could be achieved. For the townsman the road might seem still easier — as witness William de le Pole, a merchant in trade, whose son became an earl and whose great grandson a duke.

As the system of leasing land grew, the bonds of servitude gradually loosened and in the early years of the fifteenth century the peasant, formerly totally subject to his lord's will, with all claims in his land vested in his master, came to regard himself as having occupation rights tantamount to moral title, and the idea of 'customary tenancy' and 'copyhold' achieved near-legal status. By 1439 the law courts had started to protect the tenant and hence admit he had long-term custody of his acres. The structure of village life evolved, and the bondsman of earlier centuries became steadily more prosperous as his security of tenure grew.

At the more general, national level prosperity fluctuated, and the power of the Crown waned. Henry V, so rightly proud of his great victories at Harfleur and Agincourt, died in 1422 aged thirty-five, and the reign of his son, Henry VI, was a disaster. Lords struggled with each other, as the Houses of York and Lancaster took turn and turn about with the throne. By 1450 English trade was at a low ebb; war and jealousy robbed the country of its French and Iberian markets, and Venice and Genoa were the powers in the Mediterranean.

But the accession of Edward IV in 1461 brought something of a trade revival, and by 1475 England was more prosperous than at any prior time in the century. However, the depression had left its mark, particularly on towns, and some (like Leicester, Lincoln, Northampton and Nottingham) actually became smaller. Others, especially ports such as Bristol and Southampton, weathered the storm and soon recovered; while the wealth of the London merchants remained renowned. Edward died suddenly in 1483 at the age of forty-one. On the murder of his small son (Edward V), he was succeeded by Richard III, an able administrator and soldier. This monarch died two years later, fighting for his kingdom at the battle of Bosworth Field. He had had no time in which to prove his worth — his legacy for the local historian: the founding of the College of Arms.

Sources

The fall of the house of Plantagenet on 22 August 1485 marks the second point at which to conveniently turn away from a skeletal account of relevant national events, to consider some of the sources to which a local historian may refer for a perception of the larger scene.

The three avenues described in Chapter 1 as valid for the ages up to the Norman conquest remain equally germane for the periods now discussed — contacts with archaeologists and museums, reference to manuscripts and printed works.

Contacts with archaeologists and museums

As before, it will be especially useful to discuss points of outstanding general concern with professionals at county, town or city level. Archaeologists and museum staff will readily be able to comment on finds of national importance and relate them to local places or events. It is also important to maintain contact with the British Museum and the Archaeology Branch of the Ordnance Survey. If the research being caried out is of an extensive kind, likely to be spread over months or even years, and is undertaken on a basis of one historical period at a time, then it is as well to make enquiries accordingly. This has two great advantages: the first is that the information being gathered is more amenable to discipline, and the second is that the professional person concerned is far more likely to take a genuine interest in a project if the seeker after wisdom and truth seems to be pursuing a rational and logical course of action.

Manuscripts and printed works

As the local historian's studies move progressively from the ages about which only the archaeologist's trowel can inform to time when the written word was firmly established in England, it will be apparent that there is a mass of contemporary works and an even greater mass of later commentaries and analysis.

Manuscript sources What now follows must, therefore, be highly selective, and no more than an indication of the material at the disposal of the diligent researcher.

A splendid place to start is with *Historical Interpretation* by J.J. Bagley (Penguin Books 1965), the subtitle of the first volume of which is 'Sources in English Medieval History 1066-1540'. The book is organised on a century-by-century basis, covering works from Ordericus Vitalis' history of England and Normandy, the Anglo-Saxon chronicles, the Domesday survey, the *Gesta Stephani* (the deeds of Stephen), and the works of the twelfth-century historian William of Malmesbury, to letters written after the battles of Towton and Bosworth. The book refers to many other manuscripts, some of which will be mentioned later in Chapters 4-9. J.J. Bagley's book contains bibliographies and a glossary of archaic and technical words. *The Norman Conquest* by R. Allen Brown (London 1984) is a work in the series 'Documents of Medieval History'. It deals with literary, narrative and other manuscripts dubbed Norman, Old English and Anglo-Norman; documents from charters, writs and leases; through laws, customs and customals to surveys, and ends with letters and artistic sources. As may be expected it discusses the Bayeux tapestry as primary research material. It contains a bibliography, but no index.

The first four volumes in the authoritative *English Historical Documents* series published under the general editorship of Professor D.C. Douglas may be noted here, but they are of such consequence as to be dealt with at some length in later chapters.

General books There are four very substantial works dealing with the years between the great survey of King William I and the death in battle of King Richard III. They are all published by Oxford University Press. The first is *Domesday Book to Magna Carta* by A.L. Poole (reprinted 1975). The bibliography is sectionalized and runs to twenty-six pages. The second book, *The Thirteenth Century*, is by Sir Maurice Powicke (reprinted 1970). It deals with the period between the years 1216 and 1307, and it too contains an extensive bibliographical section. The third volume, *The Fourteenth Century* by Mary McKisack (reprinted 1976), is equally authoritative, as is the final work *The Fifteenth Century* by E.F. Jacob (reprinted 1978). This book ends with the year 1485.

Less weighty, but highly readable, accounts are *English Society in the Early Middle Ages* by D.M. Stenton (describing events from 1066 to 1307), and A.R. Myers' *England in the Late Middle Ages* (covering the years 1307-1536). Both are published by Penguin Books. A valuable reference work for the medieval period (and others) is the *Historical Atlas of Britain* edited by M. Falkus and J. Gillingham (London 1981). It is a lavishly illustrated volume with contributions by many eminent experts. The general accounts of, and maps, histograms and pictures for, the period 1066-1485 are particularly useful.

A further comprehensive volume spanning the whole period under review is *Medieval England* by Colin Platt (London 1978). This is subtitled 'A social history and archaeology from the Conquest to 1600', and is well illustrated with many coloured plates. The maps, graphs, diagrams and plans are helpful and the book contains a long section of notes and references. *Feudal Britain* by G.W.S. Barrow (London 1983) outlines the 'completion of the medieval kingdoms of the British Isles 1066 to 1314', and has a bibliography. *The Batsford Companion to Medieval England* by Nigel Saul (London 1983) is, perhaps, more a pleasant acquaintance than a close friend, but it is not expensive and has uses as a first resort. *The Norman Heritage* by Trevor Rowley (London 1983) contains very pertinent graphical material which reflects the author's work in archaeology. Maps include settlements destroyed in the north in 1086, distribution of Norman castles, vineyards, monastic houses, nunneries, royal forests, medieval deer parks, and the colonization of the waste in south Lincolnshire.

Medieval England by M.W. Beresford and J.K.S. St Joseph (Cambridge 1979) is a comprehensive aerial survey (the second-named author was professor of aerial photographic studies in the University of Cambridge). The book contains a very wide range

A decorated initial from a charter of Edward III to the citizens of Bristol empowering them to imprison evildoers and disturbers of the peace, and to punish bakers found cheating on weight by drawing them through the streets on a hurdle.

of pictures 'chosen to illustrate features of the English rural and urban landscape assignable between the Anglo-Saxon settlements and the end of the reign of Elizabeth I' in 1603. It compares early village and town plans with both landscape evidence and modern layout. In many cases the similarity between the old and the new can be quite striking, the geographical evolution of the settlements being quite apparent. This is particularly so in the cases of Chelmsford from 1591 to 1952, and Winchelsea from 1292 to 1958. Numerous villages are also shown to have retained in the twentieth century their layout of the Middle Ages. The book is a treasure house for many local historians — approximately 200 settlements are dealt with, some in great detail. *The Medieval Economy and Society* by M.M. Postan (Penguin Books 1975) covers, in the course of thirteen chapters, the underlying structures of manors, villages, markets, towns, gilds, trade, industry and prices from, broadly, the earliest days for which there are useful data to the period just after the Black Death. *Rural England* by H.E. Hallam (London 1981) outlines within the covers of a short work salient features of the economic realities between 1066 and 1348. It has a useful glossary and a set of chapter notes.

The kings The structure, government, economy, social development and religious practices of England in the Middle Ages were so dependent on the abilities and personality of the monarch of the day that it is worthwhile for the local historian to learn a little of the rulers who, each in their different way, shaped the country and its destiny. At a somewhat different level it is also helpful to remember that because in the early Middle Ages the kings and their courts were itinerant, and active in campaigns, hundreds of places were marked by their presence and activities, and are very entertainingly documented. Such activities could vary from King John buying wine in Sturminster Newton in Dorset, Edward I capturing Northampton from Simon de Montfort, to the involvement of Richard III with the manor of Skipton Craven in the Pennine region of West Yorkshire.

There are literally dozens of books on the lives of the post-Conquest kings, but the following modern works are of value and easily accessed. A gentle introduction is contained in *The Lives of the Kings and Queens of England* edited by Antonia Fraser (London 1975). Each chapter is written by a specialist in the period — Norman, Angevin, Plantagenet, Lancaster and Yorkist, and later reigns. A more lengthy treatment of the rulers from 1066 to 1485 is given in *The Saxon and Norman Kings* by Christopher Brooke (London 1978), and *The Plantagenets* by John Harvey (1967).

Each of the following publications is devoted to the life of one king, they all contain lengthy bibliographies, and sometimes schedules of selected dates: *William the Conqueror* by David Douglas (London 1969); *William Rufus* by Frank Barlow (London 1983); *Henry II* by W.L. Warren (London 1977); *King John* by W.L. Warren (London 1978); *Edward III* by Michael Packe (London 1983); *Henry IV* by D. Buisseret (London 1984); *Henry V* by D. Seward (London 1987); *Edward IV* by Charles Ross (London 1983); *Henry VI* by Ralph A. Griffiths (a book of 966 pages spanning the years 1422-61); *Richard III* by Charles Ross (London 1981). At the time of writing the following volumes are in preparation: *Henry I* by Warren Hollister; *Henry III* by David Carpenter; *Edward I* by Michael Prestwick; *Edward II* by J.R.S. Phillips; *Henry V* by Christopher Allmand; *Edward VI* by Peter Ramsey. There are, of course, older treatments of the lives and works of some of these monarchs, and others not mentioned. Most are out of print but are worth searching for in the card indexes of the larger reference libraries.

Specialist works Publications dealing with particular aspects of life in medieval England line ever longer sections of the shelves of better booksellers and reference libraries. Some which, from personal experience, are especially useful are now listed. *The Constitutional History of Medieval England* by J.E.A. Joliffe (London 1937) is a seminal work now sadly out of print, covering the time from the English settlement to 1485. It is quite invaluable to the researcher who wishes to place in context the early jurisdictions, feudal rights and obligations, the constitution of the shire and the borough, and many other matters relating to the government of the day as it impinged on local communities.

Another quite basic work, also sadly out of print, but no doubt available through the British Library or local lending scheme, is *Obligations of Society in the XII and XIII Centuries* by A.L. Poole (Oxford 1946). The book is a printed version of the Ford lectures of 1944 and is divided into six sections: classification of society; the peasants; the knights; the serjeants; amercements (fines), and feudal levies. *The Nobility of Medieval England* by K.B. McFarlane (Oxford 1980) represents the Ford lectures for 1953 together with other related matter. The book *Peasants, Knights and Heretics* (Cambridge 1981) is a collection of studies edited by R.H. Hilton. It contains fifteen essays, many of which are of value to the local historian seeking to unravel some of the complexities of the medieval period. They are: three studies of the common field and open field systems; inflation in 1180-1220; the famine and agrarian crisis of 1315-22; the knight's fee; freedom and villeinage; redistribution of income in the fifteenth century; landlords and tenants; Lollardy and sedition 1381-1431; and five essays on that probably mythical medieval terrorist Robin Hood, who 'lived' in the Weald, the woods of Essex, the New Forest, Sherwood and Yorkshire. Many a chronicler of local events will be able to weave 'Robin' into his tale.

The Cistercian Abbey of St Mary ad fontes (Fountains Abbey), in North Yorkshire, dating from the 12th century, is now one of the most famous and beautiful of all monastic ruins.

Medieval Monasteries of Great Britain by L. Butler and C. Given-Wilson (London 1983) is a volume describing 'all the main monastic sites surviving in Great Britain'. Within these limits it is a very useful volume. The long introduction is an excellent survey of all aspects of monastic life. The gazetteer may be considered less satisfactory. It describes the history and architecture of eighty monasteries, but merely 'lists' more than 250 which are *not* described, and hence presumably not considered major — one

29

such is Battle Abbey at Hastings. The list is said to be a 'comprehensive guide to . . . sites . . . where remains of medieval buildings may be seen', but it is not. To quote but one example, it does not mention Newenham in Devon where remains may be visited, some free-standing and some built into the fabric of Lower Abbey Farm. These comments aside, the book is helpful on the things it *does* cover, and of great value to the local historian lucky enough to have one of the eighty monasteries described in the volume within his area of research.

Great Medieval Castles by J. Forde-Johnston is a guide to some 200 castles. It covers, in seven chapters, castle design and construction from just after the coming of the Normans to later medieval periods and developments. It is very well illustrated with photographs and plans, and the select bibliography points to further informative sources.

Christian England by David Edwards (London 1981) relates the story of English Christianity up to the Reformation in the 1540s, but the chapters dealing with the abbeys and their place in medieval society, the peasants' revolt of 1381 and the relationships between church and kings are helpful reading for present purposes. *Medieval Households* by David Herlihy (Harvard 1985) is generally valuable but particularly for its final section: 'The household system in the late Middle Ages'. *The Black Death* by Philip Ziegler (Penguin Books 1982) is a 300-page account of the plague from its introduction in Melcombe, Dorset, in June 1348, through its progress as far north as Scotland by Christmas 1349. Many places are specifically named in the text, and the book provides pertinent insights into the effects of the scourge in town and village. *Food and Drink in Britain* by C. Anne Wilson describes the gradual changes and developments in the materials used as, and in the preparation of, foodstuffs in Britain from the earliest archaeological times. Its descriptions, from contemporary records, of meals eaten by both the nobility and the common people in the Middle Ages are most useful and a valuable addition to knowledge of local customs.

Finally, *Bosworth Field and the Wars of the Roses* by A.L. Rowse (London 1971) relates in 400 pages the background to, and events of, the reign of King Richard III, which lead to his death in 1485 at the age of thirty-three.

Diners of the early seventeenth century. Of particular note are the square trencher boards.

3   1485 to 1714

The new king, Henry Tudor, victor of Bosworth, now Henry VII and first of an important line of monarchs, set about establishing the country on a sound footing. He lacked the imagination for a grand design, but he was a sound administrator and had a good grasp of financial matters. It is the view of modern historians that Henry's firm moves against the warring factions which existed within the ranks of the great nobles were effective and set England upon the road to economic prosperity.

The king had a well established government machine and became an autocrat by consent, using the tools at his disposal with great skill, not forging new ones. The great formal organs of power — law courts and parliament — operated in accordance with established precedent. The powers of the sheriffs were controlled and those of the justices of the peace enhanced, although their authority was limited to their own counties. National justice was administered from Westminster and, with the exception of Durham, the palatinates recognised the Crown as final arbiter.

Society, to begin with, remained unsettled, but piece by piece the jigsaw of local authority was reassembled, the gentry of the shire preserving good order in their lands and dealing with appropriate matters of agriculture, poverty, vagabondage, and the economy generally. In parliament the lords spiritual and temporal functioned both as a royal council and a high court, and although the commons were technically not part of parliament they were in practice — the shire-knights elected by the senior freeholders, and the representatives of the boroughs elected by the wealthy traders and most prosperous craftsmen. Parliament became the ally of the Crown because its members shared common interests with the king.

In military matters the king was equally conservative, relying on the longbowmen, avoiding cannon oftentimes, and even legislating against the use of crossbows. Henry's expeditions to France and Ireland were economically mounted and he went so far as to prepare a book of *Statutes and Ordinances of the War*. On the sea the king had a small permanent force which he augmented when necessary by hiring merchant shippers at the rate of a shilling a ton a month.

But money, not weapons of war and physical repression at home, was the keystone of Henry's policy, and for this he depended on the goodwill of his people, the

31

The court of Wards and Liveries which administered laws aimed at ending the maintenance of private armies. Also known as the Star Chamber, from the decorated ceiling in which it met.

encouragement of husbandry and the stimulation of industry and trade. There were problems with the Venetians, the French and the Flemish which brought about tariff disputes, but trade prospered and English venturers roamed the seas in search of new lands and commodities. When Henry VII died in 1509 he had set England on a prosperous road and had some claim to be regarded as the greatest of the Tudors.

At the age of eighteen years Henry VIII succeeded to the throne, and when he died thirty-eight years later at the age of fifty-six England had been transformed not, in the words of G.M. Trevelyan, 'by chance or by the whim of a king impatient to be divorced, but on account of profound changes in the habits of the English people.' There had, in the preceding centuries, been an ever increasing process in the granting of freedom to villeins, the towns had grown in importance as centres of trade, the burgher and merchant classes had emerged as a 'middle' group between the nobles and the base peasantry. Parliament had evolved and become established as two chambers, the common law had come to be respected. English had triumphed as the national language, the castle had been made obsolete by the cannon, and with the coming of printing learning flourished.

The local historian, unless he has very specialised interests, will find little of consequence in the broader religious issues of Henry VIII's reign, but the measures of 1538
requiring the provision of parish registers among other things are of some moment, as
will be discussed in Chapter 10. The wars with France and Scotland are also subjects
for specialised study, although again parish and county records, such as the muster
rolls, will be of great value, and these (together with national records) are also discussed later.

King Henry's only son, Edward VI, reigned six years before dying of consumption
at the age of seventeen. During his reign there were great religious upheavals and the
gulf between Catholic and Protestant widened. Under the 'Protector' — the Duke of
Somerset — the country's economic situation deteriorated, and following his execution
John Dudley, Duke of Northumberland, contrived to make things even worse.
Inflation ran rampant, further enclosures of common land caused disgust, rent
increases and punitive game laws made tempers rise. In 1549 the Norfolk peasants,
under Robert Kett, rose. There were risings of a religious nature in the West Country
and Oxfordshire, the army remained unpaid and all-in-all the times were miserable
indeed. Edward died leaving the country torn in several directions at once by economic, agricultural and religious stresses. Lady Jane Grey, his successor, 'reigned' for
twelve days in the summer of 1553, to be succeeded by Mary I.

A devout Catholic, the new sovereign set about undermining England's independence by marrying her cousin, the future Philip II of Spain, and plunged the country
into a religious bloodbath. Chapter 10 describes how parishes throughout England
were affected as the pendulum swung while Mary tried to enforce the wholesale
transformation of the country into a staunchly Catholic state. Latimer and Ridley, the
Protestant bishops, and Archbishop Cranmer died at the stake, and there were
rebellions. These were suppressed, but on her death Mary left England in a greater
state of chaos than ever.

From the very beginning Elizabeth I steered a wise and prudent course, steadily
reinstating Henry VIII's religious legislation and gently encouraging liberty of conscience. Individualism was fostered, and enterprise at home and abroad allowed rein.
She weathered the storms of Spain's ambitions — the king's attempts to marry her
and the coming of the Armada. The age saw great progress and adventures in the
discovery of new places — Virginia was colonised, Drake returned from a voyage
around the world lasting three years, and bringing home vast treasure. The East India
Company was founded, trade with Russia and Turkey grew; the search for a route to
Cathay led to unknown lands north of Labrador, and to mining in Canada.

At home, enclosure of arable land for pasture, the drift of an economy based on
individual enterprise rather than one on feudal tenure, allowed large estates to be
built up and the wool trade to prosper, but there was also suffering. The poorer rural
elements of the population drifted towards the towns, villages were even deserted on
occasion, and vagabondage continued to disturb the country districts.

Slowly, farming for gain asserted itself in a number of directions, and England's
ability to grow crops other than wool, for profit, increased. There was unrest in many
counties, but steadily the deployment of capital to manufacturing and merchant enterprises overcame the most vexing elements of pauperism to warrant the assumption
that extreme poverty was no longer of paramount significance.

An illustration from Holinshed's Chronicles showing the minting of new coinage in the years 1560-61. The minting displayed the confidence of the government after the debasements of several previous reigns.

Industry became a dominant feature of the queen's reign — metal-working in iron, copper, brass and tin, weaving in silk and 'cotton' (or light wool), thread and lace making, glass, parchment, and much more. Companies formed for the exploitation of natural resources mined coal and metal ore, and harvested timber. Private enterprise triumphed: money was power, and money-lenders flourished.

Strangely, the roads were neglected and their upkeep fell upon the parishes, who often ignored them. But on the main routes post-horses, pack-horses and saddle animals were used, together with carts and coaches, and trade went on in spite of this rather vague attitude to highway administration and maintenance.

Elizabeth died on 24 March 1603, in some strange way having outlived her days. Her job was done. Her brilliant statesmanship had secured the country, and the religious upheavals were a thing of the past. England was a world power. The queen had said, 'I will that a king succeed me, and who but my kinsman the king of the Scots.' On the day she died the news was carried to Edinburgh.

The reign of James I was troubled. Thomas Babington Macauley wrote, centuries later, 'He was made up of two men — a witty well-read scholar who wrote, disputed and harangued, and a nervous driveling idiot who acted.' The 'Gunpowder Plot' failed, religious factions warred, the *Mayflower* sailed for America, there were restrictions on the pulpit and the press, the Thirty Years War began in 1618, crises came and went. The distinguished historian Godfrey Davies has said that 'in certain respects, to attempt to write a social and economic history of England under the early Stuarts is like making bricks without straw. Our knowledge of many fundamental facts is imperfect, and some of it is likely to remain so. There are additional difficulties due to the failure of economic periods to coincide with political.'

In the early years of James the woollen industry reached its peak, prices continued to rise and Crown revenue became inadequate. Clamour for social change grew but

The Tudor Royal Post system established staging points (usually inns) set about ten miles apart. Between these points 'postboys' would carry letters. The innkeepers were responsible for providing horses and riders to the next stage post. Speeds depended on terrain; five miles per hour were usual, but in difficult country could fall to as little as one mile in that time.

little was effected. In 1625 the courageous and high-minded Charles I succeeded his father. He, too, had problems with parliament, and from 1629 he governed for twelve years by personal rule. Without parliament there was no money and civil war became inevitable. The king and parliament were against each other, and the High Church was against the Puritans. When war came the most prosperous areas of the kingdom were held by parliament — the great ports, the bulk of the country's wealth, some 70 per cent of the population. Given the power base it seems in retrospect inevitable that the parliamentarians should triumph and the king be executed.

At the level of the everyday life of the average Englishman there were changes, many of which were extremely minor and no doubt irritating, others were more important, particularly where they touched religion. At a higher level important men went into exile, lost their lands and in other ways became impoverished. With the Restoration in 1660 the nobility enjoyed their own again, and the puritan moral code became a memory of a short-lived imposition. The high-born, the country gentry, set up hard but largely paternalistic dominion over their broad acres, and the 'squire-archy' was born as the more affluent in trade and commerce purchased land. Mixed farming was introduced. The yeoman class prospered, the peasants did not. Industry fluctuated in the wake of moves in continental markets. The new king, Charles II, was popular and largely tolerant.

James II, brother of Charles II, ascended the throne in 1685. He was a Catholic, and was neither trusted nor liked. There followed the battle of Sedgemoor, the 'Bloody Assizes', and religious persecution. In November 1688 William of Orange, James' son-in-law, invaded at the invitation of parliament, and he and his wife Mary became joint sovereigns. The struggles between king and parliament were finally ended; constitutional monarchy would henceforth be the rule in England. Mary died in 1694 at the age of thirty-two, and William was killed in a hunting accident eight years later. His reign had been much troubled by war, and the economy of the country had suffered. The final Stuart sovereign, Queen Anne the second daughter of James II, reigned from 1702 until her death aged forty-nine in 1714. She was not a clever woman but she was served by exceptional men, the greatest of whom was John Churchill, Duke of Marlborough. This outstanding soldier won resounding victories against England's continental enemies, and public morale and support grew. Parliament was supreme and the country achieved financial soundness on a firm basis of internal harmony. The capital of world trade became London, and England prospered.

In 1701 the Act of Succession effectively barred the Stuarts from the throne and paved the way for the Protestant house of Hanover. In 1707 the Act of Union between England and Scotland created Great Britain. The queen died in 1714 and the 'century of revolution' was finally over.

Sources

The eve of the coming of 'German George' is a most convenient point at which to interrupt an outline narrative of events, to note and comment on some of the sources open to the local historian relating his studies to the greater events of the day. Perhaps more than at any period in English history there were unique and diverse events against which a local researcher may set his parochial material.

Contacts with archaeologists and museums

In addition to maintaining contacts with local authority (and national) archaeologists and curators of county and town museums, the local historian will be able to visit an ever-increasing number of grand houses as his interests move forward from the early Tudor to the late Stuart. This source of actual physical evidence regarding architecture, furnishing, decoration, costume, weaponry and everyday life will not only be of great general value but, if one of the houses lies in the actual area being studied, a whole new matrix for investigation can be developed — was the house the centre of a great estate, and if so how was the land developed and the farms or local 'industries' laid out? If the locality being studied is a town the questions to be posed are equally interesting regarding the earlier owners' activities.

Manuscripts and printed works

Mention was made in Chapter 2 of the volumes *Historical Interpretation* by J.J. Bagley, published by Penguin Books. The second of these, covering the period 1540 until the present day, is particularly valuable for the years being discussed in this chapter, and was issued in 1971. Bagley divided his volume into a series of sections, the first two of which refer to matters between the years 1540-1660 and 1660-1760. Documents discussed and described include quarter sessions and parish records, wills and inventories, lieutenancy papers, state papers, diaries, autobiographies, pamphlets, early newspapers, hearth tax and poll tax records. There is also a section on colonial records, the perusal of which may throw valuable light on papers dealing with the histories of such places as Liverpool and Bristol, which played such a great part in the activities of colonial expansion.

The authoritative works in the *English Historical Documents* series will be commented on in great detail in later chapters. Designed to deal with written sources from 500AD to the present day, they are at the time of writing not quite complete, but several refer to the centuries dealt with in the present chapter. A further significant volume is *Seventeenth Century England* Vol.I, 'Primary Sources', edited by Ann Hughes (London 1980), and this too will be dealt with later, in Chapter 12.

General books The four works in the *Oxford History of England* series are *The Early Tudors* (1485-1558) by J.D. Mackie (reprinted 1951), *The Reign of Elizabeth* (1558-1603) by J.B. Black (reprint 1959), *The Early Stuarts* (1603-60) by Godfrey Davies (reprint 1959) and *The Later Stuarts* (1660-1714) by Sir George Clark (reprint 1961). Although somewhat old, all remain valuable, indeed invaluable until succeeded by more modern works in the same series.

Slightly more recent, less weighty but well worth perusal are two volumes in the *Pelican History of England* series (Penguin Books). They are *Tudor England* by S.T. Bindoff (1950) and *England in the Seventeenth Century* by Maurice Ashley (reprint 1967). A further text, *The Century of Revolution 1603-1714* by Christopher Hill (London 1980) is commented on in the appropriate later chapter, but for the present it is sufficient to say that the former Master of Balliol College writes at one point, 'Far more than from any textbook, the student will learn about the period by reading the plays of Shakespeare, Jonson, Middleton, Wycherley and Congreve; the poems of Donne,

Herbert, Milton, Marvell, Dryden; the essays of Bacon, Addison, and Steele; the letters of Dorothy Osborne; the *Table Talk* of John Seldon; the works of Winstanley, Bunyan, Defoe, Swift.' And that is so, of course. However, the local researcher, perhaps not requiring so catholic and comprehensive a background, may wish to refer to the bibliographies in the *Oxford* books and in the *Pelican* publications. These, particularly in the first-named works, are classified according to such categories as political, constitutional, ecclesiastical, military, and so on.

The kings and queens (and Cromwell) As has been shown (or at least suggested) in the first section of this chapter, the whole business of government from 1485 to 1689 was dependent on the abilities, temperament, whims and fancies of the reigning sovereign of the time. After 1689, when constitutional monarchy was established, matters were rather different.

Once again, as for earlier reigns, there have been dozens of books written about the titular heads of the realm, and the simplest introduction remains *The Lives of the Kings and Queens of England* edited by Antonia Fraser (London 1975). Being but a single short volume, the treatment given to the life of each ruler is inevitably extremely brief, and the local researcher may wish for a fuller treatment. There are two volumes in the Collins paperback *British Monarchy* series: *The Tudors* by Christopher Morris and *The Stuarts* by J.P. Kenyon (both London 1966). Christopher Morris stresses that his book is neither a text to Tudor history nor a series of narrative biographies, and although Dr Kenyon does not make the same point it is apparent from his treatment of the subjects that he adheres to much the same concept. Each work starts with a long introductory essay on the cultural, political and religious backgrounds of the times, followed by accounts of the reigns of the monarchs concerned. As inexpensive introductions to the period which saw the quiet autocratic changes wrought by Henry VII, through the period of the 'divine right' of the early Stuarts, to the emergence of constitutional rule in the days of William III, the local historian is well served by these publications. Both books contain long bibliographies.

Today there are authoritative works on most of the sovereigns whose reigns occurred between 1485 and 1714. For the first king, Henry VII, Professor S.B. Chrimes has written a volume of that name, and it may be useful for certain purposes to compare this modern analysis of the king, his strategy and achievements with the *History of the Reign of King Henry VII*, written between 1611 and 1622 by Francis Bacon. A modern edition with a specially written introduction was published by the Folio Society (London 1971). Biographies of later sovereigns are: *Henry VIII* by J.J. Scarisbrick (London 1981), and another by Jasper Ridley (London 1984); *Queen Elizabeth I* by Sir John Neale (Pelican 1971); *King Charles I* by E. Gregg (London 1978), *Cromwell, Our Chief of Men* and *Charles II* (London 1979), both by Antonia Fraser. There are two earlier books devoted to the life of this king: *King Charles II* by Sir Arthur Bryant, and *The Life and Times of Charles II* by Christopher Falkus. Also, *The Life and Times of James II* by Peter Earle (London 1981); *The Life and Times of William and Mary* by John Miller (London 1979); and two volumes on Queen Anne: *Queen Anne* by Edward Gregg, and *The Life and Times of Queen Anne* by Gila Curtis.

Specialist books A glance through the pages of *British Books in Print* or the catalogues of our major publishers will reveal the titles of the almost bewildering array of books currently available on this period, and the open shelves of the public libraries will display some of these. What now follows can be but brief mention of a few of the books which may be found to be of value: *The Economy of England (1450-1750)* by D.C. Coleman (Oxford 1977); *Peace, Print and Protestantism* (1450-1558) by C.S.L. Davies (London 1984); *The Parliament of England (1559-1581)* and *The Tudor Revolution in Government*, both by G.R. Elton (Cambridge 1982); *Pre-Industrial England* by G. Holderness (London 1983); *The World Turned Upside Down* by Christopher Hill (Penguin 1981). The title of this last-named work is a little ambiguous; the book is, in fact, a most useful work in the field of social history and examines the responses of the population at large to the English Civil War. *The Stuart Constitution* by J.P. Kenyon (Cambridge 1984) contains extracts from essential contemporary documents as well as commentaries incorporating the very latest research up to the time of publication. *The Causes of the English Revolution 1529-1642* by Lawrence Stone (London 1984) contains an analysis of the important issues of the period, and there are a number of further books by Christopher Hill, who is an outstanding authority on seventeenth-century England, all interesting, but particularly relevant to the field of local history research are *Religion and Politics in 17th Century England*, and *Change and Continuity in 17th Century England*. The volume *The Revolution of 1688 in England* by J.R. Jones (London 1982) is of interest to local scholars for the background it gives to the 'Glorious Revolution' and the advance of William of Orange after his landing in Brixham, at the invitation of Parliament.

Finally, *The Lisle Letters* by M. St Clare Byrne (Penguin 1984) is an edited collection of nearly 2000 letters which brings 'to life the intimate concerns of the Lisle household against a backdrop of Tudor politics and court intrigue'. The book is indeed a fascinating one and, when compared with the Paston letters (of the fifteenth century), can provide valuable contrasts in attitudes, modes of life and thought.

A satire by Hogarth and another, of the events of 1745 when the Jacobites sought to put Charles Edward Stuart (the Young Pretender) on the English throne. The scene is the King's Head hostelry at Tottenham Court Road turnpike, watched over by the tavern sign showing Charles II, the Pretender's great uncle, and a noted patron of bordellos. The work is rich in symbolism, and caricatures the lack of discipline of the English foot guard charged with suppressing the rebellion, and the loose morals and conflicting forces of the day. Both the papist Jacobite Journal and the patriotic God save our Noble King (George II) are on sale.

4

1714 to the present day

This chapter covers the reigns of eleven sovereigns and spans 275 years — a far, far shorter period than that dealt with in Chapter 1, and much less time than that discussed in Chapter 2. But in so many ways the period from 1714 until the present has been more momentous than all the preceding centuries put together.

At the start of the period the industrial revolution was in the future, but smallpox was rampant and infant mortality rife. Today the great inventions of the internal combustion engine, the flying machine, the telephone, the nuclear bomb, are history. The population has exploded to unforeseen levels, infant deaths are a tiny, tiny fraction of what they were. Having visited the moon man now waits to stand on the surface of the planets. Smallpox has largely gone, but AIDS has emerged. Where tomorrow?

George I succeeded to the throne of England on 1 August 1714. William III and Mary II had had no children; the Duke of Gloucester, last of Queen Anne's children, was dead long since, and the Act of Succession of 1701 vested the future of the Crown in the nearest Protestant relatives of the Stuarts — Sophia, the wife of the Elector of Hanover, and her descendants. Come 1714, when Anne died, the 'heir' was George Louis of Brunswick-Luneburg, now George I, King of England. He was fifty-four, had never bothered to learn English and spent much of his time in Hanover. During his thirteen-year reign 'cabinet' government began, and Sir Robert Walpole, chief minister of the majority party in the House of Commons, became the country's first Prime Minister.

Indeed, the power of the House of Commons increased, and for many years the political and social power was concentrated in the hands of the men who ruled the Commons — the wealthy landowners. The 'working man' in both town and country had no power, nor vote. *Quieta non movere*, which might be rendered as 'Let sleeping dogs lie', was the cornerstone of Walpole's policy, and Georgian England has been likened to a peaceful Eden.

In 1715 there was a Jacobite rising with the objective of setting James Edward Stuart, the 'Old Pretender', on the throne, but it failed totally and marked the end of Jacobitism as a serious threat. On a somewhat different front 1722 saw the setting up of local workhouses to give work to the poor of each parish.

George II succeeded his father as king in 1727 and reigned for thirty-three years. He too was essentially a German prince, but the country was safely in the hands of parliament. It was a time of religious development and colonial exploration. In 1729 John and Charles Wesley founded the Methodist Society in Oxford, and in 1732 the colony of Georgia was founded in America.

monday Dec.r 19th 1768

A TABLE shewing the Number of People, and how they are employed, in the Work-House, at Christchurch, Weekly.

Days of the Week.	N° of People.	Spinning Flax.	Ditto Worsted.	Knitting Hose.	Making and mending Apparel for the Use of the House.	Making Beds and doing other Household Business.	Picking Hemp.	Digging and other Garden Work.	people	out of work	Old, Infirm, and Children, not able to work.
Monday	70	28	0	1	8	4	2	8	8	0	20
Tuesday	73	28	0	1	8	4	2	3	8	0	29
Wednesday	73	28	0	1	2	5	2	3	8	0	29
Thursday	73	28	0	1	8	4	2	3	8	1	29
Friday	73	28	0	1	8	4	2	8	8	1	29
Saturday	73	28	0	Beating ... a pair of hose	2	5	2	8	8	0	29

the week ends of ... Spinning 35 of Flax — 0-16-5   This Week Ends the Quarter the Earnings Spinning Flax — 10-4-11¾
                                                            Earnings out of the House — 0-2-6
                                                                                            10-7-5

Workhouse records for weekly periods in December 1768. The principal occupations are shown to be spinning flax and worsted, knitting hose and picking hemp. During the week in question no worsted material seemed available. Other tasks included darning and patching, housekeeping and gardening. It should be noted that no less than half the inmates were, for one reason or another, unable to work. Reference should also be made to page 175 of this book, for details of the diet fed to the inmates.

In 1739 war broke out with Spain, in 1743 France and Spain joined forces to fight England (more properly Britain) in both America and India. In the meantime Walpole had retired (in 1742), and the Duke of Newcastle and his brother were the great forces in the political field. The '45 Rebellion came and went with the English victory at Culloden, but in 1756 the 'Seven Years War' between England and France began. Because of early defeats the British government crumbled, and William Pitt (later, Earl of Chatham) assumed effective control. George II died in October 1760, and his grandson came to the throne as George III and was to reign for fifty-nine years, dying blind, possibly mad (and certainly as a recluse) in January 1820.

At the time of his accession George III was twenty-two years old, and it was expected of him that he should choose new ministers to run the government, but, as the twentieth-century historian J. Steven Watson has said, 'any such appointment would no more mark an epoch constitutionally than a change in Windsor coachmen marks a chapter in the history of locomotion.' We may therefore forget the great expectations with which the new reign started. Indeed the king, for the first twenty years of his reign, conspired, intrigued and contrived to create his own 'party', and for a while succeeded. His minister Lord North, together with the king, was mainly responsible for losing the North American colonies. They forfeited the support of the Commons, the merchant class, and the Whigs in general by their ineptitude in dealing with the settlers, and George III's 'personal' rule ended when, in 1783, he granted ministerial power to William Pitt the Younger, who exercised the office of Prime Minister, with just one break, from then until his death in 1806 at the age of forty-seven.

During the sovereignty of George III, Britain saw the French Revolution through and endured the Napoleonic Wars — mainly through the genius of men like Pitt, Wellington and Nelson. The reign was not all intrigue, war and confusion, however, even though from about 1810 the king was blind and often insane. The king, 'Farmer George', encouraged agricultural and farming improvements, and was a noted biblio-phile — his personal collection laid the foundation of the British Library. The Royal Academy was established, prison reform occurred, Cook voyaged to Australia, slavery began to be abolished in British possessions, a new system of poor relief was started, the first steam-boat appeared on the Clyde, and literature flourished; new roads were laid, the first canals dug and hence transport revolutionised.

The king died on 29 January 1820. His eldest son had, since 1811, ruled for him as Prince Regent, and now came to the throne as George IV. The new sovereign harmed the monarchy by his personal extravagance and immorality, and interference with the process of government. The industrial revolution was causing upheavals and distress. Reform, including the reduction of costs and the easement of poverty, was a high priority. Town life was drab, the number of labourers in both urban and rural areas was growing, and there was fear of mob violence. The king's extravagant lifestyle did not commend him to his subjects. Nonetheless, the year 1820 was at the beginning of what has come to be called the 'age of reform' — and this will be commented on in greater detail in Chapter 15. Sufficient for the present to say that the whole question of the relief of poverty was seriously enquired into. Conditions in the general mixed workhouses remained bad, but small gains were made in the care of the young, the sick and the old. Peel revised the penal code and set up a civilian police force in London. Adult education was a topic of importance, and in 1827 the Society for the Diffusion of Useful Knowledge was formed. From the vantage point of the late twentieth century the detailed analyses of many of these measures makes them appear tentative and primitive, but they were steps in the direction of easing the lot of ordinary people, of whom there were an ever increasing number as the population grew and grew.

George IV was succeeded in June 1830 by his brother the Duke of Clarence, who took the style William IV. The new king, liberal in outlook for his day, was popular and agreeable. He so hated pomp and ceremony that he even wished to dispense with the coronation ceremony. During the six years of his reign, the process of change gathered speed. In 1832 a parliamentary Reform Bill was finally passed — the artic-ulate middle class having at last succeeded in obtaining the franchise on the basis of property qualifications rather than the mere ownership of land.

The great Poor Law Reform occurred in 1834 (the first major progress since the beginning of the seventeenth century). Poor Law Unions were set up as parishes were amalgamated, and 'workhouses' were established. An act of parliament of 1833 pro-vided for the state inspection of factories, and in 1834 Robert Owen launched the Grand National Consolidated Union. The Municipal Corporations Act of 1835 ad-vanced the government of the larger boroughs. The great processes of change were to continue for many years.

Princess Victoria of Kent, grand-daughter of George III and niece of William IV, became queen in 1837 and was to reign for sixty-three years. In this long period, one of the greatest parliamentary times in history, men like Melbourne, Peel, Palmerston, Disraeli, Gladstone and others ruled over the government. An important factor in the Victorian age of progress was that there was no major military involvement in Europe (Crimea excepted) during the whole of the queen's reign. Her prime ministers could,

CAUTION.

WHEREAS it has been represented to us from several quarters, that mischievous and designing Persons have been for some time past, endeavouring to induce, and have induced, many Labourers in various Parishes in this County, to attend Meetings, and to enter into Illegal Societies or Unions, to which they bind themselves by unlawful oaths, administered secretly by Persons concealed, who artfully deceive the ignorant and unwary,---WE, the undersigned Justices think it our duty to give this Public Notice and Caution, that all Persons may know the danger they incur by entering into such Societies.

ANY PERSON who shall become a Member of such a Society, or take any Oath, or assent to any Test or Declaration not authorized by Law ---

Any Person who shall administer, or be present at, or consenting to the administering or taking any Unlawful Oath, or who shall cause such Oath to be administered, although not actually present at the time ---

Any Person who shall not reveal or discover any illegal Oath which may have been administered, although not actually present at the time ---

Any Person who shall not reveal or discover any illegal Oath which may have been administered, or any illegal Act done or to be done ---

Any Person who shall induce, or endeavour to persuade any other Person to become a Member of such Societies, WILL BECOME

Guilty of Felony,
and be liable to be
TRANSPORTED FOR SEVEN YEARS.

ANY PERSON who shall be compelled to take such an Oath, unless he shall declare the same within four days, together with the whole of what he shall know touching the same, will be liable to the same Penalty.

Any Person who shall directly or indirectly maintain correspondence or intercourse with such Society, will be deemed Guilty of an Unlawful Combination and Confederacy, and on Conviction before one Justice, on the oath of one Witness, be liable to a Penalty of TWENTY POUNDS, or to be committed to the Common Gaol or House of Correction, for THREE CALENDAR MONTHS; or if proceeded against by Indictment, may be CONVICTED OF FELONY, and be TRANSPORTED FOR SEVEN YEARS.

Any Person who shall knowingly permit any Meeting of any such Society to be held in any House, Building, or other Place, shall for the first offence be liable to the Penalty of FIVE POUNDS; and for every other offence committed after Conviction, be deemed Guilty of such Unlawful Combination and Confederacy, and on Conviction before one Justice, on the oath of one Witness, be liable to a Penalty of TWENTY POUNDS, or to Commitment to the Common Goal or House of Correction, FOR THREE CALENDAR MONTHS; or if proceeded against by Indictment may be

Convicted of Felony, and Transported for SEVEN YEARS.

COUNTY OF DORSET.
WAREHAM DIVISION.

February 20th, 1834.

JOHN BOND.
JOHN H. CALCRAFT.
JAMES C. FYLER.
GEORGE PICKARD, Junior.
NATHANIEL BOND.

C. Groves, Printer, Wareham.

A handbill warning against the dangers of joining a trade union, ranging from fines to transportation.

therefore, concentrate on domestic matters, plus the business of imperial expansion. Although the major events of empire do not impinge to any extent on the fields of study of the local researcher an awareness of the international achievements of British interests will be of value in the pursuit of studies involving trade, commerce and industrial development. In Victoria's reign, the 'British Empire' as a substantial global entity came into being. New Zealand was incorporated in 1840, Canada achieved Dominion status in 1867, to be followed by Australia, with the dignity of Commonwealth, in 1900. In 1876 Victoria became Empress of India. The empire expanded (not without conflict) in Egypt, South Africa, Burma and the Pacific. A controlling interest

Coal mining in 1788. The pit is near Broseley, where coke was first employed to produce pig iron.

in the Suez Canal was obtained in 1875. All this was good for British trade, agriculture, industry and general prosperity.

At home the process of enlightenment continued — transportation of convicts was gradually abolished; the Mines Act of 1842 forbade the employment of women and children underground; factory acts established a 10-hour working day; income tax was revived to encourage Free Trade; an Education Act of 1870 permitted the levying of rates, the building of schools and the provision of teachers, and education was granted to all children however poor their parents. Government legislation also covered such important pioneering activities as public health, artisans' dwellings and trades unions. The Reform Acts of 1867 and 1884 widened the franchise still further. In strictly material and economic fields the railways came, canals were extended, road surfaces improved, the use of electricity for power generation spread; and industrial development boomed.

Of great importance to local historians was, of course, the Local Government Act of 1888 which established elected county councils; and the setting up in 1894 of parish councils and urban and rural district councils.

Edward VII succeeded his mother on 22 January 1901, just three weeks into the twentieth century. Such things — new kings, new centuries — are not in themselves important in a parliamentary democracy. A new political party in power is more significant than a new monarch, and one year is like another in times of peace. The last two decades of Victoria's reign had been somewhat short of social reform by government, for Ireland had been a great problem and Lord Salisbury was disinclined to force social change by the enactment of legislation. Now things improved again. In 1902 Balfour's Education Act created a more uniform system of teaching and administration in England; in 1904 the Licensing Act helped to reduce drunkenness by restricting the sale of alcohol; in 1906 the Provision of Meals Act provided for feeding hungry school-children; old age pensions were introduced in 1908, labour exchanges

A suffragette meeting in Chippenham just before the Great War. Such gatherings were typical of the day, and frequently the scenes of violence. Women obtained the vote in 1918.

founded a year later, and the basis was laid for the National Insurance scheme. Further important legislation entered the Statute Book: the Workmen's Compensation Act (previously passed in 1897) was extended in 1906; in 1907 new powers provided for the medical supervision of children; an eight-hour day for coalminers became law; the Sweated Industries Act came onto the book; and in 1909 the Housing and Town Planning Act began the demolition of slums and the construction of sanitary houses.

The reign of George V began on the death of his father on 6 May 1910, and was dominated firstly by parliamentary problems at home and then by the Great War (or World War I as it is now fashionable to call it) and its economic and political consequences. In 1910 two general elections were required, but unemployment and health insurance measures were enacted.

The story of the war of 1914-18 has no place in this chapter, but it will be referred to in Chapter 16 because 'the war effort' is an important topic in local history. After the armistice the Representation of the People Act extended the electorate, redistributed parliamentary seats and changed the way elections were funded and held. Years of social unrest followed the war, and industry was much affected. A Socialist government briefly held office. There was a short 'general strike' in May 1926; the world economic crisis had an appalling effect on the country during the years 1929-32 — unemployment rocketed and national finances were on the verge of collapse. By 1933 England had begun to recover and unemployment and productive output were carried, by 1937, to an all-time high level. This, according to the distinguished historian A.J.P. Taylor, 'was done against the government, not by their aid'. The many works of Taylor are worth perusing for the light they throw on macro-economic forces at work in price fluctuations, the availability of goods and services, and in food.

Sadly, in the wake of the country's recovery came the Second World War (World War II), which lasted from 1939 to 1945, and these years as a source of studies for local history will also be mentioned in Chapter 16.

George V had died in 1936, having seen the affection of the people on the occasion of his Silver Jubilee the previous year. He was followed by his eldest son Edward VIII, who abdicated to marry a twice-divorced American. This king's reign, which lasted less than a year (January to December 1936) was followed by that of his younger brother Albert, who chose to hold the throne as King George VI. The new king was much loved, and he (together with his family) and Winston Churchill were the twin bulwarks of the country during the war years.

The period since the end of hostilities is that, to a greater or lesser extent, within the lifetime of the reader of this book, and hence there is much primary data available but not too much considered, authoritative analysis.

King George VI died in 1952 (at the tragically early age of fifty-six, worn down by duties he never expected to assume), to be succeeded by his elder daughter, who became Queen Elizabeth II.

The queen's reign has seen many changes of government as Conservative majorities have alternated with Labour, in the wake of general elections. There has been far-reaching legislation in social security provisions, fluctuations in economic prosperity and hence employment levels. State education has been remodelled several times, inflation has run rampant, the currency devalued more than once, the health service has been reorganised, and even county boundaries have been changed, causing the disappearance of some ancient shires and the creation of new ones. Local government has been revised — in 1972 the old urban district and rural district councils gave way to augmented district council areas. This has caused difficulties because of the discontinuities in authority between the parish, district, town and county councils, and some strange anomalies. Even at the time of writing further changes are rumoured.

Sources

Thus the present day is reached, in the skeletal outline of national events from the very earliest of recorded times.

For the early years covered by this chapter, discussions with industrial archaeologists will be of great value, and contact with the Museum of Rural Life (see Addresses, Appendix III) will also greatly help in the acquisition of knowledge, particularly about the revolutions in farming which have taken place. The great London-based museums may also be able to help on points where quite specific knowledge is required, and local town and county museums are frequently able to throw light on national events from local perspectives. As has already been stressed, a proper meeting with the curator or senior member of staff should be arranged — there is frequently more to be learned from the reserve collections than from the exhibits on display.

Books and other printed material

Historical Interpretation Vol.2 by J.J. Bagley (Penguin Books 1971) makes an excellent starting point for the identification of printed material and books of value for the period, but it must be stressed that the closer the researcher comes to the present the more voluminous is the information available. This may range from tax records, Hansard, Commissioners Reports, censuses, the indexes of *The Times*, various Statistical Abstracts, the publications of HMSO, and so on, and so on.

The archivist has the problem of what to keep, the researcher the problems of what to search for and what to read. The volumes in the *English Historical Documents* series will be dealt with in later chapters in this book, but the reader is warned even at this point that these tomes grow in size as the present day approaches, as do the sources to which they point grow in number.

There are five volumes in the *Oxford History of England* series. *The Whig Supremacy* by Basil Williams was originally published in 1939. It was revised by C.H. Stuart in 1962 and has since been several times reprinted with corrections as new information has been discovered and interpreted. The period covered spans 1714-60. The next book deals with 1760-1815 and is entitled *The Reign of George III*, by J. Steven Watson (1960). Strictly it finishes five years short of the end of the king's reign, but there are good reasons for this as the reader will discover. *The Age of Reform* (1815-70) by Sir Llewellyn Woodward (reprint 1962) is followed by *England* (1870-1914) by Sir Robert Ensor (1936), and finally *English History* (1914-45) by A.J.P. Taylor (reprint 1976). This last is, as may be imagined, particularly valuable.

The somewhat slimmer books in the *Pelican History of England* series are *England in the Eighteenth Century* (1714-1815) by J.H. Plumb (reprint 1963); *England in the Nineteenth Century* (1815-1914) and *England in the Twentieth Century* (1914-1963), both by David Thomson (1950 and 1965). Given that this last-named book includes data dealing with almost two decades after the Second World War, it is of great interest for the perspective it takes of the 'welfare state' and the so-called 'affluent society'.

Kings and queens The 'Glorious Revolution' of 1688, which ushered in constitutional monarchy, changed for ever the role the sovereign plays in English, and British, life. Nonetheless the individuals who occupied the throne through the modern period down to the present day have to a greater or lesser degree influenced the history of the country, and a reading of some or all of the following books may help to cast light on national events and hence perhaps more brightly illuminate local matters of consequence.

The Lives of the Kings and Queens of England by Antonia Fraser is a good introduction and may be followed by two volumes in the *British Monarchy* series, *The First Four Georges* by J.H. Plumb (London 1956) and *Hanover to Windsor* by Roger Fulford (London 1960). At the level of individual sovereigns there appear to be no volumes devoted to George II and William IV —although Dr Aubrey Newman is preparing a life of the first-named in the Eyre Methuen series. For the remainder of the kings and queens the following books may be referred to: *The Life and Times of George I* by Joyce Marlow, *The Life and Times of George III* by John Clarke, and *The Life and Times of George IV* by Alan Palmer (all published in London by Barkers). *Victoria RI* by Elizabeth Longford (1964); *The Life and Times of Edward VII* by Keith Middlemas; *King George V* by Sir Harold Nicolson (London 1952) is of special interest because it covers the period of the First World War. *Edward VIII* by Francis Donaldson and *George and Elizabeth* by David Duff bring the biographies of monarchs down to the beginning of the present decade.

Biographies of statesmen For the period covered by this chapter, the 'lives' of statesmen (particularly prime ministers) may be worthy of study. The following of pre-twentieth-century politicians are currently available: *Curzon* by Kenneth Rose; *Earls of Derby* by J.J. Bagley (the fourteenth earl was prime minister three times between 1852 and 1868); *Disraeli* by Lord Robert Blake; *Gladstone* by Sir Philip Magnus; *Lord Liverpool* by Norman Gash (Liverpool was prime minister from 1812 to 1827); *Melbourne* by Cecil Young; *Sir Robert Peel* by Norman Gash; *The Younger Pitt*, two volumes by John Ehrman. The Duke of Wellington is the subject of at least three books, all by outstanding historians: *The Great Duke* by Sir Arthur Bryant; *Wellington: Years of the Sword* and *Wellington: Pillar of the State*, both by Elizabeth Longford. The last-named book deals with Wellesley's political career, the first chronicles his great victories.

Biographies of prime ministers of the twentieth century which may be of value are: *Asquith* by Roy Jenkins (London 1976); *Winston S. Churchill* by Randolph Churchill and later by Martin Gilbert (the years so far covered, in seven volumes, are 1874-1945); *Anthony Eden* by Robert Rhodes James (London 1974); *David Lloyd George — the Early Years* by Bentley B. Gilbert (London 1980).

Finally, the three following biographies may be of interest for the part the subject played in national life: *Ernest Bevin*, the 'Dockers' KC' by Alan Bullock (Bevin was trades union leader and Foreign Secretary); *Nye Bevan* by John Campbell (Aneurin Bevan presided over the creation of the National Health Service); *Hugh Gaitskell* by Philip M. Williams (Gaitskell was the great leader of the Labour Party 1955-63).

Specialist works Of considerable interest are *English Society in the Eighteenth Century* by Roy Porter (Pelican Books 1982); *Life and Labour in England 1700-1780* by R.W. Malcolmson (London 1981); *The Rural World 1780-1850* by Pamela Horn (London 1980); *The Industrial Revolution 1760-1830* by T.S. Ashton (London 1982); *The Age of Manufactures 1700-1820* by Maxine Berg (Fontana 1980).

On slightly different aspects the following are also valuable: *British Economic History 1870-1914* by W.H.B. Court (Cambridge 1984); *Contemporary England 1914-1964* by L. Medlicott (London 1983) — this book contains an 'epilogue' assessing the years 1964-74; *Britain Since 1945: A Political History* by D. Childs (London 1982); *Post War Britain: A Political History* by A. Sked and C. Cook (Penguin Books 1981); *British Society Since 1945* by Arthur Marwick (Penguin Books 1982). The majority of the works cited above contain useful bibliographies and point readers to all manner of specialised subjects, ranging from *The English Poor Law 1780-1930* by Michael Rose (Newton Abbot 1971), through *The History and Social Influence of the Potato* by R.N. Salaman (Cambridge 1949) to *A Social History of Education in England* by J. Lawson and H. Silver (London 1973).

Local historians specifically interested in the general background to twentieth-century England and Britain may find the following additional volumes of value: *The Fifties* by Edmund Wilson (London 1979); *British Society 1914-1945* by James Stevenson (Penguin Books 1980); *England in the Twentieth Century 1914-1963* by David Thomson (Penguin Books 1982); and *Modern Times* by Peter York (London 1983).

It cannot be stressed too much that there are hundreds of specialist texts covering the history of the centuries under review. In the last analysis the final choice must be that of the individual researcher.

Letters patent 25 November 1468 carrying the Great Seal of Edward IV, empowering an almshouse to acquire lands to provide regular income. The blank spaces were intended for the decorated capital letters usually found on such formal royal documents.

5 Essential Sources

The first four chapters have indicated something of the importance of national policies and events in the shaping of the layout of English cities, towns and villages and, indeed, the lives of the people from early medieval times until the present.

It is in the nature of governments, legislators and administrations that over the centuries vast quantities of written material have been generated to initiate, control, modify and comment on all manner of such things and, in the process, record history. Aspiring local historians coming new to the subject may not be aware of the importance to them of a great deal of the material now contained in the national record collections housed in the Public Record Office and the archives of the House of Lords, but it is undoubtedly the case that material contained in those collections can inform on the structure, functioning (and malfunctioning) of local government; it is equally true that information is available on laws and impositions which affected every community; and further, there is hardly any place in the land which is not mentioned a number of times, often to significant effect, in our national records. A random check by way of example, shows one rural village is mentioned eighteen times in such rolls up to the end of the Tudor period, and more than twenty times in the years following to the close of the Hanoverian. Carefully analysed, the records show not only how the estates in the village changed hands (for it may be expected that the lords of the manor and later owners made sure their titles were recognised by the sovereign or parliament of the day), but also how the population rose and fell, how trades and crafts became established, how well armed the adult males were in Elizabethan times of national emergency, how rich or how poor families were, what roads and fields were named in the Middle Ages, and hundreds of other things. This present chapter, therefore, discusses the value of England's great national records, their types and the uses to which they may be put by the local historian. It concentrates on the records themselves — their dates, contents and relevance — matters of commentary, and critical analysis, if any, being dealt with in later pages, at the points at which the records provide data significant to the work being undertaken. Inevitably, the greatest emphasis is placed on the *published* records rather than those which have not yet been transcribed and issued. The chapter is organised on a thematic *cum* classification basis, rather than a chronological one, because this method best suits the material. Relevant supporting data and references are included where appropriate.

The Public Record Office

National records of one sort or another, complete or partial, genuine or spurious, accurate or deliberately falsified, have survived from all the centuries since mid Saxon times. They exist in the form of charters, grants, inquests, court records and business papers of government departments and commissions. Most are of interest to the local historian.

Since the beginning of the nineteenth century, national records have increasingly been made accessible in printed form, for it was recognised at that time that the original documents were not easy to access, for all kinds of reasons — the researcher may not have wished to travel to London, may not have had the linguistic or interpretive skills needed, nor, indeed, the time to devote to the detailed and intensive study required.

The Public Record Office was established in 1838, from which time the Master of the Rolls was authorised to print calendars, indexes and catalogues of the documents in his charge. Prior to that date publication was, from 1800, in the hands of a Record Commission and, from 1825, also undertaken by the State Paper Commission. Various changes in procedure occurred, and in recent years Her Majesty's Stationery Office (HMSO) has published an annual guidebook to the records available in printed form. The book is called *Government Publications, Sectional List 24 — British National Archives*. It is an essential reference, runs to more than eighty pages and contains addresses, prices, and descriptions of the records concerned. Over the nearly two centuries that publication of records has been taking place, six forms of presentation have been evolved: transcripts, calendars, lists, descriptive lists, indexes and catalogues. *Transcripts* comprise complete texts with abbreviations extended wherever possible; *calendars* are summaries, normally in English, sufficient to give a good indication of documents' contents; *lists* enumerate details of classes of records, with brief descriptions and dates; *descriptive lists* are of the same type as the foregoing but rather more brief; *indexes* contain logically arranged references to people, places and subjects mentioned in previous records; *catalogues* comprise publications made to complement exhibitions, and are normally descriptive lists of the items on display.

Chancery records

In medieval times following the Conquest, the Chancellor combined the duties of *all* the present-day Secretaries of State. In consequence there are many classes of record falling into the category of Chancery documents.

To begin with the Chancery was the royal 'writing office' called into existence, perhaps, by the need to record charters as guarantees to land titles. It was staffed by clerks of the royal chapel and headed by a 'chancellor' who was one of the king's chaplains. The writing office of the Saxon kings was a most efficient organisation. It issued 'writs', or formal written documents to officers in the shire courts, properly sealed in the king's name, and the custody of the royal seal (the Great Seal of the reign of Edward the Confessor and later monarchs) was a most important duty of the Chancellor.

After the Conquest, as the prosperity and the interest of the country grew, so did the business of efficient government become more complex, and it became increasingly important not only to keep copies of all important documents but to have an effective storage and retrieval system (to use a modern term). In 1199 the Charter Roll was started, in 1201 the Patent Roll, and in 1204 the Close Roll, all of which will be discussed later in this section. The term 'roll' comes from the curious medieval habit of storing the copies of the charters, letters patent, and letters close, etc., not in registers or some such booklike form, but as pieces of parchment stitched head-to-tail to form rolls, there being one roll for each year. To begin with, the Chancery was peripatetic, journeying with the king and his household, but by the fourteenth century at the latest it functioned from Westminster Hall and, from about 1373, moved to what is now Chancery Lane, into a building the successor to which is now called the Public Record Office.

Charter Rolls A royal charter was the most formal and solemn instrument by which English kings made original (and confirmatory) grants, in perpetuity, to their subjects — individual and corporate. The grants might be of lands, liberties, titles or immunities. The rolls cover the years 1199-1516, in which latter year they ceased, having been taken over by the Patent Rolls. Two publications were made by the Record Commission. The first is the *Calendarium Rotulorum Chartarum* (1803) which gives details of grants made between 1199 and 1483, but it contains important defects. The second volume is the *Rotuli Chartarum in Turri Londinensi asservati (1199-1216)*, which deals in detail with the rolls from the reign of King John. Contents of charters granted between

1226 and 1516 have been issued by HMSO in six books called *Calendar of Charter Rolls*, appearing during the period 1903 and 1927.

The Charter rolls are of two types, the first containing details of original grants, and the second confirmations. There are further works setting out ancient charters and their confirmation: *Cartae Antiqua Rolls* (Pipe Roll Society, New Series XVII and XXXIII); *Monasticon Anglicanum* (1655-73) by William Dugdale and Roger Dodsworth; and *Foedera* (1704-35) by Thomas Rymer. Calendars of confirmation rolls for the years 1509-14 have been published by HMSO in *Letters and State Papers, Foreign and Domestic, Henry VIII* (Vol.I, 2nd edition) by J.S. Brewer.

Patent Rolls The term 'letters patent' is given to documents which are issued openly, with seal or seals pendent. Royal letters patent, adorned with the Great Seal, announce a wide variety of royal acts, grants and leases of land, appointment to offices, licences and pardons, and ecclesiastical presentations. After the year 1516 letters patent replaced charters as the form in which royal grants were made. The Patent Rolls themselves began in 1201, are still compiled, and contain copies of the letters so issued.

In the nineteenth century the Record Commissioners published several volumes devoted to the patent rolls: *Calendarium Rotularum Patentium, John — Edward IV* edited by J. Caley and R. Lemon (1802), but this is an incomplete list and not very inform-ative; and *Rotuli Litterarum Patentium in Turri Londinensi asservati 1201-1216.* Publica-tions of twentieth-century date from HMSO are now seventy-three in number and embrace the years 1216 to 1585. The first two volumes, in Latin, have the title *Patent Rolls* and deal with the years 1216-32, the remaining books are described as the *Calendar of Patent Rolls* and are, in consequence, less detailed. It should be noted that Patent Rolls for the reign of Henry VIII (1509-47) are published in the State Papers series — *Letters and Papers, Foreign and Domestic, Henry VIII.* Further works of value to the local historian are *Calendars of General and Special Assize ... on the Dorses of the Patent Rolls,* appendices to the *Deputy Keepers' Reports* (numbers 9, 26, and 42 to 50) and the Rolls Series volume *Materials for a History of the Reign of King Henry VII.*

Close Rolls The term 'letters close' is given to writs and orders addressed by the monarch to individuals. The documents were folded, the seal being used to 'close' the ends, hence ensuring the contents remained private. The Close Rolls, which summar-ise details of the letters so issued, range over the period 1204 to 1903. The rolls record a very broad spectrum of information — the levying of subsidies, the repair of buildings, the delivery of landed estates to heirs, and more. The backs of the rolls were often used, from 1382 onwards, to record the details of private deeds of all kinds. Close Rolls are a most useful source of local history data, for a diligent search through the published volumes will disclose information on such diverse matters as definition of parish boundaries, enclosure awards, conveyances under Queen Anne's bounty, conveyances in trust for schools, and so on.

Two books devoted to Close Rolls appeared by authority of the Record Commis-sioners (in 1833 and 1844) under the heading *Rotuli Litterarum Clausarum in Turri Londinensi asservati.* They cover the years 1204-24 and 1224-27, and are full Latin transcripts. Between 1902 and 1938 (with a supplementary volume in 1975) fourteen further volumes in Latin appeared (dealing with the period 1227-72, the end of the reign of King Henry III). *Calendars of Close Rolls* have been published in some fifty volumes, dealing with the time from 1272 to 1509. A number of the books also contain supplementary rolls of writs and exchanges. It should be noted that some Close Rolls are printed in Thomas Rymer's *Foedera* and in Sir Francis Palgrave's *Parliamentary Writs*.

Liberate Rolls The word *liberate* comes from the Latin and is used to describe a class of writ under the authority of which royal officers made various payments. They grew out of the Close Rolls, but after 1226 constitute a quite distinct class of document until they ceased to be used in 1426. For the early years they are of some interest to local historians, for they mention purchases by the Crown of various items from specific localities.

In 1844 the Record Commissioners published *Rotuli de Liberate ac de Misis et Praestitis, regnante Johanne* — the rolls for the reign of King John, further fragments from this period being printed by the Pipe Roll Society (New Series XXI). The valuable documents from the reigns of Henry III and Edward I (1216 to 1307) were published in part by the commissioners in *Issues of the Exchequer Henry III to Henry VI*. Modern publications, via HMSO, from 1917 to 1964, comprise a *Calendar of Liberate Rolls* in six volumes covering the years 1226 to 1272.

Fine Rolls The Fine Rolls take their name from the 'fines' (*fin* = 'settlement') or payments made for writs, grants and licences made under the Great Seal (but there are exceptions). Such payments might be made for licence to marry, obtain release from custody, for the grant of tolls and customs, markets, freewarren and fairs, for permission to trade in corn, wine or cloth. They cover the granting of authority to undertake mining operations, assume wardship, take up livery, and many other things which are of interest. In 1835 and 1836 the Record Commission published in Latin *Rotuli de Oblatis et Finibus in Turri Londinensi asservati temp Regis Johannis* and *Excerpta e Rotulis finium in Turri Londinensi asservatis, Henry III 1216-1272*. The calendar, in English, published by HMSO (from 1911 to 1963), embraces the period 1272-1509 and is entitled *Calendar of Fine Rolls*. It should, however, be noted that the rolls for the reign of Edward VI (1547-53) appear in Vol.V (1927) of the *Calendar of Patent Rolls* for that king.

Miscellaneous Chancery Rolls The heading 'Calendar of Chancery Rolls, Various' is that given in *Sectional List 24* to three subsidiary classes: Supplementary Close Rolls, Welsh Rolls, and Scutage Rolls 1277-1326. They were published by HMSO in 1912. The calendar designated 'Supplementary' deals with such things as licences to export wool, restitution of lay fees, respite of assizes of Novel Disseizen for persons serving in Scotland 1303-04, 'Welsh' covers letters relating to Wales 1277-95, and 'Scutage' lists grants of scutage (a payment in lieu of feudal service) from 1277 to 1326.

Inquisitions Post Mortem When a tenant-in-chief of the king died, the escheator (a Crown official appointed to collect revenues) for the shire in which the deceased's estates lay, held an enquiry with a jury empanelled to swear to the state and extents of

A page from the calendar of inquisitions post mortem of the reign of Edward II, issued by the Record Commissioners in the 19th century. The inquisitions list the estates held by deceased magnates. The calendar is of importance to local historians seeking to gain information on the total holdings of a medieval person of great substance.

the lands concerned. The inquisition records are a source of great value to the local historian for they frequently give, at a defined date, the names of the tenants, and lists of rent and services, mills and fisheries, boundary data, and the name and age of the deceased's next heir. Inquisitions post mortem returns also include, where appropriate, proofs of age when the heirs achieved livery of their lands. There have been a number of publications covering these documents. The first was a four-volume set issued under the authority of the Record Commissioners between 1806 and 1828 with the title *Calendarium Inquisitionum Post Mortem sive Escaetarum*. From the outset this calendar (which dealt with the inquests from the reign of Richard II to that of Richard III) was severely criticised as being riddled with inaccuracies and omissions of all kinds, but unfortunately it remains the only printed guide to fifteenth-century inquisitions. A two-volume *Calendarium Genealogicum Henry III and Edward I* was published some years later (1865) to augment the earlier volumes, particularly in matters relating to the succession of heirs. From the year 1904 onwards a new series of publications gradually replaced the books mentioned. These are styled *Calendar of Inquisitions Post Mortem and other analogous Documents* and at present comprise eighteen volumes. Included in the calendar are notifications of all documents dealing with inheritance of land, proof of age, and acquisitions of dower; extents are not calendared. The years covered by the series are 1216 to 1392. *The Calendar of Inquisitions Post Mortem, Second Series*, published in three volumes between 1898 and 1956, records the documents for the period 1485 to 1509 (the reign of King Henry VII). Books in the List and Index series (Vols XXIII, XXVI, XXXI, XXXIII) cover the period from 1509 onwards.

Between the years 1823 and 1834 the Record Commission issued three works listing the inquisitions post mortem taken during the reigns of Edward I and Charles I — *Ducatus Lancastriae Calendarium Inquisitionum Post Mortem etc.* —dealing with the duchy and the palatinates of Chester, Durham and Lancaster, and further details of this class of enquiry appear in appendices to the *Deputy Keepers' Reports* No.39 (Lancashire IpM) and Nos 26-30 (Deeds, Inquisitions and Writs of Dower in the Chester Plea Rolls).

Inquisitions ad quod Damnum These inquisitions were held, to quote the HMSO *Sectional List*, 'when the grant of a market, fair, or other privilege was solicited, to ascertain whether such a grant would prejudice existing interests.' A *List of Inquisitions ad quod Damnum* covering 1243-1485 has been published in the List and Index series (Vols XVII and XXII). These lists are of great value, for many places are readily identified and details are given of a variety of estates and tenants.

Miscellaneous Inquisitions This term is used by the Public Record Office to describe those inquisitions which remained as returns in the Chancery after the classification of post mortem and ad quod damnum documents. The collection is a varied one and includes details of the possessions of men convicted of treason in the reigns of Richard II and Henry IV, and returns from every hundred and county of details of the estates of those involved with Simon de Montfort, the rebellious earl of Leicester in the years after 1264. The *Calendar of Inquisitions Miscellaneous* has been published in eight volumes for the years 1216 to 1485 and is complete.

Chancery Warrants, Letters and Proceedings Chancery warrants contain many items of local interest. A *Calendar of Chancery Warrants* contains documents from the years 1230 to 1326. Other warrants are noted in *Letters and Papers, Foreign and Domestic, Henry VIII*, the *Calendar of Patent Rolls, Edward VI*, and in the *Deputy Keepers' Reports* 43 and 48 for the years 1625-36. In the 'Signet Letters and Chancery Proceedings' categories there is material of interest to the local historian, but rather less so in the former than in the latter. A *Calendar of Signet Letters, Henry IV and Henry V* has been published, and for the Chancery proceedings (which began in 1393 and ended in 1875) the Record Commissioners published three volumes: *Proceedings in Chancery in the Reign of Queen Elizabeth*, with *Examples of Proceedings from Richard II*.

An 'exchequer' table of the 15th century which acted as an abacus. The picture shows the Irish Exchequer, its English equivalent being similar in all material respects.

Exchequer records

The word 'exchequer' comes from the Latin *scaccarium* ('chessboard') and by derivation has been applied to a counting table covered with a chequered cloth, and hence an accounting department. As the name of a government office it is of twelfth-century origin (*c*.1110) and the body itself may have grown out of the Treasury, which was a Saxon creation designed and staffed to ensure tax records were properly kept. 'Exchequer' (from the cloth, which performed a function similar to that of an abacus) came to be applied to the two offices jointly, the 'lower' section being the treasury, concerned with the receipt and payment of money and associated with the Treasury proper, and the 'upper' section (the true *scaccarium*) which was, in fact, a court which met twice yearly to regulate the accounts and co-operate with the *curia regis* (or king's court). At the first six-monthly session, held at Easter, each sheriff paid in a portion of the income due from his shire, and at the second session, held at Michaelmas, submitted the remainder of the 'farm', as the required amounts were described. It follows that the exchequer records in the British National Archives are numerous indeed, and many have been published, firstly by the Record Commissioners then by HMSO.

Domesday Book This mammoth document (now bound between covers and not held in 'roll' form) is the oldest surviving public record of an exchequer type. It is dealt with at some length in Chapter 7, 'The Coming of the Normans'.

The Book of Fees This work consists of a number of manuscripts known as the 'Testa de Nevill', which contain details of returns from the years 1198 to 1293 on the subject of the land holdings of feudal tenants. *The Book of Fees* was compiled around the year 1307. It has been published by HMSO in two volumes. The first appeared in 1921 and covered the years 1198 to 1242; and the second, for the period 1242 to 1293, was issued in 1923. An index followed in 1931.

Feudal Aids Originally feudal 'aids' were regarded as gifts from the free tenant to his lord, or from tenants-in-chief to the Crown, but gradually they assumed the status of taxes which might be levied on specific occasions. Six volumes giving details of the inquisitions and assessments relating to these aids were published between 1899 and 1921 and cover the period 1284 to 1431: Bedford to Devon; Dorset to Huntingdon; Kent to Norfolk; Northampton to Somerset; Stafford to Worcester; York and Additions. These volumes, entitled *Feudal Aids*, provide details of estate tenure during the thirteenth, fourteenth and fifteenth centuries. Being arranged by counties (and hundreds within counties) they provide unique records not only for the genealogist and topographer, but also the researcher studying the scattered nature of some of the estates, and the terms on which they were held.

Memoranda Rolls The scope of these rolls is very wide. They were kept by the King's Remembrancer and the Lord Treasurer's Remembrancer and deal with matters which arose during Exchequer business, especially concerning monies due to the Crown. To a marked degree they supplemented the Pipe Rolls. Many items of local interest, for many counties, occur in the rolls. One volume for the years 1326 and 1327 was published by HMSO in 1969 and details of many other related publications may be found in *Sectional List 24* (IV — *Rerum Britannicarum Medii Aevi Scriptores*). The Pipe Roll Society has issued the text of the rolls for 1199/1200, 1207/1208 and 1230/31.

Pipe Rolls This is the name given to the Great Rolls of the Exchequer which run in almost unbroken annual sequence from 1155 until 1834, when the exchequer systems were completely overhauled. The name 'pipe rolls' probably comes from the fact that the annual records, when rolled up and stacked, looked like pipes. The first extant pipe roll is that for 31 Henry I (1130/1131) and this, with the others from the medieval period, provides a unique record of the development of English towns, the descents of important manorial and merchant families, the development of administrative offices and procedures, and aspects of royal revenue. The Pipe Rolls of later centuries are perhaps of less value to the local historian. In 1883 the Pipe Roll Society, already mentioned, was formed to publish the early rolls, and has so far printed the rolls up to the year 1219 in those instances where they had not previously been issued by the Record Commissioners. The publications of this latter body are noted in *Sectional List 24* (IV and V).

Red Book of the Exchequer The *Liber Rubeus Scaccario*, edited by H. Hall, was published in 1897, as a part of the Rolls Series. It has a number of important uses for the local researcher, among which are quit-claims and the surrender of estates, and the liability of tenants for knight service, serjeanty or shield money.

Issue Rolls This term is the one given to a series of rolls which started in 1240 and continued (with a break of eighty-seven years from 1480) until the end of the seventeenth century. They record payments made from Crown revenues. A number of the

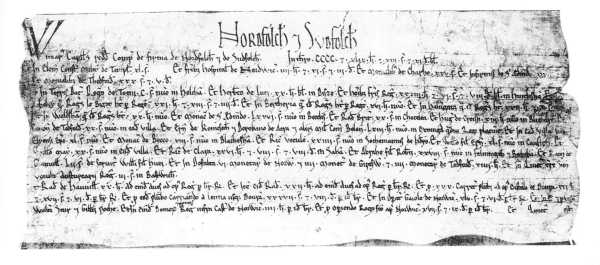

The beginning of the Pipe roll for the year 1184. The account is for Norfolk and Suffolk. The amount the sheriff of the combined counties has paid is shown, and his permitted allowances and deductions.

rolls were published by the Record Commissioners and are noted in *Sectional List 24*.

Originalia Rolls These records contain copies of charters and grants to cities, towns, companies, colleges and other foundations. They also have information regarding estates, manorial surveys, and many other similar matters of use to the local history student. Several of the rolls have been published, in abstract and in total: *Rotulorum Originalium in Curia Scaccario Abbreviatio — Henry III — Edward I* (1805-10); *Rotuli de Oblatis et Finibus in Turri Londinensi asservati, temp Regis Johannis* (1835). The Pipe Roll Society has printed a roll of the time of Richard I (new series XXI), and in Edward Jones' *Index to the Records* (1793) there is a list of *originalia* rolls from 1509 to 1714.

Register of Edward the Black Prince Four volumes of letters, writs and warrants of the Black Prince, together with petitions and other proceedings before his Council were published between 1930 and 1933: 1346-48; 1351-65, Duchy of Cornwall; 1361-65, Palatine of Chester; 1351-65, England. The books contain details of grants and warrants and are fully indexed.

Ecclesiastical records

The bulk of the ecclesiastical taxation records which have so far appeared are for the thirteenth, fourteenth and sixteenth centuries. The first volume was issued in 1802 with the title *Taxatio Ecclesiastica Angliae et Walliae, auctoritate Papae Nicholai V, c.1291*, and is a comprehensive account of medieval benefices. The second, published in 1807, *Nonarum Inquisitions in Curia Scaccarii* records the inquisitions taken on oath in parishes in twenty-seven counties, in order that the tax of 1341 should be correctly assessed and levied. The third publication was the famous *Valor Ecclesiasticus, temp Henrici VIII, auctoritate regia institutus*, made from 1810 to 1834, in six volumes. It represents a survey of all ecclesiastical property in England just prior to the Reformation. It forms an excellent reference document, compiled in the year 1534 at which time the statute giving all first fruits and tenths to the Crown was operative. There are, county by county, lists of the lands, buildings, benefactions, tithes and other incomes owned by parish churches and religious institutions. Some details for some counties are missing — Berkshire, Cambridge, Essex, Hertford, Middlesex, Northumberland, Rutland and Yorkshire — but even in these cases much of value remains.

Judicial records

The judicial records also cover a wide range of activities and authorities.

Curia Regis Rolls These record events for the period 1194 to 1272 in the court *coram rege* (the king's bench) and the bench later known as the court of common pleas. *Sectional List 24* comments: 'apart from their value for the study of medieval English law, these rolls reflect the social and economic life of all classes of English society,' and in fact the *curia regis* rolls are a quite outstanding source of information for the dedicated student. They were published in book form, in sixteen volumes, between 1923 and 1980. Information at local manor level ranges from details of land taken into the king's hands to unwarranted intrusion into woods for the purpose of stealing trees. There are details of charters and grants to individuals and institutions, private deeds and agreements, the names of local inhabitants (and local magnates) frequently giving marital and genealogical information not elsewhere available. It is important to study the contents of the volumes with great care, for the indexes, although useful, are not comprehensive. Volumes earlier than the sixteen books noted above are the Record Commissioners' issues: *Placitorum Abbreviatio Richard I to Edward III* and *Rotuli Curiae Regis* — Rolls and Records of the Court held before the King's Judiciars or Justices, 6 Richard I to 1 John (that is, 1194 to 1200). In addition, the Pipe Roll Society's publications Vols XIV and XXIV contain printed versions of some rolls not covered by HMSO books so far issued.

London Trailbaston Trials The name 'trailbaston' was that originally given to vagrants and others who trailed 'bastons' (OFr for 'stick' or 'cudgel'), but in the fourteenth century the term was widened to describe the sessions held by circuit justices of general oyer and terminer. A *Calendar of London Trailbaston Trials under Commissions of 1305 and 1306* was published in 1976. The roll is of relevance to those local historians researching the subject of crime in the Middle Ages.

Assize records The assize records are those of the appointed clerks and represent the work of the justices executing their various commissions. Six calendars of records have been published, all in 1975: from the reign of Queen Elizabeth I — Sussex, Hertfordshire, Essex and Kent; and from the years of James I — Sussex and Hertfordshire. Assize records exist from the thirteenth century down to the establishment of Crown Courts, but no plans for further publication have been announced.

A roll of 1185 deposited by an itinerant justice regarding wardships. The extract gives details of the wealth in Eton and Horton of the king's ward William of Windsor, who was in custody of his mother.

Ancient deeds The term 'ancient deeds' has been given by the Public Record Office to deeds 'earlier in date than the end of Elizabeth I's reign' (1603). The documents which have been preserved comprise deeds of conveyances of land, covenants, bonds, wills and other private documents, drawn mainly from monastic and personal muniments. The *Descriptive Catalogue of Ancient Deeds* in six volumes, published by HMSO, describes matter drawn from the Chapter House, the Augmentations Office, the King's Remembrancer's Department of the Exchequer and the Chancery. Even so the catalogue contains less than 60 per cent of the 'ancient deeds'. Others appear in *Formulare Anglicanum* by Thomas Madox (1666-1727) and in the List and Index Society's volumes 95, 101, 113, 124, 137, 151, 152 and 158.

Feet of Fines In its medieval sense a 'fine' (*finis* = 'end') was a formal legal agreement regarding the conveyance of land. The agreement itself was legal, but the dispute it settled was fictitious. In other words the 'fine' was a formula of convenience adopted to ensure the transfer was registered in a court of law. The practice began in the reign of Henry II (1154-89). To begin with the agreement between the two parties was registered in duplicate, one going to each of the litigants, but in 1195 a third copy — the 'foot of the fine' — was made for filing in the Treasury. There are in the national archives many thousand of such 'feet' and they form a wealth of evidence regarding local customs, residents, familial relationships, place and field names, local customs, and a host of other things.

The Record Commissioners issued two volumes (in 1835 and 1844): *Fines, sive Pedes Finium, sive Finales Concordiae in Curia Domini Regis 7 Richard I to 16 John* (1195-1214), Bedford to Dorset in counties. Beyond the official publication the earliest fines, from 1182 to 1199, have appeared under the imprint of the Pipe Roll Society — Vols. XVII, XX, XXIII and XXIV; and seven further books exist as unpublished Commission transcripts, Eboracum (Yorkshire) to Warwickshire. The Public Record Office also holds a series of indexes and calendars (from 1509) in manuscript form. Many local scholars have compiled, and sometimes published, feet of fines for the counties in which they have been interested. This point will be mentioned again later.

Hundred Rolls and Placita de Quo Warranto Records The 'hundred rolls' record the results of a survey of local government carried out in 1274/5 on the direct instruction of King Edward I. After the statutes of Gloucester (1278) had legislated against corruption in local administration, and the usurpation of liberties, the *quo warranto* proceedings at general eyres (travelling courts) compelled franchise holders to prove their titles. The two sets of records are, therefore, closely linked. The background to, and manner of, their compilation will be dealt with in Chapter 8, but in summary the hundred rolls are a mine of information to the researcher into thirteenth-century local government practices. Two volumes *Rotuli Hundredorum* were published, in 1812 and 1818, and an index *nominum*. A single volume *Placita de Quo Warranto* by the same editors was also issued in 1818, and contains transcripts of most of the proceedings which followed the survey of the hundreds. This book is also valuable to the local historian, providing a mass of detail on estate boundaries, charters, liberties, advowsons, and a host of other topics.

State Papers

The term 'State Papers' is accorded to the documents which have collected in the offices of the principal Secretaries of State from the time of King Henry VIII. Those held in the Public Record Office start with the year 1509 and run for about two and a half centuries. *Sectional List 24* has nine pages devoted to the titles of volumes so far published. The books are grouped under date headings: *Letters and Papers, Foreign and Domestic, Henry VIII* and *Calendar of State Papers, Domestic* (Edward VI, Elizabeth I and James I, Charles I, the Commonwealth, Charles II, James II, William III, Anne, Home Office Papers, and George III). There are many other calendars: *State Papers Foreign, Colonial* and *Board of Trade and Plantations*, but these are unlikely to be of much interest to the local historian. By contrast, the *Letters and Papers, Foreign and Domestic* contain masses of information and are in fact quite indispensable, and examples of their uses will be given in later chapters where the contents warrant.

Treasury records

Treasury records divide into two classes, 'papers' and 'books', and together they comprise the correspondence and minutes of the Treasury Board between 1557 and 1745. The *Calendar of Treasury Papers* is published in six volumes, and the *Calendar of Treasury Books* appears in thirty-two publications. For the period 1729-45 there is a set of five volumes of a combined *Calendar of Treasury Books and Papers*. Treasury records contain details of towns, harbours, roads, transport, commerce and trade; but specific interests must be prosecuted diligently, for obviously the books contain much which is of no particular moment to the local historian.

Summary

The paragraphs in this section have outlined some of the main archives held by the Public Record Office which (a) have been published, and (b) have the most 'local' value, with the advantage that the printed versions are mainly in English. There are many more lists, indexes, and registers which are available in book form, a large quantity in the original Latin. *Sectional List 24 —British National Archives* (HMSO) —

has been referred to several times. It is an indispensable aid to the historian. Two further works of considerable value are *Record Repositories in Great Britain* (HMSO) and *British National Archives and the Local Historian,* published by The Historical Association (London 1980) and subtitled 'A Guide to Official Record Publications', which of course makes the point that there are mountains of records which have *not* been published, and some of these will be dealt with in later chapters.

The Royal Commission on Historical Manuscripts

In the same way that national records of all kinds, genuine and forged, have survived from all the centuries since writing began, so have historical documents of a private nature. These include manuscripts of many sorts — belonging to colleges, cathedrals, abbeys, monasteries, guilds, corporations, and the houses of the greater and lesser nobility. They tell the history of institutions, individuals, families and causes — some remembered, many totally forgotten. In varying degrees they are all valuable, and to the end of trying to determine what papers existed, and where they were, a Royal Commission on Historical Manuscripts was established in the second half of the nineteenth century. From 1870 onwards the Commission issued reports to the Crown containing accounts of the collections of historical papers inspected. Today, *Sectional List 17* issued by HMSO records the *Publications of the Royal Commission on Historical Manuscripts.* This is periodically updated, and should be regarded as an essential part of every local historian's personal library. The latest issue has thirty pages and gives full details of all the reports made by the Commission since it was instituted. Between 1870 and the present day some eighty reports have been issued.

It is both unnecessary and impractical in a work of this size to detail all the records which have been catalogued — they vary from university colleges, towns, corporations, guilds, ducal and other noble houses to many other categories. Separate index volumes of both places and people are available (although not necessarily currently in print). *Sectional List 17* includes an invaluable alphabetical index which enables local researchers to discover not only if details have been published of the place (or interest) being studied, but also the volume number in which the information appeared. A most important section deals with the records of the House of Lords.

The Victoria County History

Although very different in kind from the great repositories described above, an essential source of reference to basic records, if not in some cases the records themselves, is the series of volumes known collectively as *The Victoria History of the Counties of England.* This undertaking, now under the direction of the Institute of Historical Research of the University of London, is an ambitious ongoing project intended eventually to cover the whole country. It was begun in 1899 and the aim of its founders was to describe the history of every English county, researched afresh from original sources. There were to be general volumes and topographical volumes, the first describing political, ecclesiastical, social and economic elements, and the second the history of each parish arranged by hundreds, wapentakes (Old Norse for 'weapon taking', the name given in the Danelaw to divisions of a shire roughly equal in status to hundreds), or wards. In all cases an academic apparatus of references to source material was to be included.

The plan has not always been adhered to. For example, in the case of Dorset, Vol.II appeared in 1908, a special volume devoted to Domesday was published (as Vol.III) in 1964, and there is almost certainly never to be a Vol.I. In some counties time, and other works, have made deep inroads into the original concept — as witness the publications of the Royal Commission on Historical Monuments (which are described in Chapter 32). Nevertheless the *VCH* works remain an indispensable guide to important records. In none of the volumes should the articles themselves be read uncritically, for they are collections of essays by various authors and are occasionally inconsistent (and some of the older ones are out of date in the light of later research). Individual volumes will be of great interest and value, but more important than these may well be the vast collection of slip references now held by the Institute of Historical Research (see Appendices II and III). These slips were compiled in the late nineteenth century by a group of ladies working in the Public Record Office. The ladies had, for the most part, attended Oxford University, but were not 'graduates' of that august institution, for the times did not permit this. Their job, as part of the *VCH* project, was to comb the public records on a manor (or parish) by manor basis for references, and produce a 'slip' for each reference, thus enabling a *corpus* of information to be assembled on which future contributors could base their articles. To date thousands of slips have not, so far, been used. They are stored, parish by parish, in manilla envelopes in the Institute. They are accessible by serious students, and their use is thoroughly recommended, for they make available avenues for research which the local historian might never otherwise find.

Other sources of national records

It is quite impossible to be exact about the number and whereabouts of the basic records not lodged with the Public Record Office or the House of Lords, and it is not possible to prepare an exhaustive list of all the printed versions. With respect to original documents, many are housed in the British Library, the Bodleian Library and the collections of the major universities, others are perhaps with the Society of Antiquaries. In the cases of the first two named there are partial catalogues, in the instances of the others specific enquiries will elicit information. There may also be published book lists — as witness the one for the library of Corpus Christi College, Cambridge, which houses the fifteenth-century *Itineraries* of William Worcestre.

With regard to published versions of national records, other than those already described (and identified in *Sectional Lists 17* and *24*) the following sources (in addition to the publications of the Pipe Roll Society and the List and Index Society) are worthy of note: Early English Text Society, Selden (and the former Camden) Society, Harleian Society, Oxford Medieval Texts (see Addresses, Appendix III).

A baptismal record for the year 1621, in Latin. When this register began in 1562 English was employed, the classical language being adopted in 1618, the vernacular tongue reappearing in 1699.

Sources of local records

Local records are to be found in many places, and not always in the most obvious. So many estates, manors and properties have changed hands over the centuries that documents recording aspects of their history may be anywhere — in record offices, in the care of trustees, in universities in both Britain and America (to cite just one example, the Sir Nicholas Bacon Collection of the University of Chicago contains hundreds of English local history manuscripts covering the years 1250 to 1700), and in private collections in a number of countries. Only the broadest guide is possible, therefore, as to where to search for what.

National Register of Archives This body was established in 1945 with the primary purpose of recording the location, extent and contents of manuscript collections in England except for those in the care of central government. The register is now part of the Royal Commission on Historical Manuscripts. It can be of immense value to the local historian. In a particular case the author was able to gain access to manorial records in the muniments of the Duke of Northumberland, the Earl of Scarborough (whose ancestors had connections with the place whose research was being undertaken) and the strongbox of a lady who was a private collector. The manuscripts when compared with those obtained from the county record offices of West Sussex, Kent and Dorset, together with two from the Public Record Office, enabled a very comprehensive picture to be built up of manorial court proceedings, land usage, local family connections, tenurial customs, and so on, for the period November 1550 to August 1607.

City and county record offices These establishments are the official depositories for local records. Each has thousands of original documents and is the collecting point for work of local importance which has been published. In many instances pertinent sections of national records have been transcribed and issued by local societies and individuals, and these are held by the local offices. Examples of such work are lay subsidy and muster rolls, protestation returns, and these and others will be called on in later chapters. In other cases, important local manuscripts have been translated and transcribed, and, even when not published, have been copied into readable form, bound into hard covers and deposited. Whilst it is not possible to list all the places where this material may be found (indeed it is probably impossible to discover just how much there is), paradoxically the existence of material of interest is easily ascertained, for the local archivist is certain to know what is available in his own collections. What he may not know is the contents of other record offices, or its possible relevance to the work being undertaken, and although the National Register of Archives may be useful it is by no means complete.

A valid method of approach is to refer to the calendars of inquisitions post mortem to discover the locations of all the properties held, at a point in history, by a magnate who was lord of the place being researched, then to write to the archivists in the corresponding counties, for details of any relevant records they may hold.

Other sources Similar approaches to those just outlined may be made to museum curators and the custodians of public 'local studies' reference libraries. A properly arranged meeting with the holders of any of the public posts mentioned, with a clear idea of the objectives to be achieved, will save days of random searching.

A further method is to trace the senior living descendant of a known early lord of the manor and enquire if he knows of any manorial papers which may be of value. The author has several times used methods such as those outlined with conspicuous success. The genealogical technique is perhaps the most difficult to use, for heiress marriages frequently complicate matters, manors were taken into the kings' hands and then granted to cadet lines or elsewhere, bloodlines became extinct, and so on. But the work *can* be done with the aid of the *Complete Peerage*, the old county histories, the *Gentleman's Magazine, The Ancestor*, a letter to the College of Arms, Burke's or Debrett's, or such nineteenth-century compendia as *Miscellanea Genealogica et Heraldica*. Like so many things in historical research the discovery of important local records depends on skill, tenacity, inductive and deductive reasoning — and the occasional happy accident, as may well become apparent in succeeding chapters.

Section III
MORE DETAILED RECORDS BY PERIOD

6 The Saxon and Danish Periods c.500-1042

The period from the time when the first Saxon and other Germanic peoples came to Britain and the death of Harthacnut (or Hardicanute) in 1042 was an important one in the formation of the 'English' nation. In the course of some six hundred years petty kingdoms came and went, the invaders and the indigenous populations were, to a greater or lesser degree, confirmed or converted to Christianity, and the country narrowly avoided becoming a Scandinavian dominion. It was eventually united under a series of undisputed monarchs; the Viking, Anglo-Saxon-Jutish and residual British cultures moved slowly together, and from this union there emerged a society which was reasonably stable and which played an important part in the development of the nearby countries of Europe.

In many ways this period is a most rewarding one to the historian researching the beginnings of his place of interest, for even though the village may be post-Conquest, or the town established as late as in the twentieth century, the land on which it stands was once in the kingdom of Wessex, Essex, Sussex, Kent, Mercia, English Northumbria, York

From the 5th century onwards, Roman Britain was invaded by initially Germanic tribes of Angles, Saxons and Jutes, and later by Scandinavian Vikings. By the 11th century the south and west of England was Anglo-Saxon-Jutish, and the north and east Danish.

A reconstruction of the timber buildings of an early Saxon village. This village, West Stow in Suffolk, was occupied from the early 5th to the mid 7th century.

or East Anglia; or perhaps Bernicia, Deira, Lindsey, or some other minor tribal unit such as that of the Middle Angles, the Hwicce, or the Magonsoete. All these (and others) enjoyed petty sovereignty for a greater or lesser span during the period being discussed.

Two very good general introductions to the times are those identified in Chapter 1. The first, *The English Settlements* by J.N.L. Myres deals with the continental backgrounds of the Germanic tribes who settled in Britain — the Ingaevones, Frisians, Eudoses and the Chauci, as well as the more well-known peoples who had absorbed them, the Angles, Jutes and Saxons — their customs, fashions, artefacts and tribal territories (which eventually became 'kingdoms') in their new homeland. The second book *Anglo-Saxon England* by F.M. Stenton follows on and describes the kingdoms of the southern English, Anglian Northumbria, Mercia; the Scandinavian years; many aspects of English society and the last years of the English state. The book is particularly valuable for its descriptions of the Reformation of the Church in the tenth century, and the conditions in England just prior to the Conquest — rural society, the Danelaw, towns and trade, and the Church itself.

A further work of much value is *The Beginnings of English Society* by Dorothy Whitelock (Pelican Books 1965) which covers much the same ground as Sir Frank Stenton's book, but in a different way. However, the great reference volume for this period is the first in the series *English Historical Documents* (London 1979). This work, also by Dr Whitelock, embraces the period *c.*500-1042, and gives the modern local historian direct access to an up-to-date, scholarly translation of primary source material of all kinds. Not the least value of the publication is a general introduction of over ninety pages, and a lengthy bibliography identifying the principal modern works recounting the country's history between the time of the Germanic settlements and the accession of Edward the Confessor.

The amount of original material available for the period is considerable, far more than the average local historian might, on first examination, suspect. Much of it is allusive, irritatingly cryptic or downright unintelligible in that it refers to people, places and events of which there are no other known records, but what remains is invaluable at both national and parochial levels.

For convenience of commentary the information may be divided into a number of classes. The first is essentially a *narrative* one, comprising 'histories', poems, sagas, 'annals' and occasional pieces. Much of the material is no doubt fanciful, distorted or embroidered, but even this can, where relevant, be woven into a local history provided the material is properly explained and the writer places it in its historical, cultural and social contexts. For example, in the biographical writings of the Scandinavian chronicler Nithard, there is reference to the 'Northmen' plundering Southampton (*Hamwig*) around the year 842, and the narrative of Simeon of Durham says that in the year 764 (following an exceptionally icy winter) 'many towns, monasteries and villages in various districts and kingdoms were suddenly devastated by fire ....' (see Whitelock).

The second class of source material comprises *laws* and this is remarkably fruitful, for not only does it give valuable insights into the way the land was governed, the social mores and the customs which became codified, but also names many places. For example, *c.*680: 'If a man of Kent buys property in London, he is to have two or three [men] as witness'; *c.*890: 'Whoever steals on Sunday, or at Christmas or Easter, or on the Holy Thursday in Rogation days [shall doubly compensate] as in the Lenten feast'; *c.*997: 'And no one is to slaughter an ox unless he has the witness of two trusty men, and he is to keep the hide and the head for three days ....'

The third class of material comprises *charters*, which were essentially confirmation of grants of land, privileges and other benefits to individuals and institutions. The earliest charters date from around the year 670, as instance a grant by Frithuwold, sub-king of Surrey (a province at that time of Mercia) to the monastery of Chertsey, of land in the area of Thorpe, Egham, Chobham, Cobham, Woodham and *Hunewaldesham* (in Weybridge), and an estate 'by the port of London where the ships come to land'; and the latest charters were granted in 1042 when, in one case, Harthacnut and his mother, Emma, gave land at Hemingford in Huntingdonshire to the church of Ramsey.

The fourth, and final, class of records may broadly be dubbed *ecclesiastical*. These documents, often dealing specifically with church matters and religious issues, nonetheless because of their very bulk often throw light on the social history and political issues of the day. Two examples will suffice to complete this introduction. In Rudolf of Fulda's 'life' of St Leofgyth, written in 836, are some fine details of the double monastery in Wimborne in Dorset, and in a letter (dated 801) from Alcuin of York 'the humble deacon' and intimate of Charlemagne, are interesting references to Northumbrian affairs.

Narrative sources

The value of the *Anglo-Saxon Chronicles* has already been stressed and, in Chapter 1, details have been given of readily available modern editions and commentaries. The Chronicles are fanciful in parts: 'The first inhabitants of this island were Britons who came from Armenia and first occupied southern Britain . . .,' and 'Five thousand and two hundred years had passed from the beginning of the world to the year AD11,' but for the Saxon (and later) times they are most useful: 'In this year [823] . . . Egbert King of the West Saxons and Berornwulf King of Mercia fought at Wroughton in Wiltshire and Egbert had the victory . . . and there was killed Hun, ealdorman of the province of Somerset, and he now rests in the city of Winchester.' 'In this year [892] the great Danish army . . . came up into the estuary of the Lympne . . . in East Kent, at the east end of the great wood which we call *Andred*,' that is to say the weald near Pevensey which the Romans called *Anderida*. Local historians with interests in eleventh-century Kent and especially the exploits of King Harold II in October 1066 will be interested to learn the narrative continues: 'the wood is from east to west 120 miles long, or longer, and 30 miles broad. The river of which we spoke before comes out of the Weald . . .'. The *Anglo-Saxon Chronicles* contain hundreds of references to places, fortresses, who fought whom and where: 'In this year [903] the army [of Ethelwold] in East Anglia . . . harried all over Mercia until they reached Cricklade . . . .' Sometimes there are references to disease (such as the great murrain of 986), trades, and adventures: 'In this year [891] three Scots came to King Alfred in a boat without any oars from Ireland . . . the boat . . . was made of two and a half hides . . . after seven days they came to land in Cornwall.'

The second great class of narrative documents comprises the histories of kings, saints and places. The most convenient initial access to these is via Dr Whitelock's book *English Historical Documents c.500-1042* (which for convenience will be referred to as *EHD1*).

Another, but far more limited, work is the *Life of King Alfred* by the monk Asser, a friend of the king, and later bishop of Sherborne in Dorset. The 'life' is of special value for there is no dominant history of this time. The text has been edited by W.H. Stevenson and published in 1904 (Oxford University Press) and reissued with notes on later scholarship in 1959. Asser provides a unique portrait of an early English king and, more importantly, details of a great Saxon royal household, institutions and contemporary events.

The *Historia Regnum* (History of the Kings) is an early twelfth-century collection of extracts from documents describing early events in Northumbria, Durham and other places. Its compilation is often credited to Simeon of Durham who, in 1104-08, wrote a history of the Church in the Palatinate. The actual authorship of the *History* may not concern local historians other than those of specialist persuasion, but it and other textual matters have been explored by Peter Hunter-Blair in his contribution to *Celt and Saxon*, edited by Nora Chadwick (London 1968). The *History* is richly laced with euphemisms for death: 'X was taken from the shipwreck of this life,' 'Y was snatched from the whirlpool of this polluted life,' 'Z left this mortal flesh for the eternity of the true light,' but many historical events are reported — the burning of York Minster in 741, the campaigns of Eadberht in 756, the burning of Catterick in 769, the subjugation of the area around Hastings in 771, the famine and deaths of 793 when 'horrible lightnings and dragons in the air . . . were often seen to fly to and fro.'

The *Flores Historiarum* (Flowers of the Histories) is a work written by Roger of Wendover, a monk of St Albans writing in the early part of the thirteenth century, and who died in 1236. He and his work are dealt with in *The Monastic Chronicler and the Early School of St Albans* by C. Jenkins (London 1922), but important extracts from the *Flores* are printed in *EHD1*, and refer to the pillage of Hartness and Tynemouth in 800, the ravaging of Thanet in 969 and many other notable events. A further manuscript describing happenings in the north of England is the anonymous *History of St Cuthbert* compiled in the mid tenth century. Reference should also be made to the section 'Early Latin Biographies' in *Anglo-Saxon England* by Sir Frank Stenton, and to *EHD1*. *St Cuthbert* is useful for the information it gives on the fluctuating fortunes of the Saxon and Viking interests in specific localities. William of Malmesbury (*c.*1095-1143) was perhaps the most important writer of history following Bede. His main work was *Gesta Regum Anglorum*, a history of England from 449 to 1120 (sometimes called *De Gestis Regum Anglorum* and hence 'On the Acts of the Kings of the English'), see *Historical Writing in England c.550-c.1307* by A. Grandsen (London 1974); 'William of Malmesbury's Life and Work' by H. Farmer in the *Journal of Ecclesiastical History* xiii (1962), and a translation in *William of Malmesbury's Chronicle of the Kings of England* by J.A. Giles (London 1876). The Chronicle contains many references to events in many places. Of particular interest is an account of the reign of King Athelstan (925-40) including events in Chester, Hereford, Exeter, York, etc. Although some of the things described are but legendary, the material usefully augments that of other writers. The writing in *Chronicon ex Chronicis* (dating from the twelfth century, but describing occurrences from the period under discussion), is by several authors and is based in part on originals now lost. Authorities are undecided as to the identity of the originator of this work, but the *Oxford Companion to English Literature* (1985) ascribes it 'traditionally' to the monk Florence of Worcester (see Chapter 7). Reference may be made to Grandsen (above) and *EHD1*. This latter carries substantial extracts relating the reigns of the Danish kings of England, and 'Florence' has much of relevance to say in augmentation of the information contained in the *Anglo-Saxon Chronicle*.

Finally, attention is well worth paying to the comparatively minor poetic and descriptive manuscripts identified in *EHD1* on pp.319-53. These include 'the battle of Maldon', and a number of Nordic sagas, many of which contain references to Scandinavian activities in England, the attack on Norwich in 1004 and the battle of Ashingdon (*Assatun*) in Essex, to name but two.

Laws

It is apparent from the general reading of historical commentaries, and Stenton's *Anglo-Saxon England* is a typical example, that at the time of the English settlement of Britain, the newcomers had a codified legal system 'agreeing in its main principles with that of other Germanic peoples, but it was not until after the coming of Christianity that any of this mass of legal custom was written down' (Whitelock *op cit*). Bede also records that King Ethelbert of Kent (*c.*610) established 'judicial decrees after the example of the Romans, which, written in the English language, are preserved to this day and observed by the people.' Indeed, these laws, and the decrees laid down by other and later kings, constitute a main source for the understanding of pre-Conquest administrative, social and economic practices. This is not to say that the laws as written are easy to understand. The terminology is of another age, and the age itself spanned four hundred years (from Shakespeare until the present day is a comparable time). Not only did the meanings of words change, but quite ordinary terms were used in special ways. The laws, however, are of very great value in assisting local historians to understand some of the conditions under which the English lived and what was expected of them by their fellows.

Useful texts (in modern translation) are *The Laws of the Earliest English Kings* by F.L. Attenborough (Cambridge 1922), and *The Laws of the Kings of England from Edmund to Henry I* by A.J. Robertson (Cambridge 1925). There are a number of valuable books in German (notably *Die Gesetze der Anglesachen* by F. Lieberman, Halle 1903-16) and readers who may find these of special interest are referred to Stenton's *Anglo-Saxon England* pp.703-05. A valuable commentary on, and quotations from, the laws appear in *EHD1* pp.357-478.

What now follows is a *very* brief selection from the laws of the ancient kings, illustrating at least a small part of the riches they contain.

Ethelbert of Kent (died 616)

Lieberman (*op cit*) suggests the laws, numbering some ninety in all, were written down in 602-03. The first group deals with the obligations of the subject to the king, punishments for offences in his presence, and so on. Later, it is possible to gain modest insight into the structure of Kentish society: after the nobles were the *ceorls* (or free peasants), a large number of half-free men termed *laets* who may have been of the pre-English population, and (law 16) at least three classes of slaves. An interesting reference (law 81) is to the custom called 'the morning gift', that made by a husband to his bride the morning after the consummation of the marriage.

Hlothhere and Eadric, Kings of Kent (673-85)

These joint kings 'added to the laws which their forefathers had made'. In the main the additions deal with keeping the peace, but some are to do with trade. Law 16.2, for example, says that if a man of the kingdom cannot purchase property with proper witness, then he is 'to declare at the altar ... with the town reeve that he bought [or bartered] the property openly by public transaction in the town, and he is then to be given back his price.'

Wihtred, King of Kent (695)

Further laws were devised on the sixth day of *Rugern* ('rye harvest', probably September) in the year 695. They were drafted mainly by bishops, hence they have a strong religious and moral tone, legislating against drunken priests, working on Sundays, and sacrificing to devils.

The laws of Ine (688-94) and the laws of Alfred (c.885-99)

Kentish laws apart, the laws of Ine are the oldest known to us, and their survival is due to their being added as a supplement to the laws of Alfred. Together with the latter they form a comprehensive statement of the West Saxon judicial climate, and throw much light on the life of the day. Examples are: 'a *ceorl's* homestead must be fenced winter and summer'; 'a ewe with her lamb is worth a shilling until fourteen days after Easter'; 'he who has ten hides must show six hides of sown land'; 'each man must keep carefully his oath and pledge'; 'if anyone is born dumb, or deaf, so that he cannot deny his sins or confess them, the father is to pay compensation for his misdeeds'; 'if anyone in a lewd fashion seizes a nun either by her clothes or her breast without her leave, the compensation is to be doubled'. There are many laws concerning personal honour, abjuring witchcraft, purchasing and exchanging goods, bribery, trial by ordeal, and much more. Read with care they are a rich source of information to the local researcher in building up a picture of Saxon life.

Further laws and ordinances

The laws of Edward the Elder (Alfred's son) and his successor Athelstan hold, with minor exceptions, little of interest to the local historian. The exceptions are those codes known as Athelstan V (issued at Exeter) and VI (concerning London). The first includes measures to be taken against reeves who accepted bribes and were neglectful, against cattle thieves, and matters of not dissimilar kind. The second text, although carrying ordinances dealing mainly with 'London', nonetheless probably relates also to Buckingham, Surrey and Kent. The rules concern the protection of property, arrangements for mutual assistance known as 'peace guilds' (which seem not unlike the present-day concept of 'neighbourhood watch'), and the assemblies of hundred-men and tithing-men. English translations appear in the volume by F.L. Attenborough cited above, and in *Ancient Laws and Institutes of England* edited by B. Thorpe (London 1865).

The hundred ordinance

In the eleventh century the territorial division known as the *hundred* was the basis for the organisation of both public finance and justice, and other administration. It operated in England south of the Thames, large areas of Mercia, East Anglia and the southern Danelaw. Useful references may be found in the bibliography on pp.716-18 in Stenton's *Anglo-Saxon England*. The 'hundred' varied in size, and also in the number of 'hides' it contained. This is not the place to explore the problem, or to examine that of the *hide* (the *English Historical Review* xvii, 1902, contains an important essay 'Large Hides and Small Hides' by J. Tait, and *The Hundred and the Hundred Rolls* by Helen Cam, London 1963, although post-Conquest in focus, is very relevant). The purpose of the present discussion is to note that about the year 950 an ordinance was issued for the government and management of hundreds, and this seems to have brought together, and recorded, practices and arrangements which had, to a greater or lesser degree, been in place for some time. *EHD1* says, 'It seems simplest to regard this ordinance as part of a movement to secure some uniformity of administrative arrangements when, after the re-conquest of the Danelaw, the kings of Wessex were ruling all England.' The ordinance appears in the books by Thorpe and Robertson which have already been mentioned. In fine it laid down that the hundred court was to assemble every four weeks, and that the common law not only be honoured but that there should be a 'day appointed when it shall be carried out'. There were clauses laying down relationships between hundreds, the pursuit and apprehension of criminals, and other things of a domestic nature all of which are material to the understanding of the times.

Later Saxon laws

The later Saxon codes and laws, spread over the years 950-1042, regulated a number of issues, and the majority appear in translation in Robertson and Thorpe. *A Handbook to the Land Charters and Other Saxonic Documents* edited by J. Earle (Oxford 1888) is also of value, especially for the reign of Cnut. The secular group of King Edgar's codes drafted at Andover 959-63 confirm the meeting of the hundred court, and laws 5.1 and 5.2 laid down that the borough court was 'to be held thrice a year and the shire court twice . . . and at the shire meeting the bishop and the ealdorman [were] to be present, there to expound both the ecclesiastical and the secular law.' Rules were laid down regarding sureties, and the hunting down of criminals that they be taken 'dead or alive'. Coinage was standardised, as was the system of measurement 'observed in Winchester'.

King Ethelred's code issued at Wantage, probably in 997, is valuable in that it gives important information on the administration of the Danelaw, and in 'the peace which the ealdorman and the king's reeve give in the meeting of the five boroughs' — that is to say Lincoln, Stamford, Nottingham, Derby and Leicester. The laws held for hundreds and wapentakes. The code dealt with a variety of matters such as trial by 'ordeal of fire or of iron'; issuing false coinage; the slaughtering of animals; and much broader matters of civil disturbance and well-being. King Ethelred's code of 1008 dealt with all manner of moral issues — 'shameful frauds', 'horrible perjuries', 'devilish deeds', 'deeds of murder and manslaughter', over-eating, over-drinking, breaches of the marriage law and 'evil deeds of many kinds'. It dealt too with the defensive works of boroughs, and with military service.

About the year 1020, Cnut, last of the Danish kings of England, developed the code which is much the longest to survive from the Old English era. It was, to a large extent, made up from the appropriate pieces of the laws of earlier monarchs, but there were new elements which this outstanding sovereign wished to be observed 'all over England'. A few extracts will illustrate a little of the range of the code. 'And he who wishes to purify the country rightly . . . must diligently restrain and shun such things as hypocrisy, lies, robbery and plundering'; 'and let us take thought very earnestly about the improvement of the peace and the improvement of the coinage . . . about the improvement of the peace in such a way as may be best for the [law-abiding] subject and most grievous for the thief . . and about the improvement of the coinage [so that there is nothing] false and no man is to refuse it.' 'It is a heathen practice [to worship] the sun or the moon, or fire or flood, wells or stones or any kind of forest trees . . . or to take part in such delusions.' The laws dealt with the rights of reeves and freemen, with buying and selling, with observing the hue and cry, the payment of *wergild* ('man-tribute') —the price set upon a man according to his rank, and paid in compensation (or fine) in cases of homicide and certain other crimes to free the offender from further obligation or punishment. They also covered the treatment of slaves, working on feast days, incest, adultery, arson and much more.

To end this section brief consideration will be given to the 'law of the Northumberland priests', committed to writing around the time of Cnut's laws, that is 1020-23. As Dr Whitelock points out in *EHD1* p.471, 'Evidence relating to the north of England in the later Saxon period is scanty. This code shows us that heathen practices had still to be reckoned with, and it reveals a three-fold division of society for certain purposes, giving a unique term to describe the lowest free class, for it seems to talk indiscriminately of a *ceorl*, a *tunesman* ['villager'], and a mysterious *faerbena* [possibly a freeman who was not a landholder]. It reveals also the organisation of the priests of

York into a community with common obligations and a common chest, the existence of the office of archdeacon in the northern province, and the toleration of the marriage of the clergy in this area.'

Charters

The point of first reference for this important material is the book *Anglo-Saxon Charters* by P.H. Sawyer (London 1968), an annotated list and bibliography issued as one of the guides and handbooks of the Royal Historical Society. It lists nearly two thousand documents under the headings of royal charters, grants by laity, the bishops, other ecclesiastics, miscellaneous texts, wills and bequests, and bounds (that is, estate or manor boundaries). The earliest charters date from the first years of the seventh century, and grants were made in the names of the kings of Kent, Sussex, Essex, Northumbria, the rulers of the Hwicce and Mercia, and all the monarchs of Wessex from Alfred to Harold II.

Charters, especially the early ones, were short and to the point, and their form may well have been based on that of the late Roman private deed. It is likely, too, that the practice of a written record confirming the transfer of land or the gift of privileges, was introduced by the Church, and secular institutions and individuals soon followed the custom. Gradually charters assumed a more inflated and convoluted style, and by the time of Athelstan had become 'absurdly elaborate and florid'. Indeed, due to the influence of Adhelm, oracular, rare and silly expressions became the fashion, but fortunately these were soon dropped in favour of a plainer form (for which modern local historians must be thankful). The volume *Anglo-Saxon Charters* by A.J. Robertson (Cambridge 1956) is worth perusing on the subject and there is a good introduction in *EHD1* pp.369-84.

By the time of Ethelred II (979-1016) a more elaborate system existed, and there seems to have been a royal writer (*scriptor*) who was well placed — he was granted land in Oxfordshire in 984 — and the practice of using a *cyrograph* was introduced. (A cyrograph is a document written in duplicate or triplicate on a single membrane, and with the word *cyrographum* — 'that which is written with the hand' — inscribed in large capital letters dividing the texts, the parchment then being cut through the centre of these characters.)

Charters are a valuable source of information to the local historian. It is worth quoting from Dr Whitelock to this end: 'They tell us of the relations between the kingdoms of the Heptarchy [and] afford incidental information on the effects of the Viking invasions, [they] are indispensable for the study of ecclesiastical history, [they] supplement the laws [both criminal] and those relating to the holding of land.' In addition they refer, from time to time, to aspects of both rural and town life, material well-being, trade and manufacture. To give just a few examples: in 681 a grant by Ethelmod the bishop to his man Beorgyth, of land by the river Cherwell, is important, for information about that part of the country in the seventh century is rare. A charter of Ethelbald, King of Mercia, dated *c.*716/717, refers to salt furnaces and salt houses near Worcester. The restoration by Cenwulf of Mercia (in 799) of lands to Christ Church, Canterbury, throws light on how overlordship was regarded at that time. A document of 804 (a declaration of Ethelric before the synod of Aclea) quotes a nuncupative (oral, unsealed) will. In 968 a charter shows 'King Edgar [giving] to Winchester Cathedral, renewal of the liberty of Taunton, Somerset, as granted by King Edward [the Elder 901-25] in exchange for land at Crowcombe, Compton and Banwell, Somerset, and at Stoke near Shalbourn, Wilts, the land having been later given to the community at Cheddar in exchange for an estate at Carhampton, Somerset.'

Sawyer's book, above, identifies the whereabouts of the charters (genuine and spurious) and their often numerous copies. These are mainly the British Museum, the Public Record Office, the Bodleian Library, or Lambeth Palace. In addition to the publications so far mentioned the following are significant: *Select Charters* by William Stubbs (Oxford 1890; the ninth edition of 1913, many times reprinted, is the best); *The Early Charters of Eastern England* by C. Hart; and a search should be made for the published cartularies (registers of charters) of abbeys — Bruton, Glastonbury, Muchelney, Worcester, Alderney, and so on — many of which have been made available by local record societies. *EHD1* has a useful bibliography on pp.385-7.

Ecclesiastical records

The pre-Viking era

The ecclesiastical history written by the Venerable Bede in 731 has been mentioned in Chapter 1 as being available under the title *A History of the English Church and People*. This volume, with a scholarly introduction by Leo Shirley-Price, is based on a specially prepared Latin text by Charles Plummer, and contains copious notes and genealogical tables. The index contains many references to settlements and other places. The importance of Bede's writings as a source of information for historians of all kinds cannot be exaggerated, particularly regarding eighth-century Northumbria. A great and influential scholar, he lived at a time of great national and spiritual awakening, a time 'during which the future shape and pattern of the English Church and nation were beginning to emerge'. In consequence his 'history', *Historia Ecclesiastica Gentis Anglorum*, is one of the fundamental reference texts which has come down to us, for Bede dealt with not only the northern provinces of England, but went to great lengths (as he outlines in his introductory passages) to obtain information on the history of all the other English kingdoms. This he gleaned from his fellow priests who visited him, and from the study of classical authors. His greatest debt was to the west of England historian Gildas (died 570), whose work *De Excidio et Conquestu Britanniae*, although not a history, contained much of value. Bede, then, was able to write of the East, West and South Saxons, the East Angles, the Jutes, Mercians, the people of Kent, the Isle of Wight, and other places, on as firm a foundation as was possible in his day. He identifies many places, and locates many events. He was the first writer to use, for historical purposes, a method of dating from the year of the incarnation of Our Lord — the system which has now become general.

Bede's history is especially valuable to local historians for the glimpses it gives of social practices. In Chapter 16, for example, he relates how King Edwin of Northumbria (*c.*628) ordered posts to be erected near clear springs adjacent to the highway 'with brass bowls hanging from them so that travellers could drink and refresh themselves.' The book ends with a chronological recapitulation of the whole work, and scholars have noted the influence of this section on the *Anglo-Saxon Chronicle*. *Bede, His Life, Times and Writings* edited by A.H. Thompson (London 1935) is useful background reading.

A number of manuscripts survive describing the lives of early saints, and these accounts are of occasional value to local researchers. It follows that all were written by literate men experienced in gathering information and recording it, and the 'lives' they described were of people who had important influences on the direction taken by society. *EHD1* contains extracts from the 'lives' of SS Gregory, Columba, Wilfrid (and these are particularly rich in describing aspects of life in the England of the seventh and early eighth centuries), Ceolfrith (which has a vivid word picture of religious life in Northumbria, as well as information on buildings and architecture), Guthlac (with insights into the life of a Mercian aristocrat), Willibrord (useful for general conditions in Northumbria), and Boniface (giving the oldest known record of a West Saxon synod). It is of interest to the specialist that this last-named work was first drafted on wax tablets, before being copied onto parchment, having in the meantime been officially 'approved'. The 'life' of St Leofgyth has already been mentioned as having valuable details regarding Wimborne in Dorset. That of St Liudger throws light on Frisian trading activities in York, and describes the working of the blood-feud.

Also surviving are dozens of letters — popes to bishops, bishops to archbishops, archbishops to kings, abbots to abbesses, and much traffic in the opposite directions. It must be admitted that many are didactic, homiletic and downright dull, and hence of limited interest, but some are of more general moment and all, to a greater or lesser degree, are of value to local historians. A wide selection is included in *EHD1* and researchers are referred to this, to the accompanying source references, and to the extensive bibliography.

A letter from the year 704 from Wealdhere of London to the archbishop of Canterbury demonstrates a little of the relations between the kingdoms of the heptarchy; one from Bede to the bishop of York (734) is very lengthy and carries information on the holding of land by title deed, and the organisation of the Church. Many others describing the organisation of monasteries and religious foundations may also be read in *Councils and Ecclesiastical Documents* edited by A.W. Haddan and W. Stubbs (Oxford 1871). There is an important body of letters from Alcuin (sometimes called Albinus or Ealhwine, 735-804) an influential theologian. Letters to ealdormen, bishops and others express views on events in Mercia, Kent and other places. Alcuin was also responsible via his writing school for the development of the Carolingian minuscule script and other innovations. Much of his correspondence appears in *Alcuin of York* by Stephen Allott (York 1974), and his life is the subject of *Alcuin, Friend of Charlemagne* by E.S. Duckett (London 1951).

The period after AD820

The records of which we have knowledge for the period after the coming of the Vikings divide, as for the years just discussed, into three main categories: prose writing, letters, and 'lives' of saints. One of the richest, perhaps *the* richest, source of prose is represented by the work of Alfred the Great, king of the West Saxons from 871 until his death in 899. Alfred, to a very substantial extent, transformed the history of pre-Conquest England and, quite apart from the 'life' by Asser, mentioned earlier, there are at least two books worthy of study: *Alfred the Great and his England* by E.S. Duckett

A page from Gregory the Great's Pastoral Care, in English (from the original Latin) made under the personal direction of King Alfred. The work of Pope Gregory is of great interest, for it was he who sent St Augustine on his mission to Canterbury in the late 6th century. The page is in insular miniscule script (with additions c.1250), with interesting decorations.

(London 1961), and *Alfred the Great*, a series of essays edited by S. Keynes and M. Lapidge (London 1983). One of this remarkable king's achievements was translating, or sponsoring the translation of, a number of historical works, the contents of some of which are useful to researchers in the field of local studies.

Alfred's version of St Augustine's *Soliloquies* (*EHD1* pp.917-18) describes the nature of 'bookland' (*bocland* = a portion of common land granted by charter, under the sovereign's orders, to a private owner), and comments on how royal expenditure should be conducted. His rendering of Boethius' *De Consolatione Philosophiae* translates passages setting out the three orders of society — there must be men who pray, men who are soldiers, and workmen — and things regarding land, gifts, weapons, food, ale and clothes. Local historians researching the history of learning may find Alfred's version of 'Pastoral Care' (*Cura Pastoralis*) by St Gregory (Pope Gregory the Great, who sent Augustine to England in the sixth century) of great interest. Of especial value are the prose and verse prefaces written in Old English by Alfred himself, published in *King Alfred's West Saxon Version of Gregory's Pastoral Care* (Early English Text Society 1871).

In the field of letters there is pertinent material, and the following works are well worthy of reference: *The Crawford Collection of Early Charters and Documents* edited by A.S. Napier and W.H. Stevenson (Oxford 1895), *Memorials of St Dunstan* by W. Stubbs (Oxford 1870), and *EHD1* pp.890-96.

In the third category of material from the years after 820 (that of the 'lives' of the saints) the *Memorials of St Dunstan* is useful for the mention of places at which important events took place. Aelfric's 'life' of St Ethelwold (included in translation in *Aelfric of Eynsham — An Anglo-Saxon Abbot* by S.H. Gem, Edinburgh 1912), and the 'life' of St Oswald, archbishop of York, included in *The Historians of the Church of York and its Archbishops* edited by J. Rame, are worthy of scrutiny. The latter 'life' (written about 1005) gives details of battles of the time of King Ethelred II (reigned 979-1016).

The Conqueror and his half-brothers Bishop Odo and Robert of Mortain.

7
The Coming of the Normans 1042-1189

The years covered by this chapter run from the accession of St Edward the Confessor until the death of King Henry II. The period was one of great upheaval and transition, and it has been said 'that between these dates there took place changes in English society ... so fundamental as to warrant their separate consideration' from all other periods.

Looked at from the broadest viewpoint this is undoubtedly true, but in many places the changes came slowly, and in some areas hardly at all, in that they scarcely affected the way people farmed the land, obtained their food or observed their religious beliefs. At the beginning of the period the kingdom, finally united under a single monarch, was already divided into shires and hundreds, bishoprics and parishes. Villages grew steadily as people co-operated to claim new areas for settlement and cultivation; and the boroughs, originally formed to meet military and defensive needs as well as trading, grew separate from the hundreds. Edward the Elder (900-925) had issued an edict that all buying and selling must take place openly before the town-reeve in the market square and this, with other measures, developed a sense of independence within the walls, and some boroughs acquired their own courts.

The local historian, researching the history of any substantial, named settlement, is well served by the work of scholars in broader studies, and the best introduction known to the author to the period under discussion remains *From Domesday Book to Magna Carta* by A.L. Poole (Oxford, reprint 1955). Dr Poole lays a groundwork for the appreciation of government and society, rural conditions, towns and trade which, used in association with the extensive bibliography, remains invaluable. His work is, nonetheless, more than thirty years old, so should be augmented by the reports of later studies such as the volumes in the *Regional History of England* series edited by Barry Cunliffe and David Hey. These volumes (not all of which have yet emerged from the press) will, when complete, number twenty-one, and are designed to be of the greatest value to local historians. The country is divided into ten regions, and, with one exception, there are two books devoted to each — one for the years up to AD1000 and one for after that date. There is extensive tabulated and bibliographic matter, identifying works covering a number of localities within the regions.

An older book, but still important, is *Life on the English Manor* by H.S. Bennet (Cambridge 1937) which, building on the foundations laid by the late Victorians Maitland (*Domesday Book and Beyond*, Cambridge 1897) and Vindogradoff (*Villeinage in England*, Oxford 1892), develops a comprehensive picture of all aspects of manorial life and government. *The Making of English Towns* by David Lloyd (London 1984), in addition to being useful in its own right, contains an extensive list of books of regional and local interest, categorized by geographical area such as South West, North East, North West, etc., and by period, Roman, Middle Ages, and so on. There is also a section naming books devoted to special themes.

The reading of modern texts and the comparison and correlation of information contained in them is an essential part of local history research, but these books, articles and technical papers are, in some fields, interpretations by twentieth-century scholars who, to a greater or lesser degree, stand between the researcher and the primary material. The local historian has at his disposal a vast quantity of early evidence and it is to this he should turn wherever possible. It is useful to consider this information under one of three headings. The first may be described as *narrative* and comprises the chronicles and annals of the kingdom; the ecclesiastical history by the monk Ordericus Vitalis, the 'modern history' of William of Malmesbury or the 'History of the English' by Henry of Huntingdon and, if the term 'narrative' is widened a little, the Bayeux tapestry. If he is lucky he will find his locality, or some person with local connections, mentioned in one of these. In the *Anglo-Saxon Chronicles* (which ended only with the death of Stephen in 1154) for example, for 1064, 'the northern men did much damage around Northampton ... they killed people and burned houses and corn and took all the cattle ... and captured many hundreds of people ... so that the shire and [its neighbours] were the worse for it for many years,' or it may simply be a picture of Robert of Mortain, the king's half-brother who held many manors, in the Bayeux tapestry.

The second source may be termed *general records* and includes documents which, although mainly applicable to the country as a whole, may nonetheless throw important light on customs, expectations and duties, which is of great value in describing how an individual village, manor or parish was organised, or how it functioned. Typical of this group is that 'mysterious document' known as the *Rectitudines Singularum Personarum* (the rights and ranks of the people), which sets out the conditions and expectations of thegns, geneats, cottars and boors in the late Saxon period: 'a thegn must contribute these things ... armed service, repairing of fortresses and work on bridges ... military watch, almsgiving and church dues ...'; a geneat 'must pay rent ... ride and perform carrying services ... bring strangers to the village ... take care of the horses ... and carry messages far and near ...'; the cottar 'must work for the lord each Monday throughout the year or three days each week at harvest time ... he should have five acres ... let him have his hearth penny on Ascension Day ... and such things according to his condition ...'; the boor must perform 'week-work for two days in each week of the year,' he must lie 'from Martinmas to Easter in his lord's fold as

81

often as it falls to his lot ... also [he must plough] three acres as boon work and two for pasturage ... and give six loaves to the herdsman of the lord's swine ... and when death befalls him the lord ... takes charge of what he leaves.'

The third group of source material comprises *specific records* such as charters, financial accounts, inquests, writs and letters and, above all, the folios of the Domesday Book which describe so many of the 'manors' of England in the year 1086: 'Ranulph holds Stoches of Turstin. Brictuin held it TRE [in the time of King Edward] and it paid geld for three virgates of land. There is land for one plough which is there and four acres of meadow and sixteen acres of wood. It is worth ten shillings.' It is unlikely that the local historian researching the story of a single place will have the resources of time, money and perhaps skill to study at first hand the membranes which record the information he seeks. There is, however, in the series *English Historical Documents* a comprehensive book (No.2 in the series compiled by D.C. Douglas and G.W. Greenaway, London 1953) which covers the period 1042 to 1189. There is also a good short guide *Historical Interpretation I* by J.J. Bagley (London 1971), and *The Norman Conquest* by R. Allen Brown (London 1984), number 5 in the *Documents of Medieval History* series. All may be recommended as invaluable cicerones.

Narrative sources

The main narrative sources are the *Anglo-Saxon Chronicles* already referred to. The chronicles' main value to the parochial researcher is that they name many individual places and hence are deeply but narrowly informative regarding some local event.

The annals ascribed to 'Florence of Worcester' are also of marginal use. Florence was a monk domiciled at Worcester and his pieces were written *c.*1113. They contain a number of references to specific localities, for example: 'In this year [1045] Edward king of the English collected a very powerful fleet at Sandwich to oppose Magnus king of the Norwegians.' Another monk, Ordericus Vitalis, wrote between 1123 and 1141 an elaborate *Ecclesiastical History*. This was translated into English by T. Forrester and published in London in 1854. It refers to many English locations. Other manuscripts of similar value are also mentioned in the reference works cited, and many are informative on matters touching local history. The more important may be mentioned here: *The Modern History* and the *Deeds of the Kings of the English* by William of Malmesbury (*c.*1125-42); *The History of the English* by Henry of Huntingdon (*c.*1129-54) which contains, among other things, a story of the Battle of Lincoln in 1140; the *Liber Eliensis*; Hugh the Chantor's *History of the Church of York* (*c.*1127); the *Chronicle of Battle Abbey* (?1155). A valuable narrative known as the *Account of the Battle of the Standard* by Richard of Hexham (*fl.*1154) contains, in addition to the story of the Scottish invasion, a useful account of conditions prevailing in the north of England during the anarchy. William of Newburgh's *History of England* is an important repository of information for the period 1154-70. It contains references to many places, describes the siege of Bridgnorth, and various provincial expeditions of a punitive nature undertaken by King Stephen. The history ends with the year 1197. The *Dialogus de Scaccario* (the 'Dialogue of the Exchequer') is printed in English in full in *English Historical Documents* 2 (*EHD2*). It takes the form of a long and detailed conversation between 'master and disciple' with the purpose of explaining the system whereby the accounts of the sheriffs were audited and enrolled around the time of King Henry II. It is extremely enlightening and should be read by every local historian wishing to unravel some of the complexities of the fiscal system of the period. Should reference be required to the Latin text, this is contained in Stubbs' *Select Charters* up to the eighth edition, and in *Dialogus de Scaccario* by Charles Johnson (London 1950). There are other narratives for the years 1042-89, and although they are of broad interest very few add to the stock of the local historian. Details of many of them appear in the reference books cited.

General records

There are literally hundreds of general records, the contents of which might be described in this chapter, but the sheer bulk of the data and the wealth (not to mention complexity) of the information contained in them precludes anything but a representative and ruthlessly pruned selection.

Royal administration

The Laws of William the Conqueror, committed to manuscript *c.*1125, set down 'what William King of the English established in consultation with his magnates after the conquest of England'. The laws stated, in the first place, that God and Christ should be honoured, but after this there was obviously one law for the Normans and one law for the Saxons. In the case of being charged with a crime, whilst the latter might 'defend' himself by ordeal of hot iron, the Frenchman might 'acquit himself by valid oath'. The laws laid down penalties for freemen who, when summoned, did not appear before the hundred and shire courts, and forbad hanging in favour of blinding, in addition to castration. The Coronation Charter of Henry I (5 August 1100) is well worth attention and contains two particularly relevant clauses: that guardianship of a dead tenant's land be vested in 'either the widow or another of their relations'; and the king's statement, 'I have retained the forests in my own hands as did my father before me.' It is interesting to note that this retention was confirmed as a main item in a charter of Stephen's in 1136.

With the end of the civil war in 1153 there followed until 1188 a series of charters and assizes, many interesting to the local historian. The documents include the *Assize of Clarendon* (1166), regarded as a landmark in the description of the administration of local justice; the *Assize of Northampton* (1176), which is to a large degree an enlargement of 'Clarendon'; the *Assize of Arms* (1181), 'let every freeman who holds chattels or rent worth 10 marks have an aubergel [a sleeveless coat of scale armour] and a headpiece of iron and a lance'; 'Let no Jew keep in his possession an aubergel but let him ... dispose of [it, that it remains] in the king's service.' The *Assize of the Forest* (1184) is of special importance in that it laid down the practices, customs and laws relating to the vast acres of the country still 'afforested' (the banning of the carrying of hunting bows, the mutilation of dogs' feet, and the appointment of verderers and foresters).

Local government and agrarian society

The *Rectitudines Singularum Personarum* has already been mentioned. It is not possible to date the document precisely, but it appears to come from about 1015 and thus gives

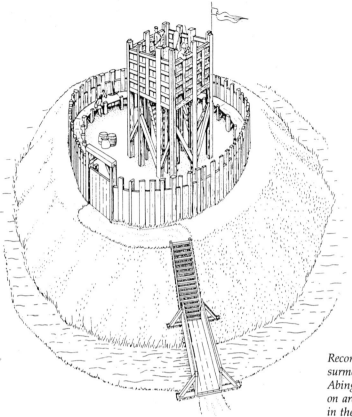

Reconstruction of a 12th century motte surmounted by a wooden tower at Abinger, Surrey. The drawing is based on archaeological studies and illustrations in the Bayeux tapestry.

an important account of the ranks and duties of the people of England in late Saxon times. There is much stress on the need to observe local customs and honour regional traditions: 'The estate law is fixed on each estate, at some places ... it is heavier, at some places, also, lighter, because not all customs about estates are alike. On some estates a boor must pay tribute in honey, on some in food, on some in ale. Let him who has the shire [and this is not necessarily the sheriff, but rather the steward of a greater thegn] always know what are the ancient arrangements about the estate and what is the custom of the district.' Of special importance are the clear definitions between freemen, half-freemen, and slaves, and also the list of the occupations performed on an estate: beekeeper, swineherd, herdsman, retainer, sower, oxherd, cowherd, shepherd, goatherd, cheesemaker, granary keeper, beadle, woodward, and hayward. Details are also given of the duties of the classes in ploughing, cutting of corn, the mowing of meadows, hunting and the care of horses. No mention is made of plough maintenance or black-smithing. There were many rights of a common nature: 'In some districts are due winter provisions, Easter provisions, a harvest feast for reaping the corn, a drinking feast for ploughing, food for making the rick, at wood carrying a log from each load, at corn carrying food on completion of the rick, and many things which I cannot recount.'

In *EHD2* the specific statements of services and rewards just outlined are augmented by details of surveys covering the period 1045 to 1189, and whilst the terminology varies (and argument waxes to this day regarding the pre-Conquest geneat's comparability with a post-Conquest villein), it is not without value or sense to match the data. William I transformed the upper levels of society, but he was at some pains to let local institutions remain insofar as possible, and let local customs prevail so that in theory at any rate 'all shall have and hold the law of King Edward in respect of their land and possessions.'

Specific records

Charters and related documents

In Chapter 6 it was pointed out that, for the period up to the accession of Edward the Confessor, charters form a quite invaluable source of information, not only with regard to the granting of lands, but also for many other purposes — records of local customs, trade, and as supplementary commentaries to other information. What was true for that period is also true for the years 1042 to 1189. *EHD2*, which deals with later Saxon and early Norman times, is, without doubt, a most convenient and authoritative reference of first resort. It contains details of many charters, a most important group of which concerns the sheriff and local government, and some of them are of quite fundamental importance. One in particular indicates the possibility of the continuity of the machinery of local government from the pre- to the post-Conquest periods, and that the Normans, recognising the strength of the Anglo-Saxon practices, left them in place. The charter concerned is that of King Henry I issued sometime between 26 July 1108 and early August 1111, and contains the directive: 'I grant and order that henceforth my shire courts and hundred courts shall meet in the same places and terms as they were wont to do in the time of King Edward [the Confessor] and not otherwise. And I do not wish that my sheriff should make them assemble in different fashion because of his own needs or interests.' There is, perhaps, an implication that William II or some of the king's officers had consistently and unwisely moved away from the tried and true system confirmed by the 'hundred ordinance' of the year 950, and that Henry, 'the Lion of Justice', was reinstating the Saxon system. The matter is obviously worthy of study. A further important instrument touching the administration of the shires is that known as the Inquest of Sheriffs, and dates from Easter 1170. It comprises the commission given by King Henry III to the barons charged to enquire into the conduct of sheriffs in all the shires, following complaints made regarding their behaviour and practices. The enquiries concerned land transfer, the collection of taxes, the trial of alleged wrongdoers, and the maintenance of the king's demesne lands.

Select Charters by William Stubbs was published first in 1870. The ninth, revised edition appeared in 1913 and has been reprinted many times by the Clarendon Press, Oxford. The book is arranged to illustrate 'English constitutional history from the earliest times to the reign of Edward the first'. The extracts are in their original Latin and Old English. Minor exceptions apart, the Latin entries are translated but Modern English texts accompany the latter. Bishop Stubbs and the late editor, H.W.C. Davis, provide many useful commentaries.

The Domesday Survey. The country was divided into seven areas (or circuits) and the thick lines on the map denote their possible boundaries. Also shown are the Domesday counties. The king's men 'made a survey of all England; of the lands in each of the counties; of the possessions of each of the magnates, their lands, their habitations, their men both bond and free, living in huts or with their own houses and lands; of ploughs, horses, and other animals; of the services and payments due from each and every estate. After these investigators came others ... to check the first description and to denounce any wrongdoer to the king.'

The Domesday texts and the Inquisitio Geldi

With certain exceptions the Domesday Book describes the whole of England south of the Tees and the fells of Westmoreland. The reasons for its compilation, the manner of the gathering of the data and their analysis do not need to be described in other than broad outline here. There are many excellent (and some not very good) books on the subject, especially following the ninth centenary of its production in 1986. A very useful modern commentary is *Domesday Book Through Nine Centuries* by Dr Elizabeth Hallam of the Public Record Office (London 1986), and an older, but still relevant volume is the Maitland book mentioned earlier. Domesday is worth studying with great care because an entry in its folios is frequently the starting point for a parish history and, equally importantly, the complexities and ambiguities are such that 'full emphasis must be given to the fact that very many local studies have a direct bearing on the interpretation of that age.' An individual entry can yield considerable information about a specific place, but to do full justice to the material the local historian will gain much of value by studying *all* the estates of a particular overlord, the entries for the villages (manors) contiguous with the one being researched and, equally, the terminology, layout, methods of compilation, shortcoming and ambiguities of the manuscripts.

By the year 1085 the Conqueror was becoming increasingly aware that, nineteen years after his coronation, he still did not have a totally clear idea of the assets and potential of his kingdom, so at Christmas that year, at one of his periodic courts at Gloucester, he ordered a special survey to be made so that he would have a better appreciation of who held what, how rich in land, animals and labour they were and, equally important, how much they should be taxed. The estimates of value were subsequently made in accordance with a system of assessment based on Anglo-Saxon practice. At the heart of that system had been the manner in which a tax, in the form of a general geld, was imposed on the shire as a whole. An arbitrary sum was laid upon the shire, and this was then apportioned onto the individual thegnly tenants in terms of the number of 'hides' (or equivalent measures) of land which they held, or were deemed to hold. There is no agreement whatsoever between scholars as to how many acres there were in a 'hide', and for the time being this topic will be ignored.

There were two other purposes behind the survey. The first was to gain an up-to-date measure of the feudal obligations laid on each tenant-in-chief, and the second was judicial in nature. The Domesday records give little information about feudal organisation, but they are arranged within each shire according to the fiefs, and hence give a good indication of its resources.

At the heart of Norman feudalism as introduced by the king, was the imposition on his senior magnates of quotas of knights' services in return for their estates. These quotas (technically the *servitia debita*) appear to have borne no direct relationship to the amount of land held, rather they seem to have been personal bargains struck between the monarch and his vassal. The tenants-in-chief in their turn enfeoffed knights on their estates in return for similar service, so that when the king summoned the feudal host he knew precisely how many knights, properly armed and caparisoned, would take the field. There is no direct reference to knight-service in the Domesday records (a later document, the *cartae baronum* of 1166 must be referred to for these data), but this aspect of the survey should be borne in mind.

The judicial element of the Domesday survey focused on the vexing subject of litigation between tenants on the subjects of possession of estates and ownership of fees. There had been many cases since the Conquest, as just one example will illustrate (reference may be made to Chapter 29 for a description of the dating conventions employed): 'In the year of the Incarnation of our Lord 1080 in the eleventh Indiction, the Epact being 26, on 2 April, an enquiry was held concerning the liberty of the abbey of Ely [at Kentford, Suffolk]. There was a danger that this liberty might be entirely extinguished since it had been neglected [and] almost destroyed by the injust exactions of [the sheriffs] . . ..' The Domesday inquest set out, therefore, to discover three major things: the size and value of land holdings for taxation purposes, the nature of the basis for the feudal obligations such as knight-service or serjeanty, and the outstanding important grievances between tenants — issues still in dispute.

The country was divided into a number of circuits, for each of which commissioners unfamiliar with the area were appointed to make enquiries of locally selected jurors, manor by manor, hundred by hundred (or the equivalent), borough by borough, for subsequent summary and rearrangement into a feudal sequence.

There are a number of special points to be borne in mind by any local historian seeking to gain the maximum amount of information about Domesday. The first is that not only were the commissioners unfamiliar with the territory they were charged with surveying, and hence not at ease with the pre-Conquest traditions of Wessex, Mercia, the Danelaw, Kent, Northumbria and so on, but were themselves mostly foreigners, Normans whose mother tongue was a form of French, and who had been born and brought up in a continental society very different from that of England. There are, therefore, many ambiguities in the data. Further, although in the vast majority of cases the unit of residence of the people actually being questioned was the village, the unit

A page from the Domesday Book describing royal lands in Yorkshire. In the original the parchment is somewhat mottled and the ink faded. The neat lines of text are in 11th century clerical Latin with Roman numerals, many abbreviations and short forms, readable only by the specialist and trained eye. Much scholarly work has been done on the manuscripts, changes, erasures, underlining, interpolations and marginalia all yielding valuable clues to both academic and local historians.

of assessment (outside the boroughs) was the 'manor', an essentially Norman concept, the boundaries of which frequently did not coincide with those of the civil or ecclesiastical unit. Some villages, or parishes, comprised two or more 'manors' (that is tenurial holdings) and some manors contained two or more villages.

Standards and customs varied from one part of the country to another, and caution must be observed to ensure that any information used is truly applicable to the place being discussed. As a general point it may be noted that in, broadly, the Danelaw shires, the unit of land-measure was 'carucate' not 'hide', and in Kent it was 'suling' (or 'sulung'), but the terms are not equivalent, some reference books to the contrary. Nor were 'hides' universally the same in area, their size depending on very localised understanding and tradition. Further, although Domesday classifies peasants as mainly freemen, sokemen, villeins, bordars and serfs, it is extremely difficult, if not impossible, to equate these classes to the Anglo-Saxon minor thegns, geneats, cottars, boors and slaves. Finally, the commissioners did not, could not, apply standard criteria of classification, so what in one shire would be a villein in another might be called a bordar.

In each instance the local jurors were called upon to answer the following questions: the name of the manor; who held it in the time of King Edward and who in 1086; how many hides were there; how many ploughs in demesne and how many belonging to the villagers; how many villagers were there and what were their ranks; how much meadow and pasture; how many mills and fisheries; how much had been added to, or taken from, the estate; what it used to be worth and what its current value; how much each freeman had. Where appropriate, each piece of financial data was required in three forms: in the time of King Edward, at the date when King William granted the tenancy, and at the time of the inquest. In general the answers appearing in the Domesday Book conform faithfully to the pattern. The survey, however, was resented in many quarters, Florence of Worcester (writing one hundred years later) going as far as to say 'the land was vexed with much violence'.

In addition to the broader statements of 'who held what' and general matters of hidage and population, the Domesday Book contains items of value, of which the following examples are indicative. In the description of Kent (printed in the *Victoria County History: Kent* Vol.III, p.213, 1932) there is a separate section allotted to the estates of the knights of the Archbishop of Canterbury in that county. The *Victoria County History: Berkshire* Vol.I, p.236, has valuable background information on local customs: 'When a thegn or a demesne warrior of the king was dying he sent all his weapons to the king as a relief.' Equally pertinent matters appear in a publication of the Chetham Society, *The Domesday Survey of Cheshire*: 'A man who shed blood from the morning of Monday to noon on Saturday paid a fine of ten shillings.' Finally, the *Victoria County History: Worcestershire* Vol.I, p.286 *et seq* has a translation on 'salt making', describing how at Droitwich a local industry employed methods more sophisticated than those normally in use.

As preserved in the Public Record Office, the resulting 'book' is bound in two sections termed 'Little Domesday' and 'Great Domesday', the former being the final returns for the eastern circuits covering the counties of Essex, Suffolk and Norfolk, and the latter the summarised information from all the other circuits, believed to be six in number.

Associated with the principal texts were a number of other records, which were direct products of the survey. These are the Cambridgeshire Survey (*Inquisitio Comitatus Cantabrigiensis*), which describes thirteen of the sixteen hundreds of the shire, and valuable to local historians for two main reasons: it is arranged territorially, hundred by hundred, instead of by tenancies, and it gives much more information than the Domesday Book both about the animals and the Saxon and Norman tenants; the Ely Inquest (*Inquisitio Eliensis*) describes the estates of the abbey of Ely, which lay in the shires of Cambridge, Hertford, Norfolk, Suffolk, Essex, and Huntingdon, and revealing comparisons can be made between the text and those of the documents mentioned earlier; Exon Domesday (*Liber Exoniensis* — the Exeter Book) is a fairly comprehensive digest of the original returns for Somerset, the bulk of Devon and Cornwall, about half of Dorset, and one manor in Wiltshire. It contains most useful data on the animals husbanded on the manors, and, on the spelling of place names, reflects the local pronunciation of the day. A comparison between the entries in Great Domesday (or the 'Exchequer Text' as it is sometimes termed) and Exon is very worthwhile; the *Monachorum* of Christ Church Canterbury, and the *Feudal Book* of the abbot of Bury St Edmunds, will be of value to historians working in those localities.

The texts of Domesday have, over the centuries, been published on a partial basis — several of the old county histories contain portions — in both Latin and English. Between the years 1861 and 1863 the Ordnance Survey issued zincographic facsimiles of the whole of Domesday. These volumes catch something of the quality of the original but totally lack the 'atmosphere' of a lithographic, full-colour edition.

For today's local historian the best starting point (at the time this is being written) is almost certainly the Phillimore edition which, in 39 county books, parallels a text by Abraham Farley published in 1783. Farley's edition was set in a specially designed 'record' type, the supposed purpose of which was to mirror the short forms and conventions of the original by employing an essentially Roman fount, which readers would find familiar, augmented by palaeographic *notanda*. Like many compromises it fell short of its creator's intentions whilst remaining useful. The parallel text produced by the Phillimore editors transliterates the Farley into twentieth-century terms. It is the outcome of a mammoth undertaking but should not be blindly accepted. Three examples will suffice to point the caution, each taken from the volume for Dorset. The name of William de *Moion* is given as William de Mohun, a form reflecting a change of pronunciation which was not adopted by the family until the early thirteenth century, and which thus completely obscures the name of the place from which the Norman tenant-in-chief came, *Moyon* in Tessy-sur-Vire in La Manche; a manor of Edward of Salisbury was said to contain a 'water meadow', but the Latin original — *brocae* — could, in the context, as easily mean 'marsh', which is rather different; a wood in a manor held by Robert FitzGerold is described as five 'rods' wide, but the original has the short-form *ḭirg*, which could be more accurately rendered as *virgate* (one-quarter of a hide) expressed as a linear measure. These are, perhaps, small differences, but they stand in the way of precise scholarship. It is also important to note that the hundreds are given their 'new' names, whereas at the time of Domesday the 'old' hundred names were still in force, the 'new' divisions not having been formed. The convention adopted by the editors need be in no way misleading but, being a considerable anachronism, should always be borne in mind.

Idem Witts de MOION ten *POLEHA*.Viginti 7 uñ teiñ tenueᵣ̄ T.R.E.7
geldb ꝑ.x.hid.Tra.ē.vIII.caᵣ̄.In dñio st.III.caᵣ̄.7 vI.ſerui.
7 xIIII.uitti 7 xxv.bord cū.vII.caᵣ̄.Ibi moliñ redd.xL.denar.7 xxxII.
aᶜ p̄ti.Silua.II.leū lḡ.7 vIII.q̨ laᶠ.Valuit x.lib.m̄.vIII.lib.
Idē Witts ten *HAME*.Godric tenuit T.R.E.7 geldb ꝑ.v.hid.Tra
.ē.IIII.caᵣ̄.In dñio st.II.caᵣ̄.7 IIII.ſerui.7 vI.uitti 7 v.bord.
cū.II.caᵣ̄.Ibi moliñ redd.vII.ſolid.7 vI.den.7 L.aᶜ p̄ti.7 III.q̨
paſturæ in lḡ.7 una q̨ in laᶠ.Valuit.Lx.ſot.modo.c.ſolid. ·

An entry from Domesday describing some manors held by William de Moyon with, beneath it, the same examples set in the specially designed 'record' type designed by Abraham Farley in the 18th century.

A system of direct taxation called 'Danegeld' had come into being in late Saxon times initially to provide funds to protect England against the Danes, and later continued almost annually as a land tax, being finally abolished in 1162. A number of records of these levies have survived, and in Exon Domesday there is a series of rolls relating to the five south-western counties of Wiltshire, Somerset, Dorset, Devon and Cornwall. These *inquisitio geldi* records (which probably date from the year 1084) are arranged hundred by hundred, broken down into holdings of each tenant-in-chief by name. The geld rolls are useful when compared with the Domesday records, providing valuable data on major holdings immediately prior to the great survey. They may also be used in other ways, as the following report of a study carried out by the author illustrates.

Over the years there has been much discussion in the south west regarding the precise size (assuming there to be such a thing) of the 'hide'. Most scholars agree that, although in later centuries the term was used as a basis for tax assessment, nonetheless there are indications that it was employed as a unit of measure containing *'n'* acres, particularly at the time of King Ethelred (979-1016). *A Key to Domesday — Dorset* by R.W. Eyton (1878) contains a chapter on mensuration which, in general terms, opts for an average Dorset hide of 240 acres but allows for so many variations as to make a generalisation useless. Eyton writes of 84 acres, an 'extreme' of 4000 (*sic*) and so on, although generally he opts for 120. The area of a hide depended on the quality of the land and the convention used in each locality. The study by the present writer has revealed that in the north of the county there are positive indications that the hide, in the eleventh century, was still regarded as containing 40 acres. The study also showed the importance of using the 'old' hundred names. One of the manors of William de Moyon (the Norman magnate already mentioned) lay in the old hundred of *Hunsberge* for, in the geld roll for that area, he is noted as having a demesne holding of *iiii hidas et dimidiam iiii agros minus,* that is four and a half hides less four acres. Reference to the Domesday record showed that in his Dorset manor of *Poleham* William held 'four hides and a virgate and six acres' (a virgate being one quarter of a hide). A detailed examination of estate acreages in Hunsberge showed that Poleham was the unnamed place referred to in the geld rolls. Then by using the figure '40' as a common factor, it could be shown that these figures summed to the same total:

four and a half hides ($4\frac{1}{2}\times40=180$) less four acres (180-4) equalled 176 acres.

and

four hides and one virgate and six acres (160+10+6) also equalled 176 acres.

Hence, at the time 1084-86 a measure of 40 acres to the hide was in use in north Dorset.

To end this section, mention must be made of the full-colour photographic facsimile edition of Great Domesday published in 1986 by Alecto Editions, to which was added in 1988, a complete translation based on the *VCH* texts, with maps and indexes. There were two complete editions, both limited in number. The first was called the Penny Edition and comprised two volumes of the manuscript in facsimile bound in leather between oak boards, with William I pennies inset in each, and two books of translation — one of maps and one of indexes — these bound in leather and linen (the published price was £5,750). The second was called the Library Edition and appeared in slightly less grand bindings (and priced at £3000). Of particular interest to the local historian is the County Edition, which provided books for each county separately, each work comprising an introduction, facsimile copies of the Domesday pages, maps and translation. The quality of the full-colour reproductions in all three editions can only be described as magnificent, and any person studying Great Domesday should make every effort to examine the work if only to gain an accurate impression of what the original membranes are now like.

The Boldon Book

This compilation dates from 1183 and was drawn up to assist in the administration of the estates of the bishopric of Durham. It is of great assistance in the understanding of the agrarian economy of the north of England. A full text in English appears in the *Victoria County History: Durham* Vol.I (1905).

The Cartae Baronum

The *cartae baronum* are among the most important records for the study of twelfth-century feudalism. They were compiled in 1166 at the command of King Henry II who required, through his sheriffs, answers from his tenants-in-chief, as follows: (i) how many knights were enfeoffed on your estates at the death of King Henry I [1 December 1135], (ii) how many hold land by the 'new enfeoffment' [that is to say, by grants since that date], (iii) how many knights, if any, are required in addition to those you have enfeoffed in order to make up the amount of knight service you owe the king, (iv) what are the names of your knights? The *cartae baronum* are discussed, with illustrations, on pp.903-15 of *EHD2*.

The Pipe Rolls

The Pipe Rolls record the annual accounts between the king and the sheriffs, by the upper Exchequer. They are discussed in some detail in Chapter 5 and are an invaluable source of detail to local historians. They are organised on a county basis and

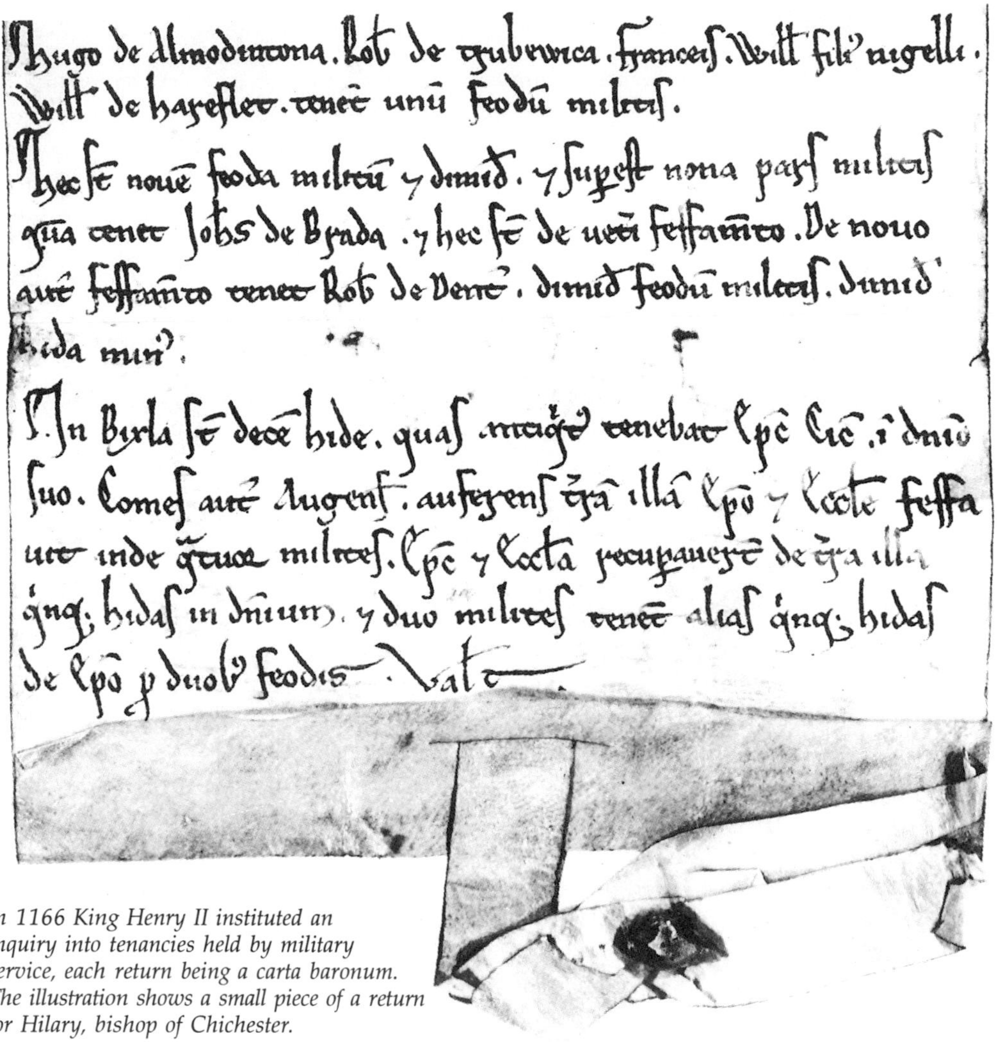

In 1166 King Henry II instituted an inquiry into tenancies held by military service, each return being a carta baronum. The illustration shows a small piece of a return for Hilary, bishop of Chichester.

many have been published either by the Pipe Roll Society (see Address, Appendix III) or by HMSO, details being given in *Sectional List 24* of Government Publications, *British National Archives*.

Ecclesiastical records

As may be imagined, there are thousands of records relating to the Church surviving from this period of history, which saw not only the arch-episcopate of Lanfranc, the papacy of Gregory VII and the Constitution of Clarendon (July 1164), but also the murder of Thomas Becket. However, there is little at national level bearing in any significant way on local studies. The local researcher is referred to the comprehensive bibliography relating to the Church of England (pp.589–97) in *EHD2*, and also to the section (p.608) describing the parochial organisation in Kent. He is also recommended to seek the help of the local studies librarian in the town or county library, and the county or city archivist, who will, quite certainly, have access to works recording the foundation of abbeys, religious institutions, chantries and chapels in the geographical area of interest. The *Monasticon Anglicanum* is also an essential text.

Town records

A considerable number of town records survive. They are at national level mainly charters and writs. Because they refer to so many town districts by name they are nevertheless of important local interest. A typical example is the charter given by John, Count of Mortain (later King John) in favour of Bristol *c.*1189: 'John, Count of Mortain, to all men and to his friends, French and English, Welsh and Irish, present and to come, greeting. Know that I have granted and by this present charter confirmed to my burgesses of Bristol dwelling within the walls and without the walls, up to the boundaries of the town, to wit, between Sandbrook and Bewell and Brightneebridge and the spring in the road next Aldebury and Knowle, all their liberties and free customs as well . . ..'

Some also provide evidence of burghal privilege and indications of the wide variations of the practices of different towns. *Early Yorkshire Charters* Vol.I by W. Farrer (1914) gives evidence of a document *c.*1124 referring to a merchant gild and free burgage; *Feudal Documents from the Abbey of Bury St Edmunds* by D.C. Douglas (1932) details customs of a borough on ecclesiastical land around the year 1130; a charter of Henry II to Cambridge *c.*1185 confirms the rent (*firma*) to the burgesses, which formerly went to the king.

The volume *EHD2* contains extracts from many records including charters granted to Gloucester, Lincoln, Hastings, Leicester, Newcastle on Tyne, Nottingham, Bury St Edmunds, Cambridge, Oxford, Beverley (Yorkshire), Bristol, Burford and Winchester. There are many documents relevant to the city of London. They begin with a writ (in Old English) of William I (sometime before 1075), 'I will that every child shall be his father's heir after his father's day', continue with charters of privilege granted by Henry I, Henry II (in favour of a gild of weavers *c.*1154-62) and others, and end with a rhetorical (but useful) description of the city at the time of Henry II, 'Among the noble and celebrated cities of the world [it extends] its glory farther than all the others . . . the matrons of this city are very Sabines.' The layout of twelfth-century London is described, and it is noted that it gave birth to many souls 'dear to all good men throughout the Latin world.' A particular feature of *EHD2* is the extensive bibliographic reference data, pointing to a wide range of books, essays and other sources.

8 The Changing Administration 1189-1327

Following the great surveys of 1086 and 1166 carried out at the commands of William I and Henry II, the most obvious and significant changes were in the highest levels of national administration and the dispensing of justice, both made in response to the perceived needs of the new dynasty in consolidating its hold on the conquered territory.

Equally important, and at a different, far less apparent, level were the shifts in the attitudes of Norman and Saxon towards one another, particularly when the memories of the events of the autumn of 1066 receded in men's minds and became hearsay merely, for their descendants. The history of the years 1189-1327, covered by this chapter, starts with the accession of King Richard I and ends with the murder of Edward II at Berkeley Castle, Gloucester, at the age of 43. At the beginning of the period the conquerors had been settled in England for more than a hundred years, and the Norman and Saxon peoples had come to tolerate, even respect, one another — 'already it was difficult to tell, among freemen at any rate, who was of English and who of Norman birth [and] all that contemporaries knew was that to speak only English was increasingly a mark of rusticity, while the possession of French was no evidence of ancestry.'

There are three books in the *Oxford History of England* series covering these times. *Domesday Book to Magna Carta* by A.L. Poole (2nd edition, 1955) stops, as indicated, in 1215/16; *The Thirteenth Century* by Sir Maurice Powicke (2nd edition, 1970) deals with the years 1216-1307, and *The Fourteenth Century* by May McKisack (1959) examines the remaining two decades, plus the years to 1399. These guides are important as sources of a wide range of pertinent material (as are their somewhat shorter companions in other series), but for the local researcher, with much narrower ranges of interest, there

95

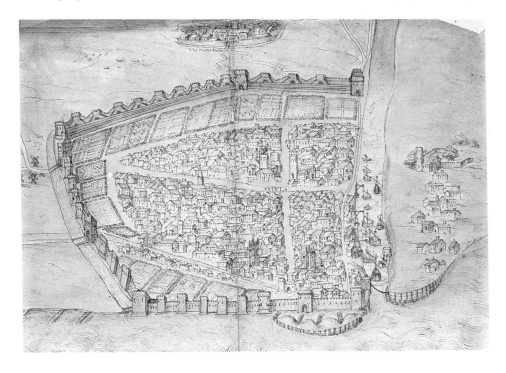

A 16th century plan of Hull. Of the many interesting features are the landing stages (bottom), the windmills (left), and the buildings outside the city confines on the far side of the river (right).

is nothing to be compared with primary material produced at, or very close to, the times in question. Fortunately, there is a great deal of such material, and much of it has been not only translated but analysed, glossed and interpreted by several generations of modern scholars.

England in the early fourteenth century was dotted with towns; London, to quote Sir Frank Stenton, was 'no mere regional market', indeed it was probably the biggest place of habitation in the country, with a population of some fifty thousand. From it a network of roads ran to the far corners of the country — to Dover in the south-east, to Winchester, Exeter and St Ives in the south-west, to Bristol on the Severn coast, north-west to Lichfield and Carlisle, north to Stamford, Doncaster, York, Durham and Berwick on Tweed. The populations of the boroughs were growing, Bristol had perhaps 20,000 people, York possibly 10,000, and several others almost 5000. There was, of course, still much woodland, and the average market 'town' was little more than a village except on market days when the populace came to trade.

All over the country in the areas that were cultivated or grazed, where the land had been claimed from marsh or forest, the fields were vast and open, and the documentary sources identified in this chapter will emphasise not only this, but the problems of travel, the cost of building and, in a notable quotation, the degree to which the inhabitants were at the mercy of the elements (to say nothing of corrupt and grasping officials).

With the increase in population, and the growing complexity of the economy and trade, the foundation of stable religious institutions and the offices of central government, the number of written documents grew and were preserved. There remain great gaps in present-day knowledge of the times, but from the mass of material which has survived much of value can be learnt. In the course of Chapter 5, 'Essential record sources', considerable reference was made to the rolls (such as Charter, Patent, Close, and so on), many of which were started during the period 1189-1327, have since been published and are available from HMSO or the public lending service. The selective use of these records is of paramount importance to the local historian as indicators and examples of social life, responsibilities, agricultural practices, lordship and many other things: 'Thomas Pycot versus Ralph le Bret [and others] that they entered into a wood of the said Thomas at Haselbere and cut down trees'; 'Ralph de Langeley versus Henry de Ekerdon for one mill in Fiffhyde which he claims as his right'; 'Stephen de Bello Monte versus Maurice de Membury to render an account while he was his bailiff in Wyneford'; 'A capital messuage held of William de Angerville, son of Hawis de Insula in free socage, rendering one pound pepper yearly for all service.'

The printed volumes of the contents of the rolls cover many thousands of pages, and it is a rare thing indeed for a place which existed in medieval times, or a person of some local note, not to be mentioned in them, together with outline information on which the assiduous researcher can build. In the case of the mill at Fiffhyde in the previous paragraph, the name of the place means 'five hides', so was it 600 acres in extent at that time (1321), or was the local hide not 120 acres in size? Could it have been in the eighth-ninth centuries the estate of a later Saxon thegn (the traditional holding of which nobleman included, quite specifically, five hides of land)? Where was the mill, of what type could it have been, is the watercourse still significant? How large is Fiffhyde now, and through what corrupting processes did its name become the present-day Fifehead? These are important questions which can be posed (and sometimes answered) with the aid of the rolls mentioned.

Over and above the records which deal with essentially parochial matters are thousands of others of varying kinds which, although of national relevance, are equally important to local historians. The Forest Charters of 1217 and 1225 are good examples of these: 'We grant that every free man can conduct his pigs through our demesne wood freely and without impediment to agist [lodge and feed] in his own woods or anywhere else he wishes'; so too is the Statute of Westminster of 1275, 'No city, borough or vill, nor any man is to be amerced [fined or similarly punished] without reasonable cause ... and this by their peers.'

The records may be divided in ways not unlike those employed in the two preceding chapters, and, as before, the first category is that of *narrative* documents and chronicles. This is followed by the class *general records*, the third category is *local matters*, and the fourth *ecclesiastical* records.

Narrative sources

A considerable selection of the numerous histories, annals and chronicles have come down to us. These range from the contemporary account by Richard of Devizes, *The Time of King Richard I*, to the *Pipewell Chronicle* of 1327. Some of the narratives, particularly the early ones, are of little local interest, but the 'Chronica Majora' and the 'Historia Anglorum' of Matthew Paris, the monk of St Albans (died 1259), are worth consulting (by way of *Matthew Paris's English History* translated by J.A. Giles, London 1852-4). The *Annales Monastici*, edited by H.R. Luard (Rolls Series 1864), are the annals of the Benedictine monastery at Burton on Trent, and contain much of interest. Other narrative works are *Chronicles of Old London* (of the thirteenth century) translated by H.T. Riley (London 1863), the 'Annals of Dunstable' issued in 1866 in *Annales Monastici*, and the 'English History' of Bartolomew Cotton of Norwich — see *Historia Anglicana* in the Rolls Series (1859), again edited by H.R. Luard. Also germane to the period are *The Chronicle of Bury St Edmunds 1212-1301* edited by A. Grandsen (London 1964), and the 'Chronicle of Peter Langtoft of Bridlington' (1297-1307). This latter may be of special value to local historians in the north of England. It was written in Yorkshire French, at the time of Edward I, is vernacular and metrical and has also been issued in the Rolls Series in an edition by T. Wright, *Chronicle of Peter de Langtoft* (1866-8). A substantial selection in metrical English appears in *English Historical Documents* (1189-1327), hereafter referred to as *EHD3*, by Harry Rothwell (London 1975).

The 'Chronicle of Lanercost' (*Chronicon de Lanercost*) describes the history of Northumberland during the years 1272-1346 and was published in a translation by Sir Herbert Maxwell (Glasgow 1913). It contains vivid illustrations of the insecurity of the north, especially around 1316. On 24 June of that year 'the Scots invaded England, burning . . . and laying . . . waste . . . as far as Richmond. But the nobles of that district, who took refuge in Richmond Castle . . . compounded with them . . . so that they might not burn that town. [Having received money] the Scots marched away . . . laying waste everywhere as far as Furness . . . taking away nearly all the goods of that district . . . [being especially] delighted with the abundance of iron which they found there, because Scotland is not rich in iron.'

General records and papers

The years under review spanned the reigns of four kings, one of whom, Edward I (called 'Longshanks', and who ruled from 1272 until 1307) was a soldier, a man of letters and a statesman who, more than any other medieval monarch, cast England in modern form. By the time of his death English government, society and law had assumed a form that was to last, more or less intact, for several hundred years. But the period also saw the 'wicked' John, the weak and untrustworthy Henry III, and the feeble, perverted Edward II.

A chapter of this length can do no more than hint at some of the very richest of the document sources and point to where transcriptions and analyses may be found. The ninth edition of *Select Charters* by William Stubbs (revised by H.W.C. Davis, Oxford 1913) contains much valuable information. *Magna Carta* by J.C. Holt (Cambridge 1965) is important, especially in respect of the preliminary draft of 15 June 1215, which dealt (as did Magna Carta itself in somewhat different terms) with all manner of what we now call 'social reforms'. These touched counties, hundreds, wapentakes, and trithings (that is, *thirdings* or ridings such as in Yorkshire until very recent times), vills, manors, and individuals of all classes — earls, barons, bailiffs, clerks, villeins, merchants, Jews, Welshmen and many others. A study of the great charter (as issued, and as later

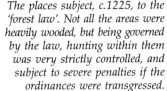

The places subject, c.1225, to the 'forest law'. Not all the areas were heavily wooded, but being governed by the law, hunting within them was very strictly controlled, and subject to severe penalties if the ordinances were transgressed.

revised) holds much for local historians. In 1217, a notable document known as the 'Charter of the Forest' was issued (and revised in 1225). It is published in *Statutes of the Realm* (London, the Record Commissioners, 1810) and extracts appear in *EHD3*. It dealt with the rights and duties of all manner of men having responsibilities, dwelling or livelihood in afforested areas. It covered hunting, the use of dogs who, to prevent them interfering with sport, were to have 'three claws of the forefoot ... cut off, but not the ball', poaching, theft, and punishment by both outlawry and ordeal for offences. It is a seminal source of record of rural local history.

Other information is provided by a group of documents which may be called dicta, statutes, proclamations and provisions. The 'provisions of Oxford' printed in *EHD3* pp.361-66 deal *inter alia* with the powers and duties of justiciars, bailiffs, sheriffs and escheators. The 'proclamation of 20 October 1258', and the 'provisions of Westminster, October 1259' (see *EHD3* pp.368-76) lay down certain rules and edicts for the conduct of local affairs. Reference should be made to *Select Charters* by W. Stubbs for the 'dictum of Kenilworth' (1266), especially for statements regarding the upholding of the charters of liberty and the forest. The dictum had, in all, forty-one clauses, of which eighteen are printed in *EHD3*.

The 'statute of Marlborough' (1267) is an important reference source for information on thirteenth-century civil, judicial and administrative procedures, as is the 'statute of Westminster I' (1275). Both appear in the Record Commissioners' publication of 1810 *Statutes of the Realm*, as does the related 'statute of Gloucester' (1278), dealing with franchises and trade. In 1285 a second 'statute of Westminster' was sealed. Stated to be a continuation of the Gloucester measure, it too dealt with trade, justice and privilege, and is found in *Statutes of the Realm* (I: pp.71-95).

The parliament of 1290 saw several pieces of legislation bearing the marks of a 'transitionary period' (to quote Bishop Stubbs). The most interesting, for present purposes, are 'summons of knights of the shire' (see *Select Charters*) and an enactment sometimes called the 'statute of Westminster III'. This, more usually known as *Quia Emptores*, from its opening words *Quia Emptores terrarum et tenementorum de feodis magnatum et alorum* ... ('Because purchasers of lands and tenements belonging to the fees of magnates and others ...'), dealt with the important subject of sub-infeudation (and led to all kinds of abuses of tenurial rights and obligations). The text is given in *Statutes of the Realm* (I: p.106), and in *EHD3* p.466. (See also 'The Period of the Statutes 1274-90' in Powicke *The Thirteenth Century* pp.322-80.)

From 1294 onwards, England was in a state of national emergency — wars in France and Gascony, expeditions to Flanders and the Scottish campaign — and these troubles led to the imposition of a number of taxes. *EHD3* contains (pp.469-76 and in-text references) pertinent information on the writs issued on the subject, and useful commentary will be found in *The Early English Customs Systems* by N.S.B. Gras (Harvard 1918). The times were unruly ones, a regent was appointed, and parliament found it necessary to 'confirm' various charters, and to enact legislation against 'mal-administration ... since the outbreak of war with France'. Again, useful starting points for the researcher investigating the nature of the duties of the sheriffs and other local officials, and the measures taken to seek to ensure the shires were well managed, are the volumes on statutes, and select charters already identified.

Local matters

Before considering the wealth of material available from contemporary sources, it is well worth while to obtain a background not only to the broader scene at the royal government level, but to situations and conditions more directly illuminating aspects of local administration, and maintenance of personal and familial prosperity. There does not appear to be a comprehensive, lengthy 'economic history' of the times (although the writing of one has often been called for by leading academic historians) and some of the early certainties are now being questioned. *The Medieval Economy and Society* by M.M. Postan (Pelican Books 1975) is a work by a distinguished economic historian, and is a fairly short but valuable contribution to the subject, and *Rural England 1066-1348* by H.E. Hallam (Fontana Books 1981) is also helpful.

Of special significance is *The Hundred and the Hundred Rolls* by Helen Cam (London, reprint 1963), which is devoted to the *rotuli hundredorum* and associated records. The book is a study of the working of local government in the thirteenth century and starts with Edward I's enquiry of 1274/5, as recorded in the hundred rolls. It describes the shire, the hundred and the function of the royal and feudal officials who served them. The book is a valuable guide to the judicial and administrative organisation of England in the thirteenth century.

The volumes in the *Oxford History of England*, already named, are useful. The books by Professor Postan, Professor Hallam, and the Oxford texts contain many pages devoted to bibliography. A significant contribution to the whole subject appears in *EHD3* (pp.783-98) and includes a select booklist under sub-headings: the land, people, and miscellaneous (this last contains much of value on towns). The paragraphs which now follow discuss a number of primary manuscripts ranging over a wide spectrum of topics. References to, and translations of, such material appear in many publications, and large numbers of these are identified in *Sources for English Local History* by W.B. Stephens (Cambridge 1981).

The countryside and the village

Interesting details of the countryside are frequently hidden away in the most unlikely document. In 1303 a case of oyer and terminer ('hear and determine' — a commission of enquiry into serious offences) contains an enlightening description of the fen country, and the areas around Peterborough, Stamford and Thorneye (*Calendar of Patent Rolls 1301-7*); and, in *Select Cases before the King's Bench* by G.O. Sayles (Selden Society Vol.55, 1936) there is, in matter referring to Lincoln, data describing 'inundation of the sea and the marsh'.

Much information on the organisation and social behaviour of village communities has been printed. The 'by laws of the village of Newton Longville, Bucks' is typical of the rules governing harvesting and pasturage. The text is given in an essay 'Open Field Husbanding and the Village Community' in the *Transactions of the American Philosophical Society* (Vol.55, part 7, 1965). It includes (1290) *inter alia* such injunctions as 'no one shall gather beans, peas or vetches in the fields ... except from the land which he himself has sown'; 'no one shall cause his beasts to graze among the corn in the night time.' No doubt such rules may be regarded as fairly typical.

Between 1187 and 1189 a treatise on the laws and customs of England appeared. This work, *Tractatus de Legibus et Consuetudinibus Angliae*, has been attributed to Ranulf Glanville (or Glanvill), chief justiciar of England (died 1190). It has been translated as *The Treatise on the Laws and Customs of England commonly called Glanvill* in an edition by G.D.G. Hall (London 1965). It contains much of value, including the ways a 'person of villein status can be made free'.

Mention has already been made of the 'Chronica Majora' of Matthew Paris (edited by H.R. Luard in the Rolls Series in 1872). One of the fascinating features of the work is the record Matthew kept of the weather between 1236 and 1259, not only in St Albans but in other places from which tales reached him. In 1236, 'the dead bodies of those drowned were seen lying unburied in caves formed by the sea, near the coast, and at Wisbeach and the neighbouring villages ... an endless number of human beings perished.' In November 1242, 'such deluges of rain fell, that the river Thames, overflowing its usual bounds and ancient banks spread itself over the countryside towards Lambeth for six miles and took possession of houses. Such was the inundation that people rode into the great hall at Westminster on horseback.'

Boroughs and towns

The information available to us from documentary sources (as distinct from archaeological reports) varies widely in content. There is, for example, an Anglo-Norman manuscript of the late thirteenth century, translated as *The Ancient Usages of the City of*

Winchester by J.S. Furley (Oxford 1927), which begins 'these are the ancient usages . . . observed in the time of our ancestors; they are, and are intended to be for the saving and sustaining of the franchise.' An earlier volume by J.S. Furley, *City Government of Winchester from the Records* (Oxford 1923), rounds out the picture. A somewhat similar account of the same date exists for the government of the city of Lincoln. The original manuscript is now missing (although it is known to have been in the city muniments as recently as 1785). Fortunately a translation was made in the eighteenth century, and has since been printed in *Medieval Lincoln* by J.F.W. Hill (Cambridge 1948).

There are many other records laying down the rules, or guidelines, for the managing of towns, and the bibliography in *EHD3* is most informative in this regard. Sadly, a number of works (transcribed into notebooks and the like) remain in local archive offices, will need diligent searching for, and much scholarly attention. It is apparent that, in the fourteenth century, the problem of urban sanitation was a grave one, and records, notably in the Close Rolls, emphasise this. Ballard and Taits' volume *British Borough Charters 1216-1307* (London 1923), by giving many instances with commentary, further augments our knowledge. A typical entry in the Close Rolls (*Calendar* of such, 1296-1302, HMSO) goes 'it is evident that the pavement in the said town of Boutham [Bootham, Yorkshire] is so very greatly broken up that all . . . passing through the town sustain immoderate . . . grievances, and the air is so corrupted and infected by the pigsties situate in the king's highways and in the lanes of that town and by the swine feeding and frequently wandering about the streets and lanes and by dung and dunghills and many other foul things placed in the streets and lanes that great repugnance overtakes [visitors and residents] and the advantage of more wholesome air is impeded . . ..'

Ports along the English Channel coasts had somewhat different problems. The *Calendar of Close Rolls 1227-31* refers to Hythe in Kent, the year being 1230: 'Word was sent to the sheriff of Kent to go in person to the port of Hythe, which is blocked, it is said, by the accumulation of sand and soil, and have the port reopened and repaired by the men of the neighbouring townships who have been accustomed and ought to open and repair that port.' Such ports were not the only ones with difficulties. In 1240, the 'goodmen of Redcliffe' (Bristol) were commanded by King Henry III to 'begin a certain trench' so that ships 'coming to our port . . . can enter and leave more freely' (*Bristol Charters 1155-1373* edited by N.D. Harding, Bristol 1930). There are other records, and for a selection reference may be made to *EHD3* p.799 *et seq*, and to *The Thirteenth Century* (Powicke, Oxford 1962/70), p.721 onwards.

Industry and trade

Sufficient manuscripts survive to give interesting insights into the trade and industry carried on in the medieval period and these, as may be expected, cover a wide range. The bibliographies mentioned at the end of the preceding section identify a comprehensive selection of texts for background reading, as well as translations of original documents. The following extracts from primary sources indicate a little of the wealth of the data.

Salt This mineral was very important, particularly for the preservation of food. In the fourteenth century a considerable amount was imported, mainly from places around the Bay of Biscay, but appreciable amounts were made in England. The coastal area of Lincolnshire had thriving businesses evaporating sea water, and the brine springs of Worcestershire and Cheshire were sources of significant output, particularly in those areas where there was ample woodland for fuelling the boiling vats. The *Calendar of Inquisitiones post Mortem III* notes (p.410), for example, that Guy Beauchamp, Earl of Warwick (died 1315), had 'a saltpit at Droitwich with a boilery of eight vats'. Reference may usefully be made to *A Medieval Society: the West Midlands at the end of the Thirteenth Century* by R.H. Hilton (London 1966). In addition to pertinent text the book contains a map showing the locations of many salt-workings.

Iron-ore The South Midlands, in addition to being a centre for salt production, was also involved in other industrial activities — coal mining, charcoal manufacture and iron smelting from ore. The *Close Rolls of Henry III 1227-31* (1902) makes particular reference to the Forest of Dean: 'Because the king is given to understand that ore for making iron can be found in his great forest at Chippenham, John de Monmouth is ordered to have that ore searched for in that forest and if it happen to be found, then to have the forges provided to go round in that forest for making the iron.' For this period (and this industry) an instructive volume is *English Industries of the Middle Ages* by L.F. Salzman (Oxford 1923).

The wool trade Already by the thirteenth century the English wool trade was flourishing, presaging the importance of the industry in centuries to come. Evidence of its thriving nature is recorded in a number of contemporary documents, and a brilliant study formed the subject of the Ford Lectures in 1941, and was subsequently published as *The Wool Trade in Medieval History* by Eileen Powers (Oxford 1941). The *Calendar of Close Rolls 1272-79* has, for the year 1276, an interesting account of the trade between Fountains Abbey, Yorkshire, and the 'fellows, citizens and merchants of Florence'. The agreement set out that deliveries would be without 'clack and lock, cot and breech wool, or black or grey inferior fleece, and without pelt wool'. Delivery was to be at specified times in the years 1277-80, to designated places at agreed prices, and the Florentines were indemnified against non-delivery.

Shipbuilding The Public Record Office accounts for 1294 contain important information on medieval methods of shipbuilding — records of the construction of a war galley at Newcastle. The data have been published as an essay 'The Newcastle Galley AD1294' by R.J. Whitwell and C. Johnson, in *Archaeologica Aeliana II* 4th series (1926). The essay is particularly important as it contains a glossary of technical terms.

Fairs For many centuries fairs were one of the foremost centres of trade. The Calendars of Patent Rolls for the period being discussed contain a number of entries touching on all manner of fairs, including the four 'great' fairs of St Ives, Boston, Winchester and Northampton. For example, on 16 November 1240 a mandate was issued from the council at Westminster 'to the bailiffs and good men of Winchester to make known to all the merchants coming to their city the provision of the king and council that all the king's prises [negotiated purchases] from merchants shall be paid for at four terms of the year.' Reference should be made to the social and economic history bibliographies in the two volumes in the *Oxford History of England* series (Powicke, and McKisack, above), and to the 'land and people' section of *EHD3*.

Weights and measures At the heart of all trading in the Middle Ages was a proper system of weights and measures. This was laid down by ordinance and a statement has been printed in *Statutes of the Realm* (Record Commission 1810). A valuable extract is included in *EHD3* pp.856-7. The local researcher in the fields of trade, commerce and industry will do well to study the standards employed; for example, a 'penny' weighed 32 grains of wheat from the middle of the ear, and an ounce was 20 pennies. There were 12 ounces to the London pound, and 12½ pounds to a stone. In less familiar terms a 'char' (cartload) contained 30 'fotmals' (70 pounds), and 'each pound has the weight of 25 shillings', 'a dicker consists of 10 hides . . . the dicker of gloves 10 pairs, the dicker of horseshoes . . . 110 shoes.' A hundredweight of wax, sugar, pepper, cumin, almonds and wormwood contained 13½ stone of 8 pounds each, and there were 108 pounds to the hundredweight. A 'seam' of glass was 20 stones and each stone was 5 pounds in weight. A hundred of linen cloth contained 6 score, a hundred of horseshoes 5 score, a hundred of dried fish 8 score, and 'in some and many places'

A page from a medieval herbal in Latin and Middle English. Throughout history medicine derived from plants has had widespread application. The page shown describes some of the uses of the Common Teazle and the Yellow Bugle.

9 score, especially the 'dried fish called Aberdeen'. The whole matter is worth close attention. There are obvious echoes of the duodecimal system, the use of the long and short hundreds, greater and lesser pounds, and so on.

Social customs and the like

The primary records which have survived contain many insights into social customs, attitudes, mores and adventures. The *Calendar of Inquisitions Miscellaneous, Close Rolls, Inquisitions post Mortem* and others contain many descriptions of local events which are well worth studying as typical of life of the day: the woman of Bursleydam (in Sussex) killed by a 'poisoned' crossbow bolt in 1267; the giving of 'love-days' in 1204, feudalism and the family (1258); provisions for mistresses and children born out of wedlock (*c.*1250); medieval courtesies (1301) and many others.

Places and their associations

In 1901 *The English Historical Review* xvi, contained an interesting list compiled in the thirteenth century of things for which various places were noted, and in the *History Teacher's Miscellany* V, No.1 (Cambridge 1927) a series of identifications were proposed for terms previously deemed obscure. The list contained such gems as 'salmon of Berwick', 'fur of Chester', 'simnel [bread] of Wycombe', 'soap of Coventry', 'blanket of Blyth', 'thieves of Grantham', 'cingles [horse furniture] of Doncaster', and so on. There were a hundred and nine references in all, some amusing, some accurate, some no doubt libellous.

Ecclesiastical records

In the Middle Ages, monasteries and cathedrals accumulated vast stores of written material, much dealing with the administration of estates and items of personal business, some with sacred and liturgical matters. There is no way, following the dissolution of the monasteries, that we can ever know just how much primary source material there was or how much irreplaceable information has been lost. This is, very naturally, a cause not only for great regret, but frustration also, but the frustration can be greatly alleviated by concentrating on the material which *has* survived — in public and private collections, libraries and museums.

The reports of the Historical Manuscripts Commission contain details of the archives of bishops, deans, and chapters in many dioceses, and these were published during the period 1876 to 1906. The bibliographies in the *Oxford History of England* volumes for the eleventh to early fourteenth centuries by A.L. Poole and Sir Maurice Powicke respectively should be used, as should that in the later volume in the same series by Professor McKisack. All are valuable in pointing to works dealing with these records. The local studies collections in the larger public libraries will contain information additional to that advised in the three works cited.

Also of special relevance is the multi-volume *Monasticon Anglicanum* of Sir William Dugdale and collaborators, published in London between the years 1655 and 1673. This majestic work is a history of religious houses, their estates and other holdings. In English and Latin, it was reprinted in 1846, and has also appeared in facsimile.

9 The Later Middle Ages 1327-1485

Edward III succeeded to the throne of England in 1327 in the wake of his father's murder, an event as significant in its way as the invasion of 1066, and one that marked 'the great divide in our later medieval history'. With the death of Richard III at Bosworth in 1485 the Middle Ages came to an end. It is with the years between these dates that the present chapter deals. It covers the reigns of eight kings, two of whom were murdered, two deposed, one was mad, two usurpers, and one killed in battle. Of the remaining two (for the previous categories are not exclusive) — Edward III and Henry V —the first was a great administrator who ruled for fifty years and the second was the victor of Agincourt.

The reign of Edward III from 1327 to 1377 saw many changes in the way the country was run. There were, for example, two houses of parliament, the office of 'Justice of the Peace' was created in 1361 (replacing that of 'Keeper' established in 1277) and English succeeded French as the language of the law courts. Respect for learning and literacy spread, the town grew, and the merchants flourished. So, on three separate occasions, did the Black Death. When Edward died, his grandson Richard, whose father had been the Black Prince, was but ten years old. The council of nine which ran the government was not a success. Taxes were levied which were hardest of all on the poor, and in 1381 the peasants revolted. Although the main risings were in Essex and Kent, they were mirrored in Norfolk, Wirral, Hampshire and the Scottish border areas. All promises made to the rebels — on the abolition of villeinage, labour services, and tenancy of land — were ignored as soon as convenient. Factions came and factions went, the king proving a faithless friend and a weak leader. Eventually, he was deposed and subsequently murdered. The new king, the usurper Henry IV, dated his reign from 30 September 1399 when he had first bid for power, but he did not easily rule. Battles raged over England as the blood descendants of Edward III fought in what subsequent generations have called the 'Wars of the Roses'. It was an unquiet time, and of general interest to local historians, not just those fortunate enough to research an area in which revolt, battle or skirmish occurred. Henry died, probably a leper, in 1413, and was succeeded by his son Henry V, who at twenty-six was in his early prime.

This is not the place to expand upon the glories of the king's victories in France —a reading of Shakespeare's *Henry V*, much less the background texts named in this chapter, will suffice for that. At home much attention was paid to the raising of money to finance the king's campaigns, and when he died in 1422 aged thirty-three the Exchequer had a deficit of about £30,000, and further debts of more than £25,000. His successors, Henry VI and Edward IV, took turn and turn about with the throne. There were further battles and rebellions, but the written records continued to mount and there remain revealing documents on such things as the working of manorial courts, borough ordinances, domestic accounts, trials for witchcraft, the schooling of children, gilds, Christmas pastimes, and many more which help round out present-day knowledge of the ordinary folk of the time. Mention, too, must be made of William Caxton who, in 1476 after an absence from England of thirty-five years, set up his printing press at Westminster and contributed greatly to the spread of learning.

Edward IV died in 1483, his two small sons were disposed of, perhaps at the instigation of the Duke of Gloucester, who assumed the throne as King Richard III, to die but two years later at Bosworth in Leicestershire, fighting bravely in his fashion for the kingdom he had so long schemed for, and the making of the 'Tudor Myth' began.

Within the *Oxford History of England* series, there are two volumes devoted to the years 1327-1485. The first is *The Fourteenth Century* by May McKisack (1959), dealing with the years 1307-99. The second text is *The Fifteenth Century* by E.F. Jacob (1961), which examines the period 1399-1485. There are other general works dealing with these periods, and each is of value, but the *Oxford* books have a great deal to commend them, not least in the detail of the indexes and the comprehensive nature of the bibliographies which run to many pages, and point to dozens of subjects of interest to local historians.

Records of places and events which did not attract national attention will be found by the thousand in the various rolls described in Chapter 5 of this present book, and a diligent study of them can be most rewarding. True, many of the entries merely record who held what on what terms, but one study carried out by the author discovered the existence of two settlements which in the fourteenth century were called by names not elsewhere recorded (one of which has since been located as a deserted site), and a record of 1385 gave the size of a manor, the names of its fields (some more than eighty acres in extent), their uses, annual rentals, and so on. The names have been analysed (thus throwing additional light on even earlier land usage), and will be included in a future volume in the *English Place Names* series.

As is the case with many other chapters in this section there is a book in the *English Historical Documents* series which will prove an invaluable aid. It will be referred to as *EHD4*, and it was published in 1969 under the editorship of A.R. Myers. Two further general reference texts are *Village Records* (Chichester 1962/82) and *Town Records* (Chichester 1983), both written by Dr John West. *EHD4* contains a general bibliography (pp.35-48) divided into original sources (public records, narrative sources, and letters and papers) and secondary sources (books, articles and commentaries, which are the work of academic historians). Primary and secondary sources may be grouped under four main headings: *general government*; *local government and related*; *everyday life, events and customs*; and *ecclesiastical*. Given the climate and difficulties of the times it

The social classes, illlustrative of the society on which the lay subsidies were laid. The figures represent the church, the nobles, and the ordinary people. In practice the clergy were partially exempted, being already taxed by decree of Pope Nicholas IV in 1291.

would be very easy to make a limited case for a further section, *battles and similar disorders*, and to collect in it references to Bamborough, Barnet, Bosworth, Gloucester, St Albans, Tewkesbury, and Towton, to say nothing of the Lincolnshire rebellion, the disorders in the north in 1410, and in the Home Counties in 1462. These are of local importance, of course, but only to a few researchers, and are thus not included.

General government sources and related documents

Lay subsidies In the late thirteenth century the system of taxation based on the number of knights' fees, or ploughlands a tenant held, was replaced by one based on that part of a person's wealth which could be classed as 'movable'. The shift in emphasis is an indirect but striking comment on the way the economy of the country was changing, and that the 'landed classes' were no longer the only wealthy groups. The subsidies started, in fact, in 1290 a little before the period now being discussed, but between that date and 1332 there were sixteen such impositions and it is more appropriate that they be mentioned here than at the outset. Between 1334 and 1434 there were a further forty-two subsidies, but on a rather different basis — and one which remained somewhat modified and supplemented, until the end of the reign of Charles I in 1649. Two essays describing the lay subsidies appear in *The Amateur Historian* (Vol.3, No.8, 1958, and Vol.4, No.3, 1959) by Maurice Beresford, who says in his introductory remarks that the subsidy records 'are chiefly important for the distinct and voluminous evidence . . . they afford . . . of personal wealth among the more well-to-do laity.' The present-day upsurge of interest in local history has stimulated the publication of the contents of lay subsidy records on a county basis, sometimes by interested individuals and sometimes by county record associations, and it is to these publications that the local researcher must turn. The 'particulars of account' given in the documents are arranged by vill and borough, hundred (or its equivalent) and county. For the years up to 1332 the names of taxpayers are given, the amounts they paid, and the names of the tax gatherers. The contents of the lay subsidy rolls may be used for a variety of purposes, not only as indicators of relative wealth (it is often possible to identify the lord of the manor), but also as a record of by-names or early occupational, locative and other types of surname. The fortunate local historian will also discover, in the published rolls for the county concerned, an introduction by the editor, giving much-welcome background to the whole subject of the subsidies, and this may be augmented by a study of *Parliamentary Taxes on Personal Property 1290-1334* by J.F. Willard (Cambridge, Massachusetts, 1934). Also of value may be another by-product of taxation, the *Nomina Villarum*, printed in county sequence in *Feudal Aids and Analogous Documents* (London 1899-1921) in six volumes. A list of printed editions of lay subsidy rolls (now somewhat out-of-date) appears in *Village Records* pp.46, 48-9.

In 1334 the system changed, the Crown ceased to be interested in individual wealth and merely levied each community with the sum required. The matter is outlined in the *Calendar of Patent Rolls* 1334-8. Although the value of the data in the later rolls is rather less to the local historian than those of the earlier — especially from 1338 when taxes could be paid in kind — they can be usefully employed. Professor Beresford's second essay is of special interest, particularly in respect of the rebates allowed for distribution to 'poor vills, cities and boroughs, desolate, wasted, destroyed or very impoverished'.

Poll taxes These impositions were later experiments in direct taxation, and came into being as a result of dissatisfaction with the subsidy method. Three poll taxes were levied between 1377 and 1380, only paupers being exempt. In practice the hardest hit of all were the poor. On pp.125-6 of *EHD4* is a schedule for the tax of 1379 showing the amount to be paid by each individual, from £4 by each earl, to single men and women (unattached to estates) 4d (old pence). Professor McKisack has said (*op cit*) that the poll tax returns are a useful guide to the distribution of population, but this is a subject which needs much more work. Local historians may wish to access *British Medieval Population* by J.C. Russell (London 1948), and *The Rising in East Anglia* by E. Powell (Cambridge 1896) has several pages listing the population of England.

The Peasants' Revolt In 1381, as a result of the iniquities of the taxes just outlined, insurrection broke out in a number of counties. *EHD4* contains a long extract from the *Anonimalle Chronicle* describing the events of the time, and many places are mentioned in which significant actions occurred. Parliament made concessions, such as grants of freedom and manumission to serfs and villeins, but these were soon repealed, as the texts printed in *Statutes of the Realm II* indicate. A relevant volume, with many indications of original sources, is *Bond Men Made Free* by Rodney Hilton (London 1973). It deals with the general background to the fourteenth-century peasant movements and their aftermath.

Further statutes If for the remainder of the period being discussed there are fewer statutes which had impact on, or initiated important data for, local communities, there is much information in the Court rolls, patents and other documents which show the effect of the legislation on nobility and commoner alike. The bibliography on pp.688-704 of *The Fifteenth Century* by E.F. Jacob points to many published versions of original documents, and that on pp.705-15 to the more important secondary material.

The business of local government and related matters

Even today distinguished historians are not agreed as to what, at various times, constituted a vill, manor, village, parish, borough, town, and so on. The changes brought about by the boundary and other amendments of the early 1970s have made things clearer only to the more dedicated amateur, and the commentary by Dr West in *Town Records* (pp.xiii-xv) is revealing in this regard. It would appear that in the fourteenth century, parliament ('the great council') itself had related problems. In the Westminster assembly of 24 February 1371, the government set out to grant the king a 'subsidy' of £50,000 to pursue the war against France. This was done on the basis that there were 40,000 parishes in England and they might thus be levied at 22s.3d each. There were, in fact, something in the order of 9,000 parishes and the tax on each was raised to 116 shillings when the more accurate figure became known.

When this evidence of appalling ignorance is added to our awareness of the lack of control parliament had over the shire and borough officers, the difficulties of communications and transport, and the preoccupations with foreign wars and domestic conflicts, the researching of local history becomes even more demanding — but also very rewarding. It must be appreciated that there is an extremely wide variety of sources available for the study of local government. A convenient and comprehensive discussion of these is contained in *Sources for English Local History* by W.B. Stephens (Cambridge 1973), 'Local Government and Politics' pp.71-98.

What now follows is a short outline of the more important elements of local government, and a selection of illustrations of the way in which a few of the national laws touched local communities.

The forest laws In the Middle Ages large areas of the country were at different times under the 'forest law', legislation that defined which areas of the country were officially forests (even if they were comparatively bare of trees and contained numerous settlements), and hence subject to many regulations as to what could or could not be done by the common folk (and to some extent their betters) living in those areas. In the fourteenth century restrictions were relaxed somewhat, and c.1369 Edward III gave permission for free men living in forest areas to collect wood for their houses and fences, and declared a general indemnity to offenders against the regulations. The easing of the laws came as a great relief to local courts and officials (although they did lead to an increase in poaching). Professor McKisack devotes a section of her *Oxford History* text to the subject (p.207 *et seq*).

Inquisitions post mortem and manorial extents When an important landowner died, who may have been a tenant-in-chief or man of equal importance, a royal writ was issued to the Sheriff (or the Escheator), demanding the answers to a number of questions. These were: What land did the deceased hold at time of death? Of whom was it held? What was its yearly value? What services did it render? Who was the heir? How old was he? Details of the inquisitions so far published appear in Chapter 5, and an examination of the answers given can be of considerable value — indeed, the information can be of primary importance not only in tracing manorial descents, the changing fortunes of notable families, but also in pinpointing the location of trades and industry, tenure by sergeanty and services and matters of like kind. It can some-times come as a pleasant surprise to, say, a local researcher in Shropshire to find that a fairly insignificant fifteenth-century lord of a manor who was not a tenant-in-chief, knight banneret, or well known courtier was in fact the important landlord of estates in Pembroke, West Wales, Gloucester, London, Essex and Suffolk; that a number of manors were held in frankpledge, or with right of free-warren, with entailed interest or some other attachment which, when fully explored, will lead to new avenues of enquiry, and reveal new data. The discovery of an entailed interest such as that of frankmarriage (implying a union between two families) can often throw light on a seeming change in manorial descent or explain an apparent discontinuity in patronage.

Closely allied with the inquisitions were the *extenta manerii* or manorial 'extents', that is to say a full description of the manors of the deceased. These too are of great value to the local historian for they may give acreages, indicate the number of acres in the local 'hide' or 'carucate', mention the classes of tenant and terms of tenancy, indicate the existence of mills (which may be checked against the Domesday information), dovecots, fishponds, orchards, vineyards, gardens and much else which may be com-pared with any sixteenth-century (or later) surveys, maps and tenancy rolls. Unfor-tunately the printed collections issued by the Public Record Office seldom give infor-mation beyond names, dates and bare facts in plain calendar form, but many 'extents' have been published by local societies.

A list of Inquisitions prepared by local societies is given in the *Handlist of Record Publications* by Robert Somerville (London 1951), further information appearing in *Village Records* by John West (pp.59-60 and 184-5), and an essay 'Inquisitions Post Mortem' by R.E. Latham is printed in *The Amateur Historian* Vol.I, No.3 (1953).

Charters For the period now being discussed the borough charter, where it exists, can sometimes be a useful source of information. *EHD4* has a number of interesting references, including (p.560) the text of a charter of 1373 to Bristol, the first provincial town to be made a county. *Town Records* by John West contains an essay introducing the subject of town charters, followed by a handlist of 194 boroughs and their charters together with references to texts by other writers (pp.81-102).

Manorial courts The main instrument of local government outside the towns was the manorial court. The function of the court (which was presided over by the lord of the manor or his agent) was to oversee the general running of the manor, ensuring the proper interpretation of its customs. It dealt with offences concerned with tenure, services, and petty grievances (more significant misdemeanors were judged by hundred, shire or other courts — even up to the king's court). In specific cases there were different kinds of court, mainly 'courts baron' and 'courts leet'; Dr West includes a valuable short essay (p.30 *et seq*) in his book *Village Records*, and lists on pp.37-42 and 180-3 details, in county sequence, of manor court rolls, accounts and customals which have been printed. Some manors were permitted 'a view of frankpledge'. Under a system of frankpledge a vill or manor was divided into tithings (groups of ten or a dozen households), each such unit having corporate responsibility for the good behaviour of its members. The 'tithing man' or head member of each group was responsible for ensuring that any member causing offence was available for examina-

111

tion by the manorial court. *EHD4* has a long and thorough account (pp.548-53) of the 'manner of holding a manorial court with a view of frankpledge, *c.*1440' taken from a Harleian manuscript in the British Museum. A useful introduction to the whole subject is contained in *Manorial Records* by P.D.A. Harvey (London 1984), and *How to Locate and Use Manorial Records* by P. Palgrave-Moore (London 1985) is also of value.

Boroughs and towns In 1414 Andrew Forsey of Bridport was selected to represent the borough in parliament, and was one of two such burgesses appointed *per ballivos per assensum communitatis* — that is to say, by the bailiffs and with the assent of the whole community. The very wording gives an important clue to the nature of the government of towns in England, for the bailiffs, merchants, tradesmen and craftsmen and their organisations were very prominent in the social and economic order of those communities. The 'organisations' concerned were the medieval gilds and they formed the backbone of urban administration. E.F. Jacob informs us (*op cit*) that 'the main problems of borough history lie in the period [ending *c.*1350]. It is to these years that the classic riddles of the relation between the municipality and the merchant gild, of the beginning of the mayorality and of the nature of burgage tenure (though the latter has far earlier origins) mainly apply.' So too the question of when English boroughs were achieving corporate existence before 'juridicial recognition was given to the fact.'

Fortunately, the local historian need not be too concerned with these complicated and absorbing topics beyond recognising that at some stage the alderman of the merchant gilds became in many cases the chief officer of the town, and eventually the title of that worthy changed to mayor. The passage from which the quotation in the last paragraph is taken recounts a synoptic history of towns that is worthy of study, and John West in *Town Records* has (pp.103-17) an equally relevant piece. The essay on pp.938-46 in *EHD4* should be studied, not least for the references included in the copious footnotes.

At one point in his account Professor Jacob describes the transition of the head of the aldermanic class in Leicester to mayoral status, and this is especially useful, for a document has survived setting out the 'borough ordinances of Leicester' in the year 1467. It is printed in *Leicester Records II* edited by M. Bateson from the original manuscript in the Leicester 'Hall Book' and extracts also appear in *EHD4*. The ordinances are of such a nature that they *must* have been of some general applicability to the other urban centres of the day. Indeed, the *Records of the Borough of Nottingham* edited by W.H. Stevenson (around 1800) tend to confirm this in a large measure, as does *The Little Red Book of Bristol* edited by F.B. Bickley (Bristol 1900). There are many manuscript records of towns lying in county museum libraries or local authority archives, waiting to be read, annotated and published. It is to be hoped that the current upsurge of interest in local history will be sustained and much-needed work carried out.

The Leicester ordinances were made by the mayor of the town and his brethren, and by 'the advice and consent of all the commons of the same town, at a common hall'. The schedule began with instructions for keeping the peace: that weapons be left indoors and that no man should 'walk after nine of the bell be struck in the night without light'; brewers were instructed to 'brew good ale ... neither raw, ropy, nor red, but wholesome for a man's body'; butchers must not 'bring any flesh to sell with any manner of sickness'; fishers and victuallers must not sell 'unseasonable victuals' and their prices must be 'reasonable'. There followed regulations regarding the disposal of refuse: 'no man lay out any muck at his door . . . to the annoying of the king's people'; there were rules for the washing of clothes, for the disposal of sweepings — no person should 'throw out sweepings when it rains upon his neighbour for the disturbing of his neighbour'. Other regulations forbad gambling ('carding and unlawful games'); dealt with scolds (punished in a ducking stool for as long as the mayor liked); and all manner of civil and commercial behaviour.

Town Records by John West contains an extensive gazetteer of sources on medieval gilds and trade (pp.122-30).

Parishes and chantries Several varieties of early records on these subjects have survived and, although specific to individual parishes and bequests, are nonetheless as valuable as more general material. They give insight into prices, wages, and the general business of parishes. One of the most valuable classes is that of the churchwardens' accounts. It must be remembered that the churchwardens of today are of very lowly and restricted status compared with the officers of the same title who exercised the duties in previous centuries. The tasks assigned to them varied from managing parish property and income, accounting for the expenditure of rates, representing the views of parishioners and maintaining the fabric of the church, to exterminating vermin.

The *Churchwardens' Accounts for the Parish of St Michael without the Northgate, Bath 1349-1575*, edited by C.B. Pearson and published in 1878 by the Somerset Archaeological and Natural History Society is, in effect, a continuous history of parish management. For 1349, for example, they record income from church tenements and land and the sale of 'old cloths', bronze, wood, wool, hay and 'lenten veils'. Records of outgoings include those for wax, oil, wattles, straw and missals, as well as a penny (old coinage) a year to the clerk for lighting the lamp, twopence for the wage of a washerwoman, and threepence for the annual wages of the warden. The clerk was paid fourpence for 'making the account', and a further threepence went on bread and ale 'bought for the expenses of the warden for the time being'.

Of similar kind are the records contained in the account book of Munden's chantry for 1456-7, published as *A Small Household of the XVth Century* edited by K.L. Wood-Legh (Manchester 1956). The foundation dated from 1361 in St Michael's Chapel, Bridport, and was, of its kind, well-to-do. The record includes pantry accounts for fish, mutton, ale, flour, 'a little pig', chickens and other comestibles as well as 'rushes for the floor', candles, spades, and so on. Expenses included material for the repair of the fabric of the buildings, screen partitions, pruning the vines, hinge bands and like ironmongery. Details of wages are also given. It is interesting to note a payment of two old pence for a cord for drawing water to 'John Forcy' (Forsey), a member of the family of the burgess mentioned under 'Boroughs and Towns' in this chapter, and whose history is touched on in Chapter 24 Surnames and their Meanings. Further records are quoted in *EHD4* pp.726-76 and reference may also be made to E.F. Jacob (*op cit*) pp.290-3.

Everyday life, events and customs

This section deals with a multitude of activities, events and practices, for the documents which have come down to us are separate, multifarious, greatly diverse and, of course, quite incomplete as records of *all* the things that went on in the country. The selection has been made to illustrate unique and terrible happenings as well as those which are trivial, everyday, mundane and sometimes downright boring. The bibliography on pp.970-83 in *EHD4*, and those on pp.558-61 in McKisack and pp.705-15 in Jacob, identify works of considerable value, and in turn many of these point to further sources from which local researchers may obtain important data.

The Black Death The great plague came first in 1348-49 and a modern, comprehensive account of its origins, causes, effects, and progress throughout England is contained in *The Black Death* by Philip Ziegler (London 1969). There are several contemporary accounts — one of which appears in the *Chronicon Henrici Knighton* edited by J.R. Lumby (Rolls Series 1895): 'in the small parish of St Leonard's there perished more than 380 people, in the parish of Holy Cross 400, in the parish of St Margaret's, Leicester, 700 ...'. The economic consequences for the country were disastrous, prices tumbled and, ironically, in a season when harvests could have been outstanding by the standards of the times, many crops perished in the fields for lack of reapers. A great deal of attention has been paid to the plague by historians.

The time of the Black Death can be a most rewarding one to research. In a specific case studied by the author, a parish which from 1316 had had two rectors each responsible for a moiety only, and living in separate parsonage houses, had after 1349 a single incumbent, both the previous rectors appearing to have died. Local lore had it that the pre-plague village had been burnt down and a new one built on high ground a mile away, but this was able to be disproved, and in the doing much new information was uncovered. A field called 'pitt mead' traditionally said to be the site of the death pit, and haunted to boot, was found in early records to be known as both *pytt* mead and, in a single case, *pyttel* mead — hence perhaps a place from which minerals had been extracted, or associated with mousehawks —although a burial pit could not be entirely ruled out.

Crime References to crime in the various rolls are numerous, and the reader is referred to *EHD4* pp. 1221-36 for a wide selection of reports of cases in Chancery and other courts, and contemporary comment on the problems of the day.

Education It was during this period that there was a great up-surge in education; Eton College was founded in October 1440, Sevenoaks Grammar School in 1432, to cite but two examples. The universities thrived — a pay award for university teachers is recorded as early as 1333 — college libraries were established, including the great Duke Humphrey library at Oxford, in 1439; Cambridge founded a training college for

Scratched into the tower wall of Ashwell Church, Herts, ten feet above the ground, when building had been abandoned because of scarcity of labour, are inscriptions in Latin written at the time of the Black Death. They read: 'The first plague was in June in the year 1349,' then 'In 1349 there was a plague and (in 13)50.' Then, in deeply incised letters, beginning, 'MCt(er) Xpenta miseranda ferox violenta ... ' the words: '1350 a pitiable, fierce violent (plague departed), a wretched populace survives to witness (to the plague), and in the end a mighty wind, Maurus, thunders in this year in the world, 1361.'

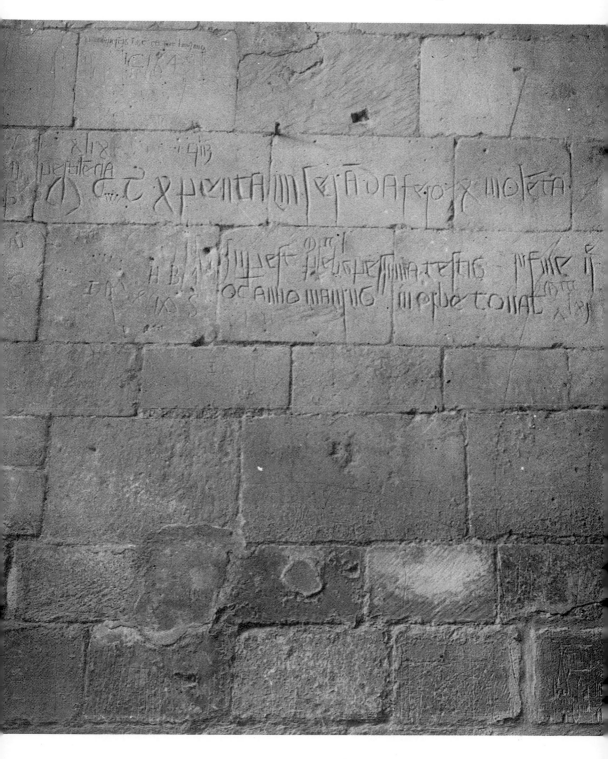

grammar school masters in the same year; the design for King's College Chapel was approved in 1447. *EHD4* contains extracts from a number of records (the sources are fully identified) including the expenses of keeping a school —'a tattered book of Horace bought for the boys, ½d' — and the cost of schooling a merchant's son in the year 1394. Details also appear on the cost of private tuition for girls between the years 1467 and 1473. Quotations given touch the setting-up of schools as far apart as Rotherham, Ipswich, Adcaster, Stratford on Avon, and London. Parliamentary and other rolls are cited and from them (together with the recommended texts) can be gained a comprehensive picture of education, from fees charged to subjects taught: 'grammar, music and singing, writing and all such things as belong to scrivenercraft'.

Entertainment It is in the records of towns and cities that the more obvious accounts of entertainment occur. An entry in 'The Old Free Book' of Norwich (*Records of the City of Norwich* edited by W. Hudson and J.C. Tingay) describes a town procession of the crafts on Corpus Christi Day *c.*1449. It is sufficiently short to be quoted in full: 'First, the light-bearers round the body of Christ in front of the procession, and each craft with a banner. Reeders, smiths, curriers, barbers, shoemakers, bedweavers, masons, carpenters, patternmakers, fletchers, bowers, fullers, shearmen, woollen weavers, pewterers, braziers, skinners, butchers, bakers, brewers, barbers with wax-chandlers, fishers, fishmongers, tailors, raffmen [timber merchants], worsted weavers, dyers, goldsmiths, drapers, grocers, mercers. The procession. Mr Sheriff's clothing. Mr Sheriff.'

In the same volume, there is an account of a pageant which took place about the same time and it includes not only the names of the crafts and gilds taking part (some of which differ from those given above) but also the themes adopted by the groups. These were: the creation of the world, hell, paradise, Abel and Cain, Noah's ship, Abraham and Isaac, Moses and Aaron with the children of Israel and Pharaoh with his knights, conflict of David and Goliath, the birth of Christ with shepherds and three kings of Cologne, the baptism of Christ, the resurrection, the Holy Ghost.

There is a financial record of a parish play in the year 1482 in the St Michael's, Bath, records mentioned in the 'Parishes and Chantries' section above. This included much expenditure on food and drink, including 'bottles of ale', corn, bread, and cheese. Also mentioned is reward to the players 'in commemoration of their plays on various occasions', to 'William for painting various properties ordered for the said play', to Richard Tanner for 'skins for the same play', and to another for 'carrying timber from the graveyard at the said time of the play'.

A remarkable collection of diaries, letters, journals and memoirs have survived from the fifteenth century. Known as 'the Paston letters' and published under that title in an edition compiled by J. Gairdner, they have recently been re-issued (in somewhat shorter form) as *The Pastons*, edited by Richard Barber (Penguin Books 1984). They are well worth serious study as an account of a family in the Wars of the Roses. One Christmas around the year 1484 Margaret wrote to her husband John (he being away) that at their home there had been 'no disguising [play acting] nor harping, nor luting, nor singing, nor any loud pastimes, but [merely] playing at the tables [back-gammon] and chess and cards,' because there had been a bereavement in the family. The latter is, of course, interesting for it indicates the pastimes normally undertaken.

A number of local societies have published extracts from family records and these are worth searching out in the specialist studies collections. Reference should also be made to two works by Iona and Peter Opie: *The Lore and Language of Schoolchildren* (Oxford 1959, and Paladin Books 1977), and *Children's Games in Street and Playground* (Oxford 1969), for interesting survivals from medieval times including *Roi qui ne ment* played by Froissart about 1345.

Healing An intriguing volume dealing with medicine, *Medical Works of the Fourteenth Century* edited by G. Henslow (London 1899), throws much light on contemporary medical practices and beliefs. A few examples are: for loss of speech 'take the juice of southern wood or of primrose, and he shall speak at once', and, to make a man or woman sleep three days, 'take the gall of a hare, and give it in his food, and he shall not wake until his face is washed with vinegar.' At an even more serious level, some of the late medieval panaceas were positively lethal: medicine for the quartan fever (a severe ague), 'take heads of garlic and the root of radish, thirty peppercorns, and crush them and mix them with wine, and give him some to drink, and let him be bled in the vein of the spleen.' According to some authorities the death of Edward IV was hastened by a surfeit of this cure.

Heraldry Although heraldry was a product of the twelfth century it arguably came to its finest flowering during the fourteenth/fifteenth centuries, when on 2 March 1484 the College of Arms received its charter of incorporation, from King Richard III. The subject of heraldry is discussed in a later chapter, but there are two points which may be mentioned here. The first is the possibility of the determination of feudal alliances through the study of heraldic charges — an outstanding example is the relationships between the Luterell, de Furnival, de Eccleshall, de Wadsley, de Wortley, and de Mounteney families, as shown by their use of six martlets and a bend (see *Boutell's Heraldry* edited by J.P. Brooke-Little, London 1983). The second point is to recommend the perusal of *The Country Gentry in the Fourteenth Century, with special reference to the Heraldic Rolls of Arms* by N. Denholm Young (Oxford 1969).

On the related subject of 'livery and maintenance' the researcher is referred to the short entry under that heading in *A New Dictionary of Heraldry* edited by Stephen Friar (Sherborne 1987), and the source material appearing in *EHD4* pp.1108-9, quoting documents in the Public Record Office.

Houses and households It is inevitable that the houses of the common people remained poor, tiny and squalid, and the homes of the nobility were large and grand. Between these, at times, distant extremes there was a range of merchant and similar dwellings, the designs of which are of value in helping modern researchers determine the lifestyles of the well-to-do. Two important books are *The English Medieval House* by Margaret Wood (London 1985), and *Medieval Households* by David Herlihy (Harvard 1985). Both contain extensive reference lists. A particular description of a merchant's town house in the early fifteenth century appeared in *Archaeologia* Vol.74 (1923-4) written by C.L. Kingsford. This is reprinted in part in *EHD4*, together with other extracts from the public records on furnishing and articles commonly found in pros-

LEFT *A prosperous merchant sits in his chamber in front of a good fire.* RIGHT *A boys' school: 'A child were better to be unborn than to be untaught.'*

perous households. The chapter 'The Peaceful Arts' in the *Oxford History* volume by E.F. Jacob should also be studied.

On the related subjects of food and drink, two fifteenth-century recipe books have been published, dating from about 1420 and 1450. They appeared under one cover as *Two Fifteenth Century Cook Books* edited by T. Austin, and issued by the Early English Text Society in 1888. They deal with all kinds of meat, pies, tarts and other delicacies. Many of the 'presentation' customs fall ill on modern ears, such as when serving roasted peacock the flayed skin complete with feathers and tail should be wound around the body 'as if the bird were still alive'. A further important work is *The Household Book of Dame Alice de Bryene of Acton Hall Suffolk* published (1931) by the Suffolk Institute of Archaeology and Natural History. The book, dating from 1412-13, has also been quoted from and examined in *Food and Drink in Britain* by C. Anne Wilson (London 1973). The household book is of great value in describing the life of a noble family over a period longer than a year. Lady Alice de Bryene was the daughter of Sir Richard de Bures, wife of Guy de Bryan (the name is spelt in many different ways) whose family gave its name to Torbryan in Devon and Hazelbury Bryan in Dorset. She was connected by marriage to the families of Montague [Montacute], Mohun, de Courtney, Maltravers, le Scrope, Poynings, Fitzpaine, Arundel, Grandison and others. It is reasonable to assume that the records contained in the account book are typical reflections of the lives of the nobility of the period. The edition published in 1931, noted above, is quite essential reading for all students of the period.

Sport and pastimes Thomas Rymer in his *Foedera*, a collection of public records published 1704-35, throws valuable light on the sports practised in the fourteenth century. In 1363 Edward III, concerned by the lack of interest in archery, proclaimed to his sheriffs that everyone in the shire 'when he has his holiday' should learn and exercise himself in the art, and use for 'his games bows and arrows or crossbolts' and not meddle or toy with 'games of throwing stones, wood or iron, playing handball, football, stick-ball [rounders, or early cricket?] or hockey or cockfighting.' In 1478 an Act of Parliament had to prohibit games in favour of practice in archery. These included quoits, football, closh (not unlike croquet), kails (a form of ninepins), half bowls, hand-in and hand-out, and chequer board.

Travel The difficulties of travel in the late Middle Ages are recounted in the publications of many local societies which quote from and analyse a wide range of primary material. Much more material remains that has yet to be translated and published, however. *The Household of Edward IV* by A.R. Myers, *Studies in Medieval History presented to F.M. Powicke* (Oxford 1948), *The Tale of Beryn* edited by F.J. Furnival and G.W. Stone (Early English Text Society 1909) provide useful data. A most interesting account of a night at an inn, *c.*1396, is printed in *EHD4* pp.1212-13, from a manual in French conversation for the instruction of Englishmen. It describes the preparation of the room: 'I do not think there are any fleas, bugs or vermin ... except there is a great quantity of rats and mice but that need not worry us ...'. The traveller is assured he will find 'two beautiful girls, as you usually have'. A later section makes it quite obvious that it was quite common for two or three travellers to share a bed. A manuscript from 1467 is also used to illustrate difficulties in undertaking long journeys: 'I abode six weeks in great sickness in London ... [and] tarried at Dover more than ten days.' Typical of town records are those edited by W.H. Stevenson (1883), *Records of the Borough of Nottingham*, which include the accounts of the bridge-wardens for 1457-8.

Ways of life For accounts of the lives of people other than the nobility and members of the wealthier groups, a useful early text is 'Piers Plowman' by William Longland. This contains, among many other pieces, an account of the peasant's life. There are several manuscript versions extant. These are noted in the *Oxford Companion to English Literature* edited by Margaret Drabble (a new edition, 1985) and extracts from one of the texts appears in *EHD4* pp.1187-91.

Witchcraft and heresy The medieval church denounced witchcraft and sorcery following the teaching of the Old Testament — 'Thou shalt not suffer a witch to live' (Exodus xxii, 18) — and the chronicles and documents of the fourteenth and fifteenth centuries contain a number of reports which are no doubt typical of the generality. Thomas Walsingham (d.1422), the monkish author of *Historia Anglicana*, tells of John Badby who, in 1410, was burnt alive in a barrel in Smithfield because he averred that it is not the Body of Christ which is sacramentally carried in the church. *An English Chronicle* edited by J.S. Davies recounts the condemnation of Eleanor Cobham in 1441 for witchcraft, necromancy, heresy and treason. Dame Eleanor was, in fact, Duchess of Gloucester, and was much persecuted but did not die at the stake. *EHD4* contains a number of stories in which political intrigue, Lollardy, heresy, jealousy, witchcraft and downright silliness are intermingled. A further reference source is *Witch Stories* by E. Lynn Lynton (London 1861, reprinted with an index 1972). This factual book contains (pp.185-90) a short section on early historic trials, which point to the widespread beliefs of the times. Local historians more deeply interested in this fascinating aspect of social behaviour are recommended to the *Malleus Maleficarum* by Jacob Sprenger and Heinrich Kramer. This work was initially compiled to give teeth to the papal bull of 5 December 1484, as a counter attack on diabolism and heresy. The 'Hammer' (*Malleus*) was republished, in English, in 1968 by the Folio Society, London, with an introduction by Pennethorne Hughes. A number of local history societies have published collections of tales about neighbourhood witches. True or not, they make interesting passages in many a parish history.

Ecclesiastical records

The importance and value of parish and chantry records have already been stressed in the course of this chapter, but these are not the only ecclesiastical documents which may be of use to the local researcher. *Sources for English Local History* (W.B. Stephens) contains in Chapter 8 a wealth of information as to where to find what, and reference should also be made to the appropriate *Victoria County History* and the *Survey of Ecclesiastical Archives* published by the Pilgrim Trust in 1951. The extracts from manuscript records printed in *EHD4* will also be of value, particularly the sections 'The administrative Structure of the Church' (pp. 698-725) and 'The Monks' (pp.779-811). Among other topics discussed are the rights and duties of an archdeacon, the closing of shops on Sundays, personal tithes, visitations, indulgences, consistory courts, delapidations, and the incomes of bishops.

A misericord, c.1379, depicting a joust. The knight on the right charges and unhorses his opponent with his lance. The knights sport drooping moustaches in the fashion of the day. The drummer and bugler add, at one level, to the excitement of the scene, and at another, complete the artistic balance of the work.

A Tudor market scene. Women trading and an apprentice fetching water. From Civitas Orbis Terrarum.

10 A new beginning? 1485-1558

Early historians regarded 1485 as the end of the Middle Ages, and although later scholarship has tended to move the date forward to, perhaps, the reign of Henry VIII, there is much to be said for using the accession of the first Tudor monarch as a point for reflection, and as the true end of an age.

For the first few years of Tudor rule a great deal of what was 'medieval' in character remained — for no mere change of kingship will materially alter how people live their lives. The private armies of the major barons continued, liveried and maintained by their masters, and life in the towns and the countryside went on much as before, and it was not until the middle of the reign of Henry VIII that the 'revolution in government', instituted by the king and his able ministers, came to complete the work his father had started after Bosworth. This chapter deals, then, with the formative period of the new society, before the great flowering of the Elizabethan Age.

England was still extensively rural but there were towns and indeed cities (notably London, Bristol, Norwich and York) which were important centres of trade and industry, although many were barely separated from the open country surrounding them. The population of the kingdom numbered something less than three million. London housed about 70,000 people, Bristol 11,000 and York 8000. The average town boasted some 3000-5000 persons.

For the bulk of his reign Henry VII worked hard to reform the machinery of government, the economic base on which the nation's prosperity could flourish, and to set a framework of laws within which the population could feel reasonably at ease. The ownership of property could be aspired to by all. Commerce was encouraged and overseas ventures promoted, and a start was made on establishing a national navy. When he died of overwork, prematurely worn out at the age of fifty-two, Henry VII had given his country peace, had largely eliminated armed factions and had instituted prudent fiscal measures.

His son, 'great golden Henry', may not have inherited all his father's gifts for administration but he was a shrewd judge of men — Wolsey, Cromwell, More and others — and with their help continued the building of the nation. The local historian is possibly not too concerned with Henry's struggles with the Church and the authority of the pope, but the Dissolution of the monasteries brought about great changes in the distribution and ownership of land that were to have far-reaching effects. It is Cromwell we have to thank for 'the parish chest', that all-encompassing term known to local researchers as indicating the wealth of information available in their own communities (some of which stems from Thomas Cromwell's mandate of 5 September 1538 that a 'sure coffer' be placed in every church for the safe keeping of parish registers).

Gradually the processes of the Reformation were completed and Henry placed himself as Supreme Head under God in both Church and State.

This is not the place to discuss Henry's continental adventures or matrimonial strategy, but simply to note that 'side by side with the kaleidoscopic changes in religion and politics there was also going on a succession of social and economic disturbances, the causes of which were not understood, but the results were all too plainly felt in rising prices, unemployment and poverty' (C.H. Williams, *EHD5*, as below). Henry VIII died aged fifty-six in 1547. In his time the great barons lost much of their power, the monasteries fell, the manors of England declined in significance, enclosures for tillage and for pasture accelerated, urban society lost some of its old security, and the coinage was debased.

After Henry's death the new king, Edward VI, aged nine and sickly, 'reigned' for just six years. The country was, in practice, in the hands of Edward Seymour, the Duke of Somerset, who, as 'protector', furthered the religious revolution. When Somerset fell and was executed, John Dudley, Duke of Northumberland, assumed command. Between them they mismanaged the country's economic situation, prices went up and the poorer elements of the population suffered. Enclosure practices caused increasing discontent, and harsh game laws and high rents were resented. In 1549, under Robert Kett, the people of Norfolk rose against their oppressions. With a force of 12,000 men he dominated the Norwich area in the summer of that year. But the rebellion was crushed, and in December 1549 Kett and his brother were hanged. The king died in 1553 to be succeeded, for twelve days, by Lady Jane Grey who was later executed at the age of seventeen. Queen Mary, the elder of King Henry VIII's daughters, came to the throne and for five years, until her death in 1558, the country was torn by strife under the guise of religious zeal.

The whole period from 1485 to 1558 is covered by one volume, *The Early Tudors* by J.D. Mackie (Oxford 1952, with many reprints). The book deals with the physical state of England, the forests, towns, suburbs, castles, ports and churches, the successes and failures of King Henry VII, the fall of the monasteries, economic development, the achievement of the age, as well as a number of other matters of more general interest to local researchers.

As may be expected from a time when the business of government was developed to new heights, and which saw such upheavals in the structure and functioning of

An official guide to weights and measures in the time of Henry VII. It was, in effect, a ready-reckoner enabling the clerk of the market to ensure fair dealing.

society, there is a vast quantity of primary material of all kinds. The publication in the *English Historical Documents* series is volume five (*EHD5*) edited by C.H. Williams (London 1967). It starts with a scholarly essay dealing with the period as a whole, the land, population, government, society and the Church, as well as observations on the Tudor dynasty itself.

Turning more directly to sources of original records, mention has been made in Chapter 5 and elsewhere of the Charter Rolls (up to 1516), the Patent Rolls, the Letters and State Papers, and the collection *Materials for a History of the Reign of King Henry VII* in the Rolls series. There are other rolls, as noted in Chapter 5, which together with all the other written material provide a wide range of interest for pursuit by the local historian. The time in England's history has now been reached when the dedicated amateur can begin to specialise in the subjects being researched. The language in which documents are written is most frequently English and becoming easier to read, contemporary printed material has survived and the range of topics available for study has increased dramatically over those of previous centuries, and may be conveniently divided into groups. In the following pages, material will, therefore, be considered under the headings: *narrative histories, national government and society, country and towns,* and *ecclesiastical.*

Narrative histories

Narrative material for this period ranges from the *Anglicae Historiae Libri* of Vergil, through the *Itinerary* of John Leland, to the diaries of men such as Henry Machyn.

The Anglica Historia Polydore Vergil (*c.*1470-1555) was an Italian scholar who came to England in 1502 as a collector of 'Peter's Pence' (a tax imposed on hearths by the pope in the tenth century and abolished in 1534). Encouraged by King Henry VII he wrote a history of England, which appeared in several versions between 1534 and 1537 and has been published in English, with a commentary, as *The Anglica Historia of Polydore Vergil, 1485-1537* by D. Hay (Camden Society LXXIV, 1950). There are many passages in Vergil which are of general interest to local historians. Two may be selected as examples. The first tells of measures instituted by the king after Bosworth to control the country, especially the 'people of the north [who were] wild and readier than others for rebellion.' In the course of the narrative there is a description of 'a new type of [sweating] sickness which swept the whole country.' The author states that of those afflicted not 'one in a hundred escaped death.' Eventually the remedy seemed to be to stay in bed and drink warm fluid, but 'in this treatment care should above all be taken that not even an arm is exposed outside the bedclothes to get cool, for this is fatal.'

The second example describes the events of 1498 when the people of Cornwall, 'a part of the kingdom as small in area as it is poor in resources', revolted against the taxes imposed on them, and the king of the Scots invaded the northern shires 'laying waste everything with slaughter, fire and pillage'.

The Chronicle of Edward Hall The complete title of Hall's history is *The Union of the Two Noble and Illustre Families of Lancastre and Yorke*, and was published in 1548, a year after his death. There have been subsequent editions, including a modernised text of the later portions by Charles Whibley (London 1904), and the definitive version of the complete work *Hall's Chronicle* by Sir Henry Ellis (London 1809). *EHD5* includes long passages from Hall which contain valuable descriptions of the life of the day with specific references to national and civic festivities and pageantry. Edward Hall was well placed in the life of the times, being member of parliament for Wenlock in 1529, Common Serjeant of the City of London in 1533 and undersheriff in 1535. His 'chronicle' was used by Shakespeare as a source of ideas and information for his early history plays.

The Itinerary of John Leland Leland (1503-52) has been described as the earliest modern antiquary. He was much involved with monastic, collegiate, and royal librar- ies and, making a tour through England in the years 1535-43, determined to write a great work 'History and Antiquities of the Nation'. The plan did not come to fruition, but he left behind a great mass of invaluable notes. A version of his *Itinerary* was published in Oxford 1710-12, edited by Thomas Hearne, and a modern edition by Lucy Toulmin Smith appeared in 1906-10. A version of the *Itinerary* was reissued in 1964. In a letter to King Henry VIII in 1546 Leland described his projected work as likely to be as 'many books as there are shires in England . . . and Wales [that is to say fifty, containing] the beginnings, increases and memorable acts of the chief towns and castles . . .'. A useful introduction to Leland and an indication of the scope of his *Itinerary* appears in Dr Mackie's book in the *Oxford* series, *The Early Tudors* pp.32-41.

Diaries as sources for local history As C.H. Williams points out in *EHD5*, from about 1500 personal diaries become useful as narrative sources, and he goes on to quote two particular instances. The first is from the journal of the king, Edward VI (the standard work of which is the edition by J.G. Nichols, *Literary Remains of King Edward the Sixth*, published by the Roxburghe Club in 1857). The young king appears to have kept a journal from about the time he was thirteen until just before his death. Of special interest to local historians in the parts of the country affected are the young monarch's accounts of the enclosure risings of 1549. These were very widespread. A good brief summary appears in Mackie p.489 *et seq*, and the bibliography in that book points to other sources of information. In writing of the revolts the king describes how, to begin with, 'the people began to rise in Wiltshire . . . then they rose in Sussex, Hampshire, Kent, Gloucestershire, Suffolk, Warwickshire, Essex, Hertfordshire, a piece of Leices- tershire, Worcestershire and Rutlandshire . . . Oxfordshire, Devonshire, Norfolk and Yorkshire.' He describes the risings from his own perspective and his account is enlightening.

The diary of Henry Machyn (published by the Camden Society in a volume edited by J.G. Nichols) looks at events from a much more lowly and unique perspective. Machyn was a citizen of London who arranged funerals. His diary ran from 1550 to 1563 and contains interesting reports on pageants and celebrations.

From time to time diaries or similar writings are found, published, deposited in local record offices or sold to private collectors. The first point of enquiry remains the county or city archive, and valuable clues will be gathered from that source. The subject of parish registers will be dealt with later in this chapter, but one item may be mentioned at this time. It was not unusual for persons to use the end papers of the early registers for noting local matters which seemed to them to be important. From personal experience the author can commend researchers to the examination of these books for 'diary' entries, which frequently comprise unique records.

Biographies The bibliography in Mackie's *Oxford History* volume has some useful data on contemporary biographies (pp.617-18) and although many of these books deal with the lives of the great, good, and not so good, the immediacy of the narratives is refreshing, and information on events in many places can be obtained.

National government and society

The increasing complexity of society, the growth of the towns and the wealth of the merchant class gradually brought about a social structure which the kings and their parliaments saw fit to try to regulate.

Sumptuary laws A revealing document is the Act against the Wearing of Costly Apparell passed in the first year of the reign of Henry VIII (1510). This is published in *Statutes of the Realm III*, 8, and also appears in *EHD5*. The Act laid down what sort of clothing the various 'degrees' should wear. This ranged from cloth of gold and purple colour for the king and his family, through what dukes, earls, lords and knights might don and how their horses might be caparisoned, through mayors, esquires, lords' sons, gentlemen, guards, grooms, university graduates, stewards, sheriffs, bailiffs and many other 'classes'. A close reading of the information yields valuable insight into class divisions, jealousies and social attitudes.

The Heralds of Arms and Visitations A further interesting comment on the times and the stratification of society appeared in *Archaeologia* LXXXIII (1933) pp.167-70. It is entitled 'A grant of arms, 1510' and was written by W.G. Clark-Maxwell. In *EHD5*, C.H. Williams comments that a grant (made to John Mundy), described in an essay, is 'an early example of the way the authority of the heralds was sought by those anxious to scale up the social ladder.'

The College of Arms was founded by letters patent in 1484. An outline of its history (written by the present author) appears in *A New Dictionary of Heraldry* edited by Stephen Friar (Sherborne 1987), and the bibliography following the entry identifies substantial background texts. One of the most important instruments placed in the hands of the heralds was the visitation, the first such being granted by warrant of King Henry VIII in April 1530. By this and other authorities (for visitations continued until the late seventeenth century) the heralds journeyed to all parts of the kingdom to determine who had the right to a coat of arms, to denounce those who had assumed such dignity without authority, and to destroy the outward symbols, such as plate, windows, gravestones, monuments and so on of falsely assumed status. Many printed records and manuscripts of the visitations are available and a complete list appears on p.366 of Friar's *Dictionary*. Visitation records are particularly valuable to the local historian, for one of their principal features was the recording of the pedigrees of armigerous families. They thus set out to the best extent then available the descent and familial alliances of local notables, making records which are quite unique and far more informative than the parish registers of the day, of which more later. Used in conjunction with the old county histories (which frequently contain references to armigerous families and genealogies), and the volumes in the *Victoria County History* series, the visitation records help build up a unique picture of local society.

References to the social classes The early Tudor period was marked by the rise of 'new' families — that is, from the advancement of individuals who, through their own efforts, acquired riches and position enabling their children to function at a higher social level than they themselves attained. Such stories form an essential part of local history. The rise of men such as Thomas Cromwell, earl of Essex, whose father was a Putney blacksmith, is well known, but there are many others — the Berties, the Wrythe (later Wroithesley) family, the Spencers whose 'founder', John, is described in a deed of 1497 as a grazier. In the present writer's own village a family with a sheep farm of 47 acres in early Tudor times went on to achieve a barony, and their story became an essential part of the development of the international wool trade, as well as the local scene.

The source of quite indispensable material is *Peerage and Pedigree* by J. Horace Round (London 1910), and the same author's 'Studies in Peerage and Family History' in the *Victoria County History : Northants* (Vol.II). The bibliography in *EHD5* pp.230-48 points to dozens of texts of relevance, and on pp.268-76 are extracts from works describing the gentry (good and bad), yeomen, and the villein (whose status was still a reality in the social system of the day).

The Common Weal Reference has been made to the records in the diaries of Edward VI of the risings *c*.1549. The background to the situation is complex and the basic text remains *A Discourse of the Common Weal of this Realm of England*, a contemporary work of uncertain authorship, edited by Elizabeth Lomond (Cambridge, reprinted 1929). The whole question of agrarian reforms, enclosures, rents and wages is worthy of study by local historians working in rural areas, and the bibliography in Mackie points to valuable sources of study. A useful section, 'The Theory of the Commonweal' appears in *EHD5* pp.276-302, and includes 'A Supplication of the Poore Commons', 1546, and the 'Dialogue between Pole and Lupset', *c*.1539. Further comment appears later in this chapter in the 'Country' and 'Town' sections.

New agencies of government The processes of strengthening and refining the machinery of government took many forms, and for a conveniently short overview the reader is referred to Chapter XVI in Mackie (*op cit*) 'The Achievement of the Age'. One of the posts created as a part of the development of the system was that of the lord lieutenant. These officers, first appointed in the reign of Edward VI (*c*.1550) took control of the armed forces in the shires (thus ousting the sheriffs in this regard), and gradually assumed the headship of the county including the responsibility for the rolls. Part of the lord lieutenant's duties was to receive the sovereign's instruction to muster the able-bodied men in each parish in times of national emergencies. These musters became an integral part of the local history of the times, and will be dealt with in greater detail in the next section.

The enclosures of 1450-1700 laid hedges across ancient ridge-and-furrow field systems.

Country and town life

Country

During the period 1485-1558 life in the shires changed in perhaps the two most important ways of all — the manner in which a living was wrested from the land and the way in which the Christian religion was decreed to be interpreted. In the manors, 'the economy of life was an endless round of ploughing, sowing, reaping, threshing and grinding, of shearing, spinning and weaving, of milking, churning, and cheese-making, supplemented by the daily activities proper to stock-breeding and poultry-keeping, and by interludes of fruit-picking, brewing, killing and salting, which came round with the revolving seasons' (Mackie). For more than a century before the Tudor era, villein tenure and villein status had been separating, and those who had held land tended to be free men rather than the totally dependent tenants of earlier years. By 1500 the process was almost complete, and it was recognised that no land held by villein tenure could make a free man a villein.

The years 1485 to 1558 form a time from which the fortunate researcher will discover the survival of court rolls and documents describing the administrative structure of the manor, and the kind of justice meted out. Typical of the information contained in a survey is the following drawn from a copy in the author's collection: 'The [manor] is a liberty of yt selfe and the Lorde may keepe two leets or lawdayes in the yere, and as many courte Barons as he please, and thereto dothe belong large and verie great royaltyes as Wayfes Strayes felons goods and chattels. The tenannts owe suyte of courte can wear no mans clothe without the lords leave and doe paye at

128

theire deathes the beste beaste for a herriott which in that place is greate profitte. The Comons and wastes belonginge to the said manor are verie large and good. The guifte of the p[ar]sonage is in the lorde of the mannor hathe belonginge to it a faire house garden orchard and backsyde with 60 acres of good meadow pasture and arrable and the tythe of the whole mannor in kynde.' The survey continues with the names of the freeholders, and the rents (plus 'suyte of court'). There were demesne acres leased for seven years, tenancies at will, for one, two and three lives; leases for thirty years, twenty-one years, and holding by widow's estate. The survey ends with a statement of the total rent and acreage of the manor, the latter divided into meadow, pasture and arable sub-totals.

From about the same time, and for the same manor, a court roll gives much insight into other practices and to justice — 'Alice Coke, widow, has not carried stone to the ways within this Homage, for the rectory there, as is the custom' (Alice was fined fourpence). 'And that one chilver hogget and lamb worth 2s came as strays, and at this Court they present they have been in the manor over a year ... and are adjudged to the lady [of the manor].' There were many other issues raised — overstinting the common with sheep beyond the permitted number, non-repair of barns and kitchens and so on. Together with records discovered in the Public Record Office, in private collections in Britain and elsewhere, a fairly complete picture of Tudor life has been assembled over a period of some ten years — local history research is not quickly done.

A number of Acts of Parliament not so far mentioned touched the life of the ordinary person. No village was without its 'stocks' and an Act of 1495 ordered local officials to set in these all idle persons. A further Act of 1531 made a distinction between impotent poor and mere wastrels, and a certain amount of begging was allowed. Should churchwardens' accounts survive for this period they may be informative.

By an Act of 1495 an agricultural labourer was required from mid March to mid September to start work before 5 a.m. and to end not earlier than 7 p.m., with two short breaks for meals. In winter he started in 'the spring of the day' and ended only when it was dark. An Act of 1515 fixed labourers' pay at about 3 pence (old pence) a day and a skilled artisan at 6 pence.

A quiet revolution had taken place in the structure of local government. During medieval times the old administrative divisions of shire, hundred (or equivalent) and tithings had prevailed, there were manors (with their courts as has been illustrated) and, of course, ecclesiastical parishes. But the Tudors found the *civil* parishes to be more practical units and organised them on a statutory basis, in some cases merely confirming existing practices. W.E. Tate's *The Parish Chest* (Cambridge 1946, reprinted 1983) is a large and exhaustive treatment of the civil parish, and *Sources for English Local History* by W.B. Stephens (Cambridge 1981) has an invaluable chapter on 'Local Government and Politics'. Both works carry extensive bibliographies.

The Highways Acts of 1555 and 1563 specified the appointment of unpaid surveyors of the 'highways' of the parish: 'the constables and the churchwardens of every parish within this realm shall yearly, on the Tuesday or Wednesday in Easter Week, call together a number of the parochians and shall then elect and choose two honest persons of the parish to be the surveyors of the highways in their parish leading to

*An almshouse account
for 1570/1.*

any market town.' (It is interesting to reflect on the non-taking of stone to the ways, quoted earlier, and a similar entry from the same roll of tenants being in mercy because they had 'not carried stone to the roads of the manor as is customary'.)

Whatever the form of parish administration — lingering manorial or the new vestry system — a further event threw greater responsibility on local governments, and that was the destruction of the monasteries in the years immediately prior to 1537, for with that turmoil went the abolition of numerous charities and hospitalities which, for centuries, had given relief to the destitute and needy. In an attempt to mitigate the immense problems created, legislation was enacted, and in 1537 the Beggars Act required each churchwarden 'to gather and procure' voluntary alms for the relief of the poor. The problem had been a long time growing, as the pages of *Statutes of the Realm II* show. In 1495 there had been an Act against vagabonds and beggars, a further

similar such in 1503-4, and legislation 'concerning punishment of beggars and vagabonds' in 1531. In 1536 there was an Act for punishment of *sturdy* vagabonds and
beggars, but the problems of the genuinely poor were steadily recognised. In 1547
'relief of the poor and impotent persons' was instituted, followed by further legislation
in 1552 and 1555. In 1572 the Elizabethan Poor Law Act came on to the statute book,
and this will be dealt with in the next chapter. For the present it is useful to note that
EHD5 contains a section 'Poverty and the Poor Law' (pp.1023-38) with extracts from
contemporary documents.

The imposition of lay subsidies continued in the sixteenth century and the Great
Subsidy Roll of 1524/5, preserved in the Public Record Office, lists people over the
age of sixteen who merited taxation. Numerous sections of this and later rolls have
been published, many by local societies or enthusiastic individuals. When compared,
like for like, they are of considerable value for, interpreted with caution, they throw
light on individual families and population movement.

Much the same can be said about the Tudor Muster rolls, a contemporary record of
which details what was expected of the lord lieutenants in mustering the local militia.
Each was required 'to choose meetest persons for captains and petty captains . . . to the
charge of certain numbers according to their qualities; those of most worship, credit
and value to have the charge of more or less according to their degrees, i.e. some of
the best worship, of two or three hundred; others of meaner degrees and values in
living, to take charge under them of each hundred apart; and also with the consent of
the captains a charge to be made of skilful and expert persons to be lieutenants of
every hundred, and necessary officers to govern and lead the said bands.' A militia
man could expect to be paid 8 pence a day when in training or service, plus one
penny for every mile he travelled between his home and place of training. At this time
a skilled tradesman was earning 4 pence or 6 pence a day, so the mustered peasant
was paid well.

The muster rolls which have been published on a county or somewhat similar basis
reveal a great deal about local social structures, and on a somewhat different level the
martial skills and weaponry available. Some of the records (e.g. the muster of 1542)
list not only the names of the militia men but their abilities as light-horsemen, users of
demi-lance, arquebus, bill, pike or bow. An entry may show that Christopher Syver-
west had a jack (leather jerkin), a sallet (helmet or head piece), a poleaxe and a sword,
and was an 'able archer'. Another might record that Laurence Meryfild had a bill, a
half sheaf of arrows (no bow being mentioned), and was an able pikeman; and so on.
Tudor Muster Rolls — Dorset by T.L. Stoate (Bristol 1978) contains a good introduction
to muster rolls and militia rolls in general, and a full listing, by county, of all the
muster rolls in the Public Record Office and a bibliography of those *printed* up to 1978.
Reference should also be made to the Society of Genealogists, London (see Addresses, Appendix III), who hold a number of typescripts.

In 1538 Thomas Cromwell, Vicar General and Vice Regent of King Henry VIII in
matters spiritual, instituted various measures and issued certain injunctions, among
which were that a bible was to be placed in every church, specific recitations were to
be made in English by the incumbent who was to preach at least once a quarter, and a
register of births, marriages and deaths was to be instituted. A number of registers
survive from this early period, but for many hundreds of parishes they do not, a more

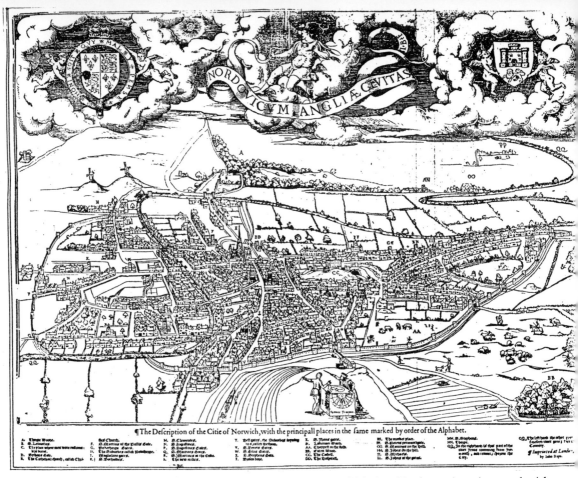

Nordovicvm Angliae Civitas. A map of Norwich in 1558, by which time 'North town' was immensely rich and for several centuries was the second city in England.

usual starting point being 1558. In 1598 it was recognised that many of the earlier records had fallen into disuse, or in some cases had actually been destroyed. So an instruction went out that registers should be reinstated (on a durable medium, vellum rather than paper) and that copying should date from at least the first year of the reign of Elizabeth (17 November 1558 to 16 November 1559), but we go too far ahead.

The early registers are of some small value to the local historian, especially if tenancies or family migrations are being studied, and they are also perhaps of value to genealogists. A baptismal entry such as 'William sonne of Edward Toppe' is of value, but 'Richard sonne of Richard Gauler' (1562) is not if, three years later (1565), 'Richard' is buried, twenty years later (1585) another Richard is interred and four years later still (1589) a third Richard is inhumed. Who was who? Were they descendants in the male line of the whole blood or from collateral branches? Is the register accurate? Were they related at all? When were they all born, which Richard married which woman (given all three were married in the same parish)? Whose son is 'John, son of Richard Gauler' baptised in 1583? Much the same problems arise with marriages. 'Edmund Joliffe married Elizabeth Tollerfield' may be useful enough, but 'Raulfe Myles married Agnes' is unlikely to be of value, and 'Aphrodosie Young and his wife' is useless saving the probability that any subsequent children of Aphrodosie were born in wedlock. A most useful reference book giving guidance on the use of parish registers is *An Introduction to English Demography* by E.A. Wrigley (London 1966).

Churchwardens' accounts for the years covered by this chapter may be of special interest. (For a brief outline of the office of churchwarden, see *Encyclopaedia Britannica* 11th edition, Vol.5, p.688). The years concerned include the Marian restoration, and the accounts possibly register such things as (1547/8) taking down images and iron in the church; (1548/9) taking down Our Lady in the chancel, purchasing 'a book called paraphtasus and Erasmus' (Erasmus's Paraphrases, see *Oxford Dictionary of the Christian Church* 2nd edition, pp.466-7). Also for this period in the reign of Edward VI, they almost certainly include such things as selling the processional cross, painting out proscribed popish pictures, and may well mention removing the stone altar with its echoes of sacrifice and its replacement with a wooden table. Then, starting in 1553, as the pendulum swung in the first year of Mary I, a new processional would have been bought, together with missal, censer, pax and corporal, and a new cloth for the pyx. The wooden table would have been thrown out and a new stone altar built as the church interior was transformed into a traditional Roman Catholic layout. In 1558 everything changed again, and this too will be mentioned in Chapter 11.

Towns

Much of the generality of the foregoing paragraphs applies equally to the towns as to the country areas, but it follows that many aspects of town life remained distinct, and different, from the rural. A good general guide to sources of an explanatory nature is the *Bibliography of British History: Tudor Period* by C. Read (Oxford 1959), and this is augmented by the *Annual Bulletin of Historical Literature* published by the Historical Association. Much information on local towns, their trading pre-occupations, gilds, liveries, economic and material matters is contained in the *Victoria County History* volumes and the older county histories.

The recommended 'further reading' section of John West's *Town Records* is also of value in indicating books on a wide aspect of life in towns up to 1600. In *EHD5* (p.901) C.H. Williams indicates that among the records of towns 'so much is recorded, connected with municipal policy and the economic life of the citizens' that it makes research 'a happy hunting ground'. There follows an extensive list of the most important collections in print which are especially valuable for the early sixteenth century. These include, among other things, records for Chester, Coventry, Guildford, Leicester, Northampton, Norwich, Nottingham, Oxford, Reading, Southampton, Worcester and York.

In addition to the foregoing, *EHD5* contains a representative selection of documents illustrating aspects and problems of daily life in towns. Such is the quantity of material available that only a brief indication is possible of information available in these present pages. No attempt has been made to classify the extracts. They are given under the headings of the various towns although it may be expected that much of the material has a wider application. In 1520, for example, Leicester set out regulations for the sale of bread —'all that bake rye bread for poor people make good bread and

Tudor town carriers sold water door-to-door and collected rubbish for dumping outside the walls.

wholesome and that it stand the more part be rye and the chesill of wheat [bran] according to the statute, and they that do not, to forfeit the paid aforesaid [that is forfeiture of their wares] and their bodies to be punished according to the law.' Extracts for London concern election of city officers, plague in the city, refuse dumping, morals, decay of buildings, inflation, and brewing; for Nottingham the documents quoted dealt with butchers, civic responsibilities, town paving, house repair, detenue (suit for the recovery) of household goods, repairs to windows, and much more. Other towns are mentioned and a wide range of matters illustrative of lives in the towns is printed. *EHD5* also has a section dealing with industry and industrial conditions (pp.995-1008). Practices and issues described include those of artificers and labourers, woollen cloth manufacture, weaving, woollen yarn, masons, metal mining, shoemaking, and glass manufacture. The bibliography identifies relevant books for further study.

Ecclesiastical material

It has been suggested in previous sections that the swings away from Rome and back again, coupled with the Reformation, the Dissolution of the monasteries, and the events taking place during the reign of Queen Mary I, impacted at local level in a variety of ways. The most immediately obvious were the changes in church interiors, as already described. With the death of Henry VIII the religious revolution had speeded up, backed with total dedication by Archbishop Cranmer (later burnt at the stake at Oxford in March 1556, in the reign of Mary I). Knox, Ridley, Latimer and Hooper were appointed court preachers. Cranmer's exquisitely written *Book of Common Prayer* was introduced on 9 June 1549, English became the language of the Church, and England a Protestant state. There was rebellion in the southwest, indeed in one Devon village 'the parishioners were so incensed that on the following day they compelled the priest to don his vestments and celebrate mass in the old fashion.' There are numerous indications in the records of folk and their priests (ordained according to the old Latin rite) disliking the new prayer book as something new-fangled and slightly heretical. A useful study may be made by local researchers into any changes in clergy at this time in parishes in which they are interested. In a specific

134

parish studied by the present author, a rector resigned in 1548/9 to be succeeded in that office by his own brother, who, no doubt, held somewhat different beliefs.

The year 1558, which marks the end of the reign of Queen Mary I and the period covered by this chapter, also marks a useful point at which the local historian may sum up ecclesiastical matters to date, and perhaps determine what customs, if any, survived the upheavals of the age. Again in a specific place, the same as just cited, a piece of land had been given in the thirteenth century in 'perpetual alms that a light should be found [*morterium vel lampas*] in the church every night in the year.' The charter of bequest also required that a light should burn at completory (i.e. *compline*, the last service of the day) until the end of that office on Easter Day; also two tapers of wax before the sepulchre of Our Lord from the ninth hour on the day of *parasceve* (Good Friday); and a man to ring the morning and evening curfew bell throughout the year. The terms of this bequest were still being honoured in 1534, for the accounts of the First Fruits Office notes the payment of 7/7d (38 new pence) against the item. No later record has been found, and it is reasonable to suppose the practices were dropped during the troubled years which followed.

There are numerous documents on religion quoted in *EHD5*, in fact the extracts and the editor's commentary cover pp.633-869. The introduction to the section says the texts selected 'illustrate the essential changes affecting the structure, organisation and profession of faith of the Church of England during some of the most critical years in its history.' The introduction, although quite short, is useful, and may be followed by a reading of the history of the Church to the Reformation in *Christian England* by David L. Edwards (London 1981), the final long chapter of which is most informative regarding the period from 1485 to 1558. The documents quoted in *EHD5* contain much of a philosophical and theosophical nature touching on doctrinal and liturgical matters and the whole complex topic of heresy, and the power of Rome. Much of the text will not be of great interest to the general local historian, but is well worth study for the indirect light it may shed on local material of seemingly puzzling kind. Of the texts of more obvious value the following in *Statutes of the Realm III* may be exemplars: 'An act concerning the taking of mortuaries' and 'An act for the submission of the clergy to the king's majesty'. In 1535 an Act gave the Crown the right to assess church incomes, and the returns were brought together in a survey called the *Valor Ecclesiasticus*. This has been published by the Record Commission (1810-34), and extracts are given in *EHD5* pp.748-58. Further documents quoted in *EHD5* deal with conditions in religious houses (including dissolution of chantries), inventories of church goods (plate, jewels, vestments, bells and ornaments), Cromwell's injunctions, the abolition of 'diversity in opinions', the disposal of monastic lands, descriptions of heresy trials, and the 'putting away of divers books and images' (1550).

1587

(132)

A trew Inventorye

of all the goods and cattels that were
John fframptons of holt within the pishe of wimborne minster
in the countye of dorst deceased made and praysed by william
fframpton Robert markham with others the second daie of September
in the yere of o[ur] lord god 1587 according to the complication
of the churche of England

In primis

iiij or Oxen praysed at .... xiij li iiij s

Item ij cows a hopper a bullock a calfe .... iij li

Item one horse praysed at .... xx s

Item v shepe praysed at .... viij s

Item v pigge praysed at .... xxiij s iiij d

Item the wood in the barkesyde .... xxvj s viij d

Item the corne & haye in the barne pfed .... xx s

Item a cart praysed at .... xx s

Item a showle a draye ij oxen pfed at .... v s

Item too ploughs wraynes ij peare of drangs ij yokes ... v s

Item in the halle a ij borde & formes .... iiij s

Item tenn powlds of porter praysed at .... ij s

Item iij candlestickes sawsers one salt a penter ... iiij s

Item to brasse potte praysed .... iij s

Item a fornace panne .... ij s

Item to kettles to little pannes .... iij s

Item a lymni forme .... iij s

Item v pykens iiij trendles ij trowghes ...... iij s

Item too spittes one brandysd ij peare of pott yokes ... xv s

Item in the chamber ij bedstede & iiij coffers ... xij s

Item iiij peare of shete to peare of blankets ... v s

Item the coverletes iij bolsters iiij pillowes ... xv s

Item about the house in stayned clothes ...... xv s

Som xxv li viij s viij d

The inventory of the goods of John Frampton, a farmer in the village of Holt in Dorset. It is dated 2 September 1587 and indicates goods to the value of £25.7s.8d. (£25.38p). His beasts are noted as four oxen, two cows, a heifer, a bullock, a calf, a horse, five sheep and five pigs. His farm implements include plough chains, harnesses and yokes. His household goods are listed after the agricultural items. It should be noticed that the values of the goods are written in Roman numerals.

136

11

The Age of Elizabeth 1558-1603

In November 1558 Queen Elizabeth entered into her kingdom and the Tudor dynasty took on new splendour. The Protestant summer had come. In May 1559 new Acts of Supremacy and Uniformity went onto the statute book, and in parishes throughout the land high altars were being pulled down again. So too were chantry altars, and most churches thus lost their relics of medieval superstition, if not genuine belief.

At a more immediate level the new queen inherited a bankrupt kingdom; there was no money in the treasury, there was an enormous debt of over a quarter of a million pounds, and ports and strongpoints were sliding into decay. Her enemies were powerful in France and Scotland.

The acknowledged authoritative work in the *Oxford History of England* series is *The Reign of Elizabeth* by J.B. Black (2nd edition 1959). At the outset Professor Black states Elizabeth 'interpreted the national inspirations and gave them articulation'. She had the loyalty of her subjects, and was the repository of their future hopes. In time she proved difficult to understand, she vacillated, temporized, was harsh, coarse and demanding, but never lost sight of her vision for the glory of England. 'It is not my desire to live or reign longer than my life and reign shall be for your good. And though you have had, and may have, mightier and wiser princes sitting in this seat, yet you never had, nor shall have, any that will love you better.' As G.M. Trevelyan said in *A Shortened History of England*, 'By the strangest chance in history, no elder statesman or famous captain in all broad Europe would have served so well to lead Englishmen back to harmony and prosperity and on to fresh fields of fame.'

This is not the place to extol the achievements and virtues of the queen, she was a monarch who matched her moment to perfection. The reign of Mary I had been popular with large sections of the clergy, but unpopular with the laity, especially those of, or aspiring to, middle-class status. With the help of this latter group (through the House of Commons) Elizabeth confirmed the sovereign nation-state, with the Church as its servant. The new Bible and Prayer Book played their parts. The vestiges of feudalism were swept aside, and the foundation of modern England laid. The state was financially poor but the people were rich in spirit — 'they gave [the queen] their lives and affections more readily than their cash' (Trevelyan).

In researching the history of towns or parishes in Elizabethan England the local historian should not overlook and never discount the spirit of the age, for out of that spirit came the legislation which governed men's lives, the well-springs for the development of their material prosperity and their attitudes to the life hereafter. At the time of publication there is no relevant book in the *English Historical Documents* series appropriate to this period, although number 6 has been in preparation for some time.

To the local historian short of financial resources and time to visit record offices or repositories this, at first sight, can be bemoaned, but other sources of information are available, for the Elizabethan age is one which has been the subject of much study by scholars. A significant work of reference is the *Bibliography of British History: The Tudor Period* by Conyears Read (London, 2nd edition 1959), and a second valuable source is *British Economic and Social History: A Bibliographical Guide* by W.H. Chaloner and R.C. Richardson (London 1976). There are two yearly publications which are useful: the *Annual Bulletin of Historical Literature* issued by the Historical Association, and the *Annual Bibliography of British and Irish History* published by the Royal Historical Society. In addition, the volumes in the *Victoria County History* series will be found to be invaluable, not least for the extensive footnotes and references pointing to further sources. *Tudor England* by S.T. Bindoff (Pelican Books 1950) is worth attention and has a substantial note on further reading. Of newer works *The Elizabethan Deliverance* by A. Bryant (London 1978) and the two books *The Parliament of England 1559-1581* and *The Tudor Revolution in Government*, both by G.R. Elton and published by the Cambridge University Press, will be helpful, as will *The Emergence of a Nation State* by A.G.R. Smith (London 1982). A further volume, *Sixteenth Century England* by Joyce Youings (London 1984) is a part of the *Pelican Social History of Britain*. In addition to providing an up-to-date analysis of the period Professor Youings includes a lengthy reading list conveniently broken down into the sections: general, occupations, landlords and tenants, people in towns, 'belonging and not belonging', rank and status, inflation of population and prices, the land market, clergy, people and schools, armed rebellion and commotions, new horizons, the poor, banishment of idleness, family and fortune, community and country, marriage and the household. It is difficult to think of a more comprehensive and up-to-date work. Taken with the other sources already mentioned and the information which follows, the local historian is well served.

The collections of the *Calendars of State Papers* published by the Public Record Office remain a prime source (and additional references appear on pp.499-506 of Black, above). On constitutional matters the appropriate volumes in *Statutes of the Realm*, edited by Luder, Tomlins and Raithby in eleven volumes (London 1810-28), are without substitute. The footnotes in *Sources for English Local History* by W.B. Stephens (Cambridge 1981) should also be addressed.

For the remainder of this chapter, written and printed material will be considered under the headings: *narrative histories, national government, country and towns,* and *ecclesiastical.*

Narrative histories and related works

Thomas Rymer's *Foedera* published in twenty volumes between the years 1704 and 1735, although not a narrative history, remains a quite invaluable work of reference for treaties and diplomatic records. The research and writing undertaken by Rymer was done on the highest authority. In 1692 at the age of fifty-one he was appointed historiographer to King William III, and a year later a warrant was issued for him to search 'all public repositories'. The resulting volumes covered the period 1115-1654. Rymer did not live to see the complete work published, as he died in 1713. For a full description of the background to *Foedera*, its models and value, reference should be made to the entry under Rymer's name in the *Dictionary of National Biography*.

Of more truly narrative histories and chronicles, the *Annales Rerum Anglicarum et Hibernicarum Regnante Elizabetha* by W. Camden (1615) has been translated twice, the later (by T. Hearne in 1717) is the more accessible and is worthy of study. *Chronicles* by R. Holinshed (1577) has been published in an edition by H. Ellis in 1807/8. A further work is the *Chronicles* (or *Annals*) by J. Stow and the edition of 1605 may be accessed through the British Library. Stow also wrote a *Survey of London* and this has been issued in an edition by C.L. Kingsford (London 1908). There are a number of more modern works. Black (pp.500-1) gives pride of place to the *History of England from the fall of Wolsey to the Defeat of the Spanish Armada* by J.A. Froude, in twelve volumes published between 1862 and 1870.

Particularly useful to the local historian is Sir John Neale's *Queen Elizabeth (I)*. First published in 1934 the book was reissued in 1971. It is not, nor does it pretend to be, a definitive history of the realm, but is invaluable background reading. Finally, mention must be made of the volumes by A.L. Rowse which illuminate the period: *The England of Elizabeth* (1950), *The Expansion of Elizabethan England* (1955), *The Elizabethan Renaissance: The Life of the Society* (1971), *The Elizabethan Renaissance: The Cultural Achievement* (1972).

National government and society

As for previous periods, the impact of national government on the local scenes both urban and rural is best illustrated by Acts of Parliament and the manner of their interpretation. As may be expected, the reign of Elizabeth, coming immediately after the troubled and oppressive reign of Mary and the ineffective sovereignty of the young Edward VI, was rich in legislation of great importance. It is impossible, and unnecessary, to point to other than a selection in these pages and for greater information the reader is referred to *Statutes of the Realm* and the other works already mentioned.

The Acts of Supremacy and Uniformity By these two Acts passed in the first year of her reign (1559), Elizabeth strengthened her hold on the religious life of the nation. The reactionary legislation of Mary's reign was set aside and supreme power over the national church was vested in the Crown. The Act of Uniformity ensured the revised Book of Common Prayer became the 'directory' of public worship, and attendance in church on Sundays became mandatory — 'Every person and persons inhabiting within this realm . . . shall diligently and faithfully . . . endeavour themselves to resort to their parish church or chapel accustomed . . . on pain that every person so offending shall forfeit for each offence 12d to be levied by the church-wardens of the parish where such offences shall be done.'

Fighting inflation A number of measures were taken during the reign to stabilise the economy. In 1561 the coinage was reformed and this helped to restore the confidence of the trading and farming interests. As a further measure the maximum rate of interest chargeable on monetary loans was set at 10 per cent. However, it followed that if these and related actions were to be successful other statutes were needed.

139

Thus comprehensive legislation was enacted (1563 and later) to encourage and control employment, and to speed the 'banishment of idleness'. By instituting systems of wage differentials based on conditions deemed to prevail in various parts of the country, prices tended to equalize. The pursuit of work was encouraged (the Statutes of Labourers, Apprentices and Artificers are relevant) by yielding 'to the hired person, both in time of scarcity and in time of plenty, a convenient proportion of wages.' In fact the legislation laid down that wage rates were to be confirmed by Justices of the Peace. Fit and able males between the ages of twelve and sixty were required to do agricultural work should this be needed, apprentices were bound for seven years, and hours of work were regulated.

The treatment of beggars and vagabonds Throughout the Middle Ages the problem of dealing with beggars and vagabonds was a vexed one and inextricably mixed with the treatment of the poor. The Dissolution of the monasteries and the fall of the chantries exacerbated the situation by terminating sources of substantial funds. In 1563 and 1572 legislation was enacted and further Acts of 1591 reinforced the measures which were authorized. The Acts are too long and detailed to be dealt with fully within these pages, and the reader is referred to Black's *The Reign of Elizabeth* p.264 *et seq*, and Youing's *Sixteenth Century England* p.254 *et seq*. It is sufficient to indicate here that *c.*1570 there were some 10,000 'sturdy' beggars in the kingdom, twenty-three classes of vagabond and swindler, and untold thousands of 'impotent, aged, and needy persons'. While the levying of rates was permitted by justices, sheriffs, mayors and bailiffs to ease the difficulties of the genuinely needy, rogues and vagabonds could be whipped and, for a time — until 1576 — bored through the gristle of the right ear, and the individual whipped 'until his or her body be bloody'.

In an attempt to mitigate the immense problems which had been building up, the Beggars Act of 1537 required each churchwarden to 'gather and procure' voluntary alms for the relief of the poor. Then in 1572 the Poor Law Act established another new parish officer, the Overseer of the Poor, who with the churchwardens, the constable and, to some extent, the Surveyor of the Highway, had to collect and dispense public money. The arrangement was a compulsory assessment for the poor and, as a consequence of the Act, the first poor rate was raised, each parish being made responsible for its own paupers. This innovation was greatly resented, and parishes tried to avoid having a destitute population which they would have to support. 'Hence a regular persecution of needy persons set in, which greatly accentuated their misery, and was an extraordinary interference with the liberty of the individual.' Just two examples will be sufficient to illustrate some of the personal problems created by the well-meant legislation. Andrew Ham of Lyme was ordered to remove his sister from his house under penalty of 40 shillings, and in the north of England a parson was called upon to give security to the overseers that he would provide for a poor man, with seven children, should this be necessary, merely because he had allowed them to come into the parish.

On the other hand, private endowment of hospitals, houses of correction and such was encouraged. As Black has said, 'It will be evident that the [Poor Law Acts of 1572, 1598 and 1601] completely secularized the whole question of relieving poverty, and at the same time established the principle of corporate responsibility as fully as the time permitted. If it showed no mercy to the "work-shy", it did everything that was humanly possible for those who were willing to work, and acknowledged a very significant obligation to the children of paupers'. As a very broad generalization this is no doubt true, but given the cases quoted above the reader may feel unable to agree that the laws 'became the final expression of Elizabethan statesmanship in the sphere of poor-law administration.' What is admirable in broad terms may not be so in specific.

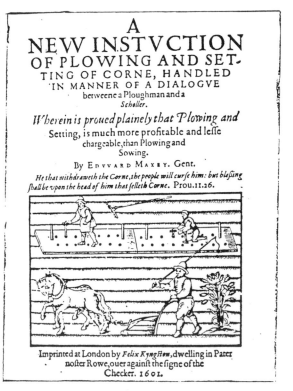

An agricultural treatise of 1601. It advocated the abolition of throwing seed about at random in favour of punching holes and setting them in regular rows. The seed-drill was invented later in the century.

Country and towns

Country life and general topics

For a broad appreciation of country life the local researcher is recommended to read *The Agrarian History of England and Wales IV* (1500-1640) edited by Joan Thirsk (London 1967), and to select books from the reading lists in Black and Youings. For specific elements of particular interest the following will be of value.

Family life Until recently there was no large-scale treatment of family life, but in 1977 *The Family, Sex and Marriage in England 1500-1800* by Lawrence Stone was published. It weighed 3lb.6oz. and ran to 800 pages, hence an abridged version followed two years later (Pelican Books). Much of the scholarly apparatus has been dispensed with in the smaller publication, but the extensive index is valuable. For illustrative aspects of Elizabethan familial life the reader is recommended to these works. The national archives — letters and papers, etc. — reflect family life, and the *Victoria County History* should be consulted as occasionally throwing light on the subject.

Tenancies As in all other centuries land-holding was important in Elizabethan times. The estates of the nobility remained substantially intact — indeed a number, because of well arranged heiress marriages, grew bigger, and the local historian may well find valuable information through the careful researching of these alliances. It is, however, mainly with tenant land that this present section will deal. Although a substantial number of acres were farmed in demesne (that is, held as the lords' or other larger owners' estates), many thousands more were tenurial holdings, the terms of which varied from place to place according to custom. The volume on agrarian history already mentioned, edited by Joan Thirsk, remains an important text, and Joyce Youings in *Sixteenth Century England* points (pp.391-2) to further relevant works. Many of these deal with matters at county level, or with family estates, and are hence worthy of special attention not only by the historians in the localities in which the estates lay but by others who wish to seek similarities or point to differences. Not to be over-looked, for example, are the practices adopted in the Percy (Earls of Northumberland) estates, which lay in many counties from Northumberland itself to Dorset and Kent. The Percy earls were inheritors of Poyning, Fitzpaine, de Bryan and other family lands and Dr J.M.W. Bean's *The Estates of the Percy Family* (1958) well illustrates how the tenancies, rents, fees and fines were handled.

The matter of terms of tenure in a specific parish (or manor) needs careful study, for frequently the records say, after a particular statement, 'according to the custom', no further information being given. The interested parties knew what the custom was and there was no need at the time for it to be specified. But the local researcher may not know and hence must tread carefully. Fortunately there frequently are, for the Elizabethan period, many records in the Public Record Office and in private hands, which deal with the same place. The Royal Commission on Historical Manuscripts (National Monuments Record) may also be consulted. In a specific instance the present writer was able to locate no fewer than six manorial 'surveys' for one small manor, covering the period 1550-1603. They were well spread over the time span and, used in conjunction with the parish register, enabled a fairly clear picture to be assembled of the tenancy structure. Indeed, of the records in private hands one was held by a duke, another by an earl and a third by a baron, all of whose noble ancestors had had an interest in the manor in Elizabeth I's reign. These records thus yielded information on how the manor was held during the material period: '23rd April in the 21st year of the reign of Queen Elizabeth [1579]. Philip Phillipps holdeth by copy of the grant of the earl of Arundel and the lord Lumley 1 tenement and a cottage containing 34 acres to him Walter and Alfradosis Phillipps and to the longest liver. Memorandum: that the said Phillip surrendered to the earl of Arundel his copy which he had of the grant of Thomas earl of Northumberland and took for the same lives again for the lives before written and are all yet living.' In addition, by naming succeeding (and in several cases preceding) generations of tenants, terms of tenancy and so on, much insight was gained into aspects of manorial administration. Typical entries were: 'term of life of the longest liver of three; 2 heriots on alienation; right of common pasturage; agent to the earl; wife of John Ellis the earl's agent; for his life which followed the holding by his mother, Parnell, who held by her widows estate; in right of his wife'.

The holding of tenancies for three lives was a fairly common (though by no means exclusive) practice at the time. Normally the 'lives' were those of close relatives — father, son and grandson, father and two sons, etc. — but occasionally the system was abused. Cases are on record of old men marrying very young girls to perpetuate the family hold on the land, and in one instance a tenant endeavoured to have the two infant sons of a friend admitted as the second and third 'lives'. For further details of practices in a variety of places reference may be made to 'Leases and Tenancy Agreements' by P. Roebuck in *Local Historian* x (1972-3), and in works identified in the bibliographies in the major volumes cited earlier in this chapter.

Enclosure of land The matter of enclosure of land was the subject of legislation as early as 1235/6, when the Statute of Merton had authorised manorial lords to enclose portions of the commons (and wastes), provided sufficient grazing land remained for their tenants. Fifty years later, in 1285, the Statute of Westminster authorised these same owners to enclose such land where the rights belonged to tenants of other manors. Over later times up to the Elizabethans, as copyhold or customary tenure (implying service to the lord) changed to leasehold (such as the 'three lives' mentioned earlier), the rolls contain many references to enclosure or attempted enclosure of common land, for the grazing of large flocks and herds. Youings cites (p.51) an instance in a Cambridgeshire manor where the lessee of the demesne exercised seignorial right over so much other village land that all the other inhabitants were effectively prevented from keeping sheep.

The Dissolution of the monasteries had made so many ecclesiastical demesne acres available that some leaseholders were able to create large farms (several hundred acres in extent) and the smaller holder was squeezed sometimes to the point of total poverty, as his common rights were lost. In many cases remaining areas of common land were grossly over-grazed and the rolls mention numerous instances of tenants 'overstinting the lord's common' by hundreds of sheep beyond their tally.

An anti-enclosure Act of 1550 had been aimed at ensuring the availability of small family farms (a size of thirty to fifty acres was the norm for the time), but for the whole of the Elizabethan period the problem of enclosure (and hence denial of right of common pasturage) remained acute. *Sources for English Local History* by W.B. Stephens contains (pp.166-80) an extensive section on agriculture and many references to specialist articles and essays. Reference should also be made to pp.252-3 of Black *op cit* and *The Anatomie of Abuses* (Philip Stubbs *c.*1590; edited by F.J. Furnivall, London 1877-9): 'These inclosures be the causes why rich men eat up poor men as beast do eat grass ... they take in and inclose commons, moors, heaths and other pastures, whereout the poor commonality were wont to have all their forage and feeding for their cattle and [which is more] corn for themselves denied to live upon.'

Diet As early as 1517 Cardinal Wolsey had laid down by proclamation how many dishes might be served at one meal, carefully identifying the social classes from high-born or eminent who might have nine, to people with goods valued at £500 who were permitted three, not counting soups. No mention was made of the lower orders.

For detailed information of all kinds — including the identification of cookery books — the reader is referred to *Food and Drink in Britain* by Anne Wilson (Penguin Books 1984). This important work (which covers many ages beside the Elizabethan) is especially rich in information for the period 1558-1603, when social class was such an important factor to government and individuals alike. It deals, in separate chapters, with fish, beasts, fowls, milk products, bread and pastry items, spices, fruit and salad vegetables, and drink. Of special interest for both country and town areas are the details of how food might be preserved and the roles played by the gilds (such as the Worshipful Company of Fishmongers) in developing the practices adopted. Much of what was common habit in earlier times falls oddly on modern ears (and, no doubt, would sit heavily in modern stomachs): 'The meat of a spayed goat of six or seven years is best . . . very sweet and fat . . . [it] makes an excellent pasty . . . .' Birds of the thrush family were trapped alive in nets 'crammed for ten days or so on bread and milk until each was a lump of fat, when they were beheaded with scissors and roasted.' In the making of rennet a calf's vell was used as the container (the vell being the stomach of the animal which had been fed solely on milk). Brine was added to the contents — curd, cream, eggs, spices — and herbs were used 'to conceal ill flavours if the vell deteriorated.' It is apparent that all classes save the desperately poor 'fed liberally', to quote Professor Black. He goes on to say that these folk 'confined themselves to white meats, bread made of rye or barley . . . and a coarser bread of beans, oats, or acorns in time of dearth.' Philip Stubbs (or Stubbes) wrote in the *Anatomie of Abuses*, 'Nowadays if the table [of the well-to-do] be not covered from one end to the other as thick as a dish can stand by another, with delicate meats of sundry sorts, one clean different from another, and to every dish a [separate] sauce appropriate to his kind, it is thought unworthy of the name of dinner.' The more well-off in season ate beef, mutton, lamb, veal, goat, pork, venison, fish and fowl, the yeoman and husbandman mainly beef and venison (and fish if they lived near the sea or full running river), and the poor very little, as noted above.

Regarding drink, common ale was for the common people, but another contemporary historian (Moryson, see Black *ibid*) speaks of the wealthy with their 'fifty-six different kinds of French wine, their thirty brands of Italian, Grecian, Spanish and Canary.'

The use of tobacco must not be overlooked. From about 1566, when it was introduced by Hawkins (rather than Raleigh), the 'Nicotian weed' grew in popularity, until by 1598 smoking was general. The 'common pipe' in the tavern, alehouse and inn placed the indulgence within everyone's reach. A continental visitor, Hentzner, wrote that smoking had become a social necessity practised by all, including 'sweet ladies'.

Markets and fairs As with the subject of diet it is difficult to separate markets and fairs into country and town varieties, for one was but a smaller version of the other; and it is as impossible adequately to define a town as it is to differentiate between a fair and a market, except that the latter was held more frequently and was smaller. What follows is, then, applicable to towns and country parishes.

Markets (and fairs) are of great antiquity. Indeed, until the advent of 'towns' they were the sole means of trading on any scale. There is evidence to indicate that very ancient such gatherings were held on hilltops, junctions of roads and tracks, even funeral barrows and, later, churchyards (although from 1285 this was technically forbidden). It was the custom to hold markets weekly, but in the reign of King Henry VI it was deemed illegal they should occur at times of important religious festivals and on Sundays, other than those at harvest time. In 1889 the government of the day published a list of market and fair charters prepared from a document in the Public Record Office known as 'Palmer's Index No.93'. This gave details of markets and fairs from the reign of King John onwards. The list, rearranged into county sequence, was published in the first edition of *The Local Historian's Encyclopaedia* by John Richardson (New Barnet 1974), but dropped from the second (1986).

Fairs usually occurred annually — probably soon after harvest — and were spread over several days (much like the so-called 'country fayres' of the present time), attracting dealers and important buyers from a wide area. Gradually only the larger towns could afford to hold fairs, and the subject will be discussed in the 'Town' section.

Churchwardens' duties As early as 1532 a statute had been passed that in consequence of the number of rooks, crows and choughs abounding, every parish was to provide itself with a net for their capture. Then in 1566 the Queen's government made churchwardens responsible for the destruction of vermin. They were given the duty of collecting a parish rate and using the money gathered for the rewarding of parishioners who presented the beaks or eggs of 'noyful fowls'. The new Act went much further than the older legislation and stipulated that the wardens with the assistance of six local men should assess the holders of land and fix the level of tax for the generation of the necessary funds. For the destruction itself the rewards were set at one penny for every three heads of 'crows, chowes, pyes or Rockes', one penny for every six young owls, and one penny for every six unbroken eggs. There were provisions in the Act for animals 'locally classed as vermin' to be added to the list — hedgehogs, polecats, sparrows and such — the heads of which 'shall be ... in the presence of the churchwardens ... burned, consumed, or cut asunder'. (The word *consumed* is an intriguing one.) Typical entries in the churchwardens' accounts for one village are: 'Pd John Upsalls wife for five higgoges 10d; for a pollcats head 4d; Payd for 2000 and 3 quarters of sparoes 3/2½d; for 2 foxes and a stote 2/2d; for 4 martenes hedes 4/-.' A useful article on churchwardens' accounts (and vestry minutes) was published in the *Amateur Historian* Vol.I, No.8 (1953).

Parish constables In its turn the post of parish constable was demanding, and if credence can be placed on references to officers in Shakespearean texts, they often failed to match up to their duties. 'You are thought to be the most senseless and fit man for the constable,' one such is told in *Much Ado*, and, when the poor fellow asks what action to take if a challenged 'vagrom man' does not halt, is advised to 'let him go and ... thank God you are rid of the knave.'

The duties of the constable included the arrest of the vagrants to which the above exchange refers, and the raising of the 'hue and cry' in his own parish in the pursuit of local malefactors. If, however, the guilty (or suspected) person fled the parish, the constable merely passed on details to his colleagues in adjoining territories. Thus the constable could make a perfunctory search — worth perhaps 4d in income — then pass details on to any parish he saw fit. In the reign of Elizabeth the parish constables were paid out of funds held by the churchwardens, but in Jacobean times they were empowered to levy their own rates. The constable had the authority to punish all those who took part in unlawful games, tippled too much in the alehouses or broke the Sabbath. He had to ensure the whipping of vagabonds from other parishes before they were sent home, the proper repair of the stocks, the maintenance of parish arms, the care of the parish bull, the compilation of jurors' lists, the convening of parish meetings and other administrative duties. If his parish bordered on the sea he was required to render assistance at shipwrecks in the locality. A useful article, 'The Constables' Accounts', was published in the *Amateur Historian* Vol.I, No.11 (1954).

Further local offices and records

In addition to the churchwardens and parish constables, two important local officers were the overseers and the highway surveyors. The office of overseers was instituted by statute in 1597 and was not abolished until 1925. The principal task of the men chosen was the collection of a compulsory rate for the relief of poverty. Many parish records have survived and a pertinent starting point to their study is the essay 'Overseers' Accounts' in the *Amateur Historian* Vol.I, No.9 (1954). By an Act of 1555 each parish was required to elect two 'surveyors and orderers for one year of the works for amendment of the highways'. Such statute labour lasted until 1835, when the raising of funds on a local basis was replaced by a general highway rate. Highway surveyors' accounts survive in many county record offices, and a good introduction to them was published in the *Amateur Historian* Vol.I, No.10 (1954).

Towns and town life

For records of events in towns, sometimes their physical descriptions, and occasionally maps, reference should be made to the old county histories and the *Victoria County History*. Reference may also be made to Leland's *Itinerary* (see Chapter 10, 'Narrative histories'). Also for the period, wills and testaments may be of value in indicating not only names of townsfolk, their occupations, rank and status, but also what property they held and who their neighbours were. Extracts from a single such document will suffice to illustrate the point: 'I give and bequeath to Ema my wife all my burgage [tenure in one ancient borough] situated in West Street on the south side between Mundens garden of St Michael on the east side and the land or garden next to St Michaels lane on the west side . . .'.

At a considerably more general level there are many publications describing town layout and life in Elizabethan times, and some of these will be noted here and others in Chapter 19. To a substantial degree the map of England had stabilized by the mid sixteenth century (a few towns had been created in medieval times — Bewdley is an example — but no new town of consequence followed in England during the period being discussed). What *was* noticeable, however, was the growth of existing towns, of which the most striking example was London, which engulfed Westminster and Southwark. York and Norwich developed — the latter after a period of decay — and the medieval 'new town' of Newcastle upon Tyne prospered by virtue of its export of coal. Bristol, Exeter, Salisbury and Worcester throve. *The Landscape of Towns* by Michael Aston and James Bond (Gloucester 1987) has a valuable chapter 'Tudor and Stuart Towns', divided into helpful sections: 'the social structure', 'the town plan', 'streets and squares', 'buildings — domestic, civic, ecclesiastical', 'town defences', 'the industrial character of towns', 'new market centres', 'new ports', and 'resorts'. The authors

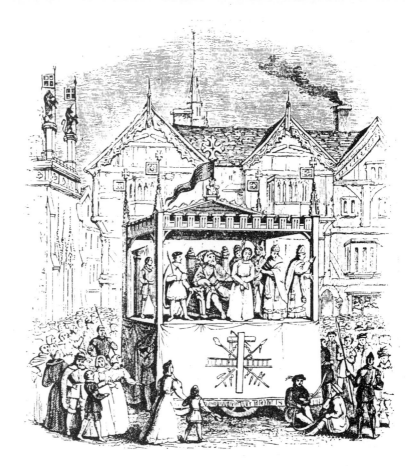

An open-air portable theatre in the town square. In this case the town is Coventry and the play is 'The Life of Pontius Pilate'.

conclude that the Elizabethan period (and just later) was one of important transition: 'The small-scale medieval market town with its basis firmly in the local rural area was in the process of evolving into a very different community with social and industrial functions on a much grander scale. The result was soon to be a divorce between the character of the town and that of its local surroundings, and a much greater uniformity in towns across the country with alien styles of architecture and new notions of town planning gaining the ascendancy.' The bibliography included in the book is valuable, and, as may be expected, the index refers to dozens of specific places.

Sixteenth Century England by Joyce Youings has a chapter 'People in Towns', which, by concentrating on social aspects of urban life, usefully complements the writing of Aston and Bond. The bibliography specifically devoted to works on Tudor towns includes many pointers to important sources, particularly in the *Transactions* of the Royal Historical Society, the *English History Review* and the *Economic History Review*. *Sources for English Local History* by W.B. Stephens has, in 'The Town', much of value, particularly referring to the use of borough (and similar) archives in tracing the development of local government and administration, and the researching of local customs, the history of the gilds, privileges and exemptions.

Local researchers should be warned that the histories of most towns have already been written — some well, some badly — but there is always new material to be found, ancient errors to be corrected and received wisdom to be challenged.

Ecclesiastical matters

The Acts of Supremacy and Uniformity of the beginning of Elizabeth's reign have already been mentioned. In the wake of the religious upheavals during the earlier Tudor period it was inevitable that there were problems but, to quote Professor Black, 'the bulk of the laity found no great difficulty in transferring its allegiance from the old church to the new. The queen, for her part, had made the establishment as comprehensive as possible, taking her stand on the principle that all members of the state were *ipso facto* members of the state church. Consequently, since the existence of dissent was not admitted, there could be no persecution.' So be it, but 1571 saw several enactments by parliament to affirm the queen's position and denounce the 'false, usurped, and alien authority of Rome'. Black's *Elizabethan England*, under the heading 'Catholic and Puritan', carefully summarizes and illuminates the ecclesiastical history of the times, and the bibliographical section 'The Church Settlement' points to many works of great interest to the local researcher wishing to gain a balanced perspective of the stresses and strains at parish level.

For that local level a good introductory publication is *Parish History and Records* by A. Hamilton Thompson, issued by the Historical Association in 1926. There is also a useful chapter 'Church, Chapel and School' in *Local History in England* by W.G. Hoskins (London, reprinted 1972), which describes church goods, the spiritual life of the parish, and incumbents and benefices. Reference should also be made to W.B. Stephens, *op cit* pp.248-9, especially the paragraphs dealing with the question of differentiating between rectors and vicars and hence touching on questions of the advowson, greater and lesser tithes, and glebe lands. *The Dictionary of Ecclesiastical Terms* by J.S. Purvis (London 1962) will also be useful on this and related topics.

Envoi

On the morning of 30 November 1601 one hundred and forty members of parliament had crowded into the Council Chamber at Whitehall to hear Elizabeth, last of a line of statesmen-monarchs, address them. In the person of the sixty-eight year old queen the flower of her dynasty had come to full and matchless bloom. England never had before, nor ever since, a reigning house of such transcendent ability.

Rome had been put aside and the power of the monasteries broken; the earlier hopes of Spain, buoyed up by the marriage of Mary and Philip, were finally shattered on the rocks of the English coast, as their great Armada, driven before the wind, fled northwards from Drake and his West-countrymen; the threat personified by Mary Queen of Scots was disposed of; Jonson, Shakespeare and a dozen others had tuned the English language to concert pitch; the prow of the *Golden Hind* rode the pacific waves of the far western ocean. The days were long and God loved England. Against this great and golden time the map of the towns and villages unrolled complete, and if events at local level were less stirring than those in grander places, this was no bad thing. All great adventures, enterprises, excursions and excitements demand a stable foundation from which they may be launched if they are to succeed. And the parishes of England in those far days were that foundation, providing its industry and manpower, the economic and agricultural well-springs of an adventurous people.

In Puritan times the Sabbath was not to be 'prophaned' by the selling of drink and meat.

12 *Royalty and rebellion 1603-1660*

A note regarding dating During the period covered by this chapter two calendars were in use, and for a detailed discussion on the problems of dating the reader is referred to Chapter 29 'Chronology'. England employed the Julian (Old Style) calendar, while most continental countries used the Gregorian (New Style), which was ten days in advance of the old. Further, the continental year began on 1 January, whereas in England a start date of 25 March was used for most purposes. If the date of the execution of King Charles I is taken as an example, this would, in modern English practice, have occurred on 30 January 1649; in the practice of the English seventeenth century it would have taken place on 30 January 1648; whereas a continental person would have said it happened on 9 February 1649. The point is an important one, particularly for local historians whose researches deal with trade with Europe, or with the occasional English document which does not conform to the Lady Day (25 March) system.

When Queen Elizabeth died in 1603 she had indicated that King James VI of Scotland should succeed her on the English throne. His accession as James I of England was peaceful and welcomed. In turn he was courteous and 'familiar', which endeared him to his new subjects. The same cannot be said for his son Charles.

During the early years of the seventeenth century large sections of the population became increasingly disenchanted with their lot. There were many reasons for this, but high on the list was the reaction to the disdainful habits of the early Stuart kings pursuing their own interpretations of the way monarchs should behave, and the role of parliament in the management of the country. In 1642 things came to a climax. King

Yorkshire & the North
1

Lancs, Cheshire & Staffs
2

Worcs, Hereford, Monmouth, Shropshire & Wales
4

Lincs, Leics, Derby Notts & Warwick
3

Beds. Hunts, Rutland & Northants

Oxford, Bucks, Herts, Essex, Norfolk & Suffolk

5   6

The West Country
8

7

9   10

London & Middlesex

Kent & Surrey

Sussex, Hants & Berks

The map shows the military districts into which England was divided in Commonwealth times. Over each district a Cromwellian major general had substantial executive, near dictatorial powers.

Charles' standard was raised at Nottingham and a four-year-long civil war began. Broadly, the nobility and the peasants were for the king, the middle classes for Parliament. In the end the Royalists were defeated, the king executed, and in 1649 Oliver Cromwell assumed the office of Lord General of the Commonwealth. In 1653 he became Lord Protector and, in effect, dictator. England was divided into military districts with a major-general over each. The condition of the country became chaotic and by 1659, a year after the Protector's death, reaction against the joyless rule of the military governors was such that the martyred king's son was invited from his exile on the continent, to be crowned as King Charles II. This did not, however, mean a return to the autocratic ways of 1642, or even the high-handed regime instituted by James I in 1603, and the powers and standing of parliament were greatly strengthened.

The Early Stuarts by Godfrey Davies (2nd edition, Oxford 1959) gives an excellent overview of the period and contains much of value for the local researcher. At the time of writing, the promised volume in the *English Historical Documents* series (*EHD7*) has not appeared, but there are many other guides to important contemporary documents and numerous scholarly commentaries on them. The *British Economic and Social History: A Bibliographical Guide* by W.H. Chaloner and R.C. Richardson (London 1976) remains most valuable, as do the *Annual Bulletin(s) of Historical Literature* of the Historical Association, and the *Annual Bibliography of British and Irish History*, issued by the Royal Historical Society. The contents of various collections from the British National Archives (as noted in *Sectional List 24*, see Chapter 5) will prove useful, as will some of the publications of the Royal Commission on Historical Manuscripts noted in *Sectional List 17* (also mentioned in Chapter 5).

Of particular and outstanding value is the *Bibliography of British History, Stuart Period 1603-1714* by G. Davies (London 1928, updated by M.F. Keeler in 1970). There is no complete guide to manuscript sources but in the absence of *EHD7* an important work is *Seventeenth Century England — A Changing Culture* Vol.I *Primary Sources* edited by Ann Hughes (London 1980). Also of value is the companion volume *Seventeenth Century England* Vol.II, *Modern Studies* edited by W.R. Owens (London 1980).

There can be no doubt that the happenings of 1603-60 were among the most disruptive in England's history, as the following bald chronology of events shows. In 1605 the Gunpowder Plot was discovered; in 1620, in the face of great persecution, the Pilgrim Fathers sailed for America. The Duke of Buckingham was assassinated in 1628. In 1629 Charles I dissolved parliament and ruled for twelve years without one. In 1640 came both the 'short' and the 'long' parliaments. Then in 1642 the first civil war began — there were battles at Edgehill, Roundway Down, Newbury, Cheriton, Marston Moor, Lostwithiel, and Newbury again. Naseby followed in 1645 and, a year later, Charles I surrendered. Then in 1648 came the short-lived second civil war — the battle of Preston — and in 1649 the king was executed. In 1651 came the battle of Worcester and the escape of Charles II. Cromwell became Lord Protector in 1653 and died in 1658. In 1660 Charles II was restored and the Act of Indemnity and Oblivion passed onto the statute book.

There are numerous early guides to local history, the more important being *A Handbook to County Bibliography* by A.L. Humphreys (London 1917) and *A Bibliography of British Municipal History* by Charles Gross (London 1897). Two useful modern works are *A Guide to the Bishops' Registers of England and Wales* (to the end of the Episcopacy in 1646) edited by D.M. Smith (1981), and *The Civil War and the Interregnum: Sources for Local Historians* by G.E. Aylmer and J.S. Morrill (London 1979).

Particular attention should be paid to the extensive bibliography in Godfrey Davies' *The Early Stuarts*, and while this contains much that will be only of marginal interest to most users of this book, the following classes are most relevant: general, political, constitutional and legal, ecclesiastical, economic, and social. A more up-to-date bibliography (1966) appears in the later editions of *England in the Seventeenth Century* by Maurice Ashley (Penguin Books 1952). The reader should be warned that Dr Ashley says at one point 'On the average at least one new book on the history of seventeenth-century England is published every week in Great Britain or the United States of America; and half a dozen first-class articles appear a month in the learned journals.'

Nevertheless, there are two critical histories of the period which will be found to be of particular value. The first is *The Century of Revolution* by Christopher Hill (Wokingham, reprinted 1980). Reference may also be made to the many other works examining the seventeenth century by Professor Hill. The second history is a three-volume publication *The History of the Great Civil War* by S.R. Gardiner (London, reprinted 1987). As may be expected these books contain hundreds of references to places touched to greater or lesser extent by the upheavals of the times. Reference should also be made to *Sources for English Local History* by W.B. Stephens for titles of articles and books of special relevance.

In addition there are several works of a biographical nature which contain much of value to the local historian. The first work comprises a pair of companion volumes by C.V. Wedgwood, *The King's Peace 1637-1641* (London 1955), and *The King's War 1641-*

1647 (London 1958). Both are useful, but the latter is especially so in charting the geography and events of the troubled period. Each book contains a useful bibliography, many of the entries pointing to records in the State Papers series or in the custody of the British Museum (now the British Library). A more recent volume is *Cromwell, Our Chief of Men* by Antonia Fraser (London 1973). This book has a lengthy bibliography and is especially useful in separating the threads of history regarding the Levellers, Anabaptists, Fifth Monarchists, Quakers and others.

It is now convenient to separate the written material for 1603-60 into the following categories: *narrative histories, national government, country and towns and county committees*, and *ecclesiastical and religious*.

Narrative histories and related works

The State of England 1600 was written by Sir Thomas Wilson (and has since been reissued by the Camden Society in 1936 in an edition by F.J. Fisher, Third Series LII, Miscellany volume XVI). The work is not a long one but gives valuable insight into the state of the common people, citizens, nobility, knights, gentlemen, lawyers and others.

Although written somewhat before 1603 (perhaps 1590) William Harrison's *Description of England* is considered by modern historians as pointing to conditions as they must have been at the start of the Stuart dynasty. Harrison was a canon of Windsor and his work contains a vivid account of English towns, villages, crops and customs. Of equal value to the local historian is the section dealing with building methods and materials, and the furnishing of houses — the use of feather beds and coverlets, metal plates to replace wooden platters, 'carpets of tapestry', bowls for wine in the houses of farmers, and much more of relevance. *Harrison's Description of England in Shakespeare's Youth* by F.J. Furnivall was issued by the New Shakespeare Society in 1877. Quite without equal to an understanding of the period is *The History of the Rebellion and Civil Wars in England* by Edward Hyde, Earl of Clarendon, who, for some six years after the Commonwealth, was the effective ruler of England. Clarendon's *History* was divided into sixteen books, beginning with the accession of Charles I in 1625 and ending with the restoration of Charles II in 1660. The great modern edition is that prepared by W. Dunn Macray in 1888, and this is worthy of study. However, there is a useful and later selection (1967) covering the period 1642-49, edited by Roger Lockyer (The Folio Society, London). This, since it deals with the time from the raising of the king's standard at Nottingham to his execution, may suffice for most purposes.

Enquiries to the record offices of local authorities will almost certainly reveal the existence of diaries and journals kept during the pre-Restoration period of the seventeenth century. Several have been published nationally, and of special interest is that of Ralph Josselin, a middle-class, middle of the road Parliamentarian cleric. This appeared as *The Diary of Ralph Josselin 1616-1683* edited by Alan Macfarlane (Oxford 1976). Josselin lived mainly in Earls Colne and most of the places he mentions are in Essex. Nonetheless what he has to say is of genuine interest, and the domestic details he records are no doubt of wide application. He is to modern ears and minds overpious, lugubrious and melancholy, but for all that worth attention.

National government

The view of the 'divine right of kings' held by the early Stuart monarchs (the sovereign's power was not limited by human law, and that people were *obliged by God's law to pay all taxes and forced loans*), together with other constitutional matters, gradually caused a total breakdown between the kings and their subjects as represented by parliament. New modes of thought stimulated ideas for a whole series of reforms: redistribution of the franchise, abolition of the monarchy and the House of Lords, election of sheriffs and Justices of the Peace, law reform, security of tenure for copyholders, throwing open of enclosures, abolition of tithes and therewith of a state church, abolition of conscription, excise, and of the privileges of peers, corporations and trading companies. This view (that of the Levellers) may have been a little extreme even for the generally radical opinion of the time, but the trend throughout England was marked. Two valuable works, for those local researchers living (or interested) in notably puritan areas of England, are *Historical Collections* by John Rushworth (London 1721), extracts from which appear in Hughes (*op cit*), and *Constitutional Documents of the Puritan Revolution* edited by S.R. Gardiner (London 1906). A close reading of Hill's sections on 'politics and the constitution', parts 1 and 2, will also be most rewarding.

There were four Acts of Parliament which came onto the statute book between 1603 and 1660 which are of special interest to local historians. They were the Protestation Oath Returns of 1641/2, the 'birth date' ordinance of 1644/5 and the Registration Acts of 1653 and 1654. With regard to the protestation oath, parliament arranged a signed protest against the possibility that a future 'arbitrary and tyrannical government' should at some time in the future interfere with what it regarded as people's beliefs and practices. It was resolved that all men over the age of eighteen years should 'protest' and that any 'person soever shall not make the protestation is unfit to bear office in the Church and Commonwealth, and it is a Shibboleth [test] to discover a true Israelite.'

The terms of the oath were as follows:

I ... doe in the presence of Almightie God, promise, vow, and protest to maintaine and defend, so farre as lawfullie I may, with my life, power and estate, the true Reformed Protestant Religion expressed in the Doctrine of the Church of England, against all Poperie and Popish Innovations within this Realme contrarie to the same Doctrine and according to the dutie of my Allegiance [to] his Ma'ties Royall person, honor, and estate. Also the Power and Privileges of Parliament, the lawfull rights and Liberties of the subject and every person that maketh this Protestation in whatsoever hee shall doe in the lawfull pursuence of ye same. And to my power, and as farre as lawfullie I may, I will opose, and by all good waies and meanes indeavor to bring to condigne punishment all such as shall either by Force, Practise, Counsells, Plotts, Conspiracies, or otherwise do anie thing in this present Protestation contained. And further, that I shall in all Just and honorable waies endeavor to preserve ye Union and Peace between the three Kingdomes of England, Scotland and Ireland. And neither for hope, feare, nor other respect, relinquish this promise, vow, and Protestation.

The returns of the protestation are kept in the House of Lords library; some have been published, and a list of these, as noted in *Sectional List 17*, is printed in *Calendar of the Manuscripts of the House of Lords* Vol.5.

The ordinance of 1644/5 laid down that birth dates should be noted in parish registers as well as parents' names, and also that dates of death as well as dates of burial should be recorded. In 1653 legislation was enacted to transfer official custody of parish registers to the government. A fee for each registration was imposed, and hence many 'registrations' were avoided. In 1654 Justices of the Peace, rather than clergy, were made responsible for marriages — again, many 'registrations' were avoided. The legislation was repealed at the Restoration.

Country and towns, and county committees

Country

To begin with, country life went on much the same as before in the 10,000 parishes of England. There were, perhaps, some 4,500,000 people in total and it follows, when allowance is made for town dwellers, the average country parish numbered no more than 300 folk — old, young, men, women and children. There is little doubt that there continued to be marked contrasts between the communities of mixed and pasture-farming areas and, in the latter, between open pastoral and forest communities. In *The Agrarian History of England and Wales IV 1500-1640* edited by Joan Thirsk (Cambridge 1969) there is a detailed examination by Professor Thirsk of the nature of the agricultural industry in a number of counties, due regard being given to the geographical (and geological) situation, the historical background (e.g. submission to the forest law), and local social conditions or aspirations. Reference should also be made to the essay 'The Changing Pattern of Labouring Life' by Alan Everitt in the same volume, for its analysis of what, today, we call 'upward mobility' — the increasing prosperity of the emerging middle-class countryman — and its opposite, the un-labelled 'downward mobility' of the non-indigenous squatters, wanderers and vagrants. The section 'Social and Economic History' in Davies (*op cit*) should also be studied, particularly for the pages on agricultural systems, enclosures and land reclamation.

At specific, and individual, parish level the local researcher is well served by many classes of document to help determine the manner of village life of the time. It matters not if some of the records are incomplete or missing — those from contiguous parishes will be of equal value, for a boundary hedge or change in rectorial jurisdiction is unlikely to be significant; and it must not be forgotten that only a few per cent of the total area of England was enclosed by 1607. Subsistence farming was very much the norm although, as communication improved, trading in food, wool, hides and such increased. Where open fields continued, the rotation of wheat, barley (or rye) and fallow persisted, but beans, peas and vetches were cultivated; and turnips, potatoes and sainfoin became more popular. Reference may be made to Davies (*op cit*) for generalities on these matters, and much of particular relevance will be found in the appropriate *Victoria County History* volumes, as well as in the 'local studies' or equivalent collections in county libraries.

In the country parishes, as in the towns, the matter of social status was important to

Part of a map of an agricultural village in the 17th century. Covering in total approximately 2400 acres, the land was mainly owned by the earl of Northumberland, who held in excess of 1800 acres. The remainder was devoted to the 'parsonage', the 'parish', or held by one of five freeholders (LEFT). It may be noted that enclosure was virtually complete, the land being divided by hedges into small fields (there were over 500 in all). Many had names denoting past (or present) usage, the name of a past (or present) tenant, or some outstanding feature. The quality of the land is indicated, one cross identifying poor ground, two indicating good. The letters 'A', 'P' and 'M' stand for 'arable', 'pasture' and 'meadow'.

many people in the early seventeenth century. In most villages the nobility, deeply attached to the purity of their ancestral blood-lines, were remote, but the country gentry — the 'squirearchy' so beloved of later writers — were not, and this was a rank to which anyone could aspire, and the tendency to secure a coat of arms and set up as a gentleman became more marked. This is not to say there was an immediate increase in the 'gentle' class in a village, but an examination of the burial registers will provide valuable pointers. In a particular case (of the author's own village) the agent of the lord of the manor is described as *generosus* on his death in 1631, and five years later his daughter is noted as *generosi* — both implying 'well-bred'. Below this class (the 'gentry') were the members of what Francis Bacon has described as 'middle people — a way between gentlemen and cottagers or peasants'. In *England in the Seventeenth Century* Maurice Ashley suggests that these folk, the yeomen, were of two kinds — those of ancient family lines of free tenants, and those who rose from the lower stratum of society by their own efforts. 'They might be freeholders, who owned land worth 40/- or more, or leaseholders with extremely long leases. All of them in any case earned their living from the land.' If the local researcher is fortunate enough to find a Jacobean map or survey for the village being studied, it will be most instructive to plot a few of the individual holdings — to determine variations in the mix of arable, meadow, and pasture, and the physical distances between some of the fields. This last will, without doubt, point to some of the practical difficulties of farming widely separated acres, and may also lead to hypotheses regarding strip layout in medieval centuries. It may also be possible to determine, from local records, more complete information — 'James Birte holdeth for term of his life onlie . . . a fair dwelling house, in good repair, with barns, stalls, stables, hayhouse, garden, orchard and yarde.' Further research may throw still more light on the practices of the day. In the specific case of James Birte above, he was, in 1607, summoned to appear before the Court of the Star Chamber to answer charges brought by the overlord (the earl of Northumberland) that he forged a lease to certain fields in the manor where he lived. Although no record has been found of the outcome, the case is indicative of the economic pressures, personal avarice, and, perhaps, social pretensions of the day.

Next in rank to the yeoman was the small farmer or husbandman, with a modest land holding, a customary rent and common grazing rights. Such men can sometimes be identified from the records by the word 'Comon' against their names indicating their supplementary rights as tenants (as distinct from 'No Comon' in other cases). At the bottom of the social scale were the very meanest of the ordinary people — cottagers and paupers. Wages for the more fortunate of these varied from 3 to 7 pence a day (by contrast a skilled mason earned 12 pence). Life was hard and many of the poorest folk needed alms to live at all. At parish level there are occasional hints in parish registers; against some names were appended such terms as *soluta, vetula-soluta, grandaevus* and so on. It does not directly follow that these very old or solitary people (who in many cases were women) were paupers, but it is most likely.

One of the beliefs held widely in the early seventeenth century was that nothing happened by chance — everything was ordained by the will of God. There was nothing that could not be explained in this way — a cattle plague was retribution for the ill-treatment of farm labourers, the decline in certain noble families was judgement for their 'stealing' of lands. Moralists taught that adultery was punished by ill-health.

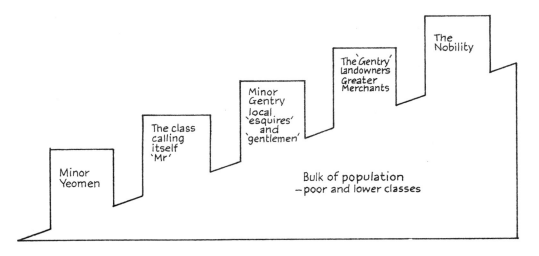

Minor
Yeomen

The class
calling
itself
'Mr'

Minor
Gentry
local
'esquires'
and
'gentlemen'

The 'Gentry'
landowners
Greater
Merchants

The
Nobility

Bulk of population
— poor and lower classes

The San Gimignano model, named after the medieval Tuscan city which had 72 towers.

But above all, the belief that people usually got their just deserts made its greatest positive appeal to those men who saw opportunities to benefit themselves. Thus the divisions between the various groups in the social scale became blurred, and between the gentlemen and the peasantry there emerged a new titular group comprising the lower end of the gentry scale and the upper section of the yeomanry. 'These were the people, the numbers of whom were steadily increasing as the 17th century wore on whose names were prefixed by the word *Mister*' (Keith Thomas, *Religion and the Decline of Magic*). English village society was tending to conform to the popular notion that, if modelled, it resembled not so much a pyramid (gentry at the peak, abject poor at the base) as a series of vertical towers on a hill (the so-called San Gimignano model). This is illustrated in the nearby diagram. The area under the slope of the hill represents the poor and lower classes of people, and the towers a series of 'more or less independent economic or status hierarchies' (Laurence Stone, *Past and Present* No.33, 1966). The towers towards the top of the hill would contain the names of mesne tenants or the local representatives of absentee lords. Lower down in an adjacent tower would be the names of local freeholders or tenants who, in local records, have been identified, such as: 'John Cooke, *gentleman*, holdeth by coppie of the courte roll . . .'. A little further down, at the bottom, would be the final towers carrying the names of the rector and the senior yeomen calling themselves (or being recognised as) 'Mister'.

Although there is a section dealing with ecclesiastical matters in this chapter, the fact is that it is difficult if not impossible for this period to separate social, moral, political, pastoral and doctrinal elements. When, finally, the civil war began in 1642, very broadly the middle classes supported parliament, and the nobility and peasantry supported the king, but there were many exceptions and cross divisions, and some folk (particularly traders in country areas) remained disaffected.

They were, inevitably, unhappy days. When law, religion, money and social standing collide there follows tragedy. The locations of the many battles of the civil wars are shown on the map of 1645, and a further map shows the areas held by the two

157

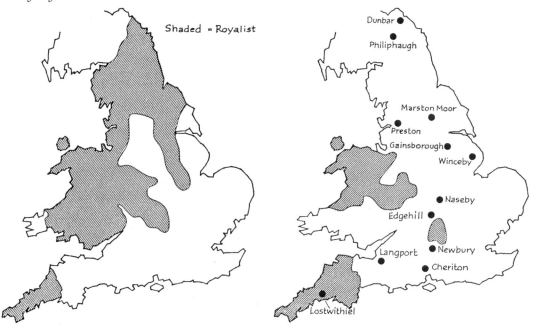

Shaded = Royalist

Dunbar
Philiphaugh
Marston Moor
Preston
Gainsborough
Winceby
Naseby
Edgehill
Langport Newbury
Cheriton
Lostwithiel

LEFT *The areas held by royalist and parliamentary factions in May 1643, with* **RIGHT** *the corresponding areas at the end of 1645 and, in addition, the sites of the civil war battles.*

sides two years earlier. Local historians are recommended to study the records of their places of interest, for hidden away may be items of moment which point to larger events. For example, a particular parish register of burials for 1645 carried, against the record of one inhumation, the words *peregrinius et eques de exercitu parliamenti* ('a horse-soldier travelling on parliamentary affairs'). An examination of the date, and further enquiries, revealed the presence of patrols in a district previously unknown to be connected with such events. In the marriage register for the same parish for 1649 are the simple words *advenae duo* ('two strangers'). They were married according to the rites of the Church, but their names were not recorded. Their story will never be known, but no doubt the uncertainty of the times had much to do with their elopement.

Turning to more peaceful matters of village layout and material prosperity, many villages of the present day contain houses dating from the early Stuart period. These may vary from the well-designed stone or brick-built manor house, with enclosed courtyard, inward-looking windows, and the slightly ponderous grandeur affected by the newly affluent, to the more humble cob-walled thatched cottage. Researchers working in those areas of the country covered by the volumes published by the Royal Commission on Historical Monuments under the heading *An Inventory of Historical Monuments in the County of* ... will find much of their work already done for them (for this and other centuries). In the secular sections for each parish will be found not only a list of buildings of note but also details of their outstanding features, materials used, and methods of construction. Failing this good fortune, the county's local studies collection may be accessed, and reference made to Chapter 28 of this present book for a list of useful texts. Contact should also be made with the Royal Commission on Historical Monuments, for access to the mass of unpublished material in their files (see Addresses, Appendix III). Respecting the contents of houses and, sometimes, their internal layout in the seventeenth century, most county record offices have inventories made by executors of deceased owners. Many of these have been published — an example is *Farm and Cottage Inventories of Mid Essex 1635-1749* edited by F.N. Steer (Chelmsford 1950), but hundreds of others await the attention of local historians willing to tease out the meanings of words rendered in the most imaginative of phonetic styles.

Three examples are now given as illustrative of estates of people of varying degrees of prosperity. That of a widow amounting to £129.16s.8d, comprised the meanest of household goods: wearing apparel, bed, bolsters, linen, dishes, spoons, table boards, chayres, deske, lumber and plate to a combined value of £22.9s.2d and *money* to the sum of £107.7.6d. Judging by an examination of all the goods, the house would have comprised but two rooms and a single hearth. The second (taken from the Essex inventories mentioned) is the inventory of a yeoman of Writtle who died in 1638. The house and outbuildings comprised a hall, parlour (with a fair jointed bedstead), a buttery, kitchen, brewhouse, milkhouse, servants chamber, chamber over the last, cheese loft, chamber over the parlour, another over the kitchen, a further room over the brewhouse, a yard (with wagon, dung carts and cradles), a stable and a hay-barn. There were a few animals (24 sheep at 10 shillings each, 2 hoggs at £1.5s.0d each), the whole estate being worth £389.4s.6d. The third inventory is that of a Dorset yeoman who left £656.10s.0d. From this it may be learnt that 46 cows and a bull were worth £185.10s.0d, horses were £5.6s.8d each, pigs 15 shillings each, and a flitch of bacon £1. The 'true and perfect inventory' gives details of the number and names of the rooms in the house, from which a layout may be attempted.

At this point the local researcher may well be able to discuss the subject of Jacobean rural vernacular architecture with the member of the county planning department responsible for the preservation of ancient buildings. These officers, invariably well qualified and knowledgeable, are in most cases very willing to discuss problems with local historians. Finally, particularly good advice is given by Stephens *op cit*, 'the study of the typology of domestic dwellings and of the regional variations and distribution patterns of the different kinds of houses is developing into a distinct branch of local and general history.

Towns

The last paragraphs of the previous section apply as well to urban as to rural studies, but if there were similarities in the matter of house buildings and contents life in the towns and villages was evolving in different ways. Stephens (*op cit*) says, 'The political upheavals of the mid and later seventeenth century lead to the alteration of many borough constitutions with the object of securing control over future parliamentary elections as well as of gaining direct influence in the local governments of the towns themselves.' He points to an unpublished paper written by R.B. Pugh (the author of *How to Write a Parish History*, London, reprint 1954) for the guidance of contributors to the *Victoria County History*, entitled 'Note on Borough Charters in the Later Seventeenth Century'. (For access to this and related work, application should be made to the Institute of Historical Research, University of London — see Appendix III).

Research into the history of a town for the early seventeenth century may (as for later and perhaps earlier times) be divided into a number of sub-headings, the three most useful of which are 'physical layout', 'local government' and 'social', with the uniquely additional 'civil wars'. In regard to all four, the early county histories will be of considerable value and may well contain maps which show the layout in, say, the eighteenth century from which useful deductions or inferences may be drawn. The appropriate volume(s) of the *Victoria County History* will also contain useful data naming roads, streets, buildings and, in some cases, their relationships to each other.

A number of towns were 'surveyed' in the seventeenth century by antiquaries and chroniclers, and extracts (with sources) appear in Hughes *op cit*. One of the best known and informative of these early works is the *Survey of London* by John Stow. This appeared in 1598 and 1603 and is invaluable for the detailed information it gives about the city. It was updated in 1720 by J. Strype and annotated editions have since been published. A full edition appeared in 1908 (Oxford) with notes and commentary by C.L. Kingsford. As an indication of the way London was changing (and, indeed, other towns were spreading) the following in the words of Stow is enlightening, concerning Spitalfields: 'Within these forty years had on both sides fair hedgerows of elm trees, with bridges and easy stiles to pass over into the pleasant fields, very commodious for citizens therein to walk, shoot and otherwise to recreate and refresh their dulled spirits in the sweet and wholesome air; which is now within a few years made a continual building throughout of garden-houses and small cottages, and the fields on either side be turned into garden plots, tenter yards [that is, yards where cloth is stretched], bowling alleys and the like, from Houndsditch in the west so far as Whitechapel and further towards the east . . . .'

The above account, describing the building in London's East End by merchants, shipwrights and other 'new' men, was mirrored by developments in other major towns. Frequently cartographic evidence is available, and street names can sometimes provide useful clues. 'New Street in Plymouth was built by one of the town's principal merchants . . . and as two other streets in the same town are also named after contemporary merchants it is likely that they have similar origin' (Hoskins *Provincial England*, London 1963). Aston and Bond in *The Landscape of Towns* point out that many new streets of this period 'followed a conservative pattern and it may be difficult to identify them without documentary evidence.' The authors go on to instance the 'medieval' layout of the seventeenth-century development at Bicester.

Around the year 1630 new ideas in town planning were introduced from Europe. These, based on concepts executed by Palladio a few years earlier, were enthusiastically taken up by Inigo Jones and applied, initially, in London. The construction of Italian-style *piazze* were undertaken (Covent Garden was a notable pioneer example, the central feature being an open square to the north of Bedford House, to be followed by well designed areas in Bloomsbury and St James). Again, reference may be made to the works of Professor Hoskins, 'The Rebuilding of Rural England' in *Provincial England*, and essays in *The Listener* Vol.XLVIII, 1953.

Aston and Bond (*op cit*) devote an important chapter to the Tudor and Stuart periods. For the years under discussion they have much of importance to say on a number of towns, including Manchester, Lavenham, Worcester, Chipping Camden, Henley in Arden, Dorchester (Dorset), Ludlow, Leominster, and many others. 'Of particular significance [was] the increasing use of bricks in towns ... More and more brick works were established in different parts of the country and [their products] seem to have been almost as common as timber in town building.' Brick began to be regarded as the hallmark of wealth and progress, while timber was characteristic of older and poorer properties. In addition to a section dealing with domestic buildings the authors include information on civic and ecclesiastical undertakings, town fortifications during the civil wars, the industrial character of towns, market towns, ports and resorts. Their conclusion is worth quoting here: 'The small scale medieval market town with its basis firmly in the local rural area was in the process of evolving into a very different community, with social and industrial functions on a much grander scale. The result was soon to be a divorce between the character of the town and that of its local surroundings, and a much greater uniformity in towns across the country, with alien styles of architecture and new notions of town planning gaining the ascendancy. During the transition, however, [there were] local building styles ... and maximum regional diversity; and the remnants of this period are an invaluable contribution to [present day] towns.'

Finally, reference should be made to *Town Records* by John West (Chichester 1983) for details of 'Town Plans and Maps' *c.*1600-1900.

Turning, then, to the matter of town records proper, it is a truism that most towns have record collections, the nature of which will vary, but information regarding them can readily be gathered from the local archivist or reference librarian. It may also be useful to refer to the *Third Report of the Royal Commission on Public Records* (1919), *Town Records*, West (*op cit*) pp.10-27, and the *Bibliography of British Municipal History including Gilds and Parliamentary Representations* (originally edited by C. Gross 1897, and updated by G. Martin 1966). The records will be of various kinds, and their nature and extent are too great to be described in detail here, but they will almost certainly include minute books (see *Amateur Historian* 1954-6, 'Borough Records, Common Council Minutes' by G.H. Tupling). For the period of the civil wars many local archives (and reference libraries) contain records of the standing committee set up by the government. In addition a number of local authorities and record societies have published portions of their records, of which the following are examples: *Beverley Borough Records 1575-1821* by J. Dennett, Yorkshire Archaeological Society lxxxiv (1933), and 'The Records of a Borough Court in the Seventeenth Century' by L.C. Lloyd in *Archives vii* (1965-6). Enquiries should also be made of the British Library, which in the Harleian, Lansdowne and Egerton manuscript collections has much of interest.

In addition to somewhat arid, but important, records of everyday business there exist, for some towns, narrative chronicles noting important events in their history, and the article by A. Dyer 'English Town Chronicles' in the *Local Historian* xii (1976-7) will be of value in this regard. Reference should also be made to the *Victoria County History* volumes, which in a number of cases have much of value in their pages. An example taken from the Dorset volume (II, published in 1908), describes events of the winter and spring of 1642/3, when Waller, the Parliamentary commander, was defeated near Bath and, in the summer, Bristol surrendered to the Royalist cavalry forces. 'Hitherto, Dorchester, Lyme, Weymouth, Melcombe and Poole had been occupied by local Parliamentary troops, under Sir Walter Erle and Sir Thomas Trenchard [the Sheriff of Dorset]; and Portland and Wareham now being garrisoned by the Parliament, Corfe only remained to the king . . . [but] in spite of the ingenious filling of their men with strong waters even to madnesse the [Parliamentary commanders] failed to inspire in them sufficient berserk courage to storm the castle.' The king's success in Bristol meant the tide had turned in his favour, and 'Dorchester, Weymouth and Portland surrendered at once, without a blow struck, [Sir William] Strode having told in Dorchester horrid tales of the valour of the Royalist soldiers.' There is further considerable narrative of this kind in the volume cited, and equally important source references such as the *Minute Books of the Dorset Standing Committee, Calendars of State Papers* and manuscripts in the Dorchester Corporation collection (now in the custody of the county record office). Such descriptions and references are features of all the general volumes in the *Victoria County History* series, and although some of the methods used to identify the sources are obscure they are well worth deciphering.

County committees
It would not be proper in a work of this nature to do other than to draw attention to the changes which the puritans (broadly the Parliamentarians) tried to introduce in the habits and customs of the country. Davies (*op cit*) says, 'They were inspired by an intense conviction of a common responsibility for sin . . . [and] during 1642-60 [they had] their one opportunity in English history to enact inhibitory laws . . .. They over-estimated the power of laws and the effectiveness of legal punishments. They did not distinguish between vice and crime, and theological considerations exercised great influence in determining their views of crime and punishment.'

In 1655 Cromwell divided England and Wales into districts, and over each one he placed a major-general who gathered taxes, acted as policeman and guardian of public morality. The measures introduced by these worthies were so draconian that the office was scrapped a year later. The legislation introduced by the Long Parliament was little better. For example (Davies p.307), the traditional method of celebrating Christmas was thought . . . to give 'liberty to carnal and sensual delights, [so in] 1644 it was ordered to be kept as a fast day.' Three years later it was forbidden to observe Easter, Whitsuntide and other festivals.

County committees were established for the better government of their areas and the proceedings of a number of these have been published, often by local record societies. The committees dealt with all manner of things, as may be expected — Staffordshire 1645: 'It is ordered that Lt Col Watson shall have liberty to fetch any malignant persons, being countrymen, for the exchange of such honest men that are taken prisoners out of his neighbourhood'; Dorset 1648: 'Uppon the peticon of Mrs Clarke [a deposed rector's widow] it is ordered that Mr James Rawson the p'sent minister [appointed by the authority of parliament] doe forthwith pay unto her the full fifts of all the tyths and p'fitts of the said p'ish for the maintenance of herself and children, accordinge to an ordynance of pliam' and an order from this Comittee.' Enquiries should be made of the local record office for any material bearing on the establishment, constitution and workings of the local committees.

Finally, although not directly touching the administrative measures of the times, searches should be made of the commonwealth memorials in parish churches, for the inscriptions on these can be very revealing, as example one from the Dorset parish of Mappowder for 1644: 'Here lyes inter'd beneath the corps of her, whoe in her lyfe

A section of a page from the manuscript of The Order Book of the Stafford County Committee. The extract shows a deleted attempt at an order, followed by a fair holograph text. The order stipulates that Richard Backhouse should be compensated for rent due on a property seized 'for the public use' by the parliamentarians.

true graces did perferr Before the world, its pleasures all therein; Such was her faith, shee ever hated sinne . . . Death hath done much for her, yt I dare say, From these sad times this saint to take away.'

Ecclesiastical and religious matters

The religious history of the times is dealt with by Godfrey Davies in two sections in his *Oxford History* volume: the first covers the years 1603-40, and the second 1640-60. Many of the issues discussed are of local moment as well as national significance. The first section may be read as giving a valuable background to the emergence of puritanism, the decline of Roman Catholicism and the seeming ascendancy of Anglican forms of worship. Of special interest to local researchers are the observations (on p.69) regarding the status and poverty of the parish priest, and these may usefully be contrasted with the duties he was expected to perform attired in 'cope and surplice'. The author deals with sabbatarianism — the suppression of games and sports, the compulsory attendance of church, and other matters bearing on everyday life, the restrictions on the press and the operation of ecclesiastical courts. In the later years of the period the problems of both the clergy and the laity grew, Anglican services were suppressed, Roman Catholics were popularly regarded as traitors and were persecuted. Only gradually did toleration justify Cromwell's boast, 'I meddle not with any man's conscience.' It is difficult to imagine that parish priests ousted from their livings to make way for 'committee men' found this much of a consolation.

This journal, a forerunner of Hansard (which began in 1774), was started in 1641 by Samual Pecke to publish accounts of parliamentary business.

13 The Later Stuart Period 1660-1714

Note regarding dating Attention is drawn to the note at the beginning of Chapter 12.

On 29 May 1660, his thirtieth birthday, Charles II arrived in London and the monarchy was restored. But the reigns of the later Stuarts were not periods of peace and order, the threat of revolution was never far away and all the kings appear to have been aware that exile might await them. Anne's years were a little better, but she died in 1714 aged forty-nine, worn with care.

The years of Charles II were plagued by religious disputes and questions regarding the powers of the monarchy. The king (1660-85) was highly intelligent but weak, and was for ever in debt. The dowry his Portuguese queen brought with her — £300,000 — was valuable, and the sale of Dunkirk to France for £400,000 helped, but the general situation of lack of funds remained.

Charles was succeeded by his brother James who reigned for three years. The new king was an avowed Catholic, and his short period as monarch saw much religious upheaval. The Monmouth rebellion was followed by the 'Bloody Assizes', Protestants were persecuted and the king appeared to ignore all advice — even that of his loyal Tories. At the invitation of parliament William of Orange initiated the 'Glorious Revolution' in November 1688, by landing in Devon with a large army, James II having fled the country to France.

The most significant point about the 'Glorious Revolution' was not so much that the new king (who ruled jointly with Mary his wife until her death in 1694) was a staunch Protestant, but that the monarchy became constitutional and parliamentary. The 'divine right of kings' was no longer an issue. Indecisive wars were fought, Jacobite plots came and went, and in 1702 William was killed in a hunting accident. Anne, the second daughter of James II, came to the throne and reigned for twelve years. To a marked degree her years were dominated by the Continental wars and the brilliant victories of Marlborough, and the age itself was outstanding. The year 1707 saw the Act of Union between England and Scotland, Isaac Newton was expounding new theories of matter and mathematics, Wren built St Paul's Cathedral, Pope and Swift, Addison and Steele were in the forefront of literature.

The Later Stuarts by Sir George Clark (Oxford, reprinted 1961) deals with the years 1660 to the death of Anne in 1714. It provides an authoritative broad outline of the period, and although perhaps concerned mainly with political and military matters nonetheless contains much of specific relevance on economic, land, agricultural and manufacturing matters, with which the local historian will be mainly concerned. *The Century of Revolution* (1603-1714) by Christopher Hill, mentioned in the last chapter, is a seminal work for the period. Hill separates events of 1660-80 from those of the later years; each section starts with a 'narrative of events' which the local historian desirous of a short but precise commentary on the national scene will find of great interest. Further sections on economics, politics, religion and ideas will round out the picture. The previous chapter noted two works in the Open University Set Books series under the title *Seventeenth Century England — A Changing Culture*; the first volume deals with primary sources, and the second with a series of modern studies interpreting various aspects of national and local life. These remain pertinent to the years 1660-1714, but may be heavily augmented by the eighth volume in the *English Historical Documents* series (*EHD8*). This work, covering the same years, was edited by Andrew Browning and published in 1966. It commences with a long introduction in which Professor Browning lays the ground for the more ready appreciation of the significance of the contemporary material comprising the bulk of the volume.

The categories *narrative histories and letters, national government and society, country and towns* and *ecclesiastical and religious* will again be used to separate the relevant classes of source material.

Narrative histories and letters

The later Stuart period witnessed the writing of many narratives describing England and its people. Some were penned by natives, some by foreigners, several are of but limited appeal, others range more widely. Among the more interesting are the records of journeys through town and countryside made by well-read and distinguished

MAGALOTTI - - - - -
BASKERVILLE ....
NORTH — — —
FIENNES ———
DEFOE -·-·-·-

The itineraries of five 18th century travellers who kept daily journals recording their impressions of the places they visited.

travellers. *EHD9* has a useful map (above) showing the routes followed by five such intrepid tourists — Count Magalotti, Thomas Baskerville, Sir Francis North, Celia Fiennes and Daniel Defoe. Between them these people covered much of England and Wales from Carlisle and Newcastle in the north to Plymouth and Dover in the south, with many places in the Midlands. A few typical extracts from the narrative may be in order.

Magalotti, who accompanied the Grand Duke of Tuscany in his travels through southwest England in 1669, kept a journal (published in London in 1821). He says, in Devon, 'Exeter . . . is a small city about ten miles from the sea. The river [Exe] empties itself into a large bay, up which the largest vessels even those of 300 tons burden, can safely pass as far as Topsham, a village three miles from Exeter whence merchandise is conveyed in smaller boats quite up to the city. The advantage of this commerce is very great, about 30 thousand persons being continually employed in the county making baize and different kinds of light cloth.' Further east he said, 'His Highness having arrived early at Basingstoke walked on foot through the town, which is wretched, both in regard to the buildings ... and the total absence of trade.' The 'tour' undertaken by Daniel Defoe covers many journeys over many years, and is represented by *A Tour through the Whole Island of Great Britain ...*, edited by G.D.H. Cole, which appeared in 1927 (London). *The Journeys of Celia Fiennes* by Christopher Morris (London, reprinted with illustrations 1987) contains descriptions and observations made over the period 1682-1703. The lady toured mainly East Anglia and the Midlands. Regarding Ipswich, she reported, 'I was there on Saturday, which is their market day, and saw they sold their butter by the pint, twenty ounces for sixpence, and often for fivepence or fourpence. They make it up into a mould just in the shape of a pint pot, and so sell it.'

Other contemporary works full of fascinating detail are *A Voyage to England containing Many Things ...* by Samuel de Sorbiere (London 1709); *Lives of the Norths* by Roger North (London 1826), which gives details of life in the north of England *c.*1676; and the writings on the southeast *c.*1670 by Thomas Baskerville. Much of this last work remains in manuscript, but some — 'An account of some remarkable things in a journey between London and Dover' — have been published by the Historical Manuscripts Commission in *The Manuscripts of the Duke of Portland* Vol.II.

Further sources of primary material are collections of family letters, such as *Memoirs of the Verney Family from the Letters at Claydon House* (four volumes, London 1892-99), and *The Flemings of Oxford ... (1650-1700)* edited by J.R. Magrath (Oxford 1904-24). References to a number of relevant texts appear in the bibliography in *EHD8*. Also, *Life in a Noble Household 1641-1700* by G.S. Thomson (London 1937) is of interest, being based on the domestic papers of the first Duke of Bedford.

National government and society

During the years 1660-1714 there was much discussion and legislation at national level of no direct interest to the local researcher. This concerned taking revenge on the Parliamentarians, an 'act for perpetual thanksgiving for the Restoration', limiting the royal and other prerogatives, determining the succession, and so on. Nonetheless there was one area, public finance, where there was great activity of particular significance. In 1660 the country was on the verge of bankruptcy. The estimate of debts inherited from the Commonwealth was in the order of £2,000,000, and the total burden after nearly twenty years of civil war and foreign expeditions may well have been almost twice this. The answer, or part of the answer, was to impose new taxes, and to institute a civil list to limit royal expenditure.

The abolition of feudal tenures In 1660 an Act of Parliament was passed 'taking away the court of wards and liveries and tenures *in capite* [held from the Crown] and by knight service and purveyance, and for setting a revenue upon His Majesty in lieu thereof.' A purist, or perhaps a pedant, might suggest that it was at this point the medieval period ended. The topic will not be pursued. The Act was fairly lengthy and appears in *Statutes of the Realm V* (pp.259-66). It may, however, be quoted in part: '[from 24 February 1645/6] all tenures by knight service of the king or any other person, and by knights service *in capite*, and by socage *in capite*, and the fruits and consequences thereof ... be taken away and discharged ... and all tenures of any honours, manors, lands, tenements or hereditaments of any estate at the common law ... are hereby enacted to be turned into free and common socage.' It was further enacted 'that it be for ever hereafter free to all and every of the subjects of His Majesty to sell, dispose or employ his ... goods to any other person or persons.' Thus the last vestiges of the *fyrd* (the feudal host) and Saxon-Norman tenurial service passed into history. There followed legislation designed to give the king an income in substitution for that gained from feudal burdens. Several of these laws are of interest to the local historian, for not only do they provide insight into the events of the years concerned, but, being imposed countrywide, are excellent bases for the comparing of one locality with another.

Hearth tax 1662 Published in *Statutes of the Realm V* (pp.390-3), the Act imposing this tax indicated that the revenue generated for the king was for the 'better support' of his Crown and dignity. The legislation stated that every fire-hearth and stove within each house and edifice, etc., be taxed at 2 shillings per year. Many of these records have been printed at county level by later historians, local record societies or interested bodies. They are quite invaluable for they give specific insight into which families lived in what sort of houses, how prosperous they were, and by patient investigation the likely *types* of houses may be determined, especially after discussion with the local authority officer responsible for the preservation of ancient buildings. The data obtained may be correlated with those in the Heralds Visitations, the memorials in the parish church, the parish register, churchwardens accounts and so on, to assemble a most satisfactory corpus of historical evidence. It should be noted that the hearth tax was abolished in 1689.

Window tax 1696 In 1696 an Act passed into the books 'for granting to His Majesty several rates or duties upon houses for making good the difficiency of the clipped money.' It is printed in *Statutes of the Realm VII* (pp.86-94), and was a tax on windows: 'for upon every dwelling house inhabited that now are or hereafter shall be erected within the kingdom of England, dominion of Wales and town of Berwick on Tweed (other than and except cottages) the annual sums . . .' as follows: 2 shillings for an inhabited house with less than ten windows, 6 shillings for those with ten to twenty windows, 10 shillings for those with more than twenty windows. Again local records are sometimes available, and in some places, in both town and country, houses from the seventeenth and earlier centuries still stand with blocked-up windows, a device adopted by the then owners to avoid paying the tax.

Other taxes In 1660 there was a poll tax graded according to rank (*Statutes of the Realm V* pp.207-25), an Act of benevolence (1661), one of royal aid (1665), tonnage (1694), a tax on births, deaths, marriages, bachelors and widowers (1695), and on land (1707). In 1711 came a Stamp Act (tax) on vellum, printed paper and so on. Details of these (with long extracts from the texts) are to be found in *EHD8* pp.313-29. The *Victoria County History* series may sometimes comment on the effects of these measures at local level, and the 'local studies' collections in the public libraries may also be of value.

A drawing of a farmyard published in Oxonia Illustrata in 1675.

Country and town life

Country

On 14 September 1668 Charles II wrote to his sister, 'The thing which is nearest the heart of the nation is trade and all that belongs to it', and this applied equally to country areas as to towns. At the highest level — the ownership of estates — there was much confusion, for during the civil war there had been confiscation and granting of land, dispossession and repossession. The Act of Indemnity and Oblivion of 1660, as a gesture of free and general pardon, was in practice a hindrance to Royalists in regaining their estates. Some families never did become restored and sank in importance, lost their competitive positions in the marriage market, and never regained their former eminence.

At the level of practice of agriculture, farming and husbandry, regional specialisation and the division of labour increased, enclosure for intensive crop cultivation became very attractive, particularly in areas near towns, and dairy farming and large-scale market gardening thrived. Lettuces, sainfoin, clover, artichokes, beans, peas, asparagus, and other vegetables and crops came in. So did turnips (the later publicity given to the agricultural reformer 'Turnip' Townshend merely highlighting the power of advertising over facts). The great age of English stock-breeding arrived. As Professor Hill wrote in *The Century of Revolution* (p.175), 'Meanwhile the abolition of feudal tenures, and the failure of copyholders to win legal protection, increased the profitability of capitalist investment in agriculture ... the liquidation of scores of ancient families, lesser gentry and freeholders, and the rise ... of vast new agglomerations of landed estates constituted a basic social revolution' at the time in question; and, on pp.189-90, Hill cites a number of relevant works of interest, some of which may be of value to local researchers. The importance of the *Victoria County History* must also be stressed, for although some of the volumes were written many years ago, they frequently throw valuable light on local practices, crops and farming methods. Reference should also be made to pp.179-80 in *Sources for English Local History* by W.B. Stephens, and three essays in Vol.2 of *Seventeenth Century England* edited by W.R. Owens: 'Social Effects of Change in Agriculture' by Joan Thirsk, 'The Changing Pattern of Labouring Life' by Alan Everitt, and 'Economics and Politics in the Seventeenth Century' by Charles Wilson.

169

YORK Four Days Stage-Coach.

Begins on Friday the 12th of April. 1706.

ALL that are defirous to pafs from *London* to *York,* or from *York* to *London,* or any other Place on that Road; Let them Repair to the *Black Swan* in *Holbourn* in *London,* and to the *Black Swan* in *Coney* ftreet in *York.*

At both which Places, they may be received in a Stage Coach every *Monday, Wednefday* and *Friday,* which performs the whole Journey in Four Days, (if *God permits,*) And fets forth at Five in the Morning.

And returns from *York* to *Stamford* in two days, and from *Stamford* by *Huntington* to *London* in two days more. And the like Stages on their return.

Allowing each Paffenger 14ˡ, weight, and all above 3d a Pound.

Performed By { *Benjamin Kingman, Henry Harrifon, Walter Baynes,*

Alfo this gives Notice that Newcaftle Stage Coach, fets out from York, every Monday, and Friday, and from Newcaftle every Monday and Friday.

Recd. in pt. 05-00. of Mr. Bodingfeld for 5 plac. for Monday the 3 of June 1706.

Although most roads were so appalling that goods were sent by packhorse or donkey, it was still possible to go by stage-coach from York to London, or London to York, in four days (if God permitted).

Towns

The legislation mentioned in the 'National government and society' section of this chapter, above, applied countrywide, and town and city archives contain, in consequence, large quantities of data which the local researcher may sift for information of relevance.

At the outset special mention needs to be made regarding London which, in the years 1665-99, was visited by plague and fire. There are a number of contemporary accounts of occurrences: Nathaniel Hodges' report of the Great Plague of 1665, 'What greatly contributed to the loss of people ... was the wicked practices of nurses ... These wretches, out of greediness to plunder the dead, would strangle their patients ... others would convey the pestilential taint from sores of the infected to those who were well.' Hodges' writing may be usefully put alongside that of Samuel Pepys, John Evelyn and others for, perhaps, not only London historians to gain insight into the squalor of urban life. Reference should be made to pp.494-503 in *EHD8* which contain details of where such accounts may be found.

In *A Plan of English Commerce* (Oxford 1927) Daniel Defoe, writing in 1728, is recorded as saying the 'sum of all improvements in trade [is] the finding out some market for the sale or vent of merchandize where there was no sale or vent before.' This had been the philosophy of merchants and traders for many years. They regarded trading as conflict — actual war with the Dutch and French, plus trade treaties, tariff barriers, and prohibitions. Their attitudes are reflected in the realities of town life in the century, particularly in the setting-up of new market centres in such places as Stevenage and Blackburn, Ambleside and Shap. New ports, such as described in Chapter 19, came into being, stimulated by government enactments or activities such as the committees for plantations, the Navigation Act, the Tobacco Act (all of 1660), the Recoinage Act (1696), the Council of Trade (1696) and the Naval Stores Act of 1704.

In *The Economy of England 1450-1750* (Oxford 1977) D.C. Coleman deals, in Chapters 8 and 9, with the transformation of trade and industry in the period after 1650, and this may be compared with the related data in *The Landscape of Towns* by Michael Aston and James Bond (London, reprinted 1987), pp.109-35.

So much has been written about the seventeenth century that it may come as something of a disappointment to local researchers to find that the work they had in mind has already been carried out — in such works as *Tudor and Stuart Lincoln* by J.W.F. Hill (Cambridge 1956), or in the chapter 'Industrial Change and Urban Growth, 1660-1815' in *Wessex from AD1000* by J.H. Bettey (London 1986), which also contains an up-to-date bibliography. The dedicated local researcher need not, however, despair. From a starting point of the *Bibliography of British History, Stuart Period 1603-1714* by G. Davies (London 1928), enquiries at reference libraries and record offices, and examination of works named in later bibliographies will soon engender ideas as to how aspects of local history in towns of the late seventeenth century may be researched and subsequently written.

Ecclesiastical and religious matters

With the coming of the Restoration the Church became more secure than it had ever been, with the king as its supreme governor. There was, in practice, a certain jockeying for position and, when James II succeeded Charles II, a certain attempt to favour Catholics. There were Test Acts, Indulgences, Tolerations, and general parliamentary attempts to permanently influence peoples' beliefs. There was the Schism Act, educational quarrels and financial crises. Presbyterianism and non-conformity grew strong, as did the Independents. The degree to which a local historian will desire to study ecclesiastical and religious matters may well be dictated by depth or direction of belief, the part of the country being studied, and the availability of records for the period. In this the bibliography on pp.362-3 of *EHD8* will be of value. On subsequent pages of that book are listed extracts from various groups of legislation: the Clarendon Code, the Indulgences, Toleration and so on. Important for present purposes among these are the Corporation Act of 1661, 'for the well governing and regulating of corporations'; the Act of Uniformity (1662), for public prayers and administration of the sacraments; the Five Mile Act (1665), for restraining non-conformists; the Test Acts (1673-8), for disabling Papists from sitting in Parliament; Toleration (1689), exempting dissenters from the penalties of certain laws; In Relief of Quakers (1696) and that against Popery (1700).

A plate from The Analysis of Beauty (March 1753) by Hogarth. In this ballroom scene the graceful lines of the noble pair on the left contrast sharply with those of the lower orders towards the right.

14 The Eighteenth Century 1714-1783

Note regarding dating Attention is drawn to the note at the beginning of Chapter 12.

In *English Historical Documents 10* (London 1957) the editors, D.B. Horn and Mary Ransome, point out in their introduction that historians, when speaking of the eighteenth century, usually mean the years 1714-83 and not those of 1701-1800. They specifically say that the shorter span presents 'the quintessence of the eighteenth century . . . at its highest point of development and least modified by residuary traces of its predecessor or the coming shadow of its successor.' Certainly, for the local historian, the period is a rewarding one, for not only were many of the early county histories written then, but numerous laws were passed which greatly affected everyday life.

This chapter deals, therefore, with the years between the accession of George I and the Peace of Versailles achieved between Britain and the American colonists in 1783, at which time George III resigned personal rule and much ministerial power to William Pitt the Younger.

George I, Elector of Hanover, had been invited to take the throne in preference to the remaining Stuart line very much as the lesser of two evils. He never bothered to learn English, and for fifty years the Whigs ruled the country. The Jacobite rebellion of 1715 failed, and the rising of 1745 was equally unsuccessful. Wars came and went, although it no doubt seemed to the ordinary person that from 1739, when hostilities against Spain began, the country was always fighting. George I died in 1727 and was succeeded by his equally alien son George II. To begin with, under the leadership of Walpole, there was a period of peace, during which a system of government through a Cabinet was established. The Cabinet was responsible to parliament, and that body, to the people — in theory at any rate. George III, grandson of George II, was twenty-two when his reign began. He was brilliantly ineffective, vindictive, weak, neurotic and not amenable to advice. He was, however, interested in agricultural improvements and in the creation of modern farms, his collection of books formed the early nucleus of the British Library, and he founded the Royal Academy in 1768.

The years now being considered are dealt with in two books in the *Oxford History of England* series. The first covers 1714-60 and is *The Whig Supremacy* by Basil Williams (1939, revised 1961). It contains long sections on local government and also the social and economic development of the people. This latter is especially useful. The second book is *The Reign of George III* by J. Steven Watson (1960), and it includes considerable discussion on economic, social and political patterns which the local researcher will find of value. Mention must also be made of *England in the Eighteenth Century* by J.H. Plumb (Penguin Books 1950). It is particularly relevant to present purposes in the section called 'The Agrarian and Social Revolutions 1742-84', and the subsequent pages which deal with the consequences of those two upheavals. A more recent and also readily available text is *English Society in the Eighteenth Century* by Roy Porter (*Pelican Social History of England* series, 1982). Based on later research than the other books mentioned it puts forward concepts and interpretations incorporating the thinking of modern historians on the subjects (amongst others) of the social order, power, politics and the law. It also contains an eleven-page bibliography.

Mention has already been made of *EHD10* which deals with events of 1714-83. There is a long, general introduction and many references to works of special relevance.

The categories of *narrative histories and letters, national government, country and towns* and *ecclesiastical and religious* will be used to classify the source material for this period.

Narrative histories and letters

There is no general history of the period for the local historian eager to obtain a contemporary view of England. A number of county histories were compiled piecemeal (rather than being conceived and written as a whole) and these may be accessed in well stocked public libraries.

Much the same goes for memoirs and diaries. The matter of letters and correspondence is, however, an entirely different one, for the eighteenth century was the age of the great letter writers. It must, of course, be admitted that much of the writing is concerned with significant political events at one end of the scale and personal domestic trivia at the other, but reference to pp.74-5 in *EHD10* and the sectional bibliography on social history may yield occasional material of value to individual researchers.

National government and society

At national level there is much of significance to the study of local history — even if some is but of background importance. An example of this is the statute of 1731 providing that all proceedings in the law courts be in English. This was deplored and opposed by many lawyers, but greatly assisted the understanding of matters, especially indictments.

In 1715 the Riot Act increased the powers of the Justices of the Peace to deal with 'tumults and riotous assemblies' and was passed as a result of the widespread disturbances which had broken out in the first few months of that year.

There were a number of Acts touching on direct taxation (and these have been conveniently brought together in the HMSO *Statutes at Large* volumes, as well as being abstracted in *EHD10*). In 1747 a new method of imposing a window tax was enacted (which varied the Act of 1696 discussed in Chapter 13), and this itself was varied by Acts of 1758, 1761 and 1766. There followed taxes of an essentially sumptuary nature — on carriages, cards and dice, and on male servants (1777): 'Every master and mistress may deliver . . . to the assessor . . . a true list of their respective servants.' All classes of servants from maître d'hôtel to stable boy were included. These impositions, designed to finance the American war, were further augmented (1778 and 1779) by taxes on inhabited houses and warehouses. *EHD10* contains (pp.323-7) useful tables of income, by county and date, generated by house taxes, window and land taxes.

A number of items of government legislation of the time were of great local significance. High on the list of these was the Workhouse Act of 1722 (the text appears in *Statutes at Large XV* pp.28-33). It provided for the setting up of workhouses in each parish and the provision of poor relief in these places only. At local level the churchwardens and overseers of the poor were responsible for the administration of the various procedures, and there is frequently a body of records which will be of value to the modern student. A useful starting point is the essay by S. Farrant, 'Some Records of the Old Poor Laws as Sources of Local History', published in *Local Historian* xii (1976-7). In addition, a great deal has been published regarding specific places — such as *Bristol Corporation of the Poor* edited by E.E. Butcher (Bristol Record Society iii, 1932) — and enquiries should be made of the local studies librarian in the appropriate public library.

The County Rates Act of 1739 (*Statutes at Large XVII*) consolidated into one general rate the various levies formerly imposed by the Justices of the Peace, and had as one of its main objects the easy assessing, collecting and levying of county rates. The justices had the power to impose the general rate, 'and the several and respective sums so assessed upon each and every town, parish or place . . . shall be collected by the high constables of the respective hundreds and divisions, in which any town, parish or place doth lie, in such a manner, and at such times, as hereinafter directed.'

In 1751 an Act substituting the Gregorian for the Julian calendar was brought in

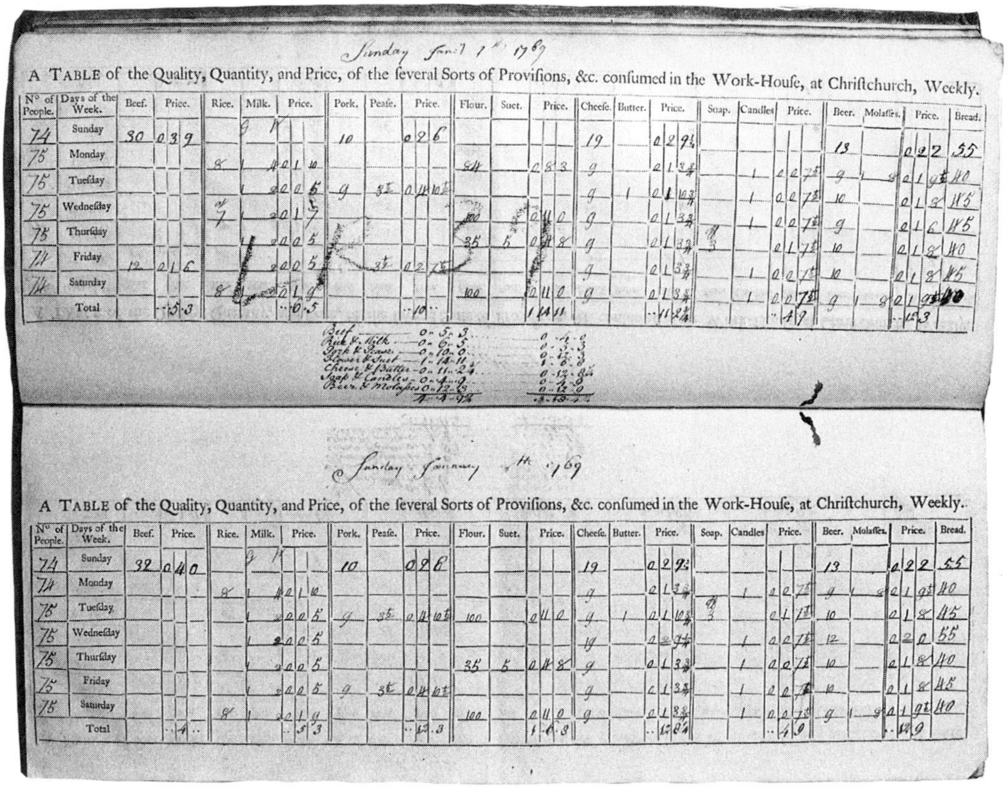

Sunday Jan.y 1st 1769

A TABLE of the Quality, Quantity, and Price, of the ſeveral Sorts of Proviſions, &c. conſumed in the Work-Houſe, at Chriſtchurch, Weekly.

N° of People.	Days of the Week.	Beef.	Price.	Rice.	Milk.	Price.	Pork.	Peaſe.	Price.	Flour.	Suet.	Price.	Cheeſe.	Butter.	Price.	Soap.	Candles	Price.	Beer.	Molaſſes.	Price.	Bread.
74	Sunday	30	0 3 9				10		0 2 6				19		0 2 9¼				13		0 2 2	55
75	Monday			8	1	0 1 10				84		0 8 3	9		0 1 3¾		1	0 0 7½	9	1	0 1 9½	40
75	Tueſday				1	0 0 5	9	3½	0 4 10½				9	1	0 1 10¾		1	0 0 7½	10		0 1 8	45
75	Wedneſday			7	1	0 1 7				100		0 11 0	9		0 1 3¾		1	0 0 7½	9		0 1 6	45
75	Thurſday				1	0 0 5				35	5	0 4 8	9		0 1 3¾	3		0 1 7½	10		0 1 8	40
74	Friday	12	0 1 6		1	0 0 5		3½	0 2 7½				9		0 1 3¾		1	0 0 7½	10		0 1 8	45
74	Saturday			8	1	0 1 9				100		0 11 0	9		0 1 3¾		1	0 0 7½	9	1	0 1 9½	40
	Total		..5.3			..6.5			..10..			1 14 11			..11 2¼			..4 9			..12 3	

Beef	0 5 3	0 4 0
Rice & Milk	0 6 5	0 5 3
Pork & Pease	0 10 0	0 12 3
Flower & Suet	1 14 11	1 6 8
Cheese & Butter	0 11 2¼	0 12 8¼
Soap & Candles	0 4 9	0 4 9
Beer & Molasses	0 12 3	0 12 9
	4 4 9½	[illegible]

Sunday January 8th 1769

A TABLE of the Quality, Quantity, and Price, of the ſeveral Sorts of Proviſions, &c. conſumed in the Work-Houſe, at Chriſtchurch, Weekly.

N° of People.	Days of the Week.	Beef.	Price.	Rice.	Milk.	Price.	Pork.	Peaſe.	Price.	Flour.	Suet.	Price.	Cheeſe.	Butter.	Price.	Soap.	Candles	Price.	Beer.	Molaſſes.	Price.	Bread.
74	Sunday	32	0 4 0				10		0 2 6				19		0 2 9¼				13		0 2 2	55
74	Monday			8	1	0 1 10							9		0 1 3¾		1	0 0 7½	9	1	0 1 9½	40
75	Tueſday				1	0 0 5	9	3½	0 4 10½	100		0 11 0	9	1	0 1 10¾	3		0 1 7½	10		0 1 8	45
75	Wedneſday				1	0 0 5							19		0 2 9¼		1	0 0 7½	12		0 2 0	55
75	Thurſday				1	0 0 5				35	5	0 4 8	9		0 1 3¾		1	0 0 7½	10		0 1 8	40
75	Friday				1	0 0 5	9	3½	0 4 10½				9		0 1 3¾		1	0 0 7½	10		0 1 8	45
75	Saturday			8	1	0 1 9				100		0 11 0	9		0 1 3¾		1	0 0 7½	9	1	0 1 9½	40
	Total		..4..			..5 3			..12.3			1.6.3			..12 8¼			..4 9			..12 9	

The weekly dietary pattern **(ABOVE)** *for a workhouse in 1769 (see also page 40). Beef was provided only on Sundays, pork and peas on Sundays, Tuesdays and Fridays, flour and suet used on Mondays, Thursdays and Saturdays. Cheese appeared every day and there was always plenty of bread, beer and molasses. No mention is made of vegetables other than peas. The simple fare may be contrasted with the two courses of the nobleman's meal* **(BELOW)**, *which include pike, pigeons, lobster, greens, apricots and artichokes.*

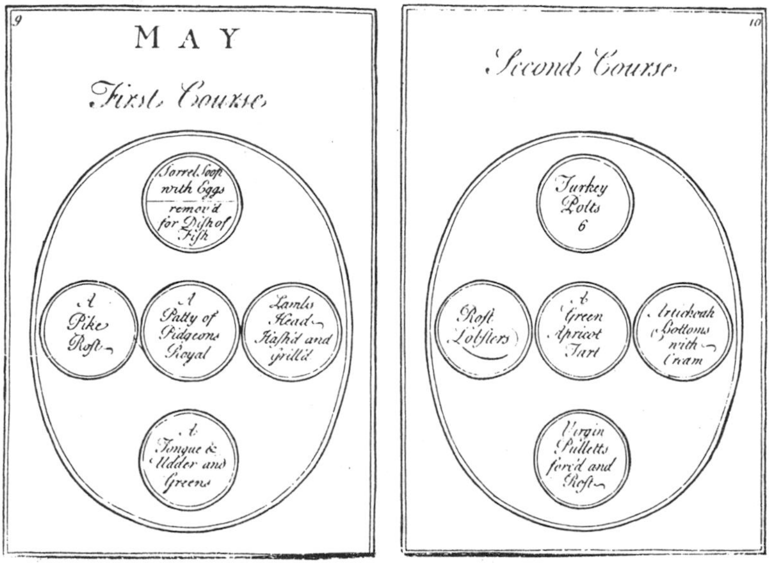
9
MAY
First Course
Sorrel Soop with Eggs remov'd for Dish of Fish
A Pike Rost
A Patty of Pidgeons Royal
Lambs Head Hash'd and grill'd
A Tongue & Udder and Greens
10
Second Course
Turkey Polts 6
Rost Lobsters
A Green Apricot Tart
Artichoak Bottoms with Cream
Virgin Pulletts forc'd and Rost

(see Chapter 29), which aligned the English calendar with that used on the Continent. It was not a popular move. Eleven days between 2 and 14 September were suppressed and a demand arose, 'Give us back our lost days'.

Finally in this section, mention must be made of the Militia Act of 1757, which remained the basis of organising the militia until the late nineteenth century. The important element of the new legislation was the raising of the force by ballot, with the aim of making it an effective second line of defence in time of war.

The local researcher should bear in mind the interaction of national and local factors of government on the parochial scene. More than ever, in the period being discussed, the wide powers exercised by county officers is in contrast with the lack of supervision from central government. The volumes by R. Burn, *Justice of the Peace and the Parish Officer* (London 1755), may be consulted if early documentation and commentary is needed; if not, then a more modern and authoritative text is *English Local Government from the Revolution to the Municipal Corporations Act* by Sidney and Beatrice Webb (nine volumes, London 1906-29). The selective *Local History Handlist* published by the Historical Association (London 1947) is still of value in the identification of pertinent material.

Country and towns

The two relevant volumes in the *Oxford History* series contain information which will set the overall scene of rural and urban life, but it must be remembered that both books were published some years ago. A more up-to-date treatment is that given by Robert W. Malcolmson in his *Life and Labour in England 1700-1780* (London 1981).

Today the hackneyed definitions of upper, middle, and working-class groups have, thanks to the popular press and endless repetition, so entered the common vocabulary that it may on occasion be difficult to remember that such stratification never was wholly accurate. Further, it has always been possible for class barriers to be transcended, and it must be recognised that in every age the abilities of people cover a wide spectrum.

The coming of national prosperity in the eighteenth century to a great degree underlines this. In 1714 England was still a mainly agricultural country, but the agrarian revolution transformed huge areas. Turnips, clover and various grasses were introduced on a wide scale, improvements in stock breeding, agricultural machinery and elaborate rotation of crops played their parts. Private enclosure Acts consolidated estates and benefited the owners. Woollen cloth manufacture was of great importance, especially in the south-west, Norfolk and Yorkshire. The silk industry developed on a 'factory system', and the cotton industry came into being. Iron smelting, using coke rather than charcoal, allowed that basic industry to develop. Coal and metal mining flourished, aided by the inventions of James Watt and others. The merchant as exporter or importer came into his own.

A useful work is *Guide to the Printed Materials for Social and Economic History, 1750-1850* by Judith Williams (New York 1926). It was exhaustive, although vast quantities of material have become available since publication, as the notes and references in both Malcolmson (*op cit*) and *EHD10* indicate; and reference should also be made to *Sources for English Local History* by W.B. Stephens (Cambridge 1981). Pages 416-23 in

EHD10 are of especial value, for they contain details of printed sources under the headings of Contemporary Works, General Histories, Population, Agriculture, Industrial Development, Wages and Prices, Transport, Trade, Banking and Commerce.

Country

One of the greatest sources of information for the local historian from the eighteenth century onwards is maps. These may be county topographic maps giving evidence of land use, or estate maps providing more detailed and, perhaps, reliable information, especially regarding enclosures. These maps are often complemented by written papers, and the local historian should not assume that all such documents have been published, or even rigorously examined. Enquiries at the local county record office will reveal much and, equally importantly, a direct approach to the local 'great estate' will often yield the most rewarding of material. Two useful books are *Maps for Local History* by Paul Hindle (London 1988), and *Maps and Plans for the Local Historian* by David Smith (London 1988).

The files of early newspapers are mines of information, and these may be supplemented by reference to other contemporary sources, as for example the writings of Jethro Tull. This great innovator in agricultural methods wrote a treatise on husbandry, *The Horse-Hoeing Husbandry*, which was published in 1733, and there is an analytical piece, by T.H. Marshall, called 'Jethro Tull and the New Husbandry' in *Economic History Review* II. An extract from Tull's treatise also appears in *EHD10* (pp.429-32).

The works of the eighteenth-century writer Arthur Young are a detailed and prolific source of information. A great deal of his published material is accessible in original editions. Young, the son of a Suffolk clergyman, was born in 1741 and died in 1820. He was himself an unsuccessful farmer but a noted agricultural theorist. He edited the periodical *Annals of Agriculture* from 1784 until 1809. His autobiography, edited by M. Betham-Edwards, appeared in 1898, and a life, by J.G. Gazeley, in 1973. In 1770 Young wrote *A Six Months Tour through the North of England*, and in it he tabulated his estimate of the 'state of the nation'. The figures he provides give the total acreage made over to grass and to arable, and its estimated financial value. He essays the incomes of the various classes of people, the size of the population by class, and revenues from agriculture and manufacture. In the same book there is a long item on enclosures, in which he makes two salient points: that the high cost of enclosure by Act of Parliament frequently made enclosure much less profitable than is sometimes supposed, and that the formation of large farms led to rural depopulation.

The next year, 1771, Young's *The Farmer's Tour Through the East of England* dealt with the agrarian improvements of the age. These included advances in stock breeding, particularly of small-boned cattle, the Lancashire being judged the best. Also covered were improvements in arable farming which, in eastern England, Young lists as: enclosure without the assistance of parliament; the liberal use of marl and clay; an excellent course of crops; the culture of turnips; the culture of clover and rye grass; the grant of long leases; the setting up of large farms. A recommended course (rotation) of crops was turnips, barley, clover (or rye grass) and wheat. Of equal value are the data Young provides on the average prices of provisions and labour. Some

The Holstein or Dutch Breed   The Improved Holstein or Dutch Breed

The selective breeding of cattle greatly improved the strains for both breeding and eating. Judging by the background scenes, it also did wonders for their temperaments.

extracts from Young's writings are given in *EHD10*, but the original works should be obtained through the British Library's lending scheme.

At individual parish level the most important records, apart from maps and estate papers, are the accounts of the overseers, the churchwardens, the inventories and wills of inhabitants, and, in fortunate cases, terriers and related documents. These may be found in the local record office.

Towns — with special reference to industry and trade

The geographical structure of towns is dealt with in Chapter 19, so this particular section deals with aspects of trade and industry.

There are two generalities which must be borne in mind: the power of the local burgesses and merchants over the 'government' of the towns; and the improvements in the road and canal systems which enabled goods to be transported long distances to the benefit of both buyer and seller.

A useful contemporary starting point is *The British Merchant: A Collection of Papers Relating to Trade and Commerce* by Charles King, published in 1721, which set out the 'General Maxims in Trade which are assented to by every body.' This may be supplemented by the sources referred to in *EHD10* pp.448-508, which cite not only Defoe's (and others') valuable descriptions of trade and commerce in towns, but also contain useful tabulations which may be employed for comparison purposes. A particularly valuable section deals with combinations of workmen (or trade unions, as they may more familiarly be called).

Regarding social life in towns (and indeed elsewhere) attention should initially be paid to the bibliography on pp.513-20 of *EHD10*, followed by the works cited on pp.521-40 which deal with the style of the trading classes, habits, holidays, architecture and other diverse matters.

Finally, attention should be directed to the broad importance of the transportation and communication systems of turnpike trusts and canals. Many works dealing with these matters are identified in the bibliographies in the *Oxford History of England* volumes, in the books in the *Victoria County History* series, and in the local collections maintained in the larger public libraries.

Ecclesiastical and religious matters

There were radical changes in the position of the English Church in the eighteenth century. The two great political parties — the Whigs and the Tories — were loyal to the ecclesiastical establishment. The Church itself was rent by intrigues, and Methodism as a manifestation of evangelical revival came to the fore. Nonconformity as displayed by the Presbyterians and Independents was no longer a crime. The numbers of dissenters and Catholics declined during the years covered by this chapter, and finally the Catholic Relief Act of 1778 was a further step towards toleration of views not in accord with the official church.

Pages 343-7 of *EHD10* contain an extensive bibliography — the Church of England, Evangelism, Non-Jurors, Protestant Nonconformists, Quakers, Methodists, Roman Catholics and Jews — which will be of great value to local researchers studying the religious history of the places of their choice. These works may be augmented by a reading of the extracts from contemporary works on pp. 349-409 of *EHD10*. Typical of these are: the position of the established Church in 1736; the aims and organisation of the Methodist Societies (1749); and the legal position of nonconformists and papists (1775).

Local historians wishing but a brief outline of the religious organisations of the day are referred to the *Encyclopaedia Britannica* (particularly the 11th edition), and *The Oxford Dictionary of the Christian Church*.

A churchwarden's record for April 1740. In addition to limiting the wages of the bellringers, it stipulated that no relief should be given to travellers.

179

Stephenson's locomotive 'Northumberland' in 1831.

15
The Later Hanoverian Period 1783-1833

The eighteenth century saw the greatest progress in the evolution of the British Constitution, an acceptable balance of power being achieved between the monarch, the Lords and the Commons. For the closing years of his reign, 'farmer George' (III) lived in seclusion and had little influence on affairs. He was, with all his failings, held in high regard by his people, but after 1811, when he was at times insane and then blind, his son (also named George) ruled as Prince Regent. During the French Revolution and the Napoleonic Wars England was well served by its senior ministers and commanders, and the prosperity of the country continued. When he succeeded his father, George IV reigned for nine years, and on his death in 1830 his younger brother — William IV — came to the throne.

It was the age of parliamentary reform and many changes had taken place in England. The population had greatly increased in number, there were far-reaching advances in both agriculture and industry to keep pace with demand, transport and communications were revolutionised.

The *Oxford History* volumes, *The Reign of George III* by J. Steven Watson (Oxford 1960) and *The Age of Reform 1815-1870* by Sir Llewellyn Woodward (Oxford 1962), remain of great value in gaining an overall perspective of the period. They deal with much of interest to the local historians and contain important bibliographies. In the *English Historical Documents* series, the 11th volume (*EHD11*) is edited by A. Aspinall and E. Anthony Smith and was published in 1969. It deals specifically with the years 1783-1832.

The immediately preceding chapters have been structured in a uniform manner.

The changes in economic and social life during the late eighteenth and early nine-teenth centuries now demand a somewhat different approach. The section headings will, therefore, be: *economic development, local government and poor law administration,* and *social and religious life.*

Economic development

The period now being discussed represents the high-water mark of the two great revolutions which led to the world as we know it today — the agricultural and the industrial. It was, above all, the time of transition from the agrarian society of earlier times to the urbanized, industrial age.

In agricultural areas the period was one of suffering and unrest, especially for and among the small farmers and landless labourers. In industrial areas there was the alternation of boom and slump.

Local studies collections are full of works of local interest — papers and books written by modern historians, professional and amateur — which will illuminate various aspects of the economic growth (or decline) of the area being studied. At the general level J.B. Williams' *Guide to the Printed Materials for English Social and Economic History, 1750-1850* (New York 1926) is a mine of information, and the annual biblio-graphies (since 1927) in *English Historical Review* are equally important. There remains, as may be expected, a mass of contemporary literature and statistical data. A valuable guide to this appears on pp.456-7 of *EHD11*, and there are many works of more modern, and critical, vintage listed in that volume.

For the economic development of agriculture, reference should be made to a work already cited, *Sources for English Local History* by W.B. Stephens (Cambridge 1981) pp.180-202. Not only is the essay on these pages of importance, but the references given are to seminal works. *The English Villages and the Enclosure Movements* by W.E. Tate (London 1967), and *The Village Labourer* by J.L. and Barbara Hammond (London 1978), are significant in their contribution to the study, and the subject is also dis-cussed in *The Rural World* by Pamela Horn (London 1980).

The writings of Arthur Young (1741-1820) are of great value. They were published in the *Annals of Agriculture* between 1784 and 1815, but the London School of Economics, in its *Reprint 14*, made the texts for the years covered by this chapter available in a 1932 edition prepared by J.C. Loudon. *The Disappearance of the Small Landowner* by A.H. Johnson (Oxford 1909) is a useful reference book, and further books are noted on pp.458-9 of *EHD11*.

On the industrial front there is much to be studied. The *Oxford History of Technology* Vol.IV, *The Industrial Revolution c. 1750-1850* edited by C. Singer and others (1930) is quite basic, and there are dozens of references identified under the heading 'Industry' on pp.459-62 in *EHD11*. For the cotton industry, contemporary works include *A Compendious History of the Cotton Manufacture* by R. Guest (1832); and *The Progress of the Nation* by G.R. Porter (1836) is valuable for many industries, including cotton and linen. The iron trade is dealt with in *A Comprehensive History of the Iron Trade* by H. Scrivenor (1841); coal is discussed in *Parliamentary Papers, 1st Series X* (1800).

In his book *The Progress of the Nation* (1851) G.R. Porter includes tables, by county, of the mileage of turnpike roads in England in 1829. These range, in a total of 18,244,

An Assessment made for one years Land Tax for the Parish of Pentridge from the 6th of April 1823 to the 6th of April 1824

Names of Proprietors	Names of Occupiers	£	s	d
Earl. of Shaftesbury	Wm. Spear	14	08	0
Revd. T Hobson	Do.	9	04	0
Joseph Rogers	Wm. Goddard	0	15	0
Earl. of Shaftesbury	Saml. Brook	1	04	0
Earl. of Shaftesbury	Wm. Herrington	0	07	0
Robt. Scott	H. Herrington	1	10	0
Earl. of Shaftesbury	Wm. Spear	0	12	0
Earl. of Shaftesbury	Wm. Spear	2	00	0
Sarah Goddard	Wm. Goddard	2	12	0
Wm. Spear	Wm. Spear	0	13	0
John Butler	John Butler	3	06	0
Sarah Goddard	Wm. Goddard	1	03	0
Henry Herrington	H. Herrington	0	14	0
H. Herrington	Do.	0	07	0
Robt. Selwood	Robt. Selwood	0	06	0
Earl. of Shaftesbury	Wm. Spear	0	13	0
H. & T. Herrington	H. Herrington	1	06	0
R. White & Hardiman	R. White & Hardiman	0	06	8
Earl. of Shaftesbury	Saml. Brook	0	13	4
	£	42	00	0

This assessment for a rural parish 1823/4 gives a good impression of the relative wealth of the proprietors, from a tax of £14.8s.0d down to one of 6/- (six shillings).

from 1,448 in Yorkshire down to 18 in Rutlandshire. When the evidence of this is compared with the description by J.L. Macadam in his *Present System of Road Making* (Bristol 1816) a very good insight may be gained into the surfaces over which the 'flying coaches' and other vehicles ran. Canal transport played a considerable part in industrial development, and J. Phillips' *A General History of Inland Navigation* (1792-1803) is recommended for the early period. Later information is given in *Historical Account of navigable rivers, canals and railways ...* by J. Priestley (London 1831). The period covered by this chapter saw the first railways. Much has been written on the subject, and a good checklist is that by C.R. Clinker, 'Sources of Railway History' in *Amateur Historian* Vol.I (1952-3).

It must be re-emphasised that the volumes in the *Victoria County History* series are frequently invaluable on matters of local economic consequence.

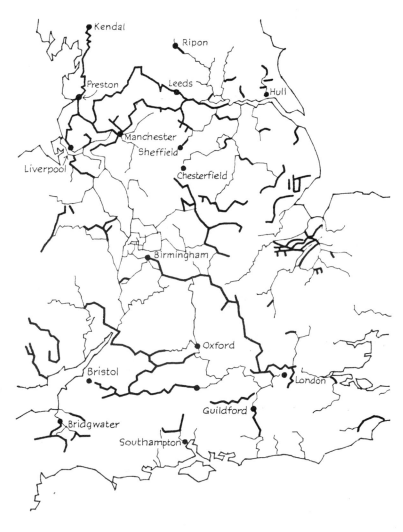

The cutting of deadwater canals started around 1760, and by about 1830 there were some 4000 miles of navigable waterway, comprising rivers, broad and narrow canals. These arteries, augmented by coastal shipping, facilitated the transport of bulk cargoes such as coal and iron ore. The steam railways of the later 19th century gradually eclipsed water transport.

Local government and poor law administration

In the eighteenth century the pivot of local government was the parish vestry, even in the boroughs. The exact functions of the vestry varied from place to place, depending on local custom as overlaid by the multitude of statutes which had been enacted over the years. In some boroughs, especially those with charters, the corporations regulated fairs and markets, managed corporation prosperity and so on, but from the point of view of civic control the parish, under the supervision of the Justices of the Peace, reigned supreme. Individuals were still required to serve as unpaid constable, overseer of the poor, churchwarden, or surveyor of the highways. Local taxes were levied at parish level in the form of rates, and the parish was responsible for the relief of its own poor.

The local customs which had held sway for so long dictated that some parishes were 'open', some were 'close', others 'select'. The first of these had some of the *prima facie* appearances of being democratic, but the others were frankly oligarchical. Various Acts, such as those of Sturges-Bourne (1818-19) attempted certain rationalisations, but practices were too diverse and the problems too great for piecemeal modification, and matters remained unsatisfactory.

The most awesome and intractable problem was the relief of poverty. Effective action and control by central government had, in effect, ceased in the middle of the seventeenth century, at which point (*c*.1660) the parishes had more or less been left to their own devices, subject only to the degree of supervision thought appropriate by the local Justices of the Peace. In some rural areas local charities helped out — the researcher will have access to many records of these bodies, some of which still exist today (there being three in the author's own village). But, as the editors of *EHD11* say (p.404), 'in the more crowded towns and industrialised regions many parishes [combined] into unions for the more economical administration of a workhouse, where segregation of the old, the sick, the children, the insane and the workshy was rarely practised and the result tended to be the horror of the general mixed workhouse.'

Special attention should be paid to the Speenhamland System (see Hammond and Hammond *op cit*, and Horn, also cited, for details too extensive to quote here), which, by allowing wages to be 'topped up' from the poor rate, instituted a method which was to have disastrous consequences for the labouring classes. As *EHD11* concludes (p.405): 'By the end of the period it was generally recognised that the [poor laws of early generations may have] saved thousands from the worst consequences of [the times] but had become a wasteful, expensive, unprofitable and demoralizing exercise in philanthropy.'

The authoritative work, for those local researchers wishing to delve deeply into this question of parish government, is the nine-volume series by Sidney and Beatrice Webb *English Local Government from the Revolution to the Municipal Corporations Act* (London 1906-29); and numerous other works are identified on pp.405-6 of *EHD11*. The pioneer book *The Parish Chest* by W.E. Tate is of great value at this stage, especially with regard to records of poor law administration, which it deals with (p.188 *et seq*) under the headings of settlement and removal, parochial experiments, overseers accounts, vagrants and vagrancy, bastards and bastardy, apprenticeship, in-relief and out-relief (workhouses), the last days of the old system, and the poor and poor laws. Reference should also be made to the two books by Dr John West, *Village Records* (Chichester 1982) and *Town Records* (Chichester 1983). *EHD11* contains (pp.407-48) many extracts from contemporary records which greatly illuminate the organisation and functioning of local government, the administration of the poor laws and the operation of workhouses. Of particular interest are tabulations (by county) of parochial expenditure for all purposes, related to population, the parliamentary debates on wages, and the (no doubt representative) financial accounts of the guardians and overseers of Birmingham for 1818/19.

Social and religious life

A reading of the general books recommended at the beginning of this chapter and in Chapter 31 will confirm that the years 1783-1832 were ones of outstanding economic and material growth, while at the same time the standard of living did not rise. The reasons are complex enough even with late twentieth-century hindsight, but they no doubt included the costs of the French wars and a series of bad harvests. Added to these were the population explosion and, in spite of everything, the greater expectation of life due to improvements in medical knowledge and hygiene. In the sphere of religion the evangelical movement was affecting the established order, and the Wesleyan and other not unrelated popular uprisings of spiritual rebirth galvanised the people into recognising that the Church of England was ill-adapted to the needs of the times. The dissenting sects, unhampered by parish boundaries, ancient traditions and old buildings, grew in influence, and the attention of the local historian may be drawn to such legislation as the Test and Corporation Acts (repealed 1828) and other relevant statutes and material identified in *Sources for English Local History* (*op cit*) pp.270-4.

The educational needs of the population were catered for in a variety of ways from the well-endowed public and grammar schools, through private day and boarding schools to the Sunday, charity and dame schools attended by the poor. It must, of course, be recognised that there were many children (employed in factories and workhouses, and on the land) who benefited little if at all from schooling of any kind.

There is a vast amount of material both primary and secondary on the social and religious life of the times, not least of which is that contained in the various local studies collections and in the archives of the local record offices. So far as the main secondary material is concerned the bibliography on pp.620-6 of *EHD11* is not only comprehensive, but is broken down into sections — population and public health, the Church and dissent, education, factory legislation, and trade unions. Extracts from the parliamentary papers and related documents (pp.629-31) give useful data on population, life expectancy and mortality.

Regarding primary sources, *A Practical View of the Prevailing Religious System of Professed Christians* (1797) by William Wilberforce was a most influential work. Wilberforce, a Member of Parliament for Yorkshire, devoted himself to philanthropic causes and the abolition of the slave trade. On the matter of dissension John Wesley's *Journal* as edited by N. Curnock (1909-16) is of immense value. Reference should also be made to the tabulation on p.667 of *EHD11* of the number of Methodists and

Circuits by county in the year 1824. A wide selection of documents on education are quoted on pp.694-722 of *EHD11*, and pp.203-47 of *Sources for English Local History* point to many other relevant publications.

During the years in question there was much factory legislation and this, with many useful tables, is identified and quoted from in *EHD11* pp.723-45. Data on trade unions, co-operative societies, savings banks and friendly societies are also cited in the volume.

Dorset) Militia List

A true List of all Persons usually, and at this Time dwelling within the West Tithing of the Parish of Fontmell Magna between the Ages of 18 and 45 Years Dated the 15th Day of November 1798

Names	Occupations	Family		Size		Exemptions and Infirmities
		Wife	N.º Child.	Feet	Inch	
Ja.ª Lawrence	Miller		-	5	10	- Yeoman Cavalry
W.ᵐ Monkton	Thetcher	Wife	6	5	8	- Serv'd Personly
Tho.ª Foot	Blacksmith	Wife	1	5	11	- Serv'd by Substitute
W.ᵐ Hill	Labourer	Wife	2	5	5	- Provisional Cavalry
Sand.ˡ Gifford	Labourer	-	-	5	6	- One Eye
W.ᵐ Gifford	Labourer	-	-	5	5	- Great Neck
Cha.ª Lawrence	Labourer	Wife	7	5	10	
Geo. Still	Labourer	Wife	4	5	7	
Steph.ⁿ Tucker	Labourer	Wife	4	5	11	
Steph.ⁿ Spicer	Carpenter	Wife	4	5	6	
Jo.ⁿ West	Butcher	Wife	6	5	11	
Jos.ⁿ Richards	Labourer	Wife	2	5	8	
Phil.ᵖ Dibben	Labourer	-	2	5	8	
Jn.º Dibben	Labourer	Wife	1	5	7	- Balloted and Refus'd
Geo. Dibben	Labourer	Wife	3	5	5	
Ja.ª Lawrence	Labourer	Wife	2	5	6	
Arthur Baker	Taylor	Wife	1	5	10	
Jn.º Tanswell	Servant	-	-	5	6	
Tho.ª Plowman	Labourer	-	-	5	5	
Tho.ª Ruttley	Grocer	Wife	-	5	7	
Jos.ª Still	Labourer	-	-	5	4	
Jn.º Wareham	Labourer	-	-	5	5	
Joshª Lawrence	Miller	-	-	5	8	
Isaac Still	Labourer	-	-	5	4	
Jos.ª Feltham	Labourer	-	-	5	4	
Tho.ª Feltham	Labourer	-	-	5	10	
Jn.º Foot	Yeoman	-	-	5	9	
Ja.ª Gifford	Labourer	-	-	5	1	
Geo. Hayter	Labourer	-	-	5	7	

Nº 14

If any Person thinks himself aggrieved by having his Name inserted in this List they may make their Appeal on Thursday the 22 November now Instant at Swan Inn in Sturminster Newton After which Day no Appeal will be heard

Charles Davis Tithingman

In this militia list for 1798 the men's names, ranks, occupations, family details and size ('as near as maybe' was the criterion) were noted. Exemptions and Infirmities are given as One Eye, Great Neck, Served by Substitute, etc. Other infirmities could include Having the Evil, Withered Leg, and Subject to Fits.

16
Workhouse to Welfare State
1833- present day

The closer we come to the present, with the tradition and practice of constitutional monarchy well established, the farther the acts of individual sovereigns recede from the sphere of interest of the local historian. The coming, finally, of universal suffrage has made the elected governments the central and representative power in the land. This is not to say that the opinions and wishes of the sovereign are of no account, but that the individual is no longer the ruler.

The present chapter spans more than one hundred and fifty years and the lives of six monarchs. When Victoria came to the throne there was no internal combustion engine, no widespread use of electricity, no wireless transmission of sound, no telephone, no nuclear weapons, no AIDS. In the time since 1833 the world has, in material senses, been transformed. In Britain there have been great advances, through legislation, in industry, agriculture, town and country planning, public safety and other fields — many of distinct interest to the local history researcher. The impact of all the wars — particularly that of 1914-18 — has left marks on the parochial scene.

The onward rush of material progress and prosperity means, in unbiased terms, that in the second half of the reign of Queen Elizabeth II even the now desperately poor would, in Victorian times, have been regarded as moderately well cared for, even fortunate.

Researchers who wish to give more than passing reference to the national scene are well served by the three final volumes in the *Oxford History of England* series. The first, *The Age of Reform* by Sir Llewellyn Woodward, has been mentioned in Chapter 15. The other two are *England 1870-1914* by Sir Robert Ensor (Oxford, reprinted 1980), and *English History 1914-45* by A.J.P. Taylor (Oxford 1965). Ensor's book has long sections on 'Economics and Institutions' and 'Mental and Social Aspects', conveniently divided into the periods 1870-86, 1886-1900 and 1901-14. The manner of sub-division and the presentation of the subject matter are both ideally suited to the needs of local historians for gaining wide perspectives into which more limited material may be set. The book by A.J.P. Taylor, dealing as it does with the war and inter-war years at the highest level, is probably of less value to the parochial historian. It should not, however, be ignored and it may be noted that the bibliography has been updated to include work published up to 1973. The books mentioned on pp.635-7 of Taylor's book may be of special interest. The two final volumes in the *Pelican History of England* are shorter than the *Oxford* books, but of slightly later vintage. They are both by Professor David Thomson, the distinguished Cambridge historian, and are entitled *England in the Nineteenth Century* (1950) and *England in the Twentieth Century* (1965). Each is of value in the gaining of historical perspective.

Because of the range of material to be covered the remainder of this chapter will be divided into two parts and a number of individual sections. The first part deals with the years 1833-74 (precisely those encompassed by the penultimate volume of *English Historical Documents*, Vol.12 Part One — *EHD12/1*— by G.M. Young and W.D. Hancock, published in 1956). The second part covers the years 1874 to the present. The final work in the *English Historical Documents* series (*EHD12/2*), by W.D. Handcock, was published in 1977 and deals with the period 1874-1914.

The period 1833-74

The high Victorian period was the one in which England's influence on the world was greatest, and that which witnessed a significant transformation of society — the important move from agriculture to industry as the basis of national prosperity, and the application of science and engineering to manufacture and transport. It also saw important legal measures affecting national and local government, poor relief, education, public health and industrial conditions.

Local government

The greatest issues of the day were the proper financing of the counties and the towns, and the relief of poverty. These were followed by the recognition of the need for proper policing. *EHD12/1* has, on pp.617-18, details of a number of books devoted to these subjects.

During the period 1834-68 various Select Committees reported on fiscal issues. In 1834, for example, the committee suggested 'that in every County a Finance Committee should be appointed ... Estimates for every year should be submitted by the Treasurer of the County to the Finance Committee ... [and] discussion of Estimates for future Expenses should take place in open Court.' This type of sentiment set the scene for the Committees of 1850, 1868 and the Goschen Report of 1870. Details of the uses to which the money generated might be put was a matter of considerable discussion and the reader's attention is directed to pp.619 *et seq* in *EHD12/1*, which give extracts from official reports and comments. In 1835 a report by the Royal Commission on Municipal Corporations led to an Act of Parliament (published in *Statutes of the Realm V and VI* William IV), which stipulated how boroughs and towns should be governed by Watch Committees, and how these bodies should be appointed and operate.

So far as effective policing is concerned the County and District Constabulary Act is important. This, in 1839 (*Statutes of the Realm II and III* Victoria), set up a general structure under a Chief Constable and in 1842 was followed by the Parish Constables Act. The text is printed in part in *EHD12/1* (pp.652-4) and in full in *Statutes of the Realm V and VI* Victoria. The Act directed how parish constables should be appointed, how they should operate, and how paid. It also directed the manner in which the local lock-up should be funded, managed and inspected. The actual office of parish constable is, of course, of great antiquity, and readers interested in this special aspect of local history may care to refer to *Amateur Historian* Vol.I No.11 (1954) for an article on the subject by Dr G.H. Tuping.

Coleshill model farm, built in 1852 for the earl of Radnor. This ambitious project included barns, granary, rick-yard, tramways, cutters, choppers, gravity-fed effluent disposal and livestock feeding, and much more.

Many previous chapters of this book have commented on the problems associated with easing the burdens of the poor, and have paid attention to the relevant various pieces of legislation. In 1834 the first of a series of Poor Law Commission reports set in train a sequence of events designed to overhaul the existing systems and to remedy some of their defects. There is an ever increasing mountain of literature on the subject, from contemporary official papers to modern interpretation. A 'select bibliography' appears on pp.695-6 of *EHD12/1*. There is little doubt that the dedicated or determined local researcher will want to study the text of the original reports, and these were officially published as the *Report on the Administration and Practical Operation of the Poor Laws* (12 volumes, *Parliamentary Papers 1834* Vol.XXVII to XXXIX, the *Report* itself being in Vol.XXVII and the Assistant Commissioner's reports in the succeeding books). Less specialist researchers may be satisfied by the extracts given in *EHD12/1* on pp.697-747, together with relevant commentaries.

Of special interest are the workhouse rules on 'dietaries' — bread, cheese, gruels, suet puddings, broth, meat, but a total absence of fruit (p.710) — and the general order rules (p.725).

Censuses of population

Although censuses of population had started in 1801 and had been conducted at ten-year intervals thereafter, it was not until 1841 that names of people were recorded. Prior to that time the numbers of people in each parish were collected, together with crude classifications of occupations. These returns are of some interest to local historians but perhaps of more value to genealogists. From 1851 places of birth were given, and some details of physical and mental handicap also appear — blind, deaf, dumb and lunatic — and it follows that the data are of great value to a local researcher in constructing a model of the community as it existed in 1851, 1861, 1871 and 1881. Information gathered after 1881 is not yet published, but specific points may be raised with the Registrar General (see Addresses, Appendix III).

Industrial conditions

It is generally accepted that industrial conditions during this period were both appalling and chaotic, and much attention was given to their improvement. An excellent background appears in the *Oxford History of England* volume by Woodward, and the reader's attention is drawn to the 'Introduction' (pp.916-30) in *EHD12/1*. The bibliography on pp.931-2 of that volume is of value, together with the excerpts from Hansard and parliamentary papers which follow it, the writings on early trade unionism being frequently of relevance, as are the data on the employment of women and children. Reference should also be made to *Sources for English Local History*, specifically pp.122-63.

The period 1874-1914

The year 1874 saw the coming to office of Benjamin Disraeli, together with a powerful majority which, on the domestic front, concerned itself with major social issues, and these continued to be of importance to subsequent administrations up to the outbreak of the Great War in 1914.

Local government

The period saw two important local government Acts — those of 1888 and 1894 — complete texts of which are in *Public General Statutes LI and LII* Victoria C41 (for the 1888 Act which deals with county councils, boroughs, the Metropolis and certain special counties), and *LVI and LVII* Victoria C73 (for the 1894 Act which covers parish meetings and parish councils, guardians and district councils). Researchers in the London area may consult *Public General Statutes LXII and LXV* Victoria C14 for the Act of 1899, which deals with the establishment of metropolitan boroughs. Extracts from the texts are also printed in *EHD12/2*, p.465 *et seq.*

For an understanding of the structural basis of local government and the constitution of parish councils the texts of the Acts are essential reading. The coming of the legislation of 1894 meant that written records of management of parishes became formalised and are in the vast majority of cases extant, either in the care of the local record office, or in the custody of the parish (or other) clerk. These records are of great value, not only for the light they throw on local government but on all manner of other things. A very brief instance may be cited from the author's own parish: (1895) 'The ratepayers and inhabitants in parish meeting assembled hereby accord the Revd R. Burdon their grateful thanks for the great interest he shows ... by carrying on the schools free of expense to the inhabitants of the parish.' (The schools were purchased by the county in 1919 for £775.) Read with care, the minutes of parish council (and parish) meetings assist in the development of quite comprehensive pictures of parish life from 1894 onwards — the rise and fall of families, the impact of all the wars, the

In this 'cottage industry' the family is making brushes on the piece-work system. The scene is Bethnal Green in the late 19th century. It was sometimes necessary to work up to eighteen hours at a stretch.

relevance of social and local issues all find their places. Occasional reference may also be found to greater events such as the raising of money for the Transvaal Fund to finance the war in South Africa in 1899-1901.

Education

The study of education on the local scene is inextricably bound up with the measures and advances taken and made at a higher level. General reading matter is identified on pp.493-5 of *EHD12/2*, and reference should also be made to the appropriate volumes in the *Oxford History* series. The Elementary Education Acts from 1870 onwards established and perpetuated secular and undenominational schools. These schools substantially replaced the earlier forms of establishment — the Common Day, Dame, District, Industrial, Factory, National, Ragged, Workhouse and others which had come into being in prior years, details of which may be found in works in the bibliography in *EHD12/2*. Enquiries made at the appropriate county hall will unearth a mass of material for the researcher, and the texts of Acts 'expedient to make provision for the education of children, and for the securing of parental responsibility in relation thereto' will also be readily available at local level.

On the subject of adult education there will be a wealth of data in the local studies collection in the major public library in the county. The nineteenth century saw much energy put into the education of the adult poor — from the establishment of national bodies such as the Adult School Movement of the Quakers, to the Workers' Educational Association (founded in 1903), to the 'reading room' set up in many a village hall. The literature is vast, but a good starting point is *Local History of Education in England and Wales: A Bibliography* by P. Cunningham (London 1976), and this may be augmented (over the whole field of education) by the extensive references in Chapter 7 of *Sources for English Local History* by W.B. Stephens (Cambridge 1981).

The relief of poverty and improvement in health

The coming of the modern era, ushered in by the later manifestations of the industrial revolution, better roads and advances in medicine, saw what may be described as a revolution in public and ministerial attitudes to poverty and, later, public health. The sectional Introductions (pp.535-43 and 605-11 of *EHD12/2*) are sound bases on which to work, and the pages which follow them contain many extracts from relevant documents, all of which illuminate the attitudes of senior politicians, influential private individuals, government inspectors, charity organisations and authors, to the various problems posed by poverty and sickness.

Although well-fed and decently clothed, the inmates of this almshouse in 1893 were dressed in 'uniforms'.

There were a number of pieces of official legislation seeking to attack the problems. On the subject of poverty there was the Unemployed Workmen Act of 1905, the Old Age Pensions Act of 1908, and the great National Insurance Act of 1911, all of which appear in the texts of the *Public General Statutes* for the years in question. The Public Health Act of 1875, the Artizans' and Labourers' Dwellings Improvement Act (appropriate to large towns) of the same year, the Factories Act of 1891, the Housing and Town Planning Act of 1909, and other measures all sought to alleviate problems of public health. The texts of all these are also to be found in the pages of the published *Public General Statutes*. At local level the diligent local historian will find much of relevance in county and other record offices and in the pages of the newspapers of the day.

The years after 1914

The years after 1914 are well within the living memories of many people. Lots of folk alive today will remember the parish as it was in the days of the First World War. Then later they will have seen the coming of main drainage and electricity in rural areas, the motor car, the telephone, effective refuse collection, the benefits of refrigeration in food preservation, and a whole host of life-enhancing medicines. But their memories are not always to be too much relied upon. Many works recommending that elderly inhabitants be interrogated (or gently encouraged to reminisce) do not suggest sufficiently strongly that everything they say should be checked. This may be done against the memories of other aged folk, against newspapers, parish records (including church magazines) and so on. Where such verification is not possible, the 'facts' should be reported in strictly qualified form.

On more general matters three books already mentioned will be of great service in assembling a framework into which local studies may be set. They are *The Parish Chest* by W.E. Tate (Cambridge, reprinted 1983), and *Town Records* (1983) and *Village Records* (1962), both by John West. At national level there is much of relevance in *A Social History of England* by Asa Briggs (Penguin Books, reprint 1986), which also contains a bibliography of work published up to 1986.

Local government

Perhaps the most important event of the period was the Local Government Act of 1972 which came into force in 1974. This set up a three-tier non-hierarchical structure of county council, district council (also known where appropriate as city or borough council), and parish council (also known as town council where relevant). The full text of the *Local Government Act 1972* (specifically Chapter 70) may be obtained from HMSO, or referred to in the larger libraries. *Local Government Administration* by Charles Arnold-Baker (London 1981) is a valuable, very detailed work. Following on from the 1972 Act, the Local Government Boundary Commission recommended the formation and naming of districts in the wake of an earlier Bill which had created new counties, changed the boundaries of others and eliminated a third group. The *Local Government Boundary Commission for England Report No.1* (HMSO, November 1972) has the text, but

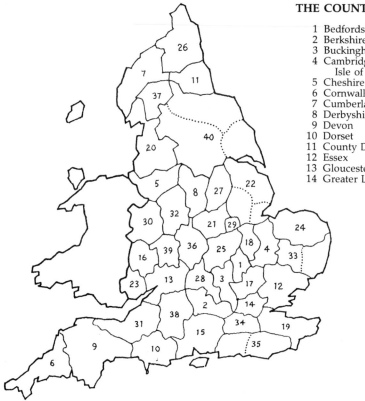

THE COUNTIES OF ENGLAND (pre 1974)

1 Bedfordshire	15 Hampshire
2 Berkshire	16 Herefordshire
3 Buckinghamshire	17 Hertfordshire
4 Cambridgeshire and	18 Huntingdon and
Isle of Ely	Peterborough
5 Cheshire	19 Kent
6 Cornwall	20 Lancashire
7 Cumberland	21 Leicestershire
8 Derbyshire	22 Lincolnshire (Holland,
9 Devon	Kesteven, and Lindsey)
10 Dorset	23 Monmouthshire
11 County Durham	24 Norfolk
12 Essex	25 Northamptonshire
13 Gloucestershire	26 Northumberland
14 Greater London	27 Nottinghamshire
	28 Oxfordshire
	29 Rutland
	30 Shropshire
	31 Somerset
	32 Staffordshire
	33 Suffolk (East and West)
	34 Surrey
	35 Sussex (East and West)
	36 Warwickshire
	37 Westmorland
	38 Wiltshire
	39 Worcestershire
	40 Yorkshire (East, North,
	and West Ridings)

THE COUNTIES OF ENGLAND (post 1974)

A	Avon	25	Northamptonshire
1	Bedfordshire	26	Northumberland
2	Berkshire	NY	North Yorkshire
3	Buckinghamshire	27	Nottinghamshire
4	Cambridgeshire	28	Oxfordshire
5	Cheshire	30	Salop/Shropshire
CL	Cleveland	31	Somerset
6	Cornwall	SY	South Yorkshire
CU	Cumbria	32	Staffordshire
8	Derbyshire	33	Suffolk
9	Devon	34	Surrey
10	Dorset	TW	Tyne and Wear
11	Durham	36	Warwickshire
ES	East Sussex	WM	West Midlands
12	Essex	WS	West Sussex
13	Gloucestershire	WY	West Yorkshire
14	Greater London	38	Wiltshire
GM	Greater Manchester		
15	Hampshire		
16/39	Hereford and Worcester		
17	Hertfordshire		
H	Humberside		
IW	Isle of Wight		
19	Kent		
20	Lancashire		
21	Leicestershire		
22	Lincolnshire		
M	Merseyside		
24	Norfolk		

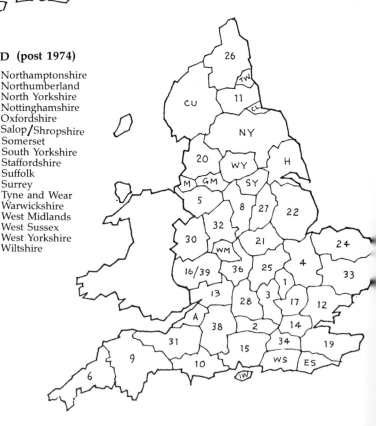

194

the reader should know there have been hundreds of modifying and clarifying documents since that date (all published by HMSO).

Specific questions regarding local government may be addressed to district councils, the National Association of Local Councils (see Addresses, Appendix III), or the county Community Council (whose address may be obtained from the county council office).

Parish layout

Since 1914, and particularly since 1945, the physical layout of hundreds of parishes has been drastically changed. In some cases, as in Plymouth, Bristol and Coventry, the war-time devastation caused by bombing created new opportunities for development. In other urban centres the decline of traditional industries and the sheer age of some buildings has stimulated planners to design new schemes. In rural areas the 'discovery' of country living, the EEC regulations on farming, and other factors, have encouraged widespread development.

In every instance there will be, in the county or city archives, plans and written matter describing the developments which have taken place. They may take a little searching out, but will be worth the effort. It will at this stage be sensible to refer to the Structure Plan produced by the senior local council in accordance with Town and Country Planning Acts, for approval by the Department of the Environment. This plan will outline in some detail the possible 'future history' of the parish and will include maps. It must, however, be borne in mind that everything is subject to change. The Structure Plans *are* only plans, but are, nonetheless, very valuable as source material.

The relief of poverty and improvement in health

In modern decades these issues have been largely removed from the list of responsibilities laid on parishes as administrative entities, and are dealt with by government departments. This does not mean that the local researcher is totally lost for material. On the subject of poor relief an important question is the uses to which the incomes from such things as 'poor lands' charities are put now that the Department of Health and Social Services (DHSS) has overall responsibility, and volunteer organisations are manifold. In matters of health, the change from the family doctor to the group practice may be relevant and worth studying. Both issues may be addressed through the use of local records and from discussions with people associated with them.

Education

A valuable local study is the impact of the 1944 Education Act on the parish school or schools. It may be recalled that, among other things, the Act reorganised elementary education and established new grades of schools, raising the school leaving age to 15 years. It followed the legislation of 1918 which had raised the age to 14. Still later changes, up to and including those still envisaged, may be discussed with senior officers of the local education authority who are almost without exception willing to help genuine enquirers. Also for the modern period many references to valuable material appear on pp.224 *et seq* of Stephens' *Sources for English Local History*.

195

The two World Wars and the local scene

Before 1914 the principal impacts of foreign wars on the local scene had been the disappearance of some of the men to the battlefront, and the raising of money to finance the conflict. After that date the effects were much greater. The demands of modern methods of warfare required the setting up of armaments factories, the intensive production of foodstuffs, and that women change their traditional roles to work on the production lines and staff public services. The stories of the Land Army, the Home Guard and all the other home-based services are part of local history. So too are the depredations wrought by the Zeppelins and, some three decades later, by the Luftwaffe and the 'doodlebugs'.

Much of the raw material needed is available on the shelves of public libraries — particularly in the local studies sections. There are, in addition, many good books giving background information, among them *The Deluge* by Arthur Marwick (London 1965) which tells of the social impact of the Great War of 1914-18, *The Phoney War on the Home Front* by E.S. Turner (London 1961), and *How We Lived Then* by Norman Longmead (London 1971). Additional material can be gleaned from *First World War* by K. Robbins (Oxford 1979), the *History of the Second World War* by Winston Churchill (now available in paperback), and *Problems of Social Policy* by R.M. Titmus (London 1950). Much of value can also be obtained from the local newspaper files of the day, and the first-hand stories of people who were alive during one or both conflicts.

Religion from 1833 to the present day

The subject of religious observance may be dealt with for the period as a whole, although the recent acceleration in the process of amalgamating Church of England parishes and the institution of team ministries may be worthy of separate study at local level.

At the beginning of the period, although Dissent was not a major issue, the Evangelical movement was gaining in influence and laying its greatest appeal in practical Christian living and devotion. The spread of Methodism and other non-conformist organisations is worthy of the attention of the local researcher and some interesting stories may be uncovered. In the author's own parish the Methodists, having obtained land on which to build a chapel, found that they were bounded on three sides by glebe acres over which the local rector held sway. That gentleman refused permission for any access over his land and the Methodist Chapel walls were built from the inside. A stone engraving over the chapel porch 'Persecuted But Not Forsaken' marks to this day their feelings in the face of the rector's attitude. Between 1851 and 1853 a number of census reports were published which may be of value. These appear in *Parliamentary Papers* 1852-3 (LXXXIX), and cover such items as church building, accommodation of worshippers, the rate of increase by decade of Wesleyan Methodists, Independents and Baptists. The essence of the data may be accessed in *EHD12/1* pp.339-98, and augmented by recourse to such books as identified on pp.337-8 in the same volume.

It must be said that the twentieth century has seen a great decline in attendance at Church of England religious services, although it is probably quite impossible to determine if this means present generations have lost faith in God or no longer feel obliged to be seen going to church and observing the outward signs of piety. Recent years have witnessed new editions of the Bible, revised liturgy, and new methods of training clergy, all of which may be reflected on the local scene.

At the general level, A.J.P. Taylor (*op cit* pp.168-9) is worth reading, and may be quoted (p.568): 'Makers of previous education acts [that is, pre-1944] had assumed that all schools could be counted on to provide religious worship without being told to do so. Education Acts were only concerned to ensure that the worship in schools, maintained by public money, was not denominational. The 1944 Act made religion compulsory for the first time ... Christianity had to be propped up by legislative enactment.' Taylor was writing *c.*1960, and since then other factors, particularly the immigration of non-Christian communities, have greatly influenced the local (and indeed national) scene. The modern religious histories of, say, Bradford and Bodmin, Woking and Walsingham could only be contrasted not compared, and can only be researched at local level from, predominantly, local records.

Conclusion

The material at the disposal of the researcher for the years 1833 until the present is so vast as to be overwhelming, and the temptation to overweight local history projects with the happenings of the last 150 years must at all costs be avoided. Nevertheless, a new road through a country area, bypassing a town for example, gives scope to investigate what was discovered during the excavations, what archaeological evidence has been destroyed, and how social patterns of communities have been affected in both positive and negative ways.

Section IV SPECIALIST TOPICS

17 Geological and geographical factors

Geology

It would be a brave, and perhaps foolhardy, person who ventured to say that geological factors have ever played an overwhelmingly important part in the choice of a site for permanent settlement. That is not to say that the local history researcher should ignore the subject. The kinds of crops which can be grown and harvested, and the types of industry and commerce which can be established, depend to a greater or lesser extent on geological features. The run of roads, the siting of bridges and the location of tunnels are all dependent on geological conditions. The materials used for houses, churches, indeed buildings of many kinds, depend on the mineral resources of the geological strata.

With a few exceptions (such as towns and settlements established to *exploit* coal, metal and other vegetable and mineral deposits), man has never looked much below the earth's surface when deciding the sites of long-term habitation. The skyscrapers of New York securely stand on the deep-seated bedrock of their foundations, but New Amsterdam (as it was called earlier) was settled without knowledge of the future needs and culture of a vast population and the type of architecture required to serve it. And so with London, with its great tower blocks which now dominate the skyline, overshadowing the works of Wren and his predecessors.

Geology in the widest application of the term is concerned with discovering the history of the earth, but the local researcher may need only regard those aspects of geology which merge into geography and history. In practical terms this means paying attention to physical geology (the study of the form of the earth's surface in the locality in question), and stratigraphical geology (the history of the relevant area through the investigation of the rocks and fossils it contains). The related subjects of cosmogony, petrology, and palaeontology can almost certainly be set on one side.

A good point of first general reference is the *Encyclopaedia Britannica* (11th edition onwards), which contains a valuable long article on the whole subject, and this can, if necessary, be followed up by reading some of the volumes mentioned in the extensive bibliographies which accompany the main text. It is also important to have at least a nodding acquaintance with the nomenclature adopted (and used in the British Isles), for many of the names are quite arbitrary, being geographical and derived from localities where the rocks and other minerals are well represented, or were first discovered.

To start at the beginning: there is very little point in attempting to put *dates* as we understand them to geological time — there is too much uncertainty. What has been possible, however, is to divide geological history into periods and to assign each a name and characteristics. This is best shown in a simple table:

Age (in millions of years) to base of:

	Quarternary	2
Cainozoic	Pliocene	7
	Miocene	26
	Oligocene	38
	Eocene	54
	Palaeocene	65
Mesozoic	Cretaceous	135
	Jurassic	200
	Triassic	240
Palaeozoic	Permian	285
	Carboniferous	375
	Devonian	420
	Silurian	450
	Ordovician	520
	Cambrian	580
	Precambrian	

The labels given to the 'ages' of the periods, Palaeozoic, Mesozoic and Cainozoic, mean *ancient, middle* and *recent* life, whilst Cambria was merely the Roman name for Wales. The first three terms are sometimes replaced by Primary, Secondary and Tertiary. Confusingly, the Tertiary period [of *Palaeocene* ('ancient') and *Neocene* ('new')] is further divided into Eocene ('new dawn'), *Oligocene* ('few fruits'), *Miocene* ('less new') and *Pliocene* ('more new'), according to the number of marine fossil organisms they contain. The terms are hardly exact. Within these periods, the names given to the geological formations and the rocks are purely arbitrary. For example, whilst *Devonian* is obvious as to its meaning, *Torridonian* comes from Lake Torridon in Scotland, and *Jurassic* from the Jura mountains. Some names are based on those of ancient places or tribes, such as Cambrian (already mentioned), *Ordovician* and *Silurian*, while still others come from the composition of the rocks themselves: Red Sandstone, Carboniferous (or coal bearing) and Cretaceous (from *creta* = chalk).

The reasons for the rough-and-ready names used in connection with geology lie in the pioneering work of the man who first classified the British rocks — William Smith (1789-1839). Smith, 'the father of British geology', was a canal engineer and land agent who produced a large coloured map of geological importance in 1815, showing the succession of stratified formations according to their fossil content. The names he coined for the different formations are largely descriptive of the characters of the rocks, and some have, in addition, geographical names such as Oxford Clay, Stonesfield Slate and Lincolnshire Limestone. Some, like Lias and Gault, are dialect words; others, like Lower Greensand and Magnesian Limestone, are descriptive; still others are old names in classical guise — Corallian and Callovian. In truth the system is chaotic, but it is time-honoured, used worldwide and now much loved by professionals.

Turning now to the geology of particular places, the *Encyclopaedia Britannica* includes in the description of each English county an outline of the underlying geological structure. At a more parochial level, those local historians whose counties have been the subject of detailed attention in the volumes published by the Royal Commission on Historical Monuments will find in the relevant volume, under the name of each individual parish, a very short statement along the lines: 'The parish covers almost 5900 acres; it lies on undulating ground which rises gradually from about 170 feet above sea level in the E to nearly 450 feet in the W ... The E and S parts of the area are on Oxford Clay, the W is on Forest Marble, and the centre is on a band of Cornbrash Beds,' or, 'A broad band of Corallian Limestone traverses the area [of the parish] from SW to NW; to the NW is Oxford Clay, to the SE it is Kimmeridge Clay.' In addition, the English Place-Name Society's later volumes contain geological maps of the areas they cover. These, although using general terms — 'mainly clay', 'alluvium and valley gravels', 'other formations' — give a useful, easily perceived picture.

Further enquiries may then be made to the Geological Society (see Addresses, Appendix III), the Royal Commission on Historical Monuments (particularly for those counties which have not yet been dealt with in published volumes), and the Ordnance Survey (see Addresses). This last body prepared, between the years 1835 and 1888, a 1-inch-to-the-mile geological survey of England and produced three kinds of map: *Solid* describing the nature of the rocks beneath the surface; *Drift* describing the surface only; and a combination series known as *Solid with Drift*. These are now being revised. In addition, HMSO publishes pamphlets entitled *British Regional Geology*, which have been prepared by the Geological Survey of Great Britain (later the Institute of Geological Sciences). In addition the following may be of value: *The Geological Map* by K.W. Earle (London 1936).

Geography

The science of geography is somewhat wider in scope than is sometimes thought, for it covers not only the study of the earth's surface and physical features but also its political divisions, climate, industry and population. The local historian, however, will be interested in three main things: what factors led to any particular town or village being established where it was, what was its geography in past centuries, what is its geography today.

The first question may not be easy to answer — early man built on hills, in valleys, on downs and open country, even in swamps, as recent studies in the Somerset Levels have shown. But it is a question worth addressing. Answers to the second point will depend on whether there have been any local archaeological studies, aerial surveys, early map making or the production of ground plans. The third issue is easily address-ed by simple perambulation and observation.

There are numerous volumes on the geography of English villages and towns, and many will be of value to the local researcher. An excellent starting point is with the books in the 'Archaeology in the Field' series, published between 1975 and 1979. These are listed in the reference books sections in this chapter.

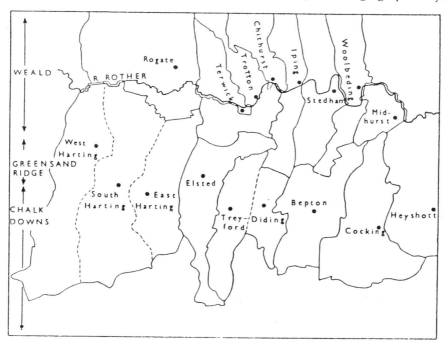

Parishes in Sussex related to villages sited on crossing points on the River Rother, or on the spring line at the foot of the chalk escarpment. Later parishes, south of the river, break the original regular pattern.

The geography of villages

In *Medieval England - An Aerial Survey* by M.W. Beresford and J.K.S. St. Joseph (Cambridge, 2nd edition 1979), the authors say: 'Villages [in early medieval times] were created in waves of colonization; the impetus for each was the acquisition of fertile land. Where field-land proved productive and easily augmented, villages grew and multiplied: where field-land was unproductive, villages remained small and widely scattered.'

A comparison of the large number of settlements mentioned in the Domesday Book, with the population distribution data from the same source, will show how thinly people were scattered and hence how dependent they were on local soil fertility and water supply. Very few places (except in Norfolk, Suffolk and Sussex) had more than twenty people per square mile, and the vast bulk of the country averaged about five inhabitants in the same area.

In pre-Conquest times, especially when colonisation was proceeding apace in the wake of the Romans' departure, it was only natural for men to band together for mutual support. The first imperative was defence — against other men, beasts and the hazards of nature. The second was staying alive by means of the cultivation of land and the herding and slaughter of animals for food.

The importance of an adequate water supply has already been touched on, for the survival of men, animals and crops. An important feature of the geography of a village is the run of its streams, the rising of its springs and the location of its ponds; in days when local fresh natural drinking water was vital, and the proper location of the

201

watermill essential, these factors were significant indeed, and such things are sometimes overlooked in local history studies. In the village in which the author currently lives a most interesting study involved not only confirming the present-day paths of the streams and brooks and the location of the ponds, but also where all the wells were situated. Much to most people's surprise there was a large number of indoor wells, some of which had been covered, some turned into 'features', and some still in service. When plotted on a large-scale Ordnance Survey map much new information was obtained (or rediscovered) regarding the location of underground streams. In addition a very useful hypothesis was able to be formed regarding the probable site of a medieval pottery ('cruckern') on the basis of adequate supplies of water, wood (for firing) and clay, and suggestions made regarding the location of the eleventh-century mill.

The true beginning of life in 'villages' must, however, be sought long before the post-Roman period. Ever since the Middle Stone Age, when man tended to become a settled farmer, a closely knit community was preferable to scattered farms for reasons already dealt with. From time to time archaeological investigation uncovers traces of Neolithic, Bronze Age or Iron Age settlements in pound or hill-fort form. Similar excavations have revealed considerable evidence of nucleated settlements dating from the Romano-British period — especially in lowland England. It is a fortunate local historian who discovers evidence of such early habitation on the sites he is studying, for all this evidence may be included in a subsequent narrative. There is little, if any, evidence to show how any one rural settlement changed over the succeeding centuries up to the Saxon, and precious few suggestions to indicate total continuity of occupation. There truly is no really satisfactory evidence on which hypotheses may be founded. It may, therefore, be far more practical to use Domesday geography as the starting point, with increasing certainty for the centuries following that date, and increasing uncertainty for the time before 1086.

For the Norman and subsequent periods an important feature in the determination and interpretation of village geography is the church. Many of our present churches survive from medieval times, and some can also be shown to stand on even earlier foundations or to incorporate pieces from previous structures. The village church was an important centre of congregation. In consequence, streets, paths, lanes and tracks led to it, and houses and hamlets thereafter followed in accordance with its location. The same considerations apply to the early village 'meeting' site, market place and fair. These were almost always close to, if not actually in, the churchyard, and may be presumed to have been so unless there is strong evidence to the contrary.

In rare instances there are villages with two churches and in such unusual cases there may be one of several explanations. The more usual answer is that there was once a much more scattered population necessitating an additional centre of worship, and the later settlement patterns obscured the original layout. In further cases an isolated church may indicate the desertion of an early village site in favour of a later. In extreme instances ecclesiastical conflict or disputed manorial seigniory may have brought a second building into being. The answer must be sought with great care.

Further geographical features of importance in medieval times were the manor house, grange, or tithe barn. It is a fortunate village that is able to pinpoint the location of these edifices with accuracy, and an even more fortunate one which has above-ground remains. Clues may sometimes be discovered in the names of ancient fields or in crop marks. As Beresford and St Joseph have said (*op cit*): 'If the owner of a manor house wished to rebuild on a different site he found fewer obstacles than did the patron of a church. If room was needed for more outbuildings or for ornamental gardens the manor house could be rebuilt in parkland away from the original site in the village. These migrations have sometimes left the old manor sites vacant and visible from the air.'

As will also be importantly noted in the next chapter, the Tudor and Stuart ages saw much valuable work being done by professional surveyors. These men recorded village boundaries, as well as the precise dividing lines between individual properties. The techniques employed in the sixteenth and seventeenth centuries were greatly in advance of the medieval practice of perambulating the peripheries. In former ages the men of the village had fixed the bounds by walking them and describing their journeys between important landmarks of trees, bridges, stakes, roads and so on. But time moved on, and changes in land ownership demanded more accurate records. A great many maps have survived from this period, and an important contribution can be made to local history studies by comparing them (scale for scale) with nineteenth- and twentieth-century maps.

In a specific case the author was able to obtain a true-to-scale copy of a late Elizabethan village map (showing field boundaries, field names and areas, road, drove and lane names, and equally importantly the location of every house and outbuilding), and a replica of a Victorian map (with data similar to the foregoing, with the single exception of the houses and barns), and compare them in very fine detail. These were then compared with a modern Ordnance Survey map, onto which had been written the present-day field names as remembered by older village folk. The degree of correspondence was remarkable. There was no surprise that the runs of the roads and lanes were almost identical (with some of the latter having fallen into disuse and become bridle ways), but in a total of more than 500 fields some 400 had the same boundaries on all three maps, and many other boundary changes were quite minor. Hedgerow dating studies in specific cases confirmed that the hedges were indeed ancient (several being much older than the date of the Elizabethan map) and, allowing for differences in orthography, the vast majority of the names were the same. Finally, and equally importantly, the locations of the Elizabethan houses were superimposed on the modern map to present a graphic picture of changes in village layout. As may perhaps be expected these were, in overall terms, also minor.

For the centuries after the seventeenth there is considerable information village by village — some places have gone into decline, some have been abandoned. Others have grown, especially since the Second World War, as the motor car and speedy communications have had their impact on local geography.

With the coming of the local government reorganisation of 1972 and the creation of district councils, together with remodelling of county councils, increasing emphasis has been placed on 'planning'. County Structure Plans have been produced and villages accorded places in a scale of priorities for development. In many cases the realisation of the plans will effect dramatic changes in local populations and geography. In some villages the number of houses will be significantly increased, even doubled or more. In the case of nucleated villages the boundaries of the inhabited areas will widen, in the case of more dispersed villages, of the 'polyfocal' type, infilling may even connect hamlets which have been separate for centuries. The increased demands for sewage disposal, leisure facilities, public transport and so on will dramatically affect village layout. The national and local press carry frequent stories of the way these latest development programmes are bringing in their wake the destruction of old smithies, ancient trees, nineteenth-century slaughter-houses, bakehouses and other features in the landscape. The opportunities for the local historian to record such things before they are forever lost are great indeed.

Reference texts – villages *Medieval England — An Aerial Survey* has already been mentioned. To this may be added two titles in the 'Archaeology of the Field' series — *Fields in the English Landscape* by Christopher Taylor (London 1975), and *Villages in the Landscape* by Trevor Rowley (London 1978). The published volumes in the *Victoria County History* and the *Inventories* of the Royal Commission on Historical Monuments, and *Deserted Medieval Villages* by M.W. Beresford and J.G. Hurst (1971), are relevant text books. A most important reference section is 'Sources for Topography and Early Settlement' in *Sources for English Local History* by W.B. Stephens (Cambridge 1981). The section points the investigator to books and articles on the dating of hedges, field patterns and other basic considerations of rural geography, as well as sources for county, estate, and other maps and plans.

The geography of towns

In his *Towns and Cities* (London 1966) Emrys Jones poses the question 'What is a town?' and demonstrates that the answer is not easy. Indeed a town is different things to different people. To some it is a kind of human society, to others a commercial and business centre, a physical layout of streets, houses, shops, offices and recreational areas. As for a city, it is enough to regard this as an important town and not to be too fussed for present purposes whether any individual one was created by charter or contains a cathedral.

It is a moot point as to when the first 'towns' were established in England. Examining the word itself, this descends from the Old English *tūn*, a word itself related to the Old Teutonic *tûnoz* ('hedge'). As A.H. Smith says in *English Place Name Elements* (Cambridge 1970), 'The precise meaning of *tūn* at any one stage is not easy to determine.' There are associated words (such as *tȳnan*, 'to enclose'), and it is obvious that over the centuries the term has evolved semantically from meaning a hedged enclosure, through a group of dwellings on enclosed land, to walled communities, to the present-day understanding of a body of citizens living in a locality and governed (at least in part) by an elected body of its residents.

Iron Age and Roman towns Professor Barry Cunliffe suggests (*Bronze Age Communities in Britain* London 1974) that pre-Roman hill forts may be 'regarded as the towns of the Iron Age', and recent discoveries in, for example, Hod Hill in Dorset, have shown that early settlement in that place was well-ordered, densely packed with houses (in the form of circular huts) and that there were several well-defined streets. He goes on to say that there remains 'an impression of a heavily built up urban complex as it would

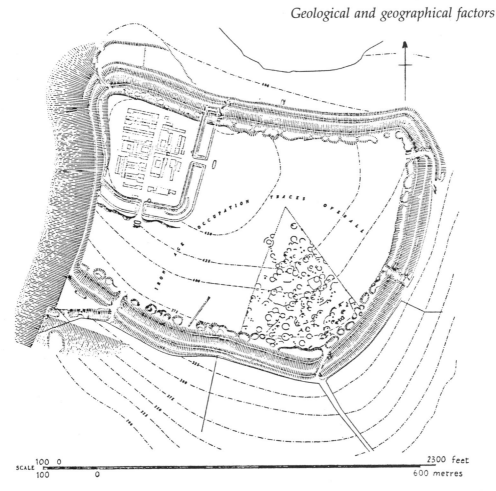

An Iron Age hill fort at Hod Hill, Dorset, its multiple ramparts enclosing some 54 acres. At one time densely packed with huts, it was, in Imperial times, the site of a Roman fort.

have been at the time of the Roman attack in AD43.' Hod Hill is by no means an isolated instance, nor were such embryonic towns unique to any one part of the country, or any one tribal area. Dr Cunliffe provides many examples and discusses the geographic layout of a number of communities.

During the years of Imperial domination many new towns were founded and existing settlements developed, and details of books devoted to the study of these are given at the end of this section. Roman implantations varied in size, character, purpose, and hence geography. A very good modern introduction to the period is *The Towns of Roman Britain* by John Wacher (London 1974). It contains many town plans, drawings of houses, villas and other buildings as well as numerous photographs. An important point to bear in mind is that the Romans occupied Britain for more than four hundred years. During this long period their needs changed, 'town planning' evolved, and there were social developments all of which had a bearing on the layout and structure of towns. Michael Aston and James Bond in *The Landscape of Towns* (London, paperback 1987) remind us that by modern standards Roman towns in this country were

205

small. They say, 'London, the largest, contained only 330 acres within its walls; Ciren-
cester, 240 acres; Wroxeter and St Albans, 200 acres each ... Brough-on-Humber,
centre of the Parisii, was just 13 acres. Everywhere regularity [in layout] exists it may
have been the result of replanning in the late first century, the final result falling far
short of original expectations. Except for the *coloniae* which were of military origin, the
shape of even the large towns was very variable, tending towards irregular ovals and
polygons rather than squares or rectangles.'

A valid aspect of local history research where modern towns include Iron Age or
Roman settlements is to plot, to a large scale, the successive geographical layouts, to
study points of difference and correspondence in great detail. The results can be most
revealing. In the case of Leicester (*Ratae Coritanorum*), for example, which was a
cantonal capital and developed over several centuries, there is no geographical similarity between the grid-like Roman layout and later town plans down to the present
day. With Gloucester (*Colonia Nervia Glevensium*), which was a foundation for army
veterans, the picture is quite the reverse — the lines of present-day main streets of
Southgate/Northgate and Westgate/Eastgate follow closely the lines of their Imperial
forerunners. Whether such coincidence (or lack of coincidence) is important is a quite
separate question, but no local history should be judged complete unless regard is
paid to the geography of earlier settlements.

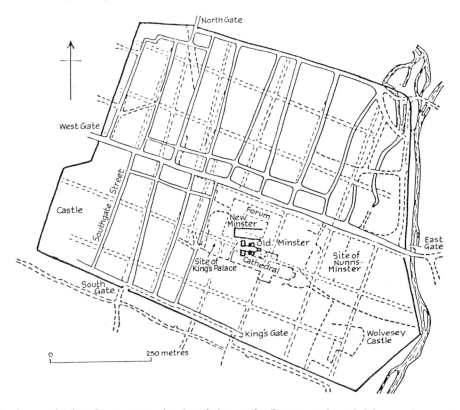

*Winchester: the late Saxon street plan in relation to the Roman roads and defences, showing that the
geography of the town remained essentially unchanged, although the earlier plan was more formal.*

206

Saxon and Scandinavian towns *The Map of Britain in the Dark Ages* (2nd edition 1974) published by the Ordnance Survey says, for the centuries from about AD400-900, 'During this period town life reached its lowest ebb.' It is apparent that during these years many towns were abandoned and some destroyed. The text goes on to say, 'The essentially rural pattern of Anglo-Saxon life postponed any revival for a long time. But knowledge of the old towns persisted. Some degree of travel must have continued along the lines of the Roman roads. These, if used at all, led to the sites of towns which in many cases were only waiting to begin a slow recovery.' And of course they did recover, particularly under the stimulus of the Scandinavian attacks of the ninth century. The need for an integrated network of fortified towns went hand in hand with genuine attempts to foster urban life. This will be mentioned again in the next two chapters.

For present purposes it is sufficient to recognise that the planting and growth of towns both in Anglo-Saxon areas and in the Danelaw could have been stimulated by a number of factors, and hence their geography varied accordingly. In one part of the country the primary aim was defence, in another the development of a market town, in a third a safe seaport, in a fourth an ecclesiastical centre. Each one of these principal considerations had a major effect on a town's layout and where, in some cases, more than one element was important (as in the instance where a seaport was also a thriving market and trading centre) the influence was even greater on the layout of the streets, the market place itself and the wharves and buildings of the port-complex.

Medieval towns According to Aston and Bond (*op cit*) there were created during the medieval period 'some four or five hundred completely new towns ... and an even greater number of rural settlements were promoted to borough status. Some of the elements making up medieval towns, particularly street plans and property boundaries, have survived to the present and provide the framework within which modern towns are accommodated.' In his book *New Towns of the Middle Ages: Town Plantation in England, Wales and Gascony* (London 1967) M.W. Beresford discussed a very wide spectrum of reasons as to why new towns were planted where they were. He excludes, however, 'promoted villages' and planned extensions to existing urban settlements.

In studying any particular medieval layout the local researcher should, therefore, investigate with great care the *type* of town which came into being, or grew on the site, during the period. Where geographical considerations permitted some new towns were planned on a fairly open grid system — Winchelsea and Salisbury are examples — others, such as Castleton in Derbyshire, on a more restricted grid layout. On rare occasions geography inspired totally unique designs. A particular case is Great Yarmouth, where the layout followed the spit of land between the sea and the River Yare. The reasons for siting a new town in a particular place may not be immediately apparent, nor easily determined, but they are things which need to be addressed.

In the same way it will be of great interest to examine the evolving geography of towns which were developed over a period of years and centuries during the medieval times. Simple answers are not always the correct ones, and mysteries may remain. In discussing a specific case Aston and Bond raise such questions as to why the town has two churches situated a long way apart, and why the town plan is, in effect, of 'hour-glass' shape. The questions which might be posed in such, or similar,

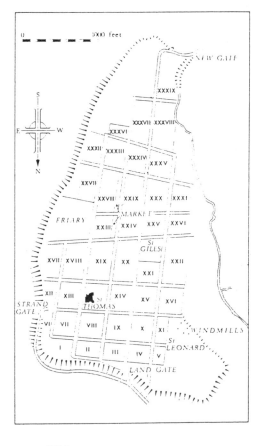

Winchelsea, Sussex. Old Winchelsea was destroyed by storms in the late 13th century, and a new town was built by Edward I on a plateau which permitted a street plan of elegance and simplicity. The diagram is based on a rental survey of 1292, the streets flanking 39 rectangles on which houses and other buildings were erected. The photograph permits a modern appreciation of the work carried out. Taken in 1967 it shows that although some thoroughfares have disappeared, and the town proper is rather smaller than in medieval times, the essential integrity of the king's layout has been retained.

situations, are: were there at one time two towns which later joined? or was there a development with an enlarged circuit of walls and a new church?

The subject of villages which became towns is also an intriguing one, and areas of successive geographical expansion well worthy of study, as is that of failed towns, which over a long period declined to villages or disappeared completely, leaving only earthworks or cropmarks.

Later towns The closer the local historian comes to the present day the more specific the topics relating to urban geography become. In the cases of modern plantation and development the whole story may be well documented — as in the cases of Milton Keynes, Skelmersdale, Welwyn Garden City, Crawley New Town and so on. For the centuries of the early modern era — Tudor, Stuart, Georgian, Regency and Victorian — the story of their geographical evolution will have to be pieced together from clues obtained from very wide reading indeed. To give but a few examples, the dominance of the eastern counties of England during the sixteenth century was an important element in the development of towns in that part of the country. The commercial revolution of the seventeenth century promoted many changes in urban layout and the facilities provided by towns. In Georgian and Regency times many towns grew in size. Defoe in writing of London described 'new squares and new streets rising up every day to such a prodigy of buildings, that nothing in the world does, or ever did, equal it, except old Rome in Trajan's day.'

In Victorian times urban populations increased dramatically, and most of the major provincial towns expanded in quite spectacular fashion. Many completely new towns were founded — sometimes they were well planned, often not, and depended on the interests of local commerce and trade for their layout.

The geography of any given town is a most absorbing subject, for if successive layers of development can be peeled away to reveal an increasingly clear picture of its growth or decay over a period of time, much will be learned of its people, their ways of life, their successes and failures.

Reference texts — towns *Medieval England - An Aerial Survey* has already been mentioned, as has *The Landscape of Towns* by Michael Aston and James Bond (London, paperback 1987), which is much to be recommended. This latter also contains a bibliography detailing works covering the period from the Iron Age to the twentieth century. In addition to the works noted above and in the *corpus* of this chapter, valuable essays will be found in the Ordnance Survey publications: *Roman Britain* (1956), *Britain in the Dark Ages* (1974), and *Britain before the Norman Conquest* (1973). *The English Medieval Town* by Colin Platt (London 1986) is also recommended.

18

Archaeological evidence

The bulk of this book concerns manuscripts and printed works which help to record the history of a town, village or parish, from Saxon days until the present. But these are not the only avenues open to researchers, for the things being studied are, after all, *places*, localities which exist in the here and now — physical, ever-changing human settlements which, were they merely forms of manuscript, would be palimpsests, erased and written on again and again, many times over. However, since places are *not* manuscripts, traces of previous usage are never quite erased, and linger on century after century as successive generations of men and women build their homes, pursue their destinies, live their lives and die. In towns and villages, houses hundreds of years apart can be seen side by side, cathedrals and churches many centuries old throw their spires skywards in competition with curtain-walled multi-storey office buildings and residential tower blocks.

The study of these ancient things, the buildings of bygone days, the layout of early towns, the settlement patterns of early villages, are as much the province of the archaeologist (and the historian) as are the excavation of vanished civilizations. It is true the *OED* defines the word 'archaeology' as 'the scientific study of the remains and monuments of the prehistoric period', and 'ancient history generally, the systematic description of the prehistoric period', but scholars in the field have gradually widened the practical application of the term until today there are many specializations including 'medieval archaeology' and 'industrial archaeology'.

Within such a framework the local historian can quite legitimately regard 'archaeology' as meaning the study of any aspect of the impact of man on the physical world, be it traces of the nomadic sites of neolithic people or the remains of Second World War deserted underground workshops. The classical archaeologist might regard the cut-off point as the seventeenth century, but his industrial counterpart can admit of no such limitation, for he would have very little of consequence on which to apply his expertise.

In *Local History in England* W.G. Hoskins wrote, 'every local history ought to begin with a chapter entitled *The Face of the Parish* or *The Face of the Town*, as the case may be', and this is an excellent idea, for although such a chapter would no doubt end with an account of present-day settlement layout, it will almost certainly begin with the evidence from the earliest possible period — evidence gathered by means of archaeological study.

Marston Magna, Somerset, a site rich in archaeological interest, and which, in post-medieval times, may have originated as a series of enclosures. The church 'A' contains Saxo-Norman elements; site 'B' is the deserted medieval village of Netherton; 'C' the site of a moated manor with fishpond.

	Third	150 B.C. - A.D. 43/85
PRE-ROMAN IRON AGE	Second	350 B.C. - 150 B.C.
	First	550 B.C. - 350 B.C.
	Late	900 B.C. - 550 B.C.
BRONZE AGE	Middle	1400 B.C. - 900 B.C.
	Early	1650 B.C. - 1400 B.C.
COPPER AGE		1850 B.C. - 1650 B.C.
	Late	2150 B.C. - 1850 B.C.
NEOLITHIC	Middle	2600 B.C. - 2150 B.C.
	Early	3000 B.C. - 2600 B.C.
	Late	5000 B.C. - 3000 B.C.
MESOLITHIC	Middle	7200 B.C. - 5000 B.C.
	Early	8000 B.C. - 7200 B.C.
ADVANCED PALAEOLITHIC		30,000 B.C. - 8000 B.C.
LOWER (& MIDDLE) PALAEOLITHIC		4/500,000 B.C. - 30,000 B.C.

The archaeology of a rural parish

With just a little, superficial investigation a local researcher can discover that at sometime in the recent past the uprooting of an ancient tree had revealed some neolithic stone tools, the running of a land drain had thrown up a broken portion of a Bronze Age bracelet, or the laying of a gas pipeline had cut across a Roman rubbish pit containing fragments of samian ware. But these are not necessarily occupation traces: the neolithic people were almost certainly nomadic, the piece of bracelet could have been dropped by an itinerant smith as he went his rounds, the rubbish pit might simply mark the line of march of a cohort of the *Legio II Augusta* on its way from a fort to the nearest town for rest and recreation. Such finds make an interesting couple of column-inches in the local newspaper, but they do not contribute very much to local history.

The archaeology of a parish can never be complete; its fields will always contain undiscovered treasures or its twentieth-century houses prevent the excavation of so far unsuspected historical remains, but a partial study can always be made on a logical basis.

Tracing the boundaries

The place to start is with the determination of old boundaries. The boundaries of civil parishes as marked on Ordnance Survey maps may be of fairly recent origin and may not be the same as the old ecclesiastical boundaries. In a way similar to the county boundaries enforced by parliamentary legislation in 1972, so nineteenth-century administrative procedures brought changes in some parish boundaries, particularly if the parish had been divided and comprised two separate parts, in which case one or the other piece was certain to be absorbed by the parish in which it lay, and the ancient boundaries modified.

A deserted medieval village at Angam in Yorkshire. The hollow depression running down the centre of the picture is almost certainly the high street and may end close to the village pond. The main centre of habitation appears to be shown in the top right quarter of the photograph.

The local historian has a personal choice to make — whether to work forwards in time or backwards. The present author has, in these circumstances, always preferred to work forwards. If the researcher is very lucky he will discover a Saxon charter in which the bounds are defined. The luck in question does not depend on the diligence of the seeker, but on whether a charter was ever granted. There are no more than some sixty-two such charters whose whereabouts are known, but most of them have been printed and details appear in *Anglo-Saxon Charters - An Annotated List and Bibliography* by P.H. Sawyer (London 1968). Most of the sixty-two define the bounds of specific parishes, but others (perhaps equally valuable) define the boundaries between contiguous parishes or, occasionally, between dioceses. If the bounds of the place being studied do not appear in one of these documents, and it must be admitted there is a high probability they will not, then it is sensible to look to monastic records such as the *Great Cartulary of Glastonbury* (which has been published by the Somerset Record Society), or the Forest Charter of Edward I granted in 1299/1300. In this latter work the bounds of a great many parishes are described in terms of perambulations and, even if difficult to follow on occasion, are very rewarding. The local historian should search in his county reference library for details of the whereabouts of printed versions of relevant sections of this and other charters for, over the years, archaeologists and historians have given such records a great deal of scholarly attention. In the original text the boundaries of a typical parish might contain such definitions as: 'from *Trehurne* on the south side of the wood of the bishop of Salisbury, leading southwards between the demesne of the earl of Cornwall, and the demesne of the abbot of Cerne,

213

then the old gate of *Hertelegh* to *La Rode* [this means a clearing or a 'ride' through a wood] then to *Staneweyesfote* [the 'stoney way'] then northwards to *Cockescruche* [Cockcross] then to *La Ruweston . . .*', and scholars have frequently translated these ancient boundary indicators not only into more readily comprehensible forms, but have identified their modern locations. The local historian should also bear in mind that there were perambulations in later times, and in some cases the data from these may be correlated with earlier information to obtain further boundary indicators. Again, discussions with local professionals will be most useful.

In Tudor, Stuart, and sometimes later ages, parishes (more strictly manors) were frequently surveyed at the direction of their owners. Many of these records have found their way into museums, but some are still in the hands of the descendants of the manorial lords of the day, or belong to private collectors. Details of the whereabouts of these maps, if known, may be obtained from the Royal Commission on Historical Manuscripts in London (see Addresses, Appendix III). In many cases the owners will allow access, and in some instances permit photographs to be taken. In a particular case the author was allowed to have a colour-washed map dating from 1607 (measuring some 8 by 6 feet) professionally photographed, the owner being not only a ducal descendant of the Jacobean lord but a noted scholar. The work was performed so accurately that a transparent overlay was made for direct same-scale comparison with a modern Ordnance Survey map, which enabled even the finest details of boundary changes to be seen. Both maps were then compared with the tithe apportionment map of 1838, and a very useful contribution made to local knowledge and county records.

The important purpose of ascertaining the run of both ancient and modern boundaries is to enable a personal perambulation to be made, and if such a tour can take place in the company of the county archaeologist, so much the better. The circuit may take some time — a typical parish confines may be ten or twelve miles in length, be partially obstructed by hedges and largely on private land — but it is well worth the making. Much will be observed from later investigation: earthen banks, back lanes, old drove ways, boundary stones, ruined walls of ancient buildings, intriguing crop marks, all of which can, if properly recorded, be of immense value during later phases of investigation. One such perambulation carried out by the author drove home an observation that the northern limits of the parish concerned comprised a series of fairly regular near-rectangular fields, the hedges of which 'dovetailed' into the neighbouring parish. Subsequent discussion with an archaeologist produced the tenable hypothesis that the two parishes were, in Saxon times, a single estate (of about twenty local hides in area). Having formulated the idea, later study of the position of the medieval 'home farm', grange, and church, together with ecclesiastical records, tended to confirm the suggestion.

The next stages

Having completed the perambulation, the next step is to seek out an authoritative volume in the *Victoria County History* series, or a relevant publication of the Royal Commission on Historical Monuments (RCHM). Where they exist, these books are of great value, containing information at parish level on geological, geographical and archaeological features of note by period — prehistoric, Roman and medieval —

traces of cultivation and earthworks, and so on. If such volumes have not yet been published there are, almost certainly, others of considerable utility.

This is not to suggest that all the work has already been done. An important study can be performed by comparing the twentieth-century information with that contained in the matching old county history published in the seventeenth to nineteenth centuries. These histories, often written by local rectors, vary in quality, but they do contain extremely pertinent items. In John Nichols' *History . . . of Leicestershire* (1795/ 1811) are details of a charter of 1448 whereby King Henry VI granted a certain man leave to establish a 300-acre deer park, the location of which is now forgotten. Nash, in his *History . . . of Worcestershire* (1781), also mentions a manorial deer park, the site of which is unknown. Dugdale's *Antiquities of Warwickshire* (1656) and Bridges' *History . . . of Northamptonshire* (1720/1791), detail 'lost' villages. Hutchins' *History . . . of Dorset* (1774) mentions several churches which pre-date by as many as four centuries the present buildings, leading to the questions of where were the old ones sited, on the present foundations or not? And are ancient fonts, corbels and other anachronistic features of the later churches incorporations from the previous structures?

Other old histories of value include: *The County Palatine of Durham* (1816/1840) by Robert Surtees; *Hertfordshire* (1870/1881) by John Cussans; *Nottinghamshire* 1790/ 1796) by Robert Thoroton; *Cornwall* (1769) by William Borlase (there is also a *Parochial History of Cornwall*, 1867/1873, by Joseph Polsoe); *Devonshire* (1793/1806) by Richard Polwhele; *Kent* (1797/1801) by Edward Hasted; and *Surrey* (1804/1814) by William Bray. If the student is very lucky he will also find more local volumes, such as *A History of Tetbury* (1857) by A.T. Lee, and *The Manors of Suffolk* (1905) by W.A. Copinger.

Thematic studies

Having thus gained a knowledge of the earlier and later boundaries and an appreciation of the generality of work already documented, there are a number of avenues to be explored.

In the current climate when country living has become popular, speculative developers are buying up old buildings and either changing them beyond recognition or demolishing them to make way for new structures. The local historian may, therefore, think it worthwhile to photograph the buildings which might fall into the speculators' ken. These may include the disused mill and its wheel, the old smithy, the bakehouse, slaughter-house, the Victorian schoolroom, almshouse, abandoned brickyard or sawmill, or an old derelict cottage, most of which will not have been mentioned in the Royal Commission's publications. There is, additionally, the splendid opportunity to investigate the reasons why so many of these buildings were built where they were, when they were built, and how long their functional life lasted.

Another useful study concerns local footpaths — not simply where they run (the Ordnance Survey map and a discussion with the county rights of way officer will determine this), but *why* are they where they are? Why do five footpaths meet in the middle of an ancient watermeadow? What buildings formerly stood on that site? Do the aerial photographs of the village yield any clues?

Almost every country parish church has its guide, describing architectural features: altar to aumbry, hagioscope to heraldic glass, *tas-de-charge* to tomb chest, a list of incumbents and their patrons, memorial tablets to bygone worthies. It is, however, a rare village that has a guide to its secular buildings. There are many villages in England which are of medieval origin, and thus have houses of great antiquity together with modern houses utilizing the latest materials and techniques in their construction. All may be worthy of attention but, within the context of this chapter, the old ones are particularly so. Local authorities have, at one level or another, with one title or another, an ancient buildings preservation officer, and there are few villages without listed buildings. A discussion with this officer will elicit all kinds of valuable information which, together with the paragraphs from the historical monuments books, will provide an excellent beginning to a research programme into local vernacular architecture. It must also be borne in mind that the London-based National Monuments Record (see Addresses, Appendix III) houses not only all the background information regarding all the items included in the published volumes, but manuscript data which did not find its way into print, and many photographs which have not been published. Copies of all these may be obtained on request. The Archaeology Branch of the Ordnance Survey should also be approached.

There are many other archaeological studies which can be undertaken: the structural evolution of any hamlets, the development of the farms, changing field sizes, shapes and land usage, to identify just a few.

A medieval encaustic tile from the floor of the Franciscan friary of Dorchester which was founded prior to 1267. Such tiles in dark clay with pale inlaid designs were widely used in religious buildings throughout England.

The archaeology of towns

Just as there are many kinds of villages, nucleated, polyfocal, pre- or post-Conquest, static, developing or declining, so there are kinds of towns. Both villages and towns are physical organic entities, but they are entities which came into being and evolved for different reasons, to satisfy different purposes, and their survival has depended on widely varying factors.

The origin and growth of towns is a complex subject, and although Professor Hoskins said as long ago as 1955, in *The Making of the English Landscape*, that the matter required a whole book to itself, recent advances in research and understanding have shown that a number of very different books might be written, the approach being

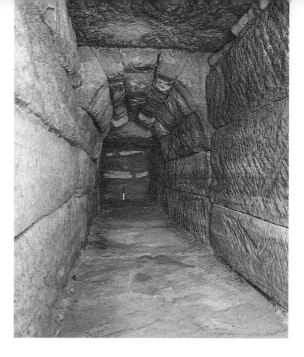

A length of sewer underneath the Roman fortress at York. Heavily built to withstand imposed loads from above, it was in part constructed of millstone grit blocks with limestone ashlars, the floor being of sandstone slabs.

thematic or chronological, social or environmental. Although there are still very few authoritative works indeed on the general subject of the English towns, there are a number, each of which is devoted to a single place, and many more given to specific subjects like *The Back-to-Back House in Leeds, The Origins of Southampton, The Georgian Buildings of Bath, The Medieval Defences of Shrewsbury, A Town Plan Analysis of Alnwick, Northumberland,* and so on.

This section of the present chapter will, therefore, be of a broad character, indicative of the type of investigation a local historian may make. Such studies will be of one of two kinds. The first will be practical and superficial — that is, of things on or at ground level. The second will be more academic, carried out in libraries and reading rooms, and will concern below-ground discoveries made in the course of excavations of a deliberate, archaeological kind, or for some other purpose which, quite incidentally, unearthed remains of value.

Without any doubt the first thing for a local researcher to determine is when did the first settlement take place on the site which is now the town (or urban parish) he is studying, for on this will depend the direction of his future work. Some towns began in Roman times, some in Anglo-Saxon (mainly the later period, after the Dark Ages), a third group comprises medieval towns, those in a fourth category developed substantially as a result of the industrial revolution, and a fifth as 'garden cities' or 'new towns' in the twentieth century. These last are hardly the subject for archaeological study, although the concept of such developments had been discussed in the nineteenth century, as witness *Garden Cities of Tomorrow* by E. Howard (1898).

Equally as important as the topic of when was a settlement founded is the two-part question of why and how. 'Why' may not be easy to answer, for initially the decision may have been for military reasons not now apparent, or for commercial advantages which in the event were of a temporary nature. For later centuries the subject is not so difficult — deliberate planning in an unoccupied area to accommodate an ever-growing workforce, a good road system being opportunely exploited to found a new centre of trade, an abundance of raw material permitting the building of new manufacturing complexes. The question of 'how' is answered by isolating those factors which permitted survival, and from the very earliest Roman towns to the very latest contemporary 'landscaped' urban centre, the overwhelmingly important thing is a proper water supply. The significance of this cannot be overstressed, for not only is a supply of good water necessary for the more obvious needs of everyday life, but it will have an important bearing on soil conditions and hence fertility. This latter is not so important today, of course, with modern transport and food preservation methods able to ensure adequate food distribution; but in early periods, poor or ill-drained soil meant poor crops and strictly limited populations. Nowhere is this more apparent than in the well-known case of the city of Salisbury in Wiltshire. The great prehistoric fortress of Sarum expanded to become the important Roman centre of *Sorbiodunum*, and by the middle of the sixth century had evolved and developed into *Searesbyrig* ('dry town'), the home of the kings of Wessex. In 1075 it became the seat of a bishopric. By the thirteenth century the wells had begun to run dry, and for this and other environmentally related reasons the town of New Sarum (New Sarisbury, Salisbury) was founded some two miles to the south, and granted a charter as a 'free city' by Henry III in 1227. The ancient town, by then 'Old Sarum', decayed and its walls were finally demolished *c.*1608.

A somewhat similar story may be told of Exeter, which in Iron Age times was the site of a Dumnonian settlement. This was followed by a Roman occupation (*Isca Dumnoniorum*), and some authorities give the title 'town', even 'city', to the place. By medieval times problems were so acute that there were water carriers selling water of dubious quality door-to-door, and it was only in later centuries that techniques for the construction of piped water supplies ensured the city's stability and growth.

Given that there were adequate water supplies, there are many other physical features involved in the siting of towns. The author's home city of Bristol is a fine example of the part a great tidal river with a wide estuary can play in a town's development. A further important requirement of the very earliest towns was that the place at which they were sited should be defensible, and this is particularly true if the term 'town' is allowed to include the more complex hill forts of the pre-Roman Iron Age. Barry Cunliffe suggests, in *Iron Age Communities in Britain* (London 1974), that some of these larger forts, densely packed with huts and with well-defined 'streets' were the 'towns' of their period. The forts and oppida which occupied these sites were larger than is sometimes thought. An important settlement of the Catuvellauni at Colchester in Essex, for example, was not in fact on a height, but nonetheless comprised a central habitation complex surrounded by a defensive system of linear dykes and ditches, the total area covering some twelve square miles of land.

Roman towns

There are dozens of Roman towns in England, ranging from the great centres, the *coloniae* of Gloucester, Lincoln, York and Colchester, through the cantonal capitals, the lesser walled towns, spas and other substantial settlements, to minor habitation groups and enclosed villas, if one allows a little latitude in terminology. And it is not only the present-day urban historian who will be fortunate enough to find an Iron Age or Roman 'town' within his area of interest. The author, living in a small rural village of some 625 inhabitants, has both a Durotrigean hill fort settlement and a quite separate Roman villa complex within his local boundary of interest. It must, however, be admitted that it is the town historian rather than the rural who will be able to show continuity of habitation. If the researcher indeed has an early Roman occupation site to study — and these can range from Lanchester and Carlisle to the Isle of Wight (as described in the *Atlas of Roman Britain* by Barry Jones and David Mattingley, London 1987) — a most fruitful line of approach is to try to trace the influence of the earlier layout on the later. Is the *forum* still the site of the market place? Is the *basilica* anywhere near the present town hall? How many stages of Roman development were there? Does the present street pattern bear any relationship to the one laid out by the Empire's engineers? Is the site of the Romano-British cemetery still used for inhumations? The potential topics are numerous. As Ashton and Bond ask, in *The Landscape of Towns*: 'How much of Roman Britain are we seeing without realising it?'

Anglo-Saxon, Mercian and Scandinavian towns

In the early eleventh century London was the most important city in England, followed by York which had by the seventh century become the capital of Northumbria. The Saxons had been slow to establish towns. Before the ninth century they appear to have lived mainly in urban centres founded by the Romans, but in time new foundations were laid — Oxford, Lewes, Hastings, Wilton, Bridport, Langport, Malmesbury, to name but a few — and some grew in size because gradually they became homes to monastic bodies, cathedrals or defensive establishments. As is the case with localities with Roman connections, there is ample scope here for specific archaeological studies of the relationships between earlier and later settlements, and the effect one had on the other. A particular instance concerns the city of Bath which, in addition to being a great Roman centre (*Aquae Calidae, Aquae Sulis*), was three times destroyed by fire. Some studies of this nature have, of course, already been carried out. A further case in point concerns Winchester, where surveys and maps exist comparing the late Saxon street plan with the Roman road layout, and much excavation done on the sites of the old ministers, the kings' palace, the castle and the Roman forum. But there are still plenty of opportunities even in the former Wessex capital. The same comments apply to the ancient towns of the kingdom of Mercia — Worcester, Hereford, Gloucester, Shrewsbury, and the capital at Tamworth — where defensive works, grid plantations and property boundaries can be shown to still have an effect on the geographical layout. Nowhere is this more so than in the towns which were *burhs* (essentially, fortified strongholds).

North of the Danelaw boundary towns were created, or adapted, when successive waves of Scandinavian invaders established Danish Viking and, later, Norse Viking petty kingdoms. The Five (Danish) Boroughs of Derby, Leicester, Lincoln, Nottingham and Stamford were of great importance. Nottingham was a new foundation based on an earlier village. Stamford ('stone ford') replaced the Roman Great Casterton as a local centre, and then in later medieval times became home to the extensive tournament ground. The foundation of Derby actually took in the more ancient Anglian settlement of Northworthy.

Throughout England in pre-Conquest times towns were founded, rose in importance, declined in some cases to mere villages, or grew and were incorporated into modern conurbations. Much work remains to be done, for example on the study of Saxon and Danish market places, and it is believed that many are yet awaiting discovery. What was the relationship in layout terms between the market place, the monastic precinct, the parish church, and the early street plan? The local historian has much to contribute, particularly if he restricts his studies to the boundaries of a town *parish* and, in the written account which follows, traces the successive layers of habitation in a degree of detail greater than would be possible in a more wide-ranging investigation.

Medieval towns

It is unlikely that the Norman Conquest, which started in 1066, appeared to the native population to usher in a new era of prosperity, but with the advantage of the historical perspective of the twentieth century it is quite apparent that the new rulers brought with them new methods, ideas and initiatives. Between the time of the defeat of Harold and the coming of the Black Death in 1349, almost five hundred new towns were founded, and many of the older towns took on new vigour, and expanded. With the coming of modern scholarship various theories have been put forward as to why new towns were established where they were, and differentiation has been made between towns of older foundation which evolved and those which were deliberately founded on new sites, but the local historian need have little truck with these *esoterica*. Indeed many of the simplistic explanations can, with detailed study, be shown to be wrong. The reasons for the creation of new towns in either category were quite certainly multi-factoral, and the criteria themselves are frequently open to different interpretations depending on the thesis being expounded. Professor Beresford, in *New Towns of the Middle Ages* (London 1967), explores the deliberate establishment of new towns in England, Wales and Gascony, on previously unoccupied sites, and makes many points of importance to the local historian, not the least of which is the need to differentiate between commercial and strategic reasons to explain the initial decision to build. The last word has not been said by any means. For example, although Beresford says that by 1967 no medieval 'plantation' evidence had been found in Worcestershire, research in later years has indicated such possibilities in at least eight places, including Evesham, Halesowen and Bromsgrove. There are undoubtedly other finds waiting to be made, both in that county and elsewhere. The question of planned 'extensions' is also worth exploring, as is the incorporation of former villages, monastic institutions and other settlements into the scheme of things, the towns thus becoming ones which grew 'organically'.

A vital point which must not be overlooked is that whatever the apparent reason for a town's beginning or growth, factors of mere geography and geology (excepting a good water supply) were almost never paramount. Somewhere along the line a powerful baron, or group of merchants, said something like, 'this matter is to our advantage, this is where we shall build.' Only when this point has been fully explored is the local historian really ready to go on to other equally intriguing and important subjects such as street plans, market sites, linear or grid layouts, property limits, town walls and defences, castles, mints, monastic properties, parish churches, suburbs and the like.

Bury St Edmunds, Suffolk. Originally a village in which, in AD908, the bones of St Edmund had been laid to rest, 'Boedericesworth' grew in medieval times, and in the centuries following the Conquest a new borough took the form of a series of north-south streets parallel to the west front of the abbey precinct.

Post-medieval towns

If it is accepted that the battle of Bosworth Field and the death of Richard III in 1485 brought the medieval period to an end, then this is a convenient point at which to begin to discuss towns of more modern development, for the Tudor dynasty brought a new initiative, especially in things commercial. This does not mean, however, that during Tudor, Stuart and subsequent periods (excluding the present) there were any further *major* foundations. What there was, essentially, was expansion, in places like Norwich which attracted Flemish weavers, and Bristol's trade with the New World, but this is not the whole story, as Chapter 19 shows.

Examination of early town plans will be of great value to the historian trying to make sense of town growth from the time of the Tudors onwards. At the beginning of the sixteenth century most towns in England contained considerable open space within their boundaries, and development from then on was by infilling on town fields, building on monastic acres which had become available after the Dissolution, and by subdivision of burgage holdings. It is sometimes difficult readily to distinguish between old and new work. In Bicester, for instance, infilling carried out in the seventeenth century is of a type almost identical to the medieval buildings. Towards the middle of the seventeenth century Italian ideas of town planning were introduced, initially by Inigo Jones, and the concept of the *piazza* took root, especially in London where re-layout was greatly facilitated by the Great Fire which destroyed about 80 per cent of the city — but London is a special case. In many towns brick construction became the hallmark of the wealthy houseowner, timber (and sometimes stone) remaining symbols of poorer and older dwellings. In any case, such instances as the appalling fires of the sixteenth and seventeenth centuries in Dorchester, Nantwich, Northampton and Warwick led, perhaps indirectly, to the use of wood being banned. The parish researcher thus needs to be very aware of the *history* of his chosen territory, using documentary evidence of all kinds, and employing this information as a reference framework against which to carry out any *archaeological* studies. It is at this point that the old county histories come in useful. Most of them include invaluable descriptions for ready comparison with present-day layout, and the investigation of intermediate development: 'This west gate was taken down in the year 1776 ... and it appears from an ancient drawing that one angle was surmounted by a lofty turret ... the space between Westgate-street and the bounds of the ancient city northwards, is filled by three avenues, or lanes ... at the top of which is a street running parallel ... and extending from the Northgate to the northwest angle of the wall ... the vestiges of which are still discernable.'

New ports were established, or existing ports expanded. Deal is a case in point, in which an old fishing village was developed at the initiative of the local community; Devonport, Falmouth (Pennycomequick), Whitehaven, Plymouth are other instances; and 'resorts' were created — Tunbridge Wells, Epsom (of therapeutic 'salts' fame), Hampstead; and watering places like Brighton and Bognor (not yet 'Regis') became famous and grew in size. All this activity provides valuable data from which the local writer may choose his themes. In the later eighteenth century the establishment of industry was a crucial factor in town growth. The basic processes of coal production, and metal mining, and the conversion industries of coke manufacture, smelting, metal foundry work, textile, and pottery making, all helped shape the faces of the towns, as did the marketing of agricultural produce. The industries left factory buildings, warehouses, and acre upon acre of workers' dwellings in their wake. Many have now gone, and written records must be relied on, but others have not — they have been converted into shopping arcades, art centres, theatres and 'desirable residences', and their stories may be uncovered by diligent research, not least in the newspaper columns of the day.

In Victorian times, the greatest influence on town development was the railway industry, the construction and maintenance sheds, the marshalling yards, the workers' homes, the lines and the stations themselves. Swindon in Wiltshire, now a centre of twentieth-century electronic and support industries, still remains essentially three towns — 'Old', 'New', and 'Railway' Swindon — and is still called so by the older

Fishwick Cotton Mill near Preston was demolished in the first decade of the 20th century, and belonged to Swainson, Burley & Co. It was regarded as one of the wonders of its day and is on record as being '7 storeys high, 158 yards long, 18 yards broad', and contained '660 windows and 32,500 panes of glass'.

inhabitants. The work of such bodies as the Society for Improving the Conditions of the Labouring Classes has no place in this chapter (it is touched on elsewhere), but the results of their efforts in housing development are well worth attention.

Industrial archaeology

The study of the premises, plant, equipment and processes such as those mentioned in the preceding section provides a valid field for the attention of the local historian. In some cases information will be found in books already published, but the bulk of these will have been written by social or economic historians, each in his own way seeking to interpret some aspect of society.

By far the more fruitful sources of information for the researcher are the companies who are the successors to the organisations and individuals who pioneered the industries. The local museums will have photographs, journals, even work books and catalogues, but the companies themselves will have archivists (under some title or other) who will be the custodians of information of value. The present author has

223

obtained a great deal of raw data regarding the woollen industry by accessing the eighteenth-century records maintained by an insurance company, most of which had not seen daylight since the reign of George III. Older established companies in the iron, steel, woollen, textile, printing and other industries have on the appropriate occasions published centenary volumes containing all manner of useful information, and often have drawings (and, later, blueprints) in their files describing their early premises. The libraries of the great engineering and industrial professional institutions should also be searched — the Institution of Mechanical Engineers, The Royal Society, The Royal Society of Arts; and such modern creations as British Coal, British Gas and the Electricity Generating Board are all normally very helpful in the face of serious enquiries. Then there are bodies like the successors to the Mersey Docks and Harbour Board.

But it is not only the local historian in the potteries, the great steel towns, the textile centres, the coalmining areas or the large ports who has the opportunity to study industrial archaeology — the cottage industries of the rural areas fed important local centres, and every parish historian has a part to play, however limited, in its exploration.

Reference books

General and landscape

Whilst there are, no doubt, many important workers in the area of archaeology applied to local history, two outstanding writers on the subject are W.G. Hoskins and C.C. Taylor. Dr Hoskins was Hatton Professor of English Local History at Leicester University and was one of the great pioneers in developing the methodology of the disciplines concerned, and raising their academic status to higher degree level. Hoskins' *Local History in England* (London 1959/1972) contains several chapters on archaeological fieldwork which were later expanded into a full-scale volume, *Fieldwork in Local History* (London 1967/1982), the second edition of which contains a long bibliography by C.C. Taylor. The book starts with an introduction to fieldwork, followed by specialized chapters devoted to Anglo-Saxon landscapes; fieldwork in medieval history; towns and villages; houses, farmsteads, hedges, walls, roads and lanes; the book ends with a penetrating valedictory. Hoskins' *The Making of the English Landscape*, first published in 1955 and reprinted and revised several times since, traces the history of landscape from before the English settlements up to the present time. It includes rural and urban landscape, the impact of the later enclosure legislation and the industrial revolution.

Christopher Taylor is on the staff of the Royal Commission on Historical Monuments, and is the author of a number of books relevant to this chapter: *Fieldwork in Medieval Archaeology* (London 1974), outlines preparation for fieldwork, discovering sites in the field, recording and interpretation in the field, discovering and interpretation of sites by documents, and the publication of fieldwork; *Fields in the English Landscape* (London 1975) discusses the subjects of prehistoric, Roman, Saxon, medieval open and enclosed, and seventeenth-century fields, the age of parliamentary enclosures, and modern fields; *Roads and Tracks of Britain* (London 1975) deals with prehistoric trackways, Roman, Saxon and Dark Age, medieval, post medieval, and modern roads and tracks. It is well illustrated in both half-tone and line, and contains a glossary. A further, very well illustrated, general book is *Archaeology in Britain Since 1945* by Ian Longworth and John Cherry (London 1986).

Trees and Woodland in the British Landscape by Oliver Rackham (London 1976) is the work of a Cambridge botanist in the discipline of the history of ancient woodlands and their management. The book is of particular interest to local historians researching villages (or towns) in what were anciently chases and royal forests. A point made strongly is the part trees played in the definition of village boundaries, as witness a document from AD901: '... then in a straight line to the pear tree ... then along the road to Withy ['willow'] Grove ... then along the road to the pollard oak ... and from there to the wood ... by the little hedge along the spinney ... from there to the hoar ['lichen covered'] apple tree ...'. (Students of more general history will also perhaps recall that Harold Godwinsson's English soldiers gathered at Colbec Hill between the Andredsweald and the Hastings isthmus, at the 'site of the hoar apple tree', as a prelude to their great battle in 1066, but this is a slight digression.) Dr Rackham's book is quite basic to the local historian's appreciation of the part woodland and timber played in the siting and development of villages. A further work by Oliver Rackham is *The History of the Countryside* (London 1986), an expanded version of his *Ancient Woodland* published in 1980. In the new volume Rackham repeats in a more informal fashion much of his earlier material, and adds excellent chapters on hedges, grassland, roads, ponds, heaths, and other features. The time-frame chosen is from about 4000BC until around the end of the seventeenth century. Later periods are touched on, but the emphasis remains with the 'ancient countryside'.

The Archaeologist's Handbook by Jane McIntosh (London 1985), and *The Penguin Dictionary of Archaeology* by Warwick Bray and David Trump (London, 2nd edition 1982), are useful basic reference texts.

Villages

Village and Farmstead by C.C. Taylor (London 1983), subtitled 'A History of Rural Settlement in England', starts with the beginning of settled habitations in prehistoric times and ends with a chapter on the modern landscape. *Villages in the Landscape* by Trevor Rowley (London 1978) covers the form and fabric of villages as they have evolved from early neolithic settlement sites, through the high points of the eighteenth and nineteenth centuries, to what the author terms the 'decline' of the twentieth. There is an extensive bibliography. *The Village and House in the Middle Ages* by Jean Chapelot and Robert Fossier, written in French and published in 1980, appeared in English in 1985. The book draws on archaeological information gathered from continental countries with which the English had ancestral and cultural affinities and, in addition, trading connections. It takes, therefore, a wider view than more insular treatises and is able to compare similarities from many nations to point generalities — examples are fossilized medieval plough marks in Holland, and thirteenth-century enclosure walls at Stannheim in Germany, the construction of which throws light on English practice of the day. The authors are, respectively, an historian and an archaeologist, hence the content ranges widely, the chapter on medieval building materials and techniques being particularly valuable.

The Lost Villages of England by Maurice Beresford (London, 1986) is a classic study of villages which, for one reason or another, have been abandoned — in some cases after more than six hundred years of continuous habitation. Beresford describes the locations of very many villages, and discusses the reasons for their depopulation. The book contains aerial photographs, ground plans and maps illustrative of typical sites, and a gazetteer giving listings by county, with map references for identification. Together with his *Medieval England* (written in collaboration with J.K.S. St Joseph, and noted more fully in Chapter 2 herein), the work is a most important source of ideas and a factual account of actual sites.

Towns

A good starting point is the section of Hoskins' *Local History in England* dealing with both the topography of urban areas and their social and economic history. There is also a chapter on fieldwork, and some notes on the drawing of plans. *The Landscape of Towns* by Michael Aston and James Bond (London, reprint 1987) is a useful book devoted wholly to urban centres. It is laid out in the conventional way (period by period) and each section is a lucid exposition of the criteria affecting the development of towns in the period under discussion. The book ends with a long bibliography, which gives details of publications dealing with individual towns. *The Making of English Towns* by David W. Lloyd (London 1984) contains many maps, town plans and photographs.

Industrial archaeology

A book of fundamental worth is *The Making of the Industrial Landscape* by Barrie Trinder (London 1985). The rise of industrial England in the eighteenth century was marked by the introduction of new manufacturing processes, the application of power-driven machinery and vast workshops devoted to spinning, weaving, iron founding, engine building and many more tasks. Coal mining became a basic industry, and the nineteenth century saw the growth of the railway network. The new endeavours changed the landscape, for in the wake of the industrial revolution came vast town developments, sometimes affecting whole regions. Dr Trinder's text is augmented by a large number of illustrations, and the local historian writing of the 'dark Satanic mills' of the eighteenth and nineteenth centuries will find both to be useful guides. Two further books of note are *The Techniques of Industrial Archaeology* by J.M. Pannell (London 1974) and *Elementary Surveying for Industrial Archaeologists* by H. Bodey and M. Hallas (London 1978).

A final word

The subject of archaeology appropriate to this chapter has many books devoted to it. There are many specialist areas, and the reader is recommended to study *The Material Heritage* section of the Phillimore Bookshop catalogue (see Addresses, Appendix III) for details of the hundreds of works published in recent years.

Soldiers manning a burh. From an early 11th century manuscript.

19 The evolution of towns

In the course of Chapter 17 a very brief indication was given of the importance of geographical factors in the siting and development of towns. This present chapter now affords an opportunity to explore the subject of evolution of towns in a little more detail, due regard also being given to the social and administrative structures as well as the purely physical.

As was seen earlier, there are some authorities who believe that in this country the 'town' had its beginnings in the hill forts and oppida (see section below, 'Roman towns') of the Iron Age. For most local historians the study of these settlements will form part of the work they are doing in *rural* districts, for it is in such localities that many may now be found. Nonetheless, there is evidence that an oppidum lies beneath present-day Canterbury, another under Rochester, and still further tribal settlements beneath the later Roman towns of Silchester and Winchester. Fortunately local archaeological societies publish details of explorations in these and other actual (or suspected) early proto-urban sites, and it is to such societies, and the county council, that the local researcher should refer; he may find drawings and diagrams showing the layout of the settlements in question. It is, however, very unlikely that there will be much evidence that these pre-Roman centres had any influence on the layout and development of later towns on the same sites.

The same cannot be said of the Roman period itself, and it is from those centuries that the natural processes of the development of urban life in England can be traced.

Roman towns

There is little or no agreement between scholars and students of the Romano-British period on the subject of the number of types of towns established in Britain. In much the way that we use the terms metropolitan borough, city, large town, municipality, market town or urban conurbation without precision, so did the writers of antiquity use a number of words to describe the urban sites of their day. These may be listed as follows:

Civitas A word in essence meaning 'citizen', but employed to describe communities in which the inhabitants were essentially non-Roman. Examples of civitates (broadly, the capital sites of British tribes during the period) are Canterbury, Chelmsford and St Albans — *Durovernum Cantiacorum*, *Caesaromagus* and *Verulamium* respectively.
Colonia Normally the term given to towns inhabited by people of Roman (or Latin) origin, frequently retired soldiers. Examples of these are York, Gloucester, Colchester and Lincoln. Such towns were governed by charter.
Municipium A term used to describe towns, also governed by charter, which housed people of varying status. Scholars have tentatively assigned *municipium* status to Dorchester (Dorset), Leicester, London and Wroxeter among other places.
Oppidum A word used loosely to describe a fortified native 'town'. Examples may be Selsey, Silchester and Stanwick.
Urbs Broadly meaning 'city', the word was used to describe large *oppida*, but there is little precision in the term and it has not uniquely been applied to any Roman town in Britain.
Vicus is also a quite difficult word to define — it was used to refer to districts, estates, centres of towns, villages with nearby forts, and so on.

The lack of true exactness in all these terms is a problem the local historian must face, but in endeavouring to achieve precision of terminology for a particular place at different times during the Roman centuries, much may be learned about the function and evolution of the town in question.

The degree to which the layout of a modern town corresponds with any part of that of the Roman which may have lain on the same site is a matter for individual study, and the question of lack of correspondence will raise that of discontinuity of occupation and re-establishment at a later date. This is not to say that specific reasons for abandonment are easily assigned, if at all. War, famine and pestilence may have played their part, but the precise stimuli, their cause and duration may never be known. A valuable commentary occurs in the chapter 'Town-life or life in towns?' in *The Towns of Roman Britain* by John Wacher (London, reprint 1981), and the reader is referred to the book as a whole for the descriptions of dozens of Roman urban settlements. We are left with the certainty that Roman Britain contained numerous walled towns of medium size, and some six or eight large ones. By and large they were well sited, but there remains little doubt that most, if not all, were desolated by the barbarian Germanic intrusions of the fifth century, and it was not until the seventh century that some began slowly to revive.

Anglo-Saxon and Scandinavian towns

The Roman era was followed by what has been called, even by serious historians, the Dark Ages, and during these centuries, up to about the early seventh, town life reached its lowest ebb.

The origins of Saxon towns are complex, for there were numerous different, and occasionally antagonistic, forces at work. Sometimes the forces were religious, at other times defensive or warlike, at still others commercial, and each was reflected in the layout of the town itself: within a quite restricted geographical area one town might have a fortress, another a market centre, a third an ecclesiastical focus.

According to sources contemporary with the period, three types of towns were recognised: the *ceaster*, meaning a town founded on a well-established Roman site; the *port* or commercial market centre, often by the sea but not always so, for some 'ports' are known to have been well inland; and the *burh*, almost without exception a fortified place.

As early as the seventh century, examples of *ceasters* were London, Canterbury, Rochester, Winchester, York, and Dorchester-on-Thames, each the site of religious see and based on an old Roman town. Monastic foundations such as those at Gloucester and Bath were also located on former Roman sites. So far as *ports* are concerned, these were innumerable and ranged in size from, for example, Southampton (Hamwich) on the coast, to the tiny inland market town of Sturminster Newton (Newentone). The subject of the *burhs* is a most interesting one, for these fortified places came into existence mainly in response to the need for a defensive system against the Danes. In fact a network of fortresses was built in the south of England, during the reigns of Alfred the Great and his Saxon successors. A royal memorandum from the time of Edward the Elder (899-925) lists the West Saxon *burhs*. Known as 'The Burghal Hidage', the document records the number of hides of land assigned to ascertain the length of the defended walls. Several scholarly works on the subject of the memorandum have appeared: 'The Burghal Hidage — the establishment of a text' by D.H. Hill in *Medieval Archaeology* 13 (1969), 'The unidentified forts of the Burghal Hidage' by N. Brooks in *Medieval Archaeology* 74-90 (1964), and others listed at the end of this chapter. *Burhs* included Warwick, Worcester, Lewes, Axbridge and Wareham.

As has been suggested, some towns were more or less created as the seats of bishoprics or adjacent to monastic foundations for purposes of trade and husbandry — Winchester, Bury St Edmunds and Peterborough are examples of such, and their layouts as pointers to generalities are worthy of study.

Elsewhere, in the southern Danelaw, and in Mercia which had, in effect, been destroyed by the Scandinavian invaders, there is evidence of *burhs* in Gloucester, Hereford, Chester and Shrewsbury. In the major areas of the Danelaw considerable urban development took place. Perhaps the most generally known area of the north Midlands — the land of the Five Boroughs of Leicester, Derby, Nottingham, Stamford and Lincoln — was the subject of varying influences: Nottingham was a new foundation and an important centre of trade; Derby, too, was new and incorporated an earlier Anglian settlement; Stamford was almost a new creation with a well defined 'plan' based on a 'high street' and subsequently developed in the late Saxon era. Leicester and Lincoln were old Roman sites and the Scandinavians seem not to have made much impression on the layout of these two places. Derby and Nottingham, together with the pre-Conquest layouts of Cambridge, Huntingdon and Northampton, are worthy of study for insights into the development of towns during the critical tenth century years. Cambridge, for example, developed as a commercial town and 'port', and Northampton, originally a Danish military centre, also expanded after its capture by Edward the Elder in 918. The multi-themed development of towns in the Anglo-Saxon period has been dealt with by a number of scholars, and some of the more pertinent articles and books are detailed at the end of this chapter.

Medieval towns

Between the year of the Conquest and the middle of the fourteenth century nearly five hundred completely new towns were created, and hundreds of villages and small rural settlements expanded and were granted borough status. The ambition of any community with urban aspirations was to obtain a charter to hold a market — for with this the possibilities for the material success and wealth-gathering by its inhabitants were greatly increased.

A number of simplistic hypotheses have been generated to explain the unprecedented expansion in urban growth, and early medieval towns have been divided into the categories of those deliberately founded or 'planted', and those which developed from existing settlements and 'grew organically'. Again, a number of erudite texts have been prepared on the various elements of the hypotheses, and some of these are noted later.

In their *Visions of the Past* (London 1983) Christopher Taylor and Richard Muir ask (p.245): 'What did the towns of medieval England look like? In many ways it is easier to generalize about the smaller and less successful creations than about the urban super-stars, where clues may survive in street patterns but where detailed proof can only be obtained through excavation.' And this, of course, is the problem in places where continuity of habitation has been maintained over many centuries. Early in the Norman period military considerations were of paramount importance in the planting of new towns, and the kings themselves played important roles in deciding what, and where, to build. Significant work was carried out in the reign of King Edward I — Winchelsea, planned on a major grid system, although never actually completed belongs to this period, as do Kingston-upon-Hull and Berwick-on-Tweed. To a marked degree a regularity of plan — the grid pattern — was a feature of these fresh sites, compact blocks of streets and houses, sometimes, as in the case of Devizes, with a castle, in others with defensive walls and ditches and entrances protected by solid gates. *Medieval England - An Aerial Survey* by M.W. Beresford and J.K.S. St Joseph (Cambridge 1979) has a valuable chapter on the 'planned towns' 1066-1307, and includes analysis and descriptions of Bury St Edmunds, Boston (Lincolnshire), Hedon (Yorkshire), Launceston, Pleshey (Essex), Chelmsford (which developed from a small Domesday agricultural manor), New Buckenham (Norfolk), Brackley (Northamptonshire) and Baldock (Hertfordshire). This last was a foundation of the Knights Templar who, in giving it the name *Baudoc* ('Baghdad') obviously wished to create a thriving trading centre. They never quite succeeded.

To return to an earlier theme, royal patronage was no certain guarantee of success, and the local historian has a fruitful field for study should a failed new town lie in the district of his investigations. Two examples are Newton in Dorset, which was founded in 1286, and Warenmouth in Northumberland, which was established in 1247 and had disappeared by Tudor times.

The market place at Cambridge. Although the original market may have been located elsewhere, it is likely that the present site has been in use since Norman times.

There remains a great deal of work to be done not only in the study of these medieval plantations, but in their very identification. As has been mentioned, Beresford (*op cit*) reported that no such towns had, up to 1967, been found in Worcestershire; yet since that date at least ten locations have been identified, although some may yet be shown to be planned extensions rather than entirely new beginnings on virgin land. Such planned additions were by no means uncommon in the period under review, and district names such as 'Newtown' in Bristol or 'Newland' in Pershore and Banbury indicate localities and themes for study. An equally important and rewarding field of investigation is that concerned with the upgrading of villages to town status — what Taylor and Muir call 'bids for urban stardom' — and the physical development of these, often based on a market, sometimes occurred in distinct and separate phases, as may be evidenced in Swindon, Brackley, and Stratford-on-Avon. Sometimes the bids for stardom failed, as in the cases (among many others) of Ripley near Harrogate, or Snitterfield in Warwickshire. The subject of medieval town plan is one which, in the past few years, has received a great deal of attention from professional archaeologists and historical geographers, and much has been written and published. A useful starting point not only for terminology but also for a good introduction remains Aston and Bond's *The Landscape of Towns*, which deals with relevant matters under the headings: street plan types — open triangular or irregular market places, defended castle-boroughs, undefended linear plan, grid plan, unique plans, composite plans; and, within the above elements, the market place, streets and lanes, and property boundaries. Other features such as monastic precincts and parish churches, and their place in medieval urban layout, are also discussed.

Tudor and Stuart towns

The visitations of the Black Death between 1348 and 1369 saw the end of major urban progress in medieval times. Queensborough on the Isle of Sheppey, founded complete with castle in 1368, was, with Bewdley in Worcestershire, the last new foundation for some two hundred years.

With the coming of the Tudor dynasty, however, and the growth in England's material prosperity, there came a great stimulus to the urban centres as foci for trade, commerce, and business in general. The outstanding development of the age was the growth of London. By the middle of Henry VIII's reign it had outstripped by more than tenfold its nearest provincial rival and thus is a very specialist subject for historical study, beyond the scope of *local* history. The same cannot be said for other towns, for their rises, and sometimes falls, come well within the scope of such research. The fluctuating fortunes of York, Norwich, Bristol, Exeter, Worcester, Newcastle-on-Tyne, and other major provincial towns, are worthy of investigation (even if much has already been done) not least for the effect such thriving places had on the countryside immediately surrounding them. In smaller towns, too, much of significance was happening as trade and local industry expanded.

Of special importance in the wake of the new prosperity was the institution of urban markets or, in some cases, the revival of markets which had fallen into desuetude or had actually lapsed. Such foundations were as far apart as Blackburn and Stevenage and the student is recommended to 'The Making of Some New Towns *c*.1600-1720' by C.W. Chalkin, in *Rural Change and Urban Growth 1500-1800* (C.W. Chalkin and M.A. Havinden, London 1974).

Equally significant was the creation of new seaports. The first of these was Falmouth (so named by Charles II in succession to the earlier name of Pennycomequick, just prior to receiving its charter in 1661). Whitehaven came, and Deal, each as a result of individual or local communal enterprise. On occasion, military and naval considerations were relevant, as is certainly the case with Chatham and Devonport, and Portsea next to Portsmouth.

Industrial considerations played a somewhat smaller part in urban development. Many industries were, of necessity, still rural — wool, food production, tanning and such — but increasingly industry demanded larger labour forces and mutual co-operation; and these in turn meant a speeding up of the urban congregation of labour — Halifax in the wool trade, and the assemblage of dwellings around clothiers' establishments in places like Stroud, and, for lace making, in Honiton. In the Midlands the metal-working industries stimulated growth in Wolverhampton and Dudley, among other places. The industrial development of Tudor and Stuart times is a rewarding subject.

At the centre of this 17th century map is Petworth House, the chief residence of the earls of Northumberland from 1574 to 1632. The town was first mentioned c.AD791 in a grant by Eardwulf, King of Northumbria; centuries later it became notable as the 'gateway' to the great house. It has many Tudor and Jacobean buildings in an intricate complex of narrow streets around a tiny market place. The classical town hall dates from the 18th century.

It is pertinent to quote Aston and Bond (*op cit*) in their conclusions regarding the evolution of towns in the sixteenth and seventeenth centuries, that there began 'a divorce between the character of the town and that of its local surroundings, and a much greater uniformity in towns across the country ... and new notions of town planning gaining the ascendancy.'

Georgian and Regency towns

During these Hanoverian years the development of towns went on apace. Few new towns were created, for by the standards and practice of the day most of the more attractive sites had been taken. What dominated the period was the creation of urban landscapes on Classical lines, the vision often being that of a local merchant who employed architects and builders inspired by the bygone worlds of antiquity. In spa towns such as Bath, Cheltenham and Leamington, crescents, squares, and circuses with broad avenues and streets were laid out in magnificent profusion, and sometimes delightfully augmented by the inclusion of old castle sites, such as was the case in Wisbech.

The foregoing, however, represents just one end of the social scale, that at which the upper-middle classes imposed their own visions on the landscape for the betterment of themselves and their peers. At the other end of the scale, urban expansion meant working-class slum quarters crammed into whatever spaces were deemed available and suitable. 'Blind back' housing became a tradition, particularly in the industrial towns like Leeds, Liverpool and Nottingham. To begin with these houses were well constructed, and although they backed against a boundary wall they did not represent a serious blot on the urban landscape. They were, however, soon succeeded by the back-to-back pattern, with houses sharing a common rear wall, and these developments were soon a regular feature of the poorer areas of the three towns just mentioned, and others — for example Birmingham. A useful text on this subject is *A History of Working-Class Housing* edited by S.G. Chapman (Newton Abbot, 1971).

Domestic buildings, however poor or grand — and with the introduction of stucco and ornamental ironwork some became very grand indeed — should not be the only ones to attract the attention of the local researcher. The building of customs houses, town halls and assembly rooms also had an important influence on urban layout and the appearance of town centres. Baroque features with ornate pilasters, statues and carved facades made their appearance; and Palladian styles introduced by Lord Burlington, John Wood, Robert Adam and William Chambers became a vogue. Churches too had an important bearing on the subject of urban layout in these times, and their locations and environs are worthy of investigation. For example, in Manchester in the forty years ending with 1795, no fewer than six new churches were built, and in half that time four were erected in Cheltenham. Styles varied from Baroque in Birmingham to near Palladian in Derby, and the Gothic Revival could be seen in Warwick and Shrewsbury, each expression having its effect on the locality. So, too, with industrial buildings — the Lancashire cotton mills, the woollen mills of Yorkshire and Gloucester, breweries at Margate, Tadcaster and Burton-on-Trent.

The Georgian and Regency years were ones of urban consolidation and internal progression, towns grew in size, the number of types of buildings proliferated and

The early 19th century area of Red Lion Street, Nottingham. An important seat of the stocking trade at that time, the city also became a noted lace-making centre.

considerable attention was paid to town planning; the gulf between town and country village grew wider and wider.

Victorian towns

When Victoria came to the throne in 1837 the population of Great Britain was about 25 million, when she died it had grown to almost 42 million. The intervening years had seen a spectacular increase in town dwelling, many new towns were built and the populations of the major provincial centres increased by as much as tenfold.

It is not possible in this brief account to more than touch on just a few points of especial relevance. There were new mining towns in tin, coal and iron-working areas where terraced houses lined the cobbled streets. There were railway towns, which transformed the faces of many an urban centre; in Birmingham, Rugby, Carlisle and York the railway dictated the razing of whole sections of older streets and the building of new to accommodate it. The planting of new towns was stimulated, Swindon is practically such, then there were Crewe, Eastleigh (Hampshire), Middlesborough and New Wolverton, among others.

The foundation and expansion of seaside resorts was much encouraged by the railways, but this merely accelerated a trend which had already begun. Names such as Fleetwood, Felixstowe, Weston-super-Mare, Lytham St Annes, Bournemouth, Southend and even Brighton itself would today hardly be known without the revolution in travel brought about by the railways. The Bank Holiday Act of 1871 and the institution of the Wakes Week played their part — especially in the case of Blackpool.

If the story of the seaside town in the wake of the railway development and the institution of regular holiday periods is one of success, that of the development of spa towns in Victorian times is less so. Bath never lost its appeal, but Tenbury and Matlock Bank were not the runaway successes their founders had hoped, although places like Harrogate and Great Malvern thrived and the evidence of their great Victorian splendour is still to be seen.

Although much of the development of nineteenth-century English towns was due to the riches, imagination and persistence of gifted (or pig-headed) individuals there was a certain attempt at what we would recognise today as town planning — the grid-system used in Bradford, the railway towns of Middlesborough and Eastleigh, Blackpool, Skegness and others; the more 'Arcadian' approach of Bournemouth, the imaginative radial plan only partially achieved in Fleetwood (Lancashire). A further feature of town development (which to date has not engaged the attention of local historians to any degree) is the re-modelling of town centres and the addition of suburbs, both of which were subjects of planning to a greater or lesser degree. London itself is an

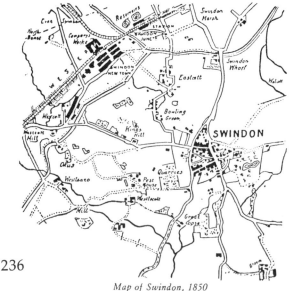

Swindon around 1850. A significant development of the period was the coming of the Great Western Railway, which not only established engine sheds, locomotive construction works and the like but also stimulated the foundation of a 'new town' to support the resulting prosperity.

Map of Swindon, 1850

This picture by the famous photographer Frank Meadow Sutcliffe (1853-1941) shows the market at Whitby, Yorkshire, around the turn of the century.

obvious and outstanding example — Farringdon Street, Queen Victoria Street, Shaftesbury Avenue, the Victoria Embankment and much else — but there were also good efforts made in the centres of places as far apart as Cambridge, Taunton, York and Norwich. The matter of suburbs is a most interesting one, and as far as the author is aware little work has been done on the social patterns maintained in planned Victorian suburbs. It is apparent that in some places working-class extensions were on the grid pattern, while middle-class areas were based on curving tree-lined avenues, large individual plots and, again, 'Arcadian' aspirations, but much investigation remains to be done.

The towns of the twentieth century

For research into towns of the present century two good introductory texts are *The Genesis of Modern British Town Planning* by W. Ashworth (London 1954), and the *Report of the Departmental Committee on Garden Cities and Satellite Towns* issued by the Ministry of Health in 1935. Both these publications deal with important matters, including the criteria regarded as relevant in the planting of towns like Welwyn, Letchworth and cities of such kind. Neither work, by its very nature, takes into account the destruction of towns by the Luftwaffe in the Second World War, and the consequent opportunities for re-planning and major rebuilding which occurred in such places as Bristol, Coventry and Plymouth.

An imaginative recent development in Exeter, in which a medieval church is incorporated harmoniously into a paved cleanly-styled shopping precinct.

Throughout the twentieth century local authorities, empowered by national legislation, have attempted with greater and lesser success, to develop their own town plans, with the main objectives of ensuring proper standards of hygiene and sanitation and maintaining 'amenities'. Hampstead Garden Suburb was developed soon after the turn of the century and was to a degree a model for expansion in provincial locations. After the First World War there was a great housing boom and the proliferation of great sprawling suburbs, and the term 'jerry building' was increasingly heard to describe cheap, ill-fitted working-class homes. The ever-growing popular practices of building council estates, and 'private' estates, influenced the townscapes and perpetuated the time-honoured pressure of segregating social groups. The inter-war years saw much development which is now regretted — tasteless speculative building and appalling ribbon development which the 1925 Restriction Act did little to combat. Suburbs in some towns comprised mere blocks of dwelling houses, badly built and without regard to social and domestic needs such as parks, shops and community halls.

After the Second World War some towns, like Bristol, Coventry and Plymouth were able to take advantage, in their bombed areas, to erect new buildings, often in well-used modern materials, and their work was echoed in similar re-building programmes in Exeter, Southampton, Hull and parts of London. In many towns elegant (and some ugly) tower blocks of offices and commercial premises were erected, and whole areas of town centres were paved over to form *piazze* (or 'piazzas' as is becoming common Anglicized usage for an elegant Italian term), with well designed recreational areas.

In some suburbs, and indeed some 'inner city' areas, the concept of the tower block became that of the multi-storey residential unit, sometimes good to look upon but increasingly difficult to live in in peace and privacy, sometimes offensive to the eye and equally inconvenient for harmonious community life to blossom. A further phenomenon which should not escape the local researcher's attention is the estates of prefabricated single-storey houses (the 'prefabs') which came in the wake of the 1939-45 war, and which in some towns still exist.

In addition to town development and extension carried out in post-war years, the 1946 New Towns Act permitted interesting developments on fourteen sites, including Bracknell, Crawley, Stevenage, Peterlea and Corby. Taking advantage of lessons learnt, these new creations included civic amenity areas, commercial, well segregated residential and industrial developments, and the provision of easily accessible shops and schools. In the 1960s there were nearly a dozen new towns as far apart as Washington in Durham, Redditch in the Midlands, and Milton Keynes some miles to the east.

Finally, the impact of the motor car, and the building of motorways, has had a significant effect on the expansion of existing towns, and the siting of new towns. All this is grist to the local historian's mill. The future of the town has no place in these pages, although individual researchers may wish to speculate.

Reference texts

There are hundreds, even thousands, of books on the emergence of towns, their growth and amenities. This short section identifies a few basic volumes and articles, and points to where useful bibliographies may be found. Works already identified in the course of this chapter are not included, although the reader is reminded that there is an extensive book-list in *The Landscape of Towns* by Aston and Bond (London, 1987). General works include *Towns in the Making* by G. Burke (London 1971), *The Geography of Towns* by A.E. Smailes (London 1973), *The Study of Urban History* edited by H. Dyos (London 1968), and *A Guide to British Topographical Collections* by M.W. Barley (London 1974). By historical period (or important topic) the following may be found to˙be of value: *The Iron Age and its Hill Forts* edited by M. Jesson 1971; *Iron Age Communities in Britain* by B. Cunliffe (London 1974); 'The Burghal Hidage' by D. Hill in *Medieval Archaeology* Vol.XIII (1969); 'Late Saxon Planned Towns' by M. Biddle in the *Antiquaries Journal* Vol.LI (1971); 'The Later Pre-Conquest Boroughs' by C.A. Radford in *Medieval Archaeology* Vol.XIV (1970). For the post-Conquest years: *Town Origins: The Evidence from Medieval England* edited by J.F. Benton (Boston USA 1968); *The English Medieval Town* by Colin Platt (London 1976); *An Introduction to the History of English Medieval Towns* by Susan Reynolds (Oxford 1977); *New Towns of the Middle Ages* by M.W. Beresford (London 1967); and, by the same author and a collaborator, *English Medieval Boroughs – a Hand-list* (Newton Abbot 1975).

Strangely, the author is unable to discover any volume devoted to an overall commentary on Tudor and Stuart, Georgian and Regency, Victorian, or Modern towns. There are vast quantities of books and scholarly papers on *individual* towns, but nothing, it would seem, on the generality of the periods in question. The following books and articles dealing with specific aspects of townscapes may be of value. 'The Provincial Towns of Georgian England: a study of the Building Process 1740-1820' by C.W. Chalkin in *Studies in Urban History* No.3 (London 1974), and, by the same author, 'The Making of Some New Towns, *c.*1600-1720' in *Rural Change and Urban Growth 1500-1800 (London 1974); Landscapes and Documents* edited by A. Rogers and R.T. Rowley (London 1974); *The Spas of England and Principal Sea-Bathing Places* by A.B. Granville (1841, reprint Newton Abbot); *The Impact of Railways on Victorian Cities* by J.R. Kellett (London 1968).

For an introduction to garden cities, the great pioneer work is by E. Howard, *Garden Cities of Tomorrow* (London, reprint 1902), and for an insight into a contemporary difficulty, *Traffic in Towns* by Colin Buchanan (Harmondsworth 1963) is most enlightening.

Finally, for specific towns, the *Victoria County History* and the *Historical Monuments* (RCHM) volumes remain invaluable.

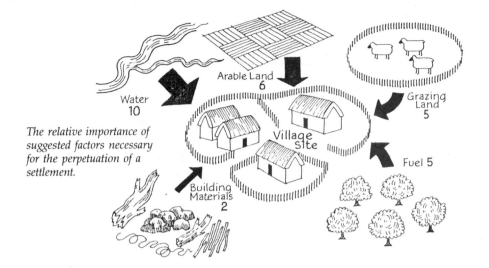

The relative importance of suggested factors necessary for the perpetuation of a settlement.

Water 10
Arable Land 6
Grazing Land 5
Building Materials 2
Village Site
Fuel 5

20 The evolution of villages

The question which must be asked at the outset is what is a village? For many local researchers whose studies are confined to those country places the matter may be academic, for received perception or common usage will provide the answer. Alternatively, the *OED* definition, 'an assemblage of houses larger than a hamlet and smaller than a town', may suffice. If, however, the research demanded is of a more penetrating kind the question may not be so easily resolved. The *Dictionary of British History* (edited by Alan Isaacs and others, Pan Books 1982) avoids the issue completely by omitting the word 'village' altogether, although it defines 'villein' (*villanus*) as a peasant who cultivated land in a village. The issue is obviously worthy of further investigation. At the root of the word is the Latin *villaticus* ('an assemblage of houses outside or pertaining to a villa'). But times move on and meanings mutate, pressed into forms to suit the requirements of the day, and currently a broadly acceptable definition of a village, in geographical terms, may be 'a nucleated rural settlement of twenty or more homesteads', and that of a hamlet as a settlement with between three and nineteen households. However, in *Villages in the Landscape* (London 1978), Trevor Rowley says, 'The analysis of villages requires that a distinction be made between the pattern of rural settlement and the morphology of individual rural communities.' He goes on to comment on the structures and changing roles of villages, indicating that in the past century or so the most profound change has been sociological. He concludes that 'the fundamental changes of status and function makes the definition of "village" very different.'

Lest the reader should now feel that complexity has been added to what, *prima facie*, is a very simple situation, he should be assured that it has only been done to point up that, with the coming of the motor car and metalled roads, the modern village of the commuter (or in which a distant person has a holiday home) is very different from the medieval settlement in which the majority of the inhabitants earned their living within

240

the accepted local boundaries. Thus in many cases a 'village' which has existed down to the present day from far earlier times, including pre-Saxon, has seen many changes of identity, has had many changes in prosperity, and these changes, and the reasons for them, should be sought out and analysed as part of the fascinating research in trying to determine the history of each individual 'village'.

Early villages

At whatever historical period a particular settlement was established, and in whatever geographical location, there were a number of things essential to its survival. At the very top of the list was water, for without this vital supply human, animal and plant life would be impossible. The next items of importance were good arable and grazing lands, the former kind being possibly slightly more necessary than the latter. Fuel as a source of comfort and for cooking was essential, and so was an availability of building material.

Archaeologists are broadly of the opinion that between around 4500 and 2500BC there were in England groups of people with advanced social structures, complex religious organisation and outstanding relative technology. Remains of villages (if the word may be employed to describe large settlements of a time long before the Romans) which have been found are generally acknowledged to date from these Neolithic centuries. What is not certain yet is how long many of them were occupied — for a few short years, or for generations? But it is apparent that even then there was no 'ideal' site for a settlement, for traces have been discovered in chalk downland, in river valleys, on heavy clayland and in coastal areas near the seashore. As Christopher Taylor says in his *Village and Farmstead* (London 1983): 'The general pattern is of total occupation, with little indication of restrictions imposed by environmental considerations.'

For these times of early settled occupation, the local historian is entirely dependent on the work, published and unpublished, of archaeologists, for even if his area of interest lies in open country it is likely that evidence of early villages will have been washed away in the chalklands, submerged under vast quantities of hill-wash and deposits in lower areas, or buried by later generations of man, as was the case of the settlement now under the main runway at London's Heathrow airport.

In a volume of this kind it is not possible to examine the various theories which have been formulated to explain the way 'villages' developed in England during the pre-historic periods of New Stone, Bronze, and Iron Ages. Books and articles on the subjects are noted at the end of this chapter, and it must be said that every year new evidence from fieldwork discredits more and more of the older concepts. One example will suffice to point the issue. These was for many years a view that at Glastonbury in Somerset there had existed an early settlement of more than ninety huts, rather splendidly making up a 'village'. Later work has shown (or has purported to show) that there were several phases of habitation and that, at its greatest extent, 'Lake Village' (as it came to be termed) consisted of no more than a dozen dwellings.

With the firm suggestion to consult the local authorities' professional archaeologists and to read the texts suggested above and in later pages, nothing more need be said until the coming of the Saxons, who, to begin with, did not live in villages at all!

Anglo-Saxon villages

It must be pointed out at the outset that the Anglo-Saxon period lasted some seven hundred years, from the days of the first Germanic migrants in the fourth century AD to the coming of the Conqueror in the year 1066. (This is the equivalent of the period from the time when Edward I had Jews hanged for coin clipping, until now, when asset stripping is a major profit-making activity.) It can, therefore, easily be imagined that there were many waves of settlers, many petty (and larger) kingdoms, and many phases of development in the structure of the 'village'. Until fairly recent times it was believed that the Germanic invaders brought with them the concept of the village as a nucleated settlement, taking over the previous foundations of the Iron Age Celts or Romano Britons and transforming them, as well as moving on to establish their own fresh settlements. The theories developed by previous generations of historians were based on true archaeological evidence, but the interpretations they placed on it have been challenged by their successors, who suggest that the first few generations of Saxons lived not in villages as we now understand the term (as implying nucleated settlements), but in linked farm clusters of two, three or four holdings spread some-what haphazardly on the landscape. They further suggest that many of our present-day villages which exhibit a poly-focal layout may well be evolved settlements from the pre-nucleation phase. Indeed, some archaeologists and geographical historians go so far as to suggest that even when such dispersed settlements have Saxon names we should not blindly assume that they were *founded* by the Saxons. In short, scholars right down to the present are not in agreement; and new evidence is being unearthed with bewildering speed, causing hypotheses to be generated and discarded with ever increasing rapidity.

The written evidence of the day — say, the Anglo-Saxon Chronicles — is mis-leading regarding settlements, and the Domesday Book of 1086 needs very cautious consideration as a source of information about the later Saxon landscape. In the early stages of research it is easy to assume that each place-name in the Domesday record identifies a village merely because it identifies a 'manor', but this is not necessarily so. Slightly deeper study will show that a substantial number of *vills* were divided into two, or more, manors — suggesting, perhaps, separate settlements. Equally, a manor was not always a single geographical location. Again a single example will suffice. The village in which the author lives was, in 1086, a manor paying geld for 10 hides and worth £8, *but* it included a garden (*et i ortum*) worth 3d more than twenty miles away. So great care is advisable when using any written evidence which may appear to have a bearing on the subject.

Returning to the early years of the Saxon era, evidence remains very patchy and open to differing interpretations, for many of the settlements appear to contrast in a marked way with those of the continental areas from which the newcomers origin-ated. As Rowley says: 'It is quite clear that we are only just beginning to understand the nature of early Saxon settlements.' For the later period the pattern is emerging of nucleated communities in predominantly Saxon areas of England where the feudal system was rigid. In the Scandinavian parts of the country the nucleation pattern appears to be accepted by historians, but there remain many unanswered questions, as a reading of the relevant literature will demonstrate.

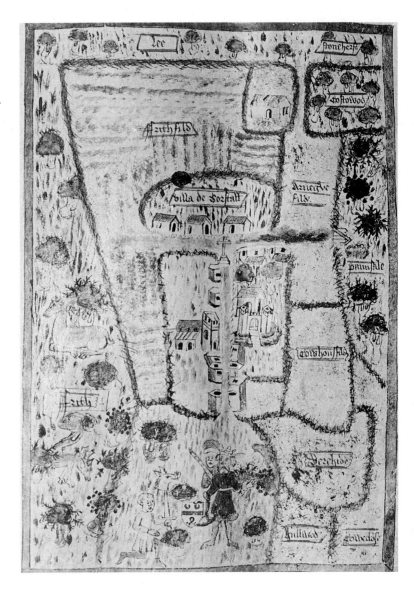

Boarstall, Bucks, in the mid 15th century. South is at the top (in the convention of the day), and in the centre is the village proper, Villa de Borstall. The church (centre left) was demolished in 1644 on the orders of the king, who held Boarstall as a stronghold. Field names (left to right, and top to bottom) are: Lee, Stoneherst, Costowod', Frithfild, Arnegrovefild, Paunsale, Cowhousfild', Frith', Derehide, Hullwod', and Coweclose.

The medieval village

The coming of the Normans united the kingdom of England in a way no other event had done. For the first time the Scandinavian and Saxon areas were governed by a ruler who owed nothing to either. For the years following Domesday up to the time of the Battle of Bosworth in 1485 (which may act as a convenient point to mark the end of the medieval period) it is quite possible that the population of the country increased by perhaps as much as twofold, even allowing for the depredation caused by the Black Death, and it must follow that during this time hundreds of new villages were founded and hundreds more expanded.

For the bulk of the period the evidence of village life is documentary in nature — ecclesiastical, social, sometimes seignorial, but seldom geographical, much less morphological. In the case of the author's own village a record of 1385 points to three large arable fields — *Estehede, Westhyde* and *le Southbreche* — of some 80 acres each in extent; two large pastures — *Northmerssh* and *Suthmersh* — and so on, but there is nothing to be learnt of the layout of the village.

Nevertheless it is true to say that archaeological investigation has shown that by the thirteenth century nucleated villages were a common and widely spread feature of the English countryside, and further studies have shown how many of them developed by very positive replanning during the whole period under review. The chapter 'The Changing Village' in Christopher Taylor's *Village and Farmstead* is worth very close reading on these topics. Although details varied from place to place it is probably fair to say, in the most general terms, that each village had its manor house, its tithe barn, church and 'green', with a cluster of tenements, large acreage of arable land with common meadows, pasture and woodland. The lord of the manor would hold so many acres in demesne (the later 'Home Farm' or 'Manor Farm'), and the peasants would have their allotted strips plus grazing, estover and similar rights. But these features did not comprise the totality of village composition in many areas of the country. There were cloth-working settlements in Suffolk, for example, coal and iron mining villages in Yorkshire, tin-mining villages in Cornwall, and, all round the coast, in bays and creeks, a whole variety of settlements. It is well worth reading Chapter 7 of *The Medieval Economy and Society* by M.M. Postan (Pelican Books 1975) on this topic, and the essay 'A Historian's Appraisal of Archaeological Research' in *Deserted Medieval Villages* edited by M. Beresford and J.G. Hurst (London 1971) is invaluable for its information regarding changes in village plans.

Recently studies have indicated that nearly all the villages currently flourishing in England were already in existence in the fourteenth century, and there were at that time many more which have, for a variety of reasons, disappeared. Indeed, a document from the year 1316 has survived which lists what is almost certainly the vast majority of the villages which existed at that date. This, the *Nomina Villarum*, when taken in conjunction with the lay subsidy rolls of a few years later, identifies by name almost fifteen thousand settlements which might qualify as being of 'village' status. Yet in spite of that we know very little about what the places were actually *like* — how the streets were laid out, precisely how the houses were constructed and so on. The survival of an early church or stone barn is interesting, but does not necessarily tell us much about the village which was contemporary with it.

Professor Maurice Beresford and others have shown, in their published works (many of which are listed at the end of this chapter) how the patterns of English villages changed during the medieval period; and it must be realised that although the population doubled between the times of the battles of Hastings and Bosworth, it was, from about 1300, actually in decline. This, and a change in farming — from arable to pasture — had a significant effect on village structure, as illustrated in Chapter 5 in *The Village and the House in the Middle Ages* by J. Chapelot and R. Fossier (London 1985).

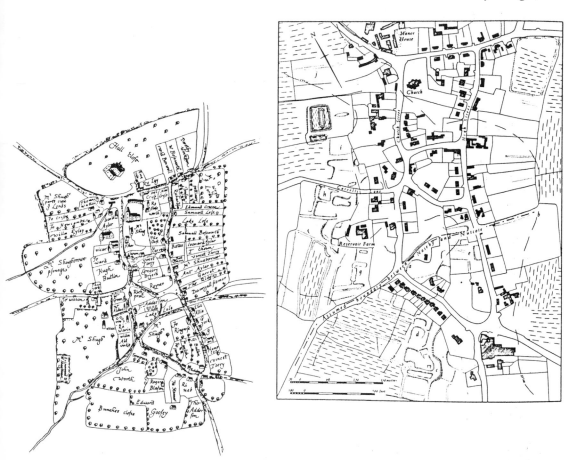

LEFT *The village of Naseby in Northamptonshire in 1630, and* RIGHT *modern Naseby. In outline very similar, the differences between the two are sufficiently marked as to warrant detailed study.*

The later village

There is no precise up-to-date information on the proportion of the population currently living in villages as compared to towns, but it has been estimated that even in the late eighteenth century no more than a quarter of the inhabitants of England were urban dwellers. Nonetheless in the time from the accession of Henry VII to the latter years of the reign of George III, although the bulk of the population remained rural, the countryside, and hence village life, was changing. It was the time of the agrarian revolution, when the great open fields of earlier centuries, with the cultivation methods which had lasted hundreds of years, gave way to enclosure into much smaller pastures and meadows. The results of the parliament-backed enclosure movement were a realignment of farm holdings and hence a wide-ranging rebuilding programme, the sheer geographical nature of which loosed the bonds of village life because it shattered much of the infra-structure of nucleated settlements by creating 'estates', the central farmhouses (or country mansions) of which were outside the conventional village boundaries which, up to that time, had prevailed.

Then came the Industrial Revolution and, in the nineteenth century, a wholesale destruction of the village for the town. The processes which since the enclosure movement had been accelerating, now did so at an unprecedented rate. Mechanization of farming procedures on the one hand, and the increasing number of urban factories on the other, combined to radically alter rural life; and when the turnpike road, the railways and the inland waterway networks are taken into account, it will be apparent that economic and technological forces were bringing wide-ranging changes. A useful reference book is *A History of the Farmstead* by John Weller (London 1982). In addition to recounting the development of farms and farming methods, and being well illustrated, it contains several bibliographies.

All through the period when the upheavals were in progress — enclosure, desertion of the countryside for the towns, the revolution in agricultural methods — there was a reasonably steady process of new village creation with, in the eighteenth century, a considerable upsurge. In places as far apart as North Yorkshire, Derby, Oxford and Dorset new settlements appeared, sometimes little better than uniform rows and blocks of houses, sometimes more imaginatively landscaped. Occasionally somewhat anachronistic Gothic styles of architecture were employed, and occasionally, as Rowley says (*op cit*), there was 'an attempt at conscious antiquarianism with inbuilt picturesqueness, use of thatch, barge boards, latticed windows and chimneys', and the reader is referred to Chapter 6 of his *Villages in the Landscape* for many other examples.

The nineteenth century saw the rise of the industrial village, a number actually designed by pioneers of the factory movement as settlements for workers in the new establishments. There were other kinds of long-term experiment. The Chartists founded 'land colonies', the Moravians planted settlements, and Robert Owen of the 'co-operative' movement attempted, at New Lanark, the foundation of a model community. Many of these experiments, successes and failures alike, have been researched and written about by modern authors, but there are opportunities still for further work.

The village today

Today, all over England, villages are in transition. The increasing availability of the motorway network and telecommunications, the long-sustained boom in house prices, government legislation regarding council houses, people taking early retirement, membership of the Common Market, have all combined to have profound effects on the structure and layout of rural settlements. Craftwork, long in decline, is beginning to grow again — decorative ironwork, upholstery, furniture making, saddlery, and other cottage-like industries are beginning to develop at an increasing rate. The incentives given to small businesses and the relaxation of regulations regarding the use of domestic premises are all playing their part. The more conventional trades of plasterer, plumber, bricklayer, mason, electrician and so on are increasingly becoming one- or two-man practices operating in a localized area.

In the past few years the County Structure Plans have pinpointed which villages are to be developed, and in what way. Estate agents in the small towns have been bought out, and now there are nationwide networks of agents, with ever-growing computer-based records and data transmission facilities. It seems, at the time of writing, the country village is being taken over by the middle class. As farms become fewer, more and more owners are selling their land for development purposes, and the houses built on the plots are of the detached, four-bedroom, two-bathroom, two-garage types. There are exceptions, of course. Here and there local housing associations are being formed to build 'starter homes' — dwellings for first-time buyers — but the process is a slow and difficult one and it is probably almost impossible to ensure such houses will always go to the kind of people for whom they are intended. The modern village is no longer an integrated community — the motor car allows more and more dwellers to 'commute' many miles to their places of employment. Some villages seem to be in decline — there is little attractive opportunity for employment in them, and they are not near flourishing towns.

Thus there are, currently, many types of village — but every one is worthy of the attention of the local historian.

Reference works

Two important works of recent years, *Villages in the Landscape* and *Village and Farmstead*, have already been mentioned. Each in a different way gives an invaluable overall picture of rural development. For the researcher who wishes to go further, the *Victoria County History* series and the RCHM volumes are indispensable for the specific places with which they deal, but to gain perspectives it is important to access general texts. For the earliest periods, the following may be of value: *Economy and Settlement in Neolithic and Bronze Age Britain and Europe* edited by D.A.A. Simpson (Leicester 1971), *Iron Age Communities in Britain* by Barry Cunliffe (London 1974), *Rural Settlement in Roman Britain* edited by A.C. Thomas (London 1966). For the Anglo-Saxon years: *Anglo-Saxon Settlement and Landscape* by T. Rowley (Oxford 1974), 'Settlement Patterns in Anglo-Saxon England' by G. Jones in *Antiquity* 35 (1961). Regarding medieval villages: *Medieval Settlement* edited by P.H. Sawyer (London 1976), *Medieval England, an Aerial Survey* edited by M.W. Beresford and J.K.S. St Joseph (Cambridge, 2nd edition 1979). Coming to the sixteenth to nineteenth centuries: *A New Historical Geography of England* edited by H.C. Darby (London 1975), and *Rural Life in Victorian England* edited by G.E. Mingay (London 1977), and *Villages of Vision* by G. Darley (London 1975) will prove of interest.

For the twentieth century there is little of a general nature, although *Villages of Vision* is relevant and *The Anatomy of the Village* by T. Sharp (London 1966) has important things to say. Perhaps the most useful sources of information are the publications of successive governments on rural development, and the County Structure Plans already mentioned. These, which were produced at great expense, frequently with the co-operation of all manner of local bodies such as the parish councils and the branches of the National Farmers' Union, are at the time of writing under review at national level, and may even now be set aside in favour of a new approach not yet defined.

A parish feast 1741. In this drawing the parish poor law authorities of chuchwardens and overseers indulge themselves at table. By contrast, their attitude to their appointed duty has been summed up as 'to maintain their poor as cheaply as they can . . . to bind out poor children apprentices [to another parish] . . . to depopulate the parish in order to lessen the poor rate.'

21 Material prosperity

This chapter considers the material well-being of individuals, villages and towns as affected by economic conditions and the rises and falls in wages and prices in advance, or in the wake, of fluctuations in agricultural and industrial prosperity. It is a subject which is wide-ranging and which has been the focus of dozens of books, numerous PhD theses and thousands of essays.

Pre-conquest period

For those local historians fortunate enough to be researching a place settled in pre-Conquest times there is, for the Roman centuries, an important section in *Roman Britain* by Peter Salway (Oxford 1981). This deals with broad 'economics' of that ancient world, food production including improvements in agricultural output; farm management; the growth of sheep rearing; the character of estates (which will be particularly informative for those parishes where Roman 'villas' were established); the roles of fuel and power; the mining of tin, lead and iron; and the industries and trades such as pottery, fine wares, wine-making, textiles and so on. The section mentions many localities, and much insight can be gained if the general picture is related not only to the details given, but also those which can be gained from perusing the transactions of the appropriate local learned society.

This may be followed by a reading of the section entitled 'Change and Decay' in *The English Settlements* by J.N.L. Myres (Oxford 1986). Topics dealt with include monetary economy, the growth of commerce and industry up to, roughly, the seventh century, the exploitation of natural resources; overseas trade; the expansion of agriculture; industrial development and export. The breakdown in urban and rural institutions and the monetary economy are also considered.

Sir Frank Stenton's *Anglo-Saxon England* (Oxford, 3rd edition 1971) has no section devoted entirely to the topic of material prosperity, but the subject is referred to many times in tracing the development of early English society, the basis of which was the free peasant. In describing the structure of that society the author deals with the sharing of fiscal burdens, the economic relationships between the classes, bookland and folkland, tribute paying, public works, systems of taxation and the law relating to property. Other passages deal with the drift of peasant life to servitude from freedom, and the fundamental lines of cleavage which so clearly defined the differing levels of prosperity between the classes. An important section deals with towns and trade, and many places are mentioned by name, and, with proper caution, valuable inferences can be drawn between what actually occurred in one locality and what may have happened in another.

Norman and early Plantagenet times

As for the pre-Conquest centuries specific and detailed records remain scarce for this period, although the general levels of prosperity may be ascertained, and particularly the great gulf which existed between the nobility and the peasants. Chapter 7 has already made mention of a number of texts, such as the *Rectitudines Singularum Personarum*; and reference has been made to *English Historical Documents* 2 and its companion volume number 3, which are important sources of information. A study of inquisitions post mortem will yield specific information on the larger or more important estates — but for information regarding the well-being of the common people there is little of a comprehensive nature available.

The Domesday records are not without value for studies in the comparative wealth of manors one with another — insofar as the information collected can be relied upon — there are some 13,000 villages and settlements mentioned, and careful research may be very rewarding. Reference to the excellent book *The Common People* by J.F.C. Harrison (London 1984) will yield much of value, but as the author says at the end of Chapter 1: 'That the people were poor, illiterate, tied to the land, and living in small and primitive houses leads to certain obvious conclusions about the sort of life that was possible for them. On the inner rituals and subtle relationships of daily life and the mental world of the peasantry our sources are silent.' Austin Lane Poole in *From Domesday Book to Magna Carta* (Oxford, 2nd edition 1955) has much of relevance to say on the subjects of feudal service, commutation, manumission, trade and industry, all of which have a bearing on the material wealth of individuals.

Later Plantagenet times

For the fourteenth and later centuries far more information is available and much of specific and general relevance may be determined by the local researcher. Although somewhat difficult to establish, a significant factor in material prosperity was rising and declining populations. As the numbers of people rose and fell the ability of the land (and trade) to support them fluctuated, and hence the quality of life suffered. The subject will require careful study by any local historian who may be interested. Professor M.M. Postan has much of importance to say in his *Medieval Economy and Society* (London 1975), which stimulates ideas regarding the use of Domesday data as a base and then relating these to (for example) lay subsidy statistics. If the researcher is lucky in finding an early manorial 'survey' giving land areas, it may be possible to draw tentative conclusions on local relative prosperity by comparing estimated numbers of households to acreage under cultivation, the number of animals the grassland would support, and so on. There are any number of works dealing with population, and among them are *British Medieval Population* by J.R. Cox (London 1948), and *Medieval Households* by David Herlihy (Harvard 1985), the latter with an extensive bibliography and copious notes.

As was suggested above, land usage played an important part in determining how families prospered; and the effect of the Black Death should be noted in this regard. For several centuries following the Conquest there was what has been termed technological stagnation in agriculture and the farming of land. All kinds of explanations have been devised to explain this — the serfdom inherent in society, the open-field system — but whatever were the causes, progress was very slow.

At the general level the balance of grain versus grass changed, the availability of manure was important and so on, but at the particular level the researcher will need the 'luck' already touched on. The author found, for his village, a record of 1385 which stated how the land was employed at that date. More importantly, it identified fields and localities the names of which were at variance with the uses to which the land was put in the late fourteenth century. For example, there were two pastures (amounting to 53 acres) whose names contained the word *fryth*, indicating they had at some time in the past been woodland. Another grazing area, of 40 acres, was called *le Southbreche*, the last syllable of which is *brēc* meaning 'land broken up for cultivation'. In other words, land usage had changed from arable to pasture. A third area, amounting to 100 acres called *Suthmersh* ('South Marsh') was also pasture in 1385; how much reclamation work had been done is impossible to say. By relating this and other information to the possible population levels as indicated by subsidy and tax records, a broad view of material well-being could be obtained. It was also possible to infer related things by analysing the meanings of by-names and surnames, for many of these were of an occupational nature, and from a time when what a man did still had *some* connection with what he was called.

Not every local researcher in rural areas will be so fortunate as to find a record of field names and uses, but a search of the local studies collection, the pages of *Notes and Queries*, the transactions and documents of the local antiquarian or historical society, will almost certainly contain something of value. General reading, such as the three *Oxford History* series volumes: *The Thirteenth Century* by Sir Maurice Powicke, *The*

Fourteenth Century by May McKisack, and *The Fifteenth Century* by E.F. Jacob will enable an overall perspective to be maintained not only for country areas, but also for towns where the main trade and industry was carried on.

As Postan says (*op cit*), 'A society like that of medieval England would nowadays be classified and described as "pre-industrial". Its income came mostly from agriculture, and by far the largest proportion of its people was engaged in growing food. The numbers engaged in industry and trade formed a relatively small proportion of the total.' Nonetheless, medieval trade and industry was very professional and, as one might expect, although mainly confined to the towns it was also carried on in the countryside, ancillary to agricultural pursuits.

The smaller markets drew peasant producers, chapmen, hucksters and 'mercators' (merchants) who traded in their lesser ways, but it was the ever expanding and proliferating towns that created environments in which protectionist gilds could be formed, non-feudal business established, and large markets permitted — it mattering not if the town was on or near the coast or deep inland. Charters of liberties combined with sound defences promoted feelings of safety, and encouraged the growth of monopolies.

The reading of the ancient county histories (the works written mainly by clerics in the eighteenth century) will be of quite inestimable value to the local researcher — as indeed will the appropriate volumes in the *Victoria County History* series. In the county histories in particular, details will be found of town markets, gilds, merchants, the rights of the bailiffs and the burgesses, charters, liberties, rents, cofferers' accounts and so on. It is also important to mount a disciplined examination of any borough or corporation archives as may have survived, plus, of course, wills and testaments of individuals, for all these sources will be germane to generating a history (partial or not) of the material prosperity of the place in question. The basic data begin to mount in volume.

Tudor and Stuart centuries

The early modern period saw an increase in population, development in trade, and considerable changes in the structure of society. The 'new men' (who considered themselves gentry) built fine houses and estates, parks and gardens. There is much documentary evidence available for the period, and it is possible to be fairly precise about industrial and agricultural practices — and hence material prosperity. Numerous wills, inventories, and account books survive as well as manorial maps, surveys, estate records, ecclesiastical muniments, and so on, and many of these may be located via enquiries at the Public Record Office, the county record office, the Royal Commission on Historical Manuscripts, or the appropriate great estate office. To give an example, the author has been able to build a fairly clear picture of the prosperity of a rural village by access to information in the *Domestic State Papers of Queen Elizabeth* (HMSO), two manorial extents (PRO), two records in the muniments of a ducal house, one in that of a baronial estate, and one in a private collection — these last being tracked down from clues contained in church records, enquiries made of the Royal Commission, and a certain amount of inductive reasoning.

Gregory King's estimate of population and wealth, England and Wales,
1688

Number of families	Ranks, Degrees, Titles, and Qualifications	Heads per family	Number of persons	Yearly income per family
160	Temporal Lords	40	6400	2800
26	Spiritual Lords	20	520	1300
800	Baronets	16	12 800	880
600	Knights	13	7800	650
3000	Esquires	10	30 000	450
12 000	Gentlemen	8	96 000	280
5000	Persons in Offices	8	40 000	240
5000	Persons in Offices	6	30 000	120
2000	Merchants and Traders by Sea	8	16 000	400
8000	Merchants and Traders by Sea*	6	48 000	200
10 000	Persons in the Law	7	70 000	140
2000	Clergymen	6	12 000	60
8000	Clergymen	5	40 000	45
40 000	Freeholders	7	280 000	84
140 000	Freeholders	5	700 000	50
150 000	Farmers	5	750 000	44
16 000	Persons in Sciences and Liberal Arts	5	80 000	60
40 000	Shopkeepers and Tradesmen	4½	180 000	45
60 000	Artisans and Handicrafts	4	240 000	40
5000	Naval Officers	4	20 000	80
4000	Military Officers	4	16 000	60
511 586		5¼	2 675 520	67
50 000	Common Seamen	3	150 000	20
364 000	Labouring People and Out Servants	3½	1 275 000	15
400 000	Cottagers and Paupers	3¼	1 300 000	6·5
35 000	Common Soldiers	2	70 000	14
849 000		3¼	2 795 000	10·5
	Vagrants		30 000	
849 000		3¼	2 825 000	10·5
511 586	Increasing the Wealth of the Kingdom	5¼	2 675 520	67
849 000	Decreasing the Wealth of the Kingdom	3¼	2 825 000	10·5
1 360 586			5 500 520	

Source: Two Tracts by Gregory King, ed. G. E. Barnett (Baltimore, 1936).

At the wider level an appreciation of material prosperity may be gained from the sources mentioned in chapters 10 to 13, and from the relevant volumes in the *Oxford History* series. In *The Early Tudors* J.D. Mackie devotes some 35 pages to the subject of economic development, including working hours and wages, the oligarchical nature of the craft gilds, and consumer protection, and points to many supporting works by other authors. *The Reign of Elizabeth* by J.B. Black is equally informative, particularly pp.250-79 which deal with such diverse matters as rising prices, the relative prosperity of the poor versus the freeholders, company promoters, and economic regulatory measures. In *The Early Stuarts* by Godfrey Davies, the various aspects of material prosperity are also well treated (pp.261-315), as indeed they are in *The Later Stuarts* by Sir George Clark (pp.36-54 in particular).

A page from a tenancy roll, temp Edward VI. Nicholas Corbin held 20 acres of land (that is arable), meadow and pasture of the lord. He was, in fact, in the same manor a freeholder. James Birte was a simple 'tennante' who, for term of his life, held of the lord (the earl of Arundel) a dwelling house, barns, hall, stable and, among other things, orchard, meadow and pasture.

The Hanoverian years

In the course of Chapters 14 and 15 much information was presented on the subject of how and where to find source material of all kinds for this period. During the years in question there was marked improvement in prosperity and rapid growth in economic terms. Town centres and market places were rebuilt, villages considerably altered in many cases, agricultural and industrial practices improved. Turnpike roads and improved harbours went hand in hand with changes in social structure. The books in the *Oxford History* series, *The Whig Supremacy* by Basil Williams and *The Reign of George III* by J. Steven Watson, are notable for background information. The first (on pp.102-50) deals with the economic and social life of the country, and the second has two long sections on the same topics (pp.10-35 and 503-34). For the later years there is much of relevance in the early sections of *The Age of Reform* by Sir Llewellyn Woodward. Reference should also be made to the bibliographies in all three volumes.

   The Parish Chest by W.E. Tate is an essential aid to local history research at this present phase, describing the specific importance of churchwardens, petty constables, highway maintenance and other accounts, as well as other ecclesiastical and civil records of many kinds. The books by Dr John West — *Town Records* and *Village Records* — will also be of value. All three volumes contain specific and implied information on material prosperity at parish level which, used in conjunction with information obtained at the local record office, will enable, in many cases, a revealing narrative to be developed.

Victorian and modern times

The publications just mentioned remain of great assistance into the modern period, as do the final volumes in the *Oxford History* series, down to the year 1945. At parish level local directories such as Kellys will give insight into the prosperity of each local community, naming traders, businessmen, farmers, craftsmen, shopkeepers and others. The information so gained may be rounded out not only with data obtained from wills and inventories, but also with that gained from the records of local auctioneers, estate agents, valuers and surveyors who, when of long standing, will have records they may be willing to access. In recent years it has been the practice of well-to-do or landed families to deposit estate and family papers with local record offices. Enquiries made by geographical area can be very rewarding, and questions posed to the more long-serving local authority employees, as well as local inhabitants, may also uncover, if not primary information, at least suggestions as to where such data may be found.

OPPOSITE *Local directories, such as this, displaying information for Over or Upper Wallop in Hampshire in 1875, are of great value in defining relative prosperity in both towns and villages. The page shown is from a Kelly's directory. Others were issued by Pigot, Hunt, Slater, Harrod, and the Post Office.*

PRIVATE RESIDENTS.

Ashworth Rev. Arthur Howard, M.A. [vicar]
Bower John Hibberd, Garlog's; & 57 Curzon street, London w
Dawkins Edward
Day John, Danebury
Enock Joseph
Hambro Percival, Wallop house
Lywood John Warwick, Broadgate
Phelps William, Manor cottage
Pothecary Walter, Fifehead manor
Wood Edward, Middle Wallop

COMMERCIAL.

Baines Jhn. B. farmer, Berry Court farm
Barnes Henry, *Five Bells*

Barnes Issac, shopkeeper
Cable John, wheelwright
Cole Benj. *George inn*, Middle Wallop
Coombs Eliza (Mrs.), shopkeeper
Dawkins Sophia (Mrs.), farmer
Day John, trainer, Danebury
French Alfred, machinist
French David, butcher & carrier
French John, beer retailer
Gale William, shopkeeper & baker
Grace John, bricklayer
Heanen Thomas, shoe maker & draper
Holloway Robert, blacksmith
Lywood John, Warwick, landowner & farmer
Maggs Philip Henry, farmer

Marshall John, farmer
Marshall Thomas, maltster
Mills Joseph, general dealer
Mouland Isaac, carpenter & builder
Paln William, farmer, Heathman street, Manor farm
Poore Robert, farmer, Wallop lodge
Pyle Richard, farmer
Round Charles, beer retailer
Seaward Stephen, farmer, Place farm
Sherwood John, beer retailer, Middle Wallop
Webb James, farmer & corn dealer
Webb Stephen, miller & coal dealer, Wallop mill
Wood Edward, surgeon, Middle Wallop

UPPER or OVER WALLOP is a parish and village, 6 miles north-west from Stockbridge, and 7 south-west from Andover, in the Northern division of the county, Thorngate hundred, Stockbridge union, Andover petty sessional division, Romsey county court district, archdeanery and diocese of Winchester, and rural deanery of Andover. The church of St. Peter is an ancient Gothic structure: it has chancel, nave, aisles, with square tower and 5 bells: the chancel was rebuilt in 1866 by the rector, the remainder (1874) is now being thoroughly restored. The register dates from 1550. The living is a rectory, value £820, with residence, in the gift of the Earl of Portsmouth, and held by the Rev. Henry John Fellowes, M.A., of St. John's College, Oxford. The charities are £7 yearly for fuel and blankets. There is a mixed school, supported by the

rector. The Baptists have a place of worship here. The Earl of Portsmouth is lord of the manor and principal landowner. The soil is chalk and a little gravel; subsoil, chalk. The chief crops are wheat, barley and turnips. The parish contains about 4,571 acres; gross estimated rental, £4,834; rateable value, £4,427; the population in 1871 was 547.

Parish Clerk, William Shadwell.

POST OFFICE.—John Mills, receiver. Letters arrive from Winchester, through Stockbridge, at 8.30 a.m.; dispatched at 6.15 p.m. The nearest money order office is at Broughton.

WALL LETTER BOX near the upper end of the village, cleared on week days at 6 p.m.; on sundays at 10 a.m.

Church School, George Rambol, master

Fellowes Rev. Hy. John, M.A. [rector]
Hillary Mrs
Saunders Miss
Wood E

COMMERCIAL.

Blake Samuel, farmer, Sudden farm
Callaway William, shoe maker
Cole William, farmer
Cooper Walter, farmer

Court Robert, wheelwright
Hatcher Mrs. *White Hart*
Hillary William, farmer, Freemantle farm
Kent Thomas, farmer
Marshman George, farmer
Pritchett William, shopkeeper
Pyle Henry, farmer
Randell Alfred, farmer, Townsend farm

Raynbird, Caldecott, Bawtree, Dowling & Co. Limited, corn &c. merchants; chief office, Basingstoke
Shephard John, mason & bricklayer
Shephard Walter, farmer
Sweet Charles, blacksmith
Webb George, blacksmith
Wood E. surgeon
Wright John, farmer

NORTH WALTHAM is a village, 4½ miles north-east from Micheldever station, 53 from London, and 7 south-west from Basingstoke, in the Northern division of the county, Bolsbott hundred, Basingstoke union, petty sessional division and county court district, and in the diocese and archdeaconry of Winchester, and rural deanery of Basingstoke south-western division. The church of St. Michael is in the Norman style, and consists of chancel, nave, and north aisle, with a handsome shingle spire and 5 bells; it was rebuilt in 1865, at a cost of £1,700, and consecrated in May, 1866. The register dates from 1664. The living is a rectory; the tithes have been commuted for a rent charge of £360, with residence, in the gift of the Bishop of Winchester, and held by the Rev. William Lewery Blackley, M.A., of Trinity College, Dublin. A National school was built in 1873 by subscription, is supported by subscriptions

and the children's pence, and has a house attached for the residence of the master. The Primitive Methodists have a chapel here. The Ecclesiastical Commissioners are lords of the manor. The principal landowner is W. W. B. Beach, esq., M.P. The soil is light; subsoil, chalk. The chief crops are wheat, barley, oats and turnips. The area is 1,938 acres; gross estimated rental, £2,633; rateable value, £2,308; the population in 1871 was 501.

Parish Clerk, Henry Beal.

POST OFFICE.—Mrs. Sarah Roe, receiver. Letters received through Micheldever, arrive at 8.25 a.m.; dispatched at 5.45 p.m.; sundays, 9.45 a.m. The nearest money order offices are at Overton & Micheldever

National School, William Langford, master

Blackley Rev. Wm. Lewery, M.A. [rector]
Blake George, baker & grocer
Blunden Edward, shoe maker
Campbell Alexander, farmer
Chalwin Henry, shopkeeper & beer retlr

Easton Richard, farmer
Gardner John, shoe maker
Hide Henrietta (Mrs.), *Flower Pot*
Oxford Andrew, *Wheatsheaf*
Payne William Penton, shopkeeper

Roe Charles, beer retailer
Roe Henry, wheelwright
Rumbolt Jaspar, farmer
Taylor James, blacksmith
Wilmott Charles, *Sun*

WARBLINGTON is a parish, in the Northern division of the county, hundred of Bosmere, Havant union and rural deanery, Fareham petty sessional division, Portsmouth county court district, diocese and archdeaconry of Winchester, three-quarters of a mile south-east-by-east from Havant station, and 66 miles from London, on the shore of Chichester Haven. The church is an ancient structure, partly Saxon and Early English, and partly in the Norman style, consisting of chancel, nave and aisles. The earliest regular registers are dated about 1660, at the Restoration: a few entries are made previous to that date as if from recollection. The living is a rectory, yearly value £585, with residence, in the patronage of, and held by the Rev. William Norris, M.A., of Trinity College, Oxford. In 1865 a school-house was built and endowed by the rector. Close to the church is the tower, the only remains of Warblington

Castle, which originally formed a quadrangle, and was in a complete state in 1633, and is supposed to have been reduced to its present proportions in the time of Oliver Cromwell. The trustees of John Fenwick are lords of the manor and principal landowners. The soil is rich loam; subsoil, marl. The chief crops are wheat, oats and barley. The area is 2,067 acres of land, and 588 water; gross estimated rental (including Emsworth), £11,999 10s. 1d.; rateable value, £10,097 19s. 11d.; the population in 1871, including Emsworth, was 2,438.

Parish Clerk, John Harden.

Letters received through Havant, which is the nearest money order office

WALL BOX cleared at 7.45 week days & 11.45 on sundays

National School, Miss Hoare, mistress

PRIVATE RESIDENTS.

Aylward Miss, Warblington villa
Bellamy Mrs. Pond cottage
Byam Mrs. Warblington lodge
Cox John Edward, Warblington house

Darell-Durell Frederick Thos. Denvilles
Norris Rev. William, M.A. [rector & rural dean], Rectory
Rawson Mrs. Warblington villa
Rawson Robert, Warblington villa

Sheppard Geo. J.P. Lymbourne house
Spencer Henry, J.P. Woodlands
Stirling Mrs. Woodlands cottage

COMMERCIAL.

Harden John, blacksmith

A unique diagram of the Benedictine monastery of Canterbury in the 12th century. Made in connection with the installation of a new water-system to serve many of the buildings including the neccessarium (centre), as distinct from the lavatorium which was merely for ablutions, it shows the cathedral and its buildings in great detail.

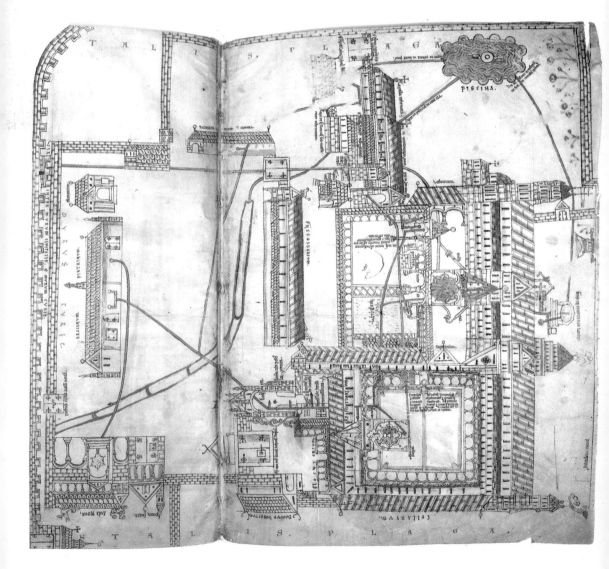

22

Social developments

As the previous chapter dealt with matters of material prosperity so this present one draws together, and comments on, complementary sources concerning social developments which came in their wake. The chapter will be divided into time periods, as before, but no further mention will be made of the volumes in the *Oxford History* series, since they, having been touched on in immediately preceding pages, may be assumed to deal, in appropriately broad terms, with the social changes that paralleled the general movements in material prosperity.

Periods up to the late medieval

Up to the late medieval period, records regarding what we now call 'social developments' are mainly of a financial nature, or of a feudal or legal kind, which state, or at any rate imply, the social status of individuals one to another. The great early source of information remains the Domesday folios, in which the male (and sometimes female) inhabitants of manors are described as bordars, cottars, villeins, etc., and these classifications provide a useful (if inexact) basis at the level of ordinary life. Before the Norman period the data are very sparse indeed, only an incomplete picture being available of the social conventions dividing the ealdormen, thegns and jarls from their ceorls and other common people.

At the higher levels of society at the time of Domesday the aristocracy were few in number, the greater and lesser magnates in their castles, the knights (and even the ordinary men of Norman blood or descent) being of far higher status than the vast majority of the Saxon, Danish and other earlier races which populated England.

The records now in the Public Record Office (and published via HMSO), which have been described in Chapter 5, give valuable insight into the social practices and customs of the day. They range over the whole or part of the period covered by this section, and are embodied in chancery records, charter and patent rolls, close and hundred rolls, and so on. Two books which have been mentioned already are of particular value in the study of social ranking and mores in preparation for work on social developments. The first is *Obligations of Society in the XII and XIII Centuries* by A.L. Poole (Oxford 1946), and the second is *The Nobility of Later Medieval England* by K.B. McFarlane (Oxford 1980). Dr Poole's book deals with many important topics — classification of society, amercements and feudal incidents among others, which have significant bearings on the structure of society at the time. In the twelfth century, for example, a person's rank and status determined how he was seen before the law. A

Norman legal expert wrote: 'There is a distinction of persons in condition, in sex, according to profession and order, and according to the law which should be observed, which things must be weighed by the judges in all matters.'

About a hundred years later the king's servants were trying to develop a much simpler 'pecking order' on the bases of frankalmoign, knight service, serjeanty, socage, and villeinage (the lower orders of peasants being hardly counted), but even this remained unsatisfactory. Sir Paul Vinogradoff, the historian and lawyer, writing in the *Economic Journal* in 1900 said, 'It would be pleasant and clear indeed, if the whole of English society could have been arranged under the headings of villeins holding by rural work, socagers holding by rent, knights and serjeants holding by military service, clergy holding by ecclesiastical obligations. The reality of things did not quite admit of such simplicity.' In the thirteenth century, in practical terms, it might be said that the status of the peasant child followed the father, and there are cases in the *curia regis* rolls of servile men being fined for falsely claiming they were free, when it was shown their fathers were also servile.

In the classes immediately above the peasantry the question of military service and service by serjeanty became more and more complex as the medieval period advanced. There is a record of a piece of land as small as 'a fifth part of a third part of a fee of one knight', and another where the service was a 'tenth part of a fee of one knight and a pair of gilt spurs or sixpence.' Gradually the intricacies were smoothed out by negotiated money payments, although the results were not quite as simple as some earlier historians believed, and the reader is referred to Poole (pp.35-76) for a most informative analysis and exposition, and in particular the roles the emerging towns played in the social developments of the years up to the end of the thirteenth century.

For the higher levels of society, in general terms secure in their large estates and familial alliances, the social strata were perhaps more simple, but as McFarlane points out (*op cit*): 'By the mid fifteenth century society was becoming more and more stratified at the top than it had been. Even "gentleman" or *generosus* had since the beginning of the fifteenth century acquired a specialized meaning. A man so described belonged to the lowest stratum of the armigerous, below that of esquire, in its turn below that of knight.' There is little doubt that society was becoming increasingly class conscious, if not class ridden, and already there was a table of precedence for use on social occasions. For local researchers of specialist turn of interest, a revealing passage occurs in *The Babees Book* edited by F.J. Furnivall for the Early English Text Society (Vol.XXXII, 1868) pp.186-94. At the head of society was the Pope who had 'no peer', at the lowest end was the gentleman 'well-nurtured and of good manners.'

As in all ages, however, in the end wealth told. As Nicholas Upton wrote, in *De Studio Militari* (1654), to be 'noble' a man could not be poor. Lord Burghley went rather further and said, 'Gentility is ancient riches', but in all but theory he was already wrong. By the late Middle Ages new money was better than none, and the records of the College of Arms bear this out. The early Tudor period was, for the kings of arms, one of their busiest times as ever-increasing numbers of letters patent flowed from the pens of their scriveners, and more and more traders and merchants saw money gentle their condition, through grants of armorial ensigns.

Further sources for the periods up to the late medieval

A good general text of recent origin is Asa Briggs' *A Social History of England* (the second edition, London 1987, is superior to the first), and the 'Selective reading list' on pp.371-9 is of great value. Earlier works of relevance include *English Society in the Eleventh Century* by Paul Vinogradoff (Oxford 1908), *Feudal England* by J.H. Round (London 1895, and although now nearly a hundred years old this book is still of fundamental interest), *Honors and Knights' Fees* by W. Farrer (Manchester 1925), *The English Medieval Borough* by J. Tait (Manchester 1936), *Peerage and Pedigree* by J.H. Round (London 1910), *The Great Revolt of 1381* by C. Oman (Oxford 1960), and *English Genealogy* by A.R. Wagner (reissued 1983).

The sixteenth to eighteenth centuries

In *Sources for English Local History* W.B. Stephens wrote: 'Up to 1538 the sources available for the study of . . . social structure in England are largely feudal or fiscal in nature; after that, until 1801, they are mainly ecclesiastical. Since such records were compiled for other purposes than the study of demography and social structure, the investigator is faced with the double problem of how reliable the records are for what they purport to be or to do, and to what extent and in what way they can be utilized to give answers which interest modern historians.' This is also true for the local historian with more limited interests than some of his colleagues, although it cannot be over-stressed that a history of a locality cannot be researched in isolation, for what is relevant to a specific place is, from the post-medieval period onwards, frequently applicable to the whole country.

As in previous ages, 'money married money' and in cases where it did not, new money married old nobility. For several centuries kings had attempted to legislate against display of wealth by over-luxurious living by enaction of sumptuary laws. As late as 1532 untitled people were forbidden to wear such things as purple silk, cloth of gold and crimson velvet lest, presumably, the burgess should be confused with the baron or the merchant with the marquess.

At another level the attitudes towards poverty relief were changing. In 1391 the Statute of Mortmain had decreed that certain tithes could be given to the poor, on the other hand legislation of 1494 condemned vagrants to whipping, loss of ears and hanging, and that of 1535/6 brought in branding on the cheek and slavery for life. Legislation of 1572 created the parish overseers of the poor, and that of 1597/8 permitted the levy of a parochial poor rate for the provision of work for paupers. By 1782 parishes were being urged to combine with one another into unions for the more efficient operation of the workhouses that had been built following Knatchbull's Act of 1723.

There are various works covering this aspect of local history (as well as the primary extracts which appear in the *EHD* series). 'Overseers Accounts' by G.H. Tupling was published in *Amateur Historian* i (1952-4), 'Vagrancy' by C.P. Ketchley appeared in *Amateur Historian* ii (1954-6), and 'Some Records of the Old Poor Law as Sources of Local History' by S. Farrant was printed in *Local Historian* xii (1976-7). More substantial works are *English Poor Law History* by Sidney and Beatrice Webb (3 volumes, 1963

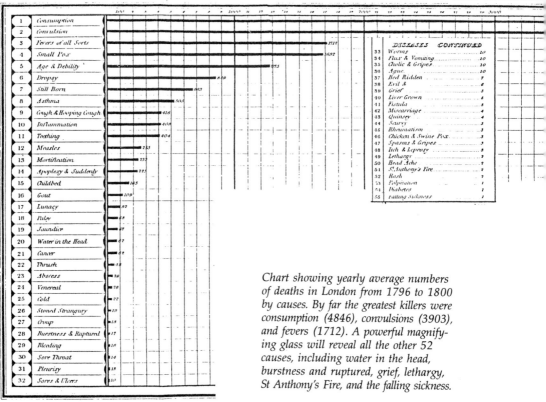

Chart showing yearly average numbers of deaths in London from 1796 to 1800 by causes. By far the greatest killers were consumption (4846), convulsions (3903), and fevers (1712). A powerful magnifying glass will reveal all the other 52 causes, including water in the head, burstness and ruptured, grief, lethargy, St Anthony's Fire, and the falling sickness.

edition), *Early History of English Poor Relief* by E.M. Leonard (London 1900), and *The Workhouse* by N. Longmate (1974).

Although the care of the sick in institutions and by acts of charity had been known from earlier times, as had public reaction to plague (*Medieval Hospitals in England* by R.M. Clay, London 1909, is a useful text and contains a comprehensive list of such institutions arranged by county), many of the major hospitals and lunatic asylums were founded in the eighteenth century and onwards. Typical of these are (Hospitals): Bath General 1738, Devon & Exeter 1753, Leicester 1771, Manchester Fever 1796, York County 1740; (Asylums): Liverpool Royal Lunatic 1792, Manchester Royal Lunatic 1766, St Lukes London 1751, York 1777. A substantial but not comprehensive list of medical institutions appears in *The Local Historian's Encyclopaedia* by John Richardson (New Barnett 1974-86). Relevant books on the subject of public health include *Doctors and Disease in Tudor Times* by W.S.C. Copeman (London 1960), *The Rise of the Medical Profession* by N. & J. Parry (London 1976), *The Story of England's Hospitals* by C. Dainton (1961), and *A History of the Mental Health Service* by Kathleen Jones (1972). A useful bibliography appears in Richardson (*op cit*) pp.151-2.

Coming now to the final topic in this section, philanthropy, this too has been known from earliest times but took a sharp upturn in the centuries now being considered. Diligent searches in the local authority record office will sometimes reveal details of charities set up by local worthies. Occasionally a commemorative plaque or board will be found in the parish church. It was not unusual for these charities to be for the benefit of the 'second poor' — that is, paupers who, for some reason, were not eligible for normal poverty relief. At national level there were set up in the eighteenth century several national philanthropic bodies, including the Thatched House Society (for those in debtors' prisons, 1773), the Relief of the Infant Poor (1769), and the Philanthropic Society (for children, 1788). Relevant texts are *English Philanthropy* by D. Owen (1964), and several books by W.K. Jordan: *Philanthropy in England 1480-1660*, and *Charities of Rural England 1480-1660*.

Bromley UNION.

REPORT of *Mr Capel* INSPECTOR

OF POOR LAWS, on the above Union, after a Visit on the *13th* day

of *January* 187*3*

1. Date of the last previous visit. *First Inspectional Visit (Major Fox July 13/72)*

2. Is the Workhouse generally adequate to the wants of the Union, in respect of size and internal arrangement? *Yes The Classification is good as also are the internal arrangements. — 114 of the old & Infirm occupy the old Infirmary and the Womens side of the building is not occupied*

3. Is the provision for the sick and for infectious cases sufficient? *The New Infirmary consists of 4 Wards with 37 Beds and two other Wards unfinished. for Men. — 4 Wards of 37 Beds (one of which is a lying in Ward) and two others unfinished for Women. They are good & sufficient There is a detached building for Infectious cases consisting of 2 Wards for each Sex. A case of Smallpox was treated here in June. The Mr O[...] whom I met embraces himself satisfied with the arrangements for the Sick There is a paid nurse.*

4. Are the receiving wards in a proper state? *There were 2 large beds in the Male Receiving W[ard] I recommended the Master to replace them with 3 small ones so as to do away with the necessity which occasionally arose of placing 2 men in 1 bed In other respects both Wards were in a proper state.*

5. Is the Workhouse School well managed? Insert a copy of any entry in the Visiting Committee's or other book, made since your last visit, by an Inspector of Schools. *17 Boys under a Master 21 Girls under a Mistress Their Lavatories are capable of improvement — They appeared healthy but the Boys are small for their age "Examined the School The children are fairly instructed The Girls reflect do credit to their Teacher The boys passed a fair examination but not equal to the examination last year and are altogether inferior to the girls E.C. Tufnell Decr 17/72"*

6. What is the number of inmates in the Workhouse not in communion with the Church of England, and what arrangements, if any, exist for affording them the religious consolation and instruction of ministers of their own separate persuasion? *2 Dissenters 3 Roman Catholics they attend their respective places of Worship*

A report for January 1873 on the condition of the Bromley workhouse which was classified as 'good'. The receiving wards were overcrowded, necessitating bed-sharing. Some of the children were 'small for their age'.

Further sources for the sixteenth to eighteenth centuries

Numerous references appear in *Sources for English Local History* already many times cited. In particular, the works named in its chapters 4, 'Poor Relief and Charities', and 9, 'Houses, Housing and Health', are most pertinent. In addition, *The Gentry 1540-1640* by Hugh Trevor-Roper (Cambridge 1951), *Social Problems and Policy during the Puritan Revolution 1640-1660* by Margaret James (London 1930), and the many original works quoted in the *EHD* volumes may be of value, as will some of the books identified in the reading lists in the *Pelican Social History of Britain* series, specifically the volumes by Joyce Youings and Roy Porter covering the sixteenth to eighteenth centuries.

Nineteenth and twentieth centuries

The last two hundred years have seen an enormous increase in population, and a process of industrial growth beyond the belief or expectations of previous centuries; and these have been paralleled by ever increasing advances (or occasionally mere changes) in social developments, ranging from the Care of Lunatics legislation of 1815 to the splitting of the Department of Health and Social Security into two separate administrations in 1988.

For the local historian, research may well begin with the official census records which date from 1801 onwards. These, especially for the decadary censuses for 1841 to 1881 (details of which have been released) provide an excellent basis for an examination of the local social structure to which social developments can be related. An appropriate commentary is *The Census and Social Structure* edited by R. Lawton (London 1978).

It is important constantly to bear in mind that the nineteenth century has been dubbed by many historians 'the age of reform', in recognition of the amount of legislation (however prompted) enacted to combat what were believed to be the major ills of English society. There were reforms in local government, in the poor laws, in public health, law, policing and prison administration, in elementary and secondary education, in the universities and in adult education. There were factory acts, coal mine acts, electoral reform. There were also riots, executions and deportations.

The situation varied from town to town, county to county, village to village. Only research at local level — the county archives, the public reference library, local newspaper files — will reveal the particular events of the day. The general background may be gained from many of the works identified in Chapters 15 and 16 and from *British History in the Nineteenth Century and After* by G.M. Trevelyan (1937 edition), and *The Age of Improvement* by Asa Briggs (London 1959). Works on specific topics of interest are noted at the end of this section.

The twentieth century saw social developments continue apace — the 'emancipation' of women led to universal suffrage, labour exchanges and unemployment insurance were introduced, the pressure of three-party politics made itself felt, and in some ways the two great wars brought the social classes a little nearer together. In recent times the great national health service has been founded and may well be unequalled in any other country. Education has been transformed at all levels, and the benefits of technology are increasingly available to all levels of society.

The kitchen at Keele Hall, Staffs, about 1890. Only a few of the staff are shown: from left to right are the culinary maid, three chefs, the butcher, fishmonger, head gardener and two 'English cooks'. Around this time there were nearly 1½ million folk in domestic service.

Further sources for the nineteenth and twentieth centuries

Books on the social progress made during the past two hundred years are almost beyond counting. Many are noted in the *EHD* volumes, and others are identified in almost every chapter of *Sources for English Local History*. Valuable lists are printed on pp.390-411 of *A Social History of England* (2nd edition) by Asa Briggs. They are classified under Industrialisation, Communication, Victorianism, The Divides of War, Poverty and Progress, and Ends and Beginnings. This last is particularly useful for the urban local historian, for it deals with race relations and inner city strife, industrial relations and the structure of industry.

The *Local Historian's Encyclopaedia* has bibliographies classified under the headings, among others, of Education, Social Welfare, Law and Order, and Trades and Occupations. Perhaps more than in any area of local history recent social developments are having an impact, and the character of local life is changing. The factors are various and many. In the towns, redevelopment of layout has changed social patterns, in some cases the high-rise tower blocks have become slums and ghettos, in other cases ethnic minorities have become majorities, in still others derelict areas have been 'gentrified' and moved up market. Equal pay legislation, and other economic pressures, have changed families' perceptions of themselves, as their disposable income has changed.

In the villages, house building has accelerated and the prices asked for dwellings have followed them. Rural industries mushroom, bringing with them demands for public services, social amenities and all that follows in the wake of population changes.

At this point the local historian becomes the social commentator.

263

23

Place and field names

Place-names

Even the most casual dip into the *Concise Oxford Dictionary of English Place Names* will show how deceptive the superficial interpretation of modern forms of place-names can be. Names which have all the appearance of the same basic word-roots can have come from different sources. Thus Highlow (Derbyshire), Highnam (Gloucester), and Highway (Wiltshire) seem to have much in common. In fact Highlow means 'high hill', from the Anglo-Saxon words *hēah* = elevated, and *hlaw* = mound or tumulus; Highnam means 'the monks' meadow or enclosure', from AS *hīwan* = religious community, and *hamm* = meadow (or the like); and Highway means 'road on which hay is carried', from West Saxon *hīeg* = hay, and AS *weg* = a road or track. Further, but misleading, impressions of similarity occur in Waterstock (Oxfordshire), Wateringbury (Kent), and Waterston (Dorset). Waterstock means 'waterplace', from *waeter* = the liquid, and *stoc* = place; but Wateringbury means 'the fortified place of Ōhthere's people,' from the AS *burg* and the (conjectured) personal name *Ōhthere*; whilst Waterston means 'the landholding of Walter', from *tun* = farmstead or estate, and the name of a thirteenth-century landowner.

The point need not be laboured by means of further examples. The fact is that English place (and field) names have, because of the country's history, been influenced by words of many different linguistic origins. These include: Anglo-Norman, British, East Frisian, East Saxon, Flemish, Frisian, German, Gaelic, Gaulish, Greek, Gothic, Indo-Germanic, Irish, Latin, Low German, Middle Breton, Middle Dutch, Middle English, Middle High German, Middle Irish, Middle Low German, Middle Welsh, Norwegian, Old Breton, Old British, Old Cornish, Old Danish, Old Dutch, Old English (Anglo-Saxon), Old East Scandinavian, and West Saxon. It is little wonder that the changes wrought by the centuries of, firstly, illiteracy and, secondly, modification in the cause of easy pronunciation, have sometimes made accurate interpretation difficult if not downright impossible.

It is, therefore, important for the local historian to acquire some understanding of the ways open to draw on this great storehouse of place-names material, the authorities to consult, and the uses to which the information gleaned may be put — and, of course, to avoid catastrophic mistakes.

The language of place-names

In her *Signposts to the Past*, subtitled 'Place-names and the history of England' (London 1978), Dr Margaret Gelling states that there are six successive linguistic layers to be

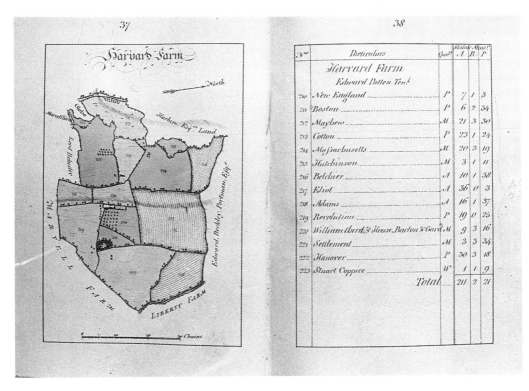

An interesting series of field names on Harvard Farm in Corscombe and Halstock, 1799. The owner, Thomas Hollis, a radical and a major benefactor of Harvard College, renamed his farms and fields after his interests, political views and friends. Hence Revolution, Massachusetts, Adams, New England, and so on.

distinguished between, in England's place-names. The first is a pre-Celtic tongue supposed to have been current in the country before the introduction of Indo-European languages. To a substantial degree the mere existence of this language is theoretical (although Basque and Pictish were non-Indo-European), but its presence in England — particularly in river names — would explain philological elements which cannot easily be accounted for in Celtic or Germanic.

The second main language whose traces can be detected is a form of Celtic (listed as 'British' above), a descendant in the Indo-European family. Elements of it are to be found in place-names, although it is generally admitted that evidence is difficult to uncover and even more difficult to authenticate. The book *Language and History in Early Britain* (Edinburgh 1950) by Professor K. Jackson includes a map showing the location of rivers whose names are 'certainly or probably' Celtic, and others whose names are 'possibly' from that language. The map does not, however, say what the names are. Fortunately, in 1956, the English Place Names Society published a two-volume set of *English Place Name Elements* by Professor A.H. Smith (Cambridge, reprinted 1970), the first volume of which contains a map of 'British Names' which can be matched against the earlier to confirm such river names as Avon, Axe, Bollin, Derwent, Nidd, Rodin, Ure, Thames and Tyne. The map also shows the *location* of dozens of places with names which contain British, Welsh and Cornish elements. It can be compared with Ordnance Survey maps to determine the *names* which match the locations — but the process is sometimes tedious.

The third layer of language to be found in place-names is Latin, but its incidence is not very great — either as a provider of complete or partial names. Dr Gelling's book (*op cit*) has a useful chapter on place-names in Roman Britain, but the definitive work on the subject is *The Place Names of Roman Britain* (Cambridge 1979), by A.L. Rivet and Colin Smith. After an introduction covering textual and linguistic problems, the book deals with literary authorities, Ptolemy's geography, the itineraries, the Ravenna cosmography, and the *notitia dignitatum*. An alphabetical list of 274 pages takes up the largest section of the book, and the work ends with an index of modern names which the local historian may use to trace any Roman name (and its derivative) which may have been given to the place he is studying.

The fourth language contributing to the naming of places is Anglo-Saxon or, as modern philologists seem now to prefer, Old English. It is Germanic, and although Indo-European it belongs to a different group from British (Celtic). During the centuries when it gradually replaced its older relative a vast number of place-names were coined in the new tongue. Indeed, the majority of location names now in use in England began life in Old English, moving through Middle to Modern and being transformed in the process. A few examples based on one simple terminator will serve to illustrate some of the difficulties the lexicographer, much less the local historian, may have. Many place-names in the twentieth century end in *bury* — Bibury (Gloucester), Newbury (Berkshire), Prestbury (Cheshire), Stockbury (Kent), Timsbury (Somerset), and Symondsbury (Dorset) are instances. But there are here, in fact, four quite separate Old English terminators involved. In the cases of Bibury, Newbury and Prestbury the word is *burh* (*burg, byrig*) = a fortified place, manor or house; in that of Stockbury it is *baer* = pasture; in Timsbury the word is *bearu* = a wood or grove; and in Symondsbury *beorg* = a hill or mound. The foregoing are fairly straightforward, but sometimes considerable uncertainty occurs — in the year 1201 the name Hazelbury (Dorset) was written *Hasebere* (*bearu* = wood or grove) and as *Haseberge* (*beorg* = hill or mound). There are dozens of other instances in which the historian must decide for himself, sometimes with the aid of topological evidence of his own discovery. On occasion he may be fortunate enough to add to the sum of knowledge about the name of the place he is studying.

The fifth language group involved is the Scandinavian, especially Old Norse — another of the Germanic languages in the Indo-European family. Place-names with Scandinavian roots occur mainly in eastern England north of the Thames, the area heavily settled from Denmark and which was known as the Danelaw — as outlined in Chapter 1. There are also names with Old Norse roots in north-west England, stemming from the Norwegian occupation in the early tenth century. *English Place Name Elements* contains in the second section two maps, one entitled 'The Scandinavian Settlement' and showing the location of parishes with names of Nordic origin (a few situated below the southern limit of the Danelaw); the other indicating the distribution of Irish-Norwegian place-names, mainly in the counties of Lancashire and Cumbria but with some in Yorkshire, a few further south, but none outside the Danelaw. Another work of distinction is *Place Name Evidence for Anglo-Saxon and*

Scandinavian Settlement, a collection of essays edited by Kenneth Cameron and published in 1975.

The final important language which has contributed to English place-names is Norman French, introduced into the country following the Conquest of 1066. When, in the tenth century, Carolingian Neustria was transformed by its Viking conquerors into 'Normandy' — the land of the Northmen — the new overlords soon adopted the French language and, after their subjugation of England, *their* descendants gradually adopted English. Nevertheless a number of French words found their way into place-names.

Major place-names

Although there have been many linguistic influences on English place-names, most are bastardized or fossilized forms of Anglo-Saxon or Middle English words. Even so the vast majority have been so contaminated over the centuries by transient vagaries of speech and spelling that their meanings require specialist investigation and interpretation.

True, Kingswood in Avon is, literally, 'the king's wood', Slough in Berkshire means 'slough' (i.e. mire), Woodford in Cheshire is 'ford in the wood', and Salthouse in Norfolk is 'the house for storing salt', but there are not too many certainties. It is, then, all the more interesting to note how the 'new towns' of the twentieth century — Cumbernauld, Welwyn Garden City, Harlow New Town — have been given not names in Modern English, but ones which at least in part hark back more than a thousand years.

As a point of first reference the local researcher is recommended to the *Concise Oxford Dictionary of English Place Names* by Eilart Ekwall (Oxford, 4th edition reprinted 1960). More basic, and of paramount importance, is the two-volume set *English Place Name Elements* (op cit), as is *Cornish Place Name Elements* by O.J. Padel (1985). These set out in a most authoritative way the words, syllables and phrases from all the source languages which have contributed to the identification of geographical areas, communities and settlements; and Dr Gelling's *Signposts to the Past* remains invaluable.

In addition to the three volumes on 'elements' the English Place Names Society has also issued (via Cambridge University Press) more than fifty books — and there are more to come — on a county by county basis. These set out to collect and define every place-name from that of the largest city to the smallest hamlet. They draw on every source known to the compilers — charters, deeds, rolls, maps, cartularies, tenancy lists, registers, testaments, calendars, fines, surveys, catalogues, itineraries, terriers, and other documents. To illustrate their approach and content a typical entry may be cited, that for the modern place-name Renscombe. The entry starts with the form *Hreminescumbe* from the charter of AD987, followed by *Romescumbe* from the Domesday folios (with a note that the 'o' is due to an orthographic confusion of 'o' and 'e'), *Rembescombe* from the feudal aid record of 1316, and so on: *Ramescome, Rennescumbe, Rymescombe, Rentscomb,* to the modern form of *Renscombe.* Based on the earliest record, the alternative meanings suggested are: 'raven's valley', from *hremn/hraefn* = raven (? the Danish flag), and *cumb* = valley; or the valley of Hremn, from the OE personal name *Hremn* followed by *cumb.*

These place-name volumes are an absolute necessity (as will be discussed later in the 'Field names' section), but they must not be regarded as the total answer, nor as completely accurate. Wherever possible everything should be checked. This recommendation may be confirmed and illustrated by reporting the case of a parish researched by the present author. The parish name appears in the relevant county volume, published in 1980, in a spelling changed in 1915 at the request of the village meeting, to be more in line with twentieth-century orthography. The revised spelling is not quoted in the place-names book; an eighteenth-century essay has been misread by the compiler, leading to a thirteenth-century lordship being attributed to the wrong magnate; the Norman commune given as the place of origin of a fourteenth-century lord is in error due to a lack of reference to, or knowledge of, a very early roll in which the definitive spelling occurs; a minor place-name (Bellipot Grene) is misinterpreted for want of reference to a seventeenth-century map showing the *shape* of the area on which the name is based; a fifteenth-century document housed in the county archive was not accessed, and which recorded place-names sworn as current in 1385. These names had not only never been collected in modern times, but threw new light on village structure and layout at a time before enclosure had begun. All the discoveries have been notified to the English Place Names Society, and details will appear in a future EPNS volume. The local historian should check everything, even when all the evidence seems to have been gathered — amateurs make new discoveries every day.

Minor place and feature names

Moving away from the names of whole settlements, be they cities, towns or villages, the names given to areas, suburbs and hamlets often retain vestiges of earlier identifications: Brislington, Hartcliffe, Redfield and Eastville in Bristol; Kings Heath, Selly Oak, Quinton and Handsworth in Birmingham, are examples of manor, settlement and local names now assigned to districts. The same pattern holds for villages — especially if they are of an early Saxon polyfocal type. In Dorset the village of Hazelbury, already mentioned, has hamlets of Kingston, Wonston and Droop, each of which is amenable to rigorous linguistic analysis, casting light on former centuries: Cynestan's tun, Wulfmaer's tun and 'outlying settlement'. In urban locations attention should be paid to the names of rivers, roads, streets, alleys and parks — Barrow Road, Herepaeth Street, Needless Alley, Stoke Park are all in current use and all in densely populated city areas. Nothing should be neglected. A city's multilevel carpark carries the name 'Culverhaye', which descends from the Anglo-Saxon *culfre* = dove, and *(ge)haeg* = enclosure or even, perhaps, 'a part of a forest fenced off for hunting'. In the London borough of Putney, an office tower block is registered as Cromwell House, not after the Lord Protector but after Thomas, Earl of Essex, vice regent in matters spiritual to King Henry VIII. Thomas's father (Walter Cromwell, otherwise Smyth) was a fuller and shearer of cloth who practised his trade in Putney.

The historian researching the story of a country parish has equally rich material at his command in the names of rivers, brooks, springs and lakes; marshes, moors and floodplains; river crossings and landing places; roads and tracks; valleys and remote places; hills, slopes and ridges; trees, forests, woods and clearings; and, richest of all, field names — pasture, arable and meadow.

The names of lost places

All over England there are abandoned centres of habitation — farm clusters, hamlets, whole villages and towns — and the reasons for their desertion may not always be clear. There are tales of villages being abandoned after Viking raids, or after the visitations of the plague, or in fear of the encroaching sea. Each can be shown to be true to a degree. Sometimes the locations of these former hamlets and vills are known but their names are lost, sometimes a name survives (or is discovered in an ancient deed) and the location is forgotten. There are many kinds of lost places apart from these obvious cases — there are whole settlements now represented by country houses, villages shrunk to farmsteads, old hamlets submerged by modern buildings, and so on.

The subject of places of which the names have been lost is not covered here (it is touched on elsewhere in this book), but the other categories are worth examining for the light an analysis of the names may throw on where the places may have been, in addition to any philological information which may be forthcoming. In case the researcher feels the study may be a minor one (although there is nothing wrong in that) there are, for example, in Dorset alone some hundred and eighty settlements whose locations are now unknown or in doubt, and this takes no account of farms. The local historian may be lucky to find a book has been written on the subject (as witness *The Lost Villages of Dorset* by Ronald Good, Wimborne 1979), or that the English Place Names Society volume gives a lead. But it is stressed that the information contained in all such publications must be checked. If no such pointers are available, then the search becomes very absorbing because an examination of Anglo-Saxon charters and other early texts is indicated, and it is from these that new discoveries can be made.

At some stage the local historian may also become the local archaeologist, for the study of lost place-names may perforce lead to field work, and perhaps a theory as to why a site was abandoned, and when.

In essence there is no difference between the names of 'lost' places and places whose locations are well known, but frequently the names themselves give clues to possible sites and are well worth recording. Sometimes names which at first sight appear to be obscure can, on closer examination, prove not to be so, whilst others, because of their construction, can be more immediately clear. A useful approach is by way of the English Place Names series which groups names according to wapentake or hundred area. A word of caution is necessary about the latter term, because there are 'old' and later hundreds — the latter dating from the thirteenth century — in much the way there are old county names and, following the enactment of the 1972 legislation, new ones.

All that aside, the approach is a valid one. If, for example, one is trying to determine the location of a specific lost place, the first thing to do is to ascertain the name of the hundred (or wapentake, lathe, rape, leet or ward, depending on local shire division), and then ascertain the language of the earliest known form of the name, bearing in mind that a simple modern name such as 'Kinson' may have been recorded in Saxon times as *Chinestanstone* = the farm of Cynestan. The name being studied may have Celtic, Latin, Scandinavian, Saxon French, or a mixture of elements, which may give a clue to its date of foundation or its peculiarities. Then from data gleaned from early charters, perambulations, the feet of fines and other property- or boundary-related documents, it may be possible to determine the names of places within the hundred near to the site of the 'lost' place, which may be helpful in a process of triangulation. That is to say that if a known place is recorded as being *south* of the lost place, and a second known place to the *east* of it, then by simple linear projection an area of likely location can be identified. For example, if a lost place called *Wodemulle* = Woodmill, is recorded as being in the fourteenth-century hundred of Whitchurch Canonicorum (AD1084 *Witchirce*), specifically in the *decenna* of Marshwood (*Mersoda*) and south of a settlement named *Heremaunseya*, known today as Harmshay Farm, and west of the hamlet of *Hokbere*, now called Hogboro Cottages, satisfying work can be done.

If, on the other hand, there are no early leads of this kind, it is unlikely that the local historian will garner much from a name like *Stocketurbervylle* (AD1318) = the place owned or rented by the Turberville family.

Field names

There is little point in setting out to research the history of field names — which in some parishes can be in excess of five hundred — without an appreciation of how land usage developed, and the effects the successive waves of settlers had on cultivation methods. The techniques used in the Midlands differ from those of Kent, the Thames basin, Northumberland and East Anglia. Bronze Age, Celtic and Roman influences persisted after the Germanic invasions and the coming of the Normans, and the enclosures which started as early as the thirteenth century (contrary to popular belief) raised hedges but did not obliterate the field names of more ancient times.

This is not the place to describe agricultural developments as they affected topographical details, but the local historian may be fortunate in discovering records which tend to suggest (or confirm) if the place he is studying was, in medieval times, farmed on a two or three, or four field system. A phrase in a fourteenth-century roll to the effect that sheep might be folded on the arable 'every fourth year' is of value, and to discover a document of like period naming pastures each of a hundred or so acres in extent, called *Estehede*, *Westhyde* and *le Southbreche* (*breche* = land broken by the plough), not only informs on the predominance of sheep farming at the time of record, and the open field nature which still prevailed, but also the use to which some of the land had been put in former centuries.

Part of an early Jacobean map displaying a wide variety of field names. (1) Portway Close, from portweg = road to the market town; (2) Corbins Frehold, after a landholder of the day; (3) The Groves, probably grof = a hollow which a stream makes; (4) Personadg Land = land set aside for the parson, i.e. glebe land; (5) Plecke/Placke Close, from plek = a small plot of ground; (6) Whiphills, from hwip = brushwood; (7) Gassons (also Garstang), perhaps gaers/graes = grass, and tun = enclosure, or the Gass family who lived in the village at the time; (8) Frogwell Mead, from frogga = frog, and Wiell = a spring; (9) Church Thorns, probably the Churche family, prominent villagers of the day; (10) The Parish, self-evidently land to let out to the poor; (11) Pidnell, arguably a Saxon personal name Pyda, plus hyll = hill; (12) Brookland, probably broc = brook, rather than brocc = badger; (13) Bresland (also Brestland), most likely from bresting = bursting with water. It may be noted that the road leading from (1) down between the two fields (5) was 'ye bowling plate'.

A careful study of all the relevant entries in the feet of fines, *curia regis*, close and other rolls, scrupulously related to the dates of the entries and the data regarding the use of the land, will assist in creating, through the field names, not only a 'map' of the village at the point of record, but also a useful indication of past layout. A pasture called *le fryth* may suggest the location of former woodland (*((ge)fyrhd* = wood, or wooded countryside); a group of messuages termed *ferthdelmen* is almost certainly a pointer to the size of a peasant's land-holding (*feardan-dael* = fourth part of, and this was surely a quarter of a hide); and the word *halfyerdlond* will indicate a holding of half a virgate (half yardland). The field name *fermeheld* (from Old French, later Middle English, *ferme* = rent) will point to land held on a lease — a farm. A field called *crukernstock* will be the site of an ancient pottery — the house (*aern*) where the earthenware (*crocc*) was made, plus *stoc* = place. (The researcher should bear in mind the need for plentiful supplies of wood and water and, probably, an east-facing slope.)

Field names have, then, a dual value for the student: as a system of labelling and, in effect, a guide book to past uses, locations, opinions and tenants. An overall appreciation of their place in local studies can be obtained from *Fields in the English Landscape* by Christopher Taylor (London 1975). This book describes systems of field layout from prehistoric times, through the Roman, Saxon, medieval, seventeenth and eighteenth centuries, the age of parliamentary enclosures to the modern. Together with *English Field Systems* by H.L. Gray, an older book reissued in London in 1969, it forms an excellent foundation on which to build an understanding of field names, and their historical significance.

A further work of general value is *English Field Names* by John Field (Newton Abbot, reprint 1982). It is not an exhaustive treatment, as the author is at pains to point out, but it is well worth referring to. It contains a glossary of denominatives commonly found. These are, perhaps unfortunately, listed in the sequence of their Modern English spellings, the root-language forms following. This leads, for example, to the dialect word *dalt* = share in the common field, being separated from, and not cross-referred to, *dole*, the Middle English form of the Anglo-Saxon *dal* = a share or a portion;· the mutated form *dael* and the West Country word *dolys* being omitted entirely.

The later books in the English Place Names series give considerable space to field names in the parishes they cover, but the reader should be warned that the lists are not necessarily complete. The books are, of course, invaluable as a basis, but may need augmenting by searches carried out with the help of the staff of the Royal Commission on Historical Manuscripts, the British Library, the county record office and the local farmers.

Field names may be classified in the way the individual local historian wishes, and his system will depend on his priorities — former land use, earlier tenants and owners, root language and so on. However, the author has found the following groupings to be generally useful. In each case typical examples are given in two categories, the first in which the meanings are transparently clear — even if the spellings are archaic — and the second in which, due to metathesis, elision and other linguistic processes, the meanings have become obscured.

Animal references Bulls Gasan, Foxhills, Frogwell Mead, Goose Close, Gilt Acres (*gilte* = a young sow).

Crops Wheatground, Rye acres, Mayes land (maize), Beere Close (barley).

Descriptions Fludlands, Northmerssh, Rushy Close, Square Ground, Copcrouch (headless cross — the field is T-shaped — from *(ge)copped* = lopped, and *cruc* = cross), Nallers ('at the alders', from *atten* = at the, and *alor* = alder), Marsh Maidens (the second word may be 'unlopped tree', but may also be *mydden* = midden).

Fertility Fat Ox (lush pasture), Goodland, Middle Breeches (*breche* = land broken up, good plough land).

Former use The Hoppeyarde, Quarry Close, Cribhouse plot (a cribhouse was used for storing receptacles for bullock fodder), Greatinox (*inhoke* = land temporarily enclosed from the fallow), The Lagge (*laege* = unploughed), Marlpits, Wortingham (*wyrtig* = full of herbs, or a vegetable garden, and *hamm* = enclosure), Yellands (*eald* = old, also land).

Location Foremead, Overhayes, Hill Close, Noremead (north mead).

Near other features Turnpike Close, Footpath Pasture, Portacres (near a road called Portway), Thrupp Hills (near the settlement called Thrupp), Stibberd Lane (next to Stibberd Bridge).

Owners Caines Meadow, Gilberts Harley, Condix (after Condit Brown, a seventeenth-century owner), Pile Mead (after the fourteenth-century de la Pile family), Iarius (Jarvis), Moyses Mead (after Moses le Bret of the thirteenth century).

Sizes Seven Acres, Yonder Four Acres, Furlong, Hide (the size depends on the part of the country).

Topography Great Wood Close, Freath (*fyrhd* = wood, or brushwood), Whiphills (*hwip* = brushwood, and *hyll* = hill).

Reference books

A most useful starting point in toponymical studies for both the rural and the urban student is *Place Names in the Landscape* (London 1984) by Dr Margaret Gelling, for this sets out *categories* of names, with hundreds of illustrations both of the linguistic foundations and their application to geographical and inhabitational features. This comprehensive work deals with names at all levels from the large cities and towns (Birmingham = the village of Beorma's people, Huddersfield = Hudraed's open land, Liverpool = creek with thick water), to the seemingly least significant landscape feature. The seventy-page glossarial index is a mine of information. Taken with the same author's *Signposts to the Past* the place-names researcher is well served.

One of the great pioneers in the field of English place-names studies was the Scandinavian scholar Eilert Ekwall. Indeed, his *Concise Oxford Dictionary of English Place Names* is a basic reference work. The following will also be of value to the researcher:

English River Names (Oxford 1928), and *Street Names of the City of London* (Oxford 1954). This last-named book is, despite its title, of wide appreciation and is of use not only to the town and city, but also the village, historian. *Cornish Place Name Elements* by O.J. Padel (Oxford 1985) is essential for the study of names in south-west England.

Not all the answers will be found in these and the other books touched on in this chapter — the last word has by no means been said on the subject of place-names, and there are new discoveries to be made at each stage of the researcher's work. The present author has found dozens of uncollected names hidden away in early tenancy lists and not-so-early terriers, many of which have added to the corpus of local history data, although it must be admitted that some have not, for they defy precise explanation. For example, what meaning is to be assigned to *Farnegoale Lane* (apart from *fearn* = fern) recorded in 1607, and which later changed to *Silly Hill*? Or a stretch of level road called *Water Knap* — can this ever have been *cnaep* = hill? And can *Kettle Lane* (for which no other spelling has been found) hark back to West Saxon *cytel* = kettle, in allusion to a bubbling spring, or was it at some stage merely 'cattle', by the same process as today's *Betty Hayes Land* was in the seventeenth century *Berryhaye*, and in the fourteenth *Byryhay*, and today's *Longlances* simply *Longlands*? The reference books do not help in cases like these.

24

Surnames and their meanings

The study of the surnames of people living in a place can be one of the most time-consuming, frustrating, baffling, but rewarding activities a researcher can undertake. In much the way that field names can reveal traces of past languages and past land usage, and street names past social values, events, local features and benefactors, so can surnames — if carefully analysed — demonstrate racial and local origins, relationships, occupations, personal attributes and even ancient street cries. However, in spite of much literature on the subject, and in spite of much scholarly attention, there are many avenues still unexplored, many names unexplained, and many experts in disagreement one with another. As with place-names, a wide background of reading and an enduring love of language is needed for the study of surnames, possibly even more so, for in twentieth-century England the population is made up of people from many lands, many languages, social attitudes, cultures and customs, all of which — since the first coining of surnames — have enlarged the vocabulary of words from which patronymics and other additional *gnomen* (early name) forms are drawn. Every one has enriched the pool of material available to the local historian.

It is only in recent centuries that surnames have achieved the status of stabilised family names and have tended to become hereditary. They started off as bynames — nicknames, sobriquets and such — to distinguish two persons in the same locality who might be called Alfred, Edgar, Edith or Ethelhild, or to mark some outstanding characteristic. Thus we have in high places Alfred the Great, Edmund Ironside, Edward the Confessor, William the Conqueror, Richard Coeur de Lion, John Lackland, Edward Longshanks, Edgiva the Fair and, for the common people, Thomas the Shepherd, Walter at the Gate, Maud the Widow, Hawisia le Webbe, Alicia Spryngabedde, Roger Mildeneye, and so on.

There is no known proof of true hereditary surnames in the period before the Conquest, and although a number of Domesday tenants of English origins have names additional to their first —such as Alnod of Kent, a byname given to a man with land in Oxfordshire — there is little or no evidence to show that these were other than personal to the individuals. However, the period immediately after the Conquest saw short-lived hereditary surnames beginning to emerge. This is especially true in the case of the families of Domesday tenants-in-chief, many of whose descendants were to play important roles in English history. To cite but one example, William de Moyon, a senior tenant of the Conqueror, brought his name from his place of origin near St Lo in La Manche, and it stayed with the family, transformed in the spoken language to Moon, and in the written to Mohun by way of such variations as Moion, Moione, Moiun, Mooun, Moun, Moune, Mown, Moyn, Moyhun, Moyun, Mahoune, Mahon,

Mohum and Mohon. The name lasted as Mohun from *c.*1245 until the eighteenth century, when the family died out. A Sir John Mohun fought in the Black Prince's wing at Creçy and was a knight of the Garter, and the fourth Baron Mohun was killed in a duel in Hyde Park in 1712, the family having in the meantime given its name to Hammoon in Dorset, Mohuns Ottery and Tormoham in Devon, and Grange Mohun in County Kildare.

However, although at the upper levels of society locative and other bynames became surnames and survived from this early period, this was not true at the lower levels and certainly there is no uniformity in the development of surnames. The matter is complicated by the fact that across the social spectrum some families changed their surnames as often as their surcoats, and individuals had, in the course of their lives, sometimes as many as three or four surnames, any of which could be adopted quite haphazardly by their progeny. The rise of hereditary surnames varies from one part of the country to another, depending on settlement patterns, the community — urban or rural — and whether the family was affluent or poor, free or servile.

The lay subsidy rolls of the fourteenth century yield much information on the subject of bynames and surnames for all categories of persons, and in many cases it seems true to say that such names were not necessarily applied to whole families nor (given that they appear in different forms in successive rolls) can they be judged to have stabilized. A man may appear as Johanne atte Asshe in one record, then a few years later as Johanne de Fraxino, but did he have a surname and if so what was it? True, both the English and the Latin forms indicate he lived by the ash tree, but did they merely permit the *taxatores* to avoid confusing him with all the other Johns who lived in the same village? In another instance a man who was recorded as Laurencio Forester in 1332, and his son as Willelmo de Fortereshaye, was himself recorded both in earlier and later documents as Laurence de Forstereshegh. What did their neighbours call them? These are obvious cases because the forms are linguistically or stylistically related, and in one of them it will be shown later that the name became hereditary — as Forsey — down to the twentieth century. But what of the case where Johanna atte Temple's father was Osberto de Arencon, and her son Edmundo de Loundres? Did any of these forms mutate into hereditary surnames? The study is a fascinating one, the answers uncertain.

Types of surname

The foregoing paragraphs notwithstanding it is possible, and indeed useful, to categorize English surnames for their better examination. There is as yet no generally accepted system of classification, and the method chosen should be the one most satisfactory to the individual researcher. To some extent local factors come into the situation — the fine-tuning, for a village in what was Wessex will be different from that of a similar place in the former Danelaw or Northumbrian areas. Also, some surnames will appear to fit with equal precision (or lack of precision) into two or even three categories, and this is particularly true with names descending from the occupation, or status, of the first user. Given these qualifications, broad categories of value are *locative* — names derived from place-names or topographical features; of *relationship* —names of fathers or mothers, with additional syllables, pet names, font names and diminutives; *occu-*

pational and social status — indications of trade, calling or office, carried down the centuries, often in mutilated or garbled form; *nicknames* — tags and sobriquets which were sufficiently distinctive, felicitous and pronounceable as to stand the test of time. There are minor categories, and sub-categories within the foregoing groups, but for purposes of local history research the types listed will be adequate in most instances.

Locative names

There are two main types of locative names (that is, names taken from geographical locations), and together they form the largest group of English surnames. Names of the first type are derived from topographical features which may be natural — woods, streams, fields, hills, brooks; or artificial — town ramparts, gates, parks, windmills. Bynames of the topographical type were, therefore, of a very parochial nature, and, if they happen to contain unusual elements, can be of both interest and value but are seldom source material for studies of migration patterns. They were, indeed, usually of the kind denoting residence, such as *atte Mede* = at the mead; *in the putte* = in the pit; which in time became just Mead or Pitt, the definite articles being dropped; or were toponymical, such as *in the hurn* (a hurn being an out-of-the-way corner), which evolved into Hurneman and Hurman. There are many topographical names which have lasted down to the present in a perfectly straightforward fashion (the articles or toponymical qualifiers being dropped), such as Field, Bridge, Ford, Green, Lake, Lane, Orchard, Townsend, Gate and so on, but others are less obvious in their modern guises — Atwell and Attwood, Byfield and Byway are clear enough as examples in which the definite article has become assimilated, but others like *Boveton* = above town, and *Binetheton* = below town, are not so obvious at first sight, neither are *Biart* = dweller near the enclosure, *Stanners* = dweller at the stone house, or *Leese* = dweller by the pasture.

Locative names such as those described above, and many others of like kind, were, as has been suggested, quite without meaning outside the limited area in which they were coined. A thirteenth-century man who was free to leave his own tithing (or who absconded) for a nearby town would not long be called Matthew atte Middele (Matthew who lives in the middle of the village), or such, but rather Matthew Longback or Matthew of (or from) Thornbury, depending on which struck his new friends as the more appropriate, and the new identification may well have turned into a surname and passed down the generations.

The second class of locative, or local names, are, as hinted in the last sentence, based on place names — such as where a man lived, where he held land, or where he hailed from. In the case of a limited number of Old English or Anglo-Saxon bynames these took such forms as *at* Dentune, *on* Lundye, *of* Wommerstone, *in* Mapeldre, but after the Conquest the prefix became, almost without exception, the preposition *de* (of or from), it mattering not whether the place was in France or England.

At the highest level of society there were the names given to the great tenants-in-chief who held their estates directly of the Conqueror, and it must be remembered that if these magnates were already powerful in their own country they may even have brought locative bynames with them, as was the case of William de Moyon already mentioned. Some of these names moved slowly into recognisably English forms and dropped the prefix, as was the case of Wydo de Brione (*fl*.1160), whose famous namesake and descendant, bearer of Edward III's standard at Creçy, was known as Sir Guy Brian, with later generations being called Bryan. Also at this senior level there were formations of a different kind, typical of which is *de la Haye* (from Haye-du-Puits in La Manche), which became both Delahaye and Delhay. At the ordinary level of society we find Richard de Derby in London, and Ingelram de Waleys (meaning Wales, though perhaps the town near Sheffield rather than the Principality) in Shropshire. Both surnames entered the mainstream of English usage as Darby and Derby, Wales and Wailes.

There are thousands of examples, and in almost every community today there are families whose surnames show that centuries ago one of their ancestors moved sufficiently far from his own country, town or village, to acquire a place-name reference, and the name adhered.

To a minor, but relevant, purpose the local historian has, ready to hand, in easily available records, a wealth of material from which to establish immigration patterns in the geographical area being researched. But there are other uses to which such information may be put, as the following example which examines what may be the evolution of a single name illustrates. Did the local fourteenth-century name *Upehull* develop into the sixteenth-century *Upsall* and the nineteenth-century *Upshall*? And what are the meanings of these three forms? 'Up' may well be *upp*, *ūp* or *uppe* = up, higher up, upon; but *hull* is a less certain element. A very likely explanation is that it is a form of *hyll* = hill, found in the West Midlands and the south-west as the Middle English *hull*, and this in combination with the first syllable forms a byname given in the fourteenth century to a person who lived 'up the hill'. In which case are *Upehull* and *Upsall* related, the 's' having been introduced by scribal error or misreading at some stage, or is the later form a name given to a family coming originally from Uppsala in Sweden? Perhaps this last suggestion is merely silly? A further small study worth making is a genealogical one. It so happens that the names Upehull, Upsall and Upshall occur in the records of one very small village —the first in a lay subsidy roll of 1327, the second in a manorial court roll of November 1550, and the third in a number of documents down to the latest twentieth-century electoral rolls. The name also appears repeatedly in the parish registers from 1562 onwards. Given that the eminent genealogist Sir Anthony Wagner has said in his book *English Genealogy*, that 'where a distinctive surname is found over the centuries in one place in successive tax returns and the like, family continuity can be presumed even if descent cannot be proved step by step', a useful study is possible.

Surnames of relationship

The word 'patronymic' is sometimes used as an easy synonym when referring to any surname, but its meaning is more limited than that, for a proper application restricts it to describing those names descending from fathers or ancestors. Thus in the full range of surnames we find examples of patronymics, metronymics — formations based on a mother's name and sometimes called matronymics — font names, personal and pet names, and diminutives all called into service. To the careful researcher there is evidence of the survival of Old English, Scandinavian, Norman, Breton and Celtic elements.

Some of the early names of this type have disappeared — Ibbotdoghter, Roger-daughter, Hannebrother, Prestebruther, to instance just a few — and the compounds which survive, such as Hickmott (which includes *magh* = brother-in-law) are very rare. But numerous patronymics of later formation have lasted — Johnson, Jackson, Peterson, Lawson, FitzPayne — perhaps to a total of more than a hundred and fifty, and to this day there are useful studies to be carried out on the distribution patterns of such rarities as *Mattimoe* = relative of Matthew. The same goes for metronymics, where a rare form is *Mattleson* = ?son of Matilda.

A very interesting sub-set in this category is that in which the Christian or baptismal name is followed immediately by one of like kind, as in the case of Johannes *Geoffrey*, where it appears that a personal name has been pressed into service as a byname. There is no generally accepted explanation of this practice, and there are examples both from within and outside the Danelaw area. Reaney in *A Dictionary of British Surnames* (London, reprinted 1987) suggests that an intermediate and usual *filius* = son of, has been totally suppressed in the written form. Reaney also deals with other interesting varieties of surnames based on relationships — those formed from pet names and diminutives. The history of pet names is a long one, there appearing to be evidence confirming their existence before the Conquest, but in those instances where pet names survive as surnames the appearance is that they are of post-Conquest foundation, and some are difficult to identify. The name *Lamb,* for example, while usually a nickname (such as Rogerus *le Lamb*), can also be descended from a diminutive of Lambert. But there are some certainties from single-source beginnings such as *Gibbe* from Gilbert, and *Pelle* from Peter. In contrast to the few pet names moving through the bynames stage to become established hereditary surnames, there are dozens of diminutives which successfully made the transition, and an example of the surnames coined from but one font-name is sufficient to make the point: from *Richard* (Reaney, as above) come almost thirty styles including Rich, Richie, Hitch, Hitchcock, Higgins, Hicks, Dick, Dickie and Diggen.

Surnames based on occupations

An important class of surnames is that based on the pursuit of occupations or the holding of various civil or ecclesiastical offices. The name *Smith* and its offshoots — Smithe, Smyth, Smythe, Syme, Smither, Smithers, Smitherman, Smythyman, Smithie, Smithye and Smythye — plus its relational offshoots Smithson, Smythson, Smission, not to mention such forms as Whitesmith and Goldsmith and the less obvious Faber (Latin *faber* = smith) and Angove (Cornish *an* = the, and Old Cornish *gof* = smith), form a formidable list of names from a single occupational group. Such names as Mercer, Shepherd, Painter, Wainwright, Fowler, Weaver, Miller, Carpenter, Slater, Cooper and Hooper are common enough, but there are many more surnames of occupation than modern spellings or general knowledge reveal. A few of these are *Arsnell* = a maker of horse nails, a shoesmith; *Horsler* = an innkeeper (from *del Hostell*); *Bolter* = a grinder of grain (a miller); *Pakeman* = a packman (hawker or pedlar); *Cordier* = a maker of cords; *Yorker* = a shoemaker; *Brayer* = a maker or seller of pestles. The mine is a rich one for the diligent researcher. Much the same can be said for the group of surnames representing the former holding of offices, which includes such obvious examples as Butler, Chamberlain, Reeve, Beadle, Granger and Steward, but some are less obvious because time has dimmed both the memory of the office concerned and distorted the spelling of the name: *Grieve* = a farm steward; *Gayler* = a gaoler; *Bailey* = a bailiff or sergeant; *Spencer* = a dispenser of provisions; *Tunnard* = guardian of the village (*tūn*) pound; *Senskell* = a majordomo (seneschal); *Wardrop* = a wardrober.

A worthwhile study is to systematically trace the linguistic structure of noteworthy names in a locality, as mentioned in poll tax, muster, protestation, tithe commutation and other returns, using as many early reference sources as possible and paying due regard to modern commentaries and analyses. However, care should be exercised in the use of dictionaries of surnames, because none is quite infallible and some entries, in even the best of them, can be positively misleading, as the detailed example which forms the last section of this chapter demonstrates.

Nicknames

The use of nicknames to identify individuals arose in England in Anglo-Saxon times (at the latest) — there are the cases of Harold Bluetooth, Svegn Forkbeard, Eadmund Ironside, all highlighting personal characteristics of men with common names. Nick-names assumed (and still assume) many forms — they can be logical or illogical — some describing physical peculiarities, others mental or moral qualities; they may take the form of animal names, being thus descriptive of appearance or disposition. They can be the names of plants, birds or insects (the author had a school friend called 'Chickweed' for no better reason than his name was Hickwood), or styles of dress, manners or speech. A nickname can mark just one incident in the life of the person concerned.

There is little agreement among philologists or social historians as to what brings a particular nickname into being, although in the days when people had just one name, of a given or baptismal kind, it was probably a necessity that an additional term be pressed into service to distinguish between folk of like name.

Many medieval nicknames were of a crude, coarse, scatological kind and have now disappeared, but others of a more acceptable and apposite fashioning passed into the language as, eventually, hereditary surnames.

In the area of physical characteristics there are some interesting survivors. Today, a man in the public bar can be known disparagingly as 'fat guts', but the modern respectable names of Pauncefoot and even Ponsford almost certainly meant 'arched belly' in their original coining, from the Middle English *panche* = stomach. The meanings of Redhead, Cruickshank, Barefoot, are obvious as are those of Thynne and Broad, but those of Callow = bald, and Pendrell = long ears, are not so well known.

In the course of one short chapter it is not possible, nor indeed necessary, to do more than suggest the richness of the material which, with a little study, can be interpreted to throw light on former ages. Names like Catchpole = constable, Benbow = archer, and Waghorn = trumpeter, all have their stories to tell, and the books listed later in this chapter are of value in this regard.

Where to find surnames

The dictionaries and reference works devoted to surnames are useful to the local historian in that they provide a framework of knowledge on which more specific researches may be built. But the fundamental data must come from original records if a truly significant investigation is to be made. There is, in most cases, very little to be gained from Saxon local documents for, as has already been pointed out, bynames were few and far between in pre-Conquest England. By the early thirteenth century the material becomes more relevant: *'Johannes de Erleia positus est loco Asciline matris sue optulit see iiij die versus Robertum de Juvenni de placito medietis tocius terre quam Robertus tenet de terra que fuit Radulfi de Insula . . .'* is a typical entry in a roll, and includes at least one name which is still found today — Erleigh (Erlé) — in the area to which the roll refers; the name probably means 'eagle wood'. True, the *curia regis*, de Banco and other rolls contain mainly names of notable, even famous, families, but they can also record the names of more ordinary folk: 1261,'Thomas Piket and his wife Cristina versus Ralph le Bret and William his son, and Richard de Langlay in a plea that they cut down trees'; 1262, 'Akyma who was wife of William de Reyney versus William de Bekeford for ⅓ of the moiety of the advowson of the church'; 1318, 'The sheriff to have here William de Bradewas, Matilda Bret, Henry de Knyghteton, Walter de Pyneford, John Keneman, John Weryng, Richard North, Thomas Tredy, and Henry Gledy to show by what right . . .', and so on. Some of the foregoing have survived to the present day — Pyneford (Pineford), Langlay (Langley), North, le Bret (Bret and Brett), whose meanings are obvious, Piket (Picot, Pykett, Piggott, etc., from the Old French personal name *Pic*), Bekeford (Beckford, from the Middle English *bekke* = brook, and ford), de Reyney (Rainey, etc., perhaps from Regny in the Loire), Keneman (Kinman, from *cyna* = cow, and *mann*, thus a herdsman). The other names are more obscure although Weryng may have survived as Waring from the Old German *Warin*, which was a popular Norman personal name.

Among later records, the subsidies of the fourteenth century and the musters of the sixteenth are all of value. Many early documents have been published, and some are mentioned in Chapter 5. Other works of reference are discussed in the next section.

Reference works

The two most valuable books remain *The Origin of English Surnames* (London, reprinted 1984) and *A Dictionary of British Surnames* (London, reprinted 1987), both by P.H. Reaney, a noted specialist in the field. The first appeared initially in 1967 and runs to more than 400 pages. Its contents are classified into chapters on spelling and pronunciation, locative names (from English, French and other continental languages), surnames of relationship, those from native and other personal names, from offices held or occupations followed, compound names and nicknames of all kinds, oaths, colloquial expressions and phrases which have given rise to family names. The book contains a bibliography of works in English, French, German, Danish and Latin, and from a number of national sources, those (in English) from Sweden being especially informative. There is an index of the surnames included in the text.

The *Dictionary*, published first in 1958, was updated by R.M. Wilson in 1976. It contains explanatory matter in the form of a long introduction which includes contributions on the development of Welsh, Scottish, Irish and Manx surnames, which are, of course, now found in England. No dictionary can ever be complete, and every user will perhaps find omissions; and there is the occasional error, as the final section of this chapter describes, but the book remains invaluable.

The new *Dictionary of Surnames* by Patrick Hank and Flavia Hodges (Oxford 1988) has 70,000 names within its pages, but even in a work of such length there must remain hundreds of omissions. *English Genealogy* by Sir Anthony Wagner (Chichester 1983) is indispensable to the researcher wishing to learn more about the social and historical background to the development of English family names. Of special relevance is the section dealing with record sources, for this will assist those students moving from the study of surnames to genealogical research.

Finally, mention should be made of the pioneer work being done within the Department of Local History of Leicester University. Since 1965 this department, which houses the English Surnames Survey, has published a number of volumes each on a county basis. Studies of Norfolk and Suffolk, West Yorkshire, Lancashire and Oxfordshire have so far appeared, and books on Sussex and Devon are scheduled. To take one of the books as an example, *The Surnames of Oxfordshire* by Richard McKinley (London 1977), this deals in great detail with the names of a single shire (which includes an important and ancient city and university). It does so more thoroughly than was possible in Dr Reaney's general exposition. In consequence the recounting of the rise of hereditary surnames is of basic worth, and the sections on the names of married women and bondsmen are seminal.

The story of a West Country name

This chapter ends with a description of a study carried out into the origin, evolution, spellings and meaning of an individual surname. It was tempting to the author to use one part of his own surname — Kease — which, so far as current research reveals, is unique to his family. It appeared in this spelling in 1698 in Worcestershire, although the form Keasse was used in Gloucestershire in 1660, and Keisse in the same county in 1583. Other spellings — Kyese, Keise, Keese — are known to have been recorded in the shires of Gloucester, Worcester and Hereford during the seventeenth and eighteenth centuries, but today only the style Keyse is found in that area, and Kease appears nowhere except in the author's own ancestral bloodline. Historically the word may come from one of several sources, but given its apparent near-restriction to the Welsh border counties, its origin lies perhaps in the Old Welsh *Cai*, the Middle Welsh *Kei*, and the Latin *Caius*, a common praenomen among the Romans. There are several other possible explanations but they are all of an uncertain nature, so the study will not be pursued in these pages, Instead, a name from the author's conjugate family will be used, because its origin and development can be traced, quite unambiguously, from the thirteenth century to the twentieth.

In its present form it is spelt *Forsey*, and its use in this chapter has the additional advantage of illustrating that various dictionaries of surnames are not accurate with regard to the meaning of this particular name; they are at best only partly right, and at worst totally wrong. A major work in the field remains *A Dictionary of British Surnames* by P.H. Reaney, in which the relevant entry reads, 'Fursey, Fussey, Fuzzey, Forsey', and goes on to instance John Forshay 1431 (Dorset) and Roger Fursey 1583 (Surrey). It interprets the name as 'dweller by the furze-covered enclosure', from the Old English *fyrs* and (*ge*)*haeg*. The *Penguin Dictionary of Surnames* says merely, '*Forsey* (see *Fursey*)', and under the latter has 'furzy enclosure — found early in Dorset just as *Forsey* is now.'

Research shows quite clearly that although the two names *may* occasionally have been confused due to scribal error, mishearing by early recorders, or poor scholarship, they are quite distinct and separate in origin and have remained separate in use by the families bearing them.

The study now reported began with the author recognising from an examination of the name 'Forsey' that although the second syllable had obviously developed from the Anglo-Saxon *haeg* (with the noun prefix *ge*) and the Middle English *hei/hey*, meaning enclosure, it seemed unlikely that the first syllables *fors* and *furs* were descended from the same root word, and the fact that Dr Reaney had cited widely separated counties for their (rather late) emergence was a further slight pointer. There could be no quarrel with *fyrs* = furze, for Fursey, but a search seemed indicated for *fors*. An obvious possibility was *forsc* = frog, but the combination with 'enclosure' appeared not to be over logical. Fortunately there is, for the county of Dorset (in which Reaney had found the name *Forshay* in a fifteenth-century deed), a mammoth 'History' by an eighteenth-century cleric, the Reverend John Hutchins. This work went through three editions, each time augmented, the last being in the mid nineteenth century. It contains a vast quantity of tabulated matter and, in the list of bailiffs for the town of Bridport, references to one man of the right name appear several times. In 1405/6 it is given as *Forsshey*, in 1408/9 as *Forshay* (the same spelling as Reaney gives for John *fl.*1431), and in 1413/14 as *Forshey*. In each case the font-name is Andrew. The search was then widened. In the Bridport archives now in the custody of the Dorset County Record Office are two ancient Dome (or Doom) books containing financial accounts of the bailiffs and cofferers of the town, from 1389/90 onwards. Also included are sundry other records, such as for the election of various officers, and for the year 1400/01 one of two chosen for a particular post was named Andrew *Forteshegh*. It is quite apparent from the context that this is the same man (apart from the supporting fact that Andrew is a name hardly used at this time). Further research revealed that in 1414/15 an Andrew *Forshey* had been chosen as one of two men to represent the borough in parliament, and it seemed sensible to hazard that a man of this standing would have held property in the area, for he would have been unlikely to have been elected by his fellow bailiffs, with the assent of the whole community, if he had not been of substantial material worth. Investigation of the feet of the fines (property documents) for the period revealed that in 1392/3, 1398/9 and 1410/11 Andrew had indeed been involved in a series of transactions concerning an estate of some 200 acres, which obviously had belonged to the family for a long time. The important points for the surname study were that his name had been spelt both as *Fortereshey* and *Forstersheigh*, as well as *Forsey* and, perhaps most significantly of all, the name of the estate itself was given as *Forstereshey*. The family had obviously taken its name from the land-holding and at some stage this was likely to have been written as *de* Forstershey, or something very similar. And this was indeed so. In 1332, in a lay subsidy roll, a family named *de Fortereshaye* was identified, and in a de Banco roll for

1310 the name appeared as *de Foresteresheye*; and in an inquisition document of 1305 it was rendered as *de Forstereshegh*. The estate itself was defined as early as 1240 in a Sarum charter as *Forestarehege*. It was, then, transparently clear that the first linguistic component of the name was not the English *fyrs* = furze (or *forsc* = frog), but the Latin *forestarius* = forester, and that the name as a whole meant 'of the forester's holding, or enclosure'. Thus the dictionaries were quite wrong regarding the Dorset family of Forsey. In the course of the years between 1310 and 1410 the spelling (and no doubt the pronunciation) had moved from *de Foresteresheye* (by way of *Fortereshey* and *Forteshegh*) to *Forsey*, the form in which it has stayed in and around the small area where the estate lay, close to Bridport, until the present time.

The progression and results of this study (which took a number of years and involved the House of Lords Record Office, the British Library, the Public Record Office and the College of Arms, as well as the Bridport manuscript books and medieval wills and testaments) have been presented not only to show that reference books can be wrong, but that the wealth of material available to the local historian can be utilized to very positive effect over an extremely narrow range as over a wide one. The final point to be made is that the local researcher should trust his instinct, and if something 'feels' wrong it may well actually *be* wrong, and with diligence can be so proved.

'The Danes sack Chertsey Abbey', part of the Runnymede Pageant 1934. Reconstructions of events such as this, organised by local groups, encourage interest in local history and may yield new information.

25 Local organisations

This chapter will discuss local organisations from two points of view: their value as repositories of local history, and the contribution their activities have made, and are making, to the social life of the community.

In any study being undertaken, the first thing to be done is the obvious one of finding out what organisations exist and whether they are part of a national body — such as the Women's Institute, Mothers' Union, Guides or Scouts — or purely local, such as the Film Club or the Debating Society. The second thing is the not quite so obvious one of discovering if the present body is the first one of its kind to be set up in the locality, and were there any local organisations which once existed but no longer do so. This last is not so easy as it may seem, but can be highly illuminating.

Repositories of local history

The list of present (and past) local bodies can be a surprisingly long one in both urban and rural areas. The following may, perhaps, be typical: the parish or town council; the parochial church council; the Royal British Legion; the working men's club (or mechanics' institute); the friendly society (Buffaloes, Oddfellows, Lions, Round Table, etc.); the history (or preservation) group; the arts and crafts society; the youth club; the 'senior citizens' group; the football, cricket, badminton, squash, or other sporting club; the Townswomen's Guild (or its equivalent), the Church Recorders' section of

NADFAS (see Addresses, Appendix III), and so on. The records of some of these bodies can go back over many years, and are frequently very rewarding.

A quite specific case may be used as an example. In the village in which the author currently lives there is now no cricket team, but rumour had it that there once was. A fairly long search produced the account book for the club which existed from 1886 until 1920 (with a break during the war years). It was in a sad state — disbound, water stained, but quite readable. In it were tucked all manner of bills, receipts and postcards bearing on the activities of the club. The accounts for the first year indicated quite clearly the recognition of the social divisions which existed at the time. The heading (on the receipts side of the ledger) read: 'Subscribed by gentlemen outside the parish for a pavilion and for the outfit of the club', and there followed a list (headed by the local member of parliament) of men described as 'Esqre', 'Mr', and in several cases no prefix at all — merely surname and initial. On the expenditure side of the book details of equipment were given: Cobbet practice bats were 8/6d, Lillywhite special drivers 15 shillings. The local gentry were prevailed upon to be such things as president, and vice president; membership fees for 'farmers and tradesmen' were 3 shillings, for 'labourers' 2 shillings, and for youths under 16 years one shilling. Details of concerts and social events to raise money for the club were given: 'Hire of Piano' £1.5.0d, 'Expenses of man coming with piano' 2/6d. The team was taken to away matches by horse-drawn transport —'Hiring horse and wagonette to carry team to match 4/-, for stabling horse 3d.' The wagonette was hired from the local Jobmaster (who was also the publican) — 'Carriages, open or closed, Breaks, Landaus, Broughams, etc. Horses let by the day, week or month. Terms moderate.' The team was careful with its equipment: 'binding a bat' 6d; 'sewing a ball' 3d. And so the records went on — 'a cap be presented to those members who perform the hat trick', 'all hat trick caps to be the same colour'. By 1893 the club was in trouble financially, but it was resolved that it be 'restarted at once'. It was restarted and, with the break during the First World War, flourished until 1920. The last entry in the book is, in fact, the score sheet for the match played on the 14 August of that year. Several of the older inhabitants of the village remember the team and filled in details — but no one was found who actually played in any of the games.

The survival of such a record cannot be a unique event — there must be hundreds of account books, minute books, and such, waiting to yield up information on past activities.

At a slightly different level the Minute Books of the Parish Council (and the Parochial Church Council) are essential research materials. For the same village in which the cricket club flourished, the parish council records (which date from 1894, the year of the Act which established such bodies) make fascinating reading — receipts for the 'Poor Lands Charity' were £76.2.8½d (mainly from renting of parish land), outgoings rather less, leaving a balance in hand at year end of £1.12.5d. It is of interest to note that the first item of non-financial business appearing in the records concerned the location of a footpath! Things seem not to change very much. The records contain much of interest (and in this regard they cannot be unique). A few short examples will indicate some of the riches in the pages. In 1896 the 'Ratepayers and Inhabitants in Parish Meeting assembled [resolved to] hereby accord the Rev R. Burdon their grateful thanks for the very great interest he continues to show in the

The Chippenham Cycling Club, 1910. Club records, and such photographs, often yield interesting and sometimes amusing information on many aspects of past local activities, and may well record architectural features long gone.

Parish ... and hereby express their ernest (*sic*) and unanimous wish that his health might very speedily be restored and his life be prolonged for many years.' Burdon, who had been Rector from 1859 to 1887, has already been mentioned as the provider of the village school. He had also built a reading room for the agricultural labourers and made other substantial gifts. He was principal landowner and, until his death in 1920, 'lord of the manor'.

For 1900 there is record of measures taken to support the Transvaal War fund; for 1901 the resolution to send King Edward VII the parish's sympathy on the death of Queen Victoria — the handsome 14 x 9½ inch black-bordered acknowledgement by the Home Office is preserved.

In many parishes the parish magazine has been in being for a number of years and is a great repository of local information — which event was held by which organisation in which year, who won prizes at the horticultural show, etc., etc. On occasion priceless material is discovered. For example, in a parish magazine for June 1925, the author found a printed list of gravestones in the churchyard compiled in 1890. The discovery was made in 1984, and a search of the churchyard at that time showed that the vast majority of the memorials had either disappeared of become illegible. The information in the parish magazine was of inestimable value and, in addition, it prompted the recording of the remaining (and later) stones for posterity.

Finally in this short section, mention should be made of 'scrapbooks' compiled by such organisations as the Women's Institute, Mothers' Union and Townswomen's Guild. From time to time these worthy bodies are moved to compile works recording the history of a parish in modern times — the Queen's Jubilee, the celebration of the wedding of the Prince and Princess of Wales, and other notable occasions. These records provide invaluable information compiled *at the time* of the event concerned, and are often illustrated with photographs, leaflets and other memorabilia. Local researchers should seek out these records — after a while they tend to go missing. There is nothing worse than being told 'Yes, we had a lovely book all about the fête we held for the coronation, but I haven't seen it for some years. There were lots of photographs, I used to have the negatives. I think I threw them away only last year.'

The foregoing paragraphs illustrate, by means of brief examples, how the history of past organisations, and the story of past events can be uncovered. Of equal importance (not least for the benefit of future researchers) is the recording of the existence and activities of present-day organisations such as those already listed. For the dedicated researcher this can be done in several ways. They are time-consuming but are worthwhile. Obviously, the very first thing is to discover what societies or bodies actually exist, and then to find out who the leaders are. At this point it is probably wise to seek out each leader and discuss their organisations with them. When some idea of the framework of objectives, aspirations and activities has been obtained it may be useful to compile a questionnaire, into which answers may be inserted, either by the leader or by the researcher. A second meeting will help to verify the answers. It is, of course, vital to confirm that the information is as complete as possible —is there an older member who remembers how the group came into being? (assuming the present leader does not), and so on. From the answers a narrative history can be written, and perhaps published in the local press or parish magazine, full credit (with photographs) being given to the people who provided all the information.

288

The second course is to write the history of the local organisation from general knowledge gleaned over the years, and to send this to the leader, or committee, for comment. There are points for and against this approach. If any of the information is inaccurate the researcher may be thought an idiot, but, on the other hand, the organisation may feel flattered to be written about and asked to vet the story.

A third way to gather information is to compile a check list of the kind of data, and anecdote, needed, and then to use this in a tape-recorded interview (or interviews, for cross-checking can be valuable) at which the list helps to ensure all the important topics are covered. It is very necessary that the information is not left on tape too long before transcription and editing — it is hoped that the reasons for this are self evident!

The subject of pictorial records should also be mentioned. In these days of the video camera and 'instant' processing it is possible to make memorable recordings of important local events — from rag-day parades to the church bazaar, the Remembrance Day service at the war memorial, or the opening of the new parish hall. This can be an expensive way of producing local history studies — especially if a duplicate copy is made for the county record office — and we do not yet know how long video film can be stored before it deteriorates. On the subject of still photographs, colour is splendid, but if economical reproduction is envisaged then black and white film is much to be recommended.

The local researcher may find this kind of work, down-to-earth and practical, a welcome contrast to the more academic kinds of study discussed elsewhere in this book.

The local 'Foresters' hold their annual fete in 1913. No doubt some of them volunteered for war service a year later.

26
Palaeography

The word 'palaeography' combines the Greek elements *palaious* ('ancient') and *graphia* (a suffix denoting styles of writing), and hence, in the words of the *Oxford English Dictionary*, means 'the study of ancient writing'.

Fortunately, the vast majority of local history projects undertaken by the amateur, part-time researcher can be brought to totally satisfactory conclusion without the need to study ancient documents at first hand, for it must be said that, quite apart from the difficulties inherent in the Anglo-Saxon, Norman French, and Latin languages, the task of reading early styles of handwriting can be formidable.

There is, of course, absolutely no doubt that even when only a facsimile of a document is available a professional historian or amateur specialist can gain a great deal from its perusal; much more so when there is the opportunity to examine the original itself. Changes of scribal hands, the use of short forms, the actual layout of the documents, all help in piecing together fragments of knowledge. Questions such as, 'Has a word been inserted, removed or altered?', and 'Who made the alterations? When, and for what reason?' may be asked. New discoveries are constantly being made through a return to original sources.

But all this is beyond the needs of the average local historian, as well as for the most part being beyond his general skills, so this chapter is devoted to giving a broad general outline of how handwriting developed, defining some of the terms used, and describing some of the early styles. The chapter also contains a number of illustrations drawn from documents of all kinds and ages relevant to the study of local history.

Palaeography is a very inexact science, and should the researcher wish to delve a little deeper an excellent starting point is *The Handwriting of English Documents* by H.C. Hector (2nd edition, Dorking 1980). The author was an Assistant Keeper of the Public Records and his book, in addition to being lucid and well-illustrated, contains a structured bibliography under the headings: general, materials and instruments, languages, abbreviation, publications in record type, miscellaneous and transcribed facsimiles, this last illustrating the appearance of a wide range of documents.

Finally, should the local researcher be fortunate enough to find an original document which has not been transcribed, and which he cannot read, then professional help will be needed. This may, or may not, be expensive — but the reward may well be worth the money, as the present author has found on more than one occasion.

Terminology

Many of the words used in palaeography have broad meanings in normal English usage, or may be used in more than one way. The following are the most important:

Cursive Writing executed without raising the pen from the vellum or paper, so that the characters are rapidly formed with a running hand. National styles evolved, hence there are, for example, English cursive and Gothic cursive hands.

Majuscule This term is used to describe letters written large; usually capitals, but not necessarily so.

Minuscule Normally a small letter, as opposed to a capital or uncial (see below). The word may also be applied to the small cursive script developed from the uncial. Various kinds of minuscule came into use, such as the humanistic and the Carolingian.

Uncial The term given to letters having the large rounded forms used in Greek and Latin manuscripts. The letters were not joined together, as occurred in cursive scripts. Later the word was applied somewhat more loosely to capital letters and others of large size, introduced in the fifth to eighth centuries.

Handwriting

All writing depends on the materials with which it is executed, so when in European countries surfaces such as vellum, and instruments like the reed pen took the place of stone and chisel, the joining of letters into cursive styles became possible. Very great freedom was attained for the introduction of new letter forms, ornamentation, the mixing of different hands, and so on.

For the study of local history there is, except in a very few cases, little need to look before Saxon times. Roman monuments and inscriptions may be found, but the majuscule writing employed on these may be regarded as a subject separate from the general theme now being explored.

Handwriting in documents before 1500

In the centuries just before and just after the Conquest, handwriting comprised a mixture of styles and letter shapes, depending on the language used (Latin, Anglo-Saxon, Norman French) and the importance of the book or document being written. To an extent the penned hands were also dependent on the nationality of the scribe or where he had been trained.

In Latin works of an important nature titles, headings and the opening words of chapters were largely based on Roman script forms, the majuscule style of writing; and the body of the text written in an uncial form which, after the coming of the Normans and the spread of their influence, was gradually succeeded by a further uncial style. The capitals (or majuscules) were of two types — 'square' and 'rustic'. The first, as may be expected from the name, had letters as wide (or half as wide) as their height, and remain quite familiar to modern eyes, as being the face from which present-day upper-case 'Roman' type has descended. Being based on characters which had been designed for incising in stone they were difficult and slow to write. Rustic capitals, on the other hand, were much easier to pen and represented a version of square capitals developed for scribal use.

Uncial styles, which were distinctive book-hands, employed open, round letter

A charter of a grant of land dating from AD965. The charter proper is in Latin; the boundaries of the grant of land are in English. The document is further described on page 70.

1278/9

Articulus. Inquiratur quantum quilibet tenet etc. Dicunt quod Abbatissa de Chateriz tenet in Foxton 300 acras terrae arabilis, 32 acras prati, 15 acras pasturae in puram et perpetuam eleemosynam episcopi Elyensis, de quo episcopo non exstat memoria, et tenet visum franciplegii, assisam panis et cervisiae per libertatum Elyensem, nescimus quo warranto.

Hundred Roll, 7 Edward I

1423/3

Subsidy Roll 1 Hen VI
Hundredum de Farnham

Farnham	116s 3¼d
Workkesham	41s 1½d
Farmesham	48s 4d
Bonewyk	40s 3¼d
Churtus	69s 0¼d
Elstede	50s 6d
Tilleford	35s 6½d
Renewalle	37s 1d
Twongham	68s 5¼d
Batshete	40s 8d
Compton	15s 4d
Taxatores	14s 8d
Summa hundredi	28l 17s 3d
cum taxatoribus	

1528/9   *This indenture made the 12th daye of June, the 20th yere of the Rayne of Kynge Harry the 8th.*

1555/6

This indenture made ye tenthe day of Januarie, in the seconde and thyrde yere of the reyne of our Sovereygne Lord and Lady Phyllyp and Marye.
1555/6

1587/8   *Three and thirteth yere of the reigne of our Soveraigne Ladie Elizabeth.*

1611

Minister's accounts for Berkshire, 9 James I
Expensa Seneschalli. Et in expensis Seneschalli et aliorum officiariorum domini Regis, et tenentium hoc anno venientium pro curia ibidem tenenda ac pro bono regimine conservando, prout per billam de parcellis indi super hunc computum ostensam et examinatam patent, 46s.8d.
Summa 46s.8d.

[facsimile of 1673 manuscript in secretary hand]

1673

This indenture made the [twentieth] day of September in the five and twentieth yeare of the reigne of our Soverayne Lord Charles the Second by the grace of God of England Scotland France and Ireland Kinge . . .

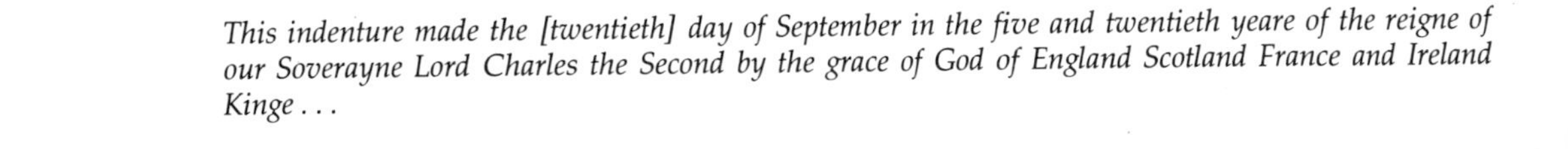

[facsimile of 1712/13 manuscript]

1712/13

This Indenture made ye twenty fourth day of February and in ye Eleventh year of ye Reign of our Sovereign Lady Anne of England Scotland France and Ireland Queen Defender of ye Faith etc.

294

1721

This, relating to the Easter offering in a parish in 1721 is in the handwriting of the rector, William Walter MA. Walter had graduated from Oxford (Magdalen Hall). This is an excellent example of what the local historian will be coping with at parish level.

1865

I Christopher Wybergh, Curate of Burneston do hereby certify, that the above is a true extract of the entry so numbered, in the Baptismal Register Book of the said parish of Burneston, Diocese of Ripon. Witness my hand this fourth day of December 1865.

295

formation and could be mixed with square and rustic characters to very pleasing effects. The Carolingian minuscules in which they typically appeared represented a hand developed in Europe. It subsequently evolved into a lower-case 'Roman' face, and with the capital lettering mentioned in the preceding paragraph is still employed by printers down to the present day.

For works written in English more 'insular', native forms of minuscule were developed. The half-uncial which was the basis of the Saxon book-hand, had originated in Ireland where, side by side with it, there had been evolved a condensed upright minuscule, used for 'glosses' (or short commentaries and explanations inserted between the lines).

In the centuries following the Conquest there gradually developed separate styles of penmanship for the two main purposes for which calligraphy was employed. These have come to be called the 'book-hand' and the related groups of 'charter', 'chancery' and 'court' hands. The first style was employed in the execution of literary and liturgical manuscripts, and those of the second in the preparation of official, royal, legal and business documents.

In the course of the Middle Ages writing, particularly the Carolingian minuscule, underwent transformation as generations of clerks succeeded one another. There remained points of contact between architecture and palaeography, and scholars have detected Romanesque and Gothic periods in both. The field is a specialised one and the study of it is still producing refinements of previous discoveries. 'But from about 1330 there is a steady decline in regularity and architectural quality: even in formal documents the writing is not only strongly cursive but wanting in discipline, and suggests an unsuccessful attempt to reconcile the claims of ceremoniousness and speed' (Hector, *op cit*). In the fifteenth century the Italian humanists introduced considerable refinement, the 'humanistic minuscule' was gradually adopted throughout the Christian world, and became the cursive hand which was eventually termed 'italic'. This style of writing began, in the early sixteenth century, to compete with Gothic cursive, and gradually the latter disappeared.

Handwriting after 1500

The invention of printing in the fifteenth century steadily did away with the need for handwritten books, and it is interesting to note that from that time onwards various styles of calligraphy developed for different purposes. The departments of central government employed writing masters who, moving through several 'bastard' phases, gradually perfected distinctive styles described below. Outside the sphere of government, in the realms of personalised correspondence, variations came with great rapidity. Individual hands contained all kinds of more or less cursive elements, but the hands themselves cease to be worth classifying except by the dedicated palaeographer, pursuing studies or hypotheses in great detail.

Secretary hands In 1571 a work written by Jean de Beauchesne and John Baildon called *A Booke containing Divers Sortes of Hands* was published. This described a form of handwriting used for everyday purposes. Cursive in nature, secretary was a distinct hand initially, and written upright, but slopes were soon introduced (in the interests of writing at speed) and by 1637 it was already possible to speak of 'sett', 'facill' and 'fast' hands, or, less opaquely, 'engrossing' 'upright' and 'sloped'. What the styles had in common was a number of letter forms.

Humanistic hands These styles started in Italy in the fifteenth century and were based on the Carolingian minuscule. During the period of their maturing, Roman capitals were introduced, and humanistic cursive became a popular hand used for private correspondence between people of sensitivity and learning. In the sixteenth and early seventeenth centuries this cursive *italic* style gained ground as an alternative to secretary, although as Hector says (*op cit*), 'By 1600 it was being written with such magnificent disregard of any calligraphical rules that it might be illegible to the writer's contemporaries and compatriots.' Indeed, in 1604 the earl of Essex's love letters were described by a contemporary as 'written in such a ragged Roman hand' as to be quite unreadable.

Round hands As has been suggested in the last section, secretary and humanistic italic, both cursive hands, were being used at the same time in England for all kinds of general and vernacular purposes. It was inevitable that they should influence each other and gradually fuse together. What emerged from this process was the English national round hand.

Because this writing was very much the style from which our modern everyday hand has descended, it is worth looking at in slightly greater detail. For example, it differentiated between the letters *i* and *j*, and *u* and *v*, which had previously caused confusion and even today transcriptions of ancient documents are being called into question, particularly in the matter of family names. Loops were provided for the ascenders (upward strokes) of *b, f, h, k* and *l*, and the descenders (downward strokes) of *f, g, j, y* and *z*. The addition of these features permitted increased legibility, a lessening of ambiguity and a speeding up of the writing process.

With the coming of the fine steel pen, further refinements were introduced. The Carstairs system (after Joseph Carstairs, died 1820) involved using the whole forearm in the business of writing, instead of just the fingers. The influence of Carstairs may still be detected in the handwriting of many Americans who, generally, apply a higher standard to calligraphy than do the English for similar purposes.

Today, the electronic typewriter with its daisy-wheel printer, and the personal computer with its ink jet dot-matrix printer, have probably put an end to *developments* in handwriting, although many people are now studying and practising the art of good penmanship, and the term a 'fine Italian hand' may yet be restored to its original meaning.

Bibliography

In addition to *The Handwriting of English Documents* by L.C. Hector already mentioned, the following books may be of value: *English Cursive Book-hands 1200-1500* by M.B. Parkes (London 1979), *Elizabethan Handwriting 1500-1650* by G.E. Dawson and L. Kennedy-Skipton (London, reprinted 1981), *Examples of English Handwriting 1150-1750* by Hilda Grieve (London, reprinted 1978).

An heraldic mystery. This panel, dated 1715, in a parish church, is clearly identified as the achievement of George I of the House of Hanover. The shield, however, is that of Anne, last sovereign of the House of Stuart, who died in 1714. With their supporters, the arms date from after 1707, when the Union with Scotland occurred. Anne's motto, however, was Semper Eadem, not Dieu et mon Droit.

27

Heraldry and local history

Although not a primary source to the local historian heraldry is, nevertheless, an important element which on occasion can contribute significantly to the progress of a study and, because of its artistic components, pleasantly illuminate it. True, the local history researcher is more likely to be pursuing investigations through source materials provided by Anglo-Saxon charters, medieval rolls, maps, land grants, muster documents and the like, but the uses of heraldry are not to be despised in the processes of rounding out historical themes. Occasionally a charge on a shield of arms, or the interpretation of a crest can be an important clue in the determination of seignorial affiliation, in linking two families with different names, or suggesting a hitherto unsuspected landholding, quite apart from the visual attraction an achievement might have as stained glass, stone carving or hatchment in the local church.

It is no part of the function of this chapter to dilate at length upon the rules (so far as they exist) or the functions of heraldry since its rise in the second quarter of the twelfth century, but a few general remarks will not be out of place. To begin with, heraldry (or, more properly, armory) comprised designs on shields and horse trappings adopted by the knightly class and above, to identify each other in tournaments. There was, and perhaps still is, a school of thought which asserted that armorial devices were assumed for identification in battle, but both research and common sense say this is probably wrong, for as so many knights chose arms of similar design, the mud, blood and turmoil of battle would have rendered such symbols on shields of little value, although the same cannot, of course, be said about armorial banners or pennons bravely waving above rallying points or on the ends of lances.

As time went on it became the custom for an armiger to display his cognizance on his seal, which thus became tantamount to his signature. Then it became a matter of convenience and practical good sense for an heir, on coming into his estate, to employ the same devices as his father, as an indication of familial continuity and lordship, so arms achieved hereditary significance and, by the end of the thirteenth century, there were both heraldic 'rules' and terminology. With the development of closed and visored helms, which effectively hid a man's face, elaborate crests in the shapes of animals, birds, fantastical creatures and other adornments were employed on helmets to signal identity, and these too became associated with particular families.

The language of blazon

Rising as it did, when the nobility and knightly classes in England were of Norman stock, it follows that the language of armory was French, and so it has remained (in remarkably garbed form with English interpolations) to the present day. Coats of arms are described according to rules known as 'blazon', a term which when used as a noun is a description in words of a coat and, when as the verb '(to) blazon', the act of so describing. A shield of arms (to cite one simple example) comprising a black cross with scalloped edges on a yellow (gold) background progressed from being described in the thirteenth century as *jaune o crois noire engrelee* to today's blazon *or a cross engrailed sable.*

At first sight both the earlier and later languages of blazon appear somewhat esoteric, but they readily yield up their secrets, being based on a comparatively small vocabulary, the words of which describe quite accurately both the colours (tinctures), layout, and principal devices used in armorial design. There are three basic books which may be studied to good effect: *A Complete Guide to Heraldry* by A.C. Fox-Davies, revised in 1969 by John Brooke-Little, the present Norroy and Ulster King of Arms; *Boutell's Heraldry*, also revised by Brook-Little (1983); and *A New Dictionary of Heraldry* (1987) edited by Stephen Friar. All three books are maintained in print.

Duplication and differencing

At all stages in the development of armory, and in all the centuries during which it has been in use, there have been two conflicting underlying factors, and it is important that the local historian be aware of them from the outset, so that if false trails are followed they are not followed for long. The first has been to satisfy the objective which has already been stated: to display identity by assuming (and from the four-teenth century being granted) arms of individual distinction. The second (not so relevant today) has, for reasons of sentiment or expediency, been to adopt arms similar to, but not technically identical with, a feudal protector or ally. The means by which this last aim is achieved is called 'differencing'.

The latest edition of *Boutell's Heraldry* gives a fine series of examples of feudal differencing of arms as assumed by the family of Luterell and their associated and dependent folk. In formal terms the Luterell arms may be described as *or a bend between six martlets sable* — that is, a gold shield carrying a black diagonal band with, on each side of this, three birds rather like house martins. This design, with colour variations and ornaments, was used by the de Furnival, Eccleshall, Wadsley, Wortley and Mounteney families. It illustrates a simple and straightforward situation, for the relationship between the Luterells and their feudal tenants is well documented. Unfortunately the local historian cannot rely on such proximity of tincture and style being always a sign of seignorial attachment. Different families are known to have employed quite similar arms to each other with apparent impunity (especially before the foundation of the College of Arms on 2 March 1484), and there is no evidence to suggest their actions were anything other than innocent.

To take but one example from the many available, a well-known medieval armorial design comprises a shield with three spike-like shapes starting from the top edge of the shield, points downward and meeting towards the bottom. In the language of blazon this is *three piles conjoined in base* (the charge being so termed, it is said, after the shape of the wooden supports early bridge-builders drove into river beds to support their structures). This shield design was used by the Earl of Chester, John le Scot

Differencing to denote cadency. LEFT *The arms of Andrew Forsey, member of parliament for Bridport in the reign of Henry V, and* RIGHT *those of Patricia, his 20th century collateral descendant.*

(*fl.*1225) as *or three piles gules* (gold with red spikes), the family of Ridel — *or three piles sable* (gold with black spikes), Basset (who succeeded Ridel) *or three piles gules within a bordure sable* (gold with red spikes all inside a black border), Bryan — *or three piles azure* (gold with blue spikes), and Wrottesley — *or three piles vert* (gold with green spikes). Members of three of the above families were, around the same time (1348 to 1369) members of the Order of the Garter, and although a connection is known to exist between Wrottesley and Basset, neither is connected with Bryan and none with le Scot. In circumstances such as this the local historian has perhaps two problems: to attempt to find a feudal or familial association or dependency, and, if the arms are uncoloured, to ascertain if they are those of le Scot, Ridel, Basset, Wrottesley or Bryan, or, indeed, some other line.

The term 'differencing' is also used in a quite distinct way from that of acknowledging feudal proximity, and that is to display family connections and descent. In the first instance, say a simple shield design (perhaps a red ground with a horizontal gold bar across the centre — *gules a fess or*) represents the bearings of the head of the main family, then offshoots might add to this stark layout crosses, birds or other charges above, below, or on the fess to mark the identity of their own branches, while honouring in their retention of the basic style the fundamental familial ties of blood. This system is known as *cadency* and marks the relationships of the cadet branches to the principal family tree.

A second method of proclaiming cadency down the male line of the whole blood is to display single marks of difference. The subject is dealt with in great detail in the more substantial books on heraldry as being one of great formality — a *label* for the eldest son, down to an *octofoil* for the ninth son. The system was standardised in the early part of the sixteenth century, and some authorities went so far as to describe the cadency symbols for the ninth son of a ninth son (an *octofoil* on an *octofoil*). In the event, the whole subject became rather fanciful in the writings of bygone heralds, their petty 'rules' never fully translated into practical expression. Even so, the local historian may find the system of value, particularly when examining rolls of arms in the county archive.

Impalement and escutcheons of pretence

Valuable clues to marital alliances are contained in two conventions for the depiction of armorial bearings of a man and his wife, known as impalement and escutcheon of pretence. Both terms refer to styles of depicting the arms of spouses on a single shield.

The first system is used when the husband is armigerous and the wife, although of an armigerous family, is not herself an heraldic heiress. The method of impalement in this situation has changed over the centuries. In early times the fashion was to cut the two shields in half down the vertical axis (the 'pale' line) and join the dexter half of the husband's to the sinister half of the wife's, thus making in many cases a very strange 'design' indeed — such as the front half of a lion joined to the right-hand portion of a spread eagle. This fashion of dimidiation was abandoned by at least the late fourteenth century and replaced by the style of compressing each set of armorial bearings onto one half of the shield — the husband's being placed on the dexter and the wife's on the sinister. The system is still in use today. (A short word of explanation is required at this point regarding the use of the words 'sinister' and 'dexter'. In heraldry the shield is described from the aspect of its *bearer*, not its *viewer*. Thus 'dexter' refers to the *left*-hand side of the shield as viewed from the *front*, and 'sinister' means the *right*-hand side.)

The second system of marshalling armorial bearings to broadcast marital relationship is to adopt an 'escutcheon of pretence'. By this method, if the wife is an heraldic heiress, the husband displays her arms on a small shield in the centre of his own, the title of the practice stemming from the fact that he is 'pretending' to represent his spouse's family, because there is no male heir to do so.

Marshalling of arms

The word 'marshalling' is used in this context in its meaning of *combining*, hence the marshalling of arms is the 'discipline of assembling the constituent elements of a coat of arms, and the various devices of which each is composed, in a manner which is in accordance with accepted armorial practice and convention. In particular, the correct ordering of combinations of armorial devices in a single coat to signify marriage, inheritance or office' (Friar *op cit*). Strictly speaking, therefore, impalement and the use of an escutcheon of pretence is marshalling at its simplest.

In more general heraldic usage the word is applied to the bringing together of two or more sets of arms to form *quarterings* — this is to say a shield divided into a number of areas, each capable of carrying a complete coat of arms as a sign of familial bonding. As with so many armorial terms the word 'quarterings' is not used in a conventional way and applied to a shield divided merely into four; indeed there can be as many 'quarterings' as there are family affiliations — perhaps the record is held by the five-surnamed Temple-Nugent-Brydges-Chandos-Grenville family, whose full achievement of arms boasts 719 quarterings. It is through the study of quartered coats, as

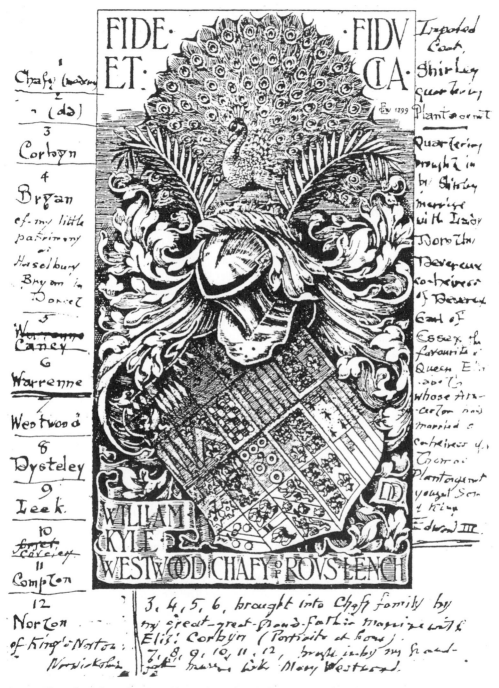

A magnificent bookplate of 1899 with, on the male side (left in picture), twelve quarterings, some of which appear to go back to the 13th century. The female side includes (second and third quarters) the royal arms of England within a bordure. The handwritten text makes reference to an heiress marriage to a grand-daughter of King Edward III.

displayed in cathedrals, county archives and other reference sources that the local historian may glean much information not only on families of note (should textual information not exist or be imprecise), but how tenure and ownership of estates changed hands in days long or recently past.

Augmentations of honour

From time to time persons distinguished in the fields of making war, healing, diplomacy, or mere grace in the sight of kings, have been granted augmentations to their armorial bearings; and the discovery of, and comment on, these can — where they are relevant — make a small but useful contribution to the rounding out of a local history.

Such augmentations are rare and signal honours. They mark especial favours from the sovereign, for although ordinary grants of arms can be purchased (subject always to the Earl Marshal's pleasure and discretion), an augmentation cannot, for its bestowal is in effect a royal warrant under the hand and seal of the reigning monarch.

Today augmentations are rarely given, but in times gone they were less rare and were granted to such as Thomas Howard, the victor of Flodden, Sir Winston Churchill of the reign of Charles II, his son John, first duke of Marlborough, Sir Frederick Treves, surgeon to King Edward VII, the Boleyn family for providing Anne to King Henry VIII, Admiral Nelson, the first Duke of Wellington and the Right Honourable Vincent Massey, a Governor-General of Canada.

To be fair, it is almost impossible to recognise augmentations at first sight, for they take many and sundry forms — such as a small escutcheon similar to that of pretence, a chief, a crest, a canton, a chevron, or, in the case of Sir Francis Drake, a complete coat of arms. Instances are known of augmentations comprising whole coats to be borne quarterly with personal arms.

A particular kind of augmentation concerns baronets. At the outset these honours were merely purchased, but in later creations the augmentations came with the grants. The gentlemen of this hereditary (non-peerage) rank, of the creations of England, Ireland, Great Britain and the United Kingdom, are permitted a canton (or an escutcheon) showing the 'bloody hand of Ulster' —*argent a sinister hand couped at the wrist gules*. Gentlemen who were early baronets of Scotland were authorised to charge their arms with a canton (or escutcheon) carrying the arms of the province of Nova Scotia — *argent on a saltire azure an escutcheon of the Royal Arms of Scotland*.

Finally there are 'augmentations of office', such as the escutcheon borne by the Kingsley family, sometime hereditary foresters of Delamere in Cheshire — *argent a bugle stringed sable* — and the 'augmentations' allowed to bishops and other dignitaries of dimidiating their personal arms with those of their office. Augmentations are worth searching out, for there is many a manor, grand house, or estate which has at one time been owned by an eminent person in receipt of an augmentation of one kind or another — and there is almost certainly a good tale to tell.

Helms and supporters

The style of helm and the direction in which it faces, whether it is open or closed, are all important pointers to the status of the person whose armorial bearings are being depicted. The subject is dealt with cogently and succinctly in the *New Dictionary of Heraldry*, and in even terser form the present practice may be stated as follows: a peer's helm is shown as a stylised silver mêlée type, facing dexter (that is *left* to the observer) and decorated with gold bars; the helmets of baronets and knights face the front (*affronty*) and are of the steel 'barrier' variety, with visors raised; esquires, gentlemen (and corporations) display closed 'tilting' helms of steel, facing dexter.

'Supporters' are figures — beasts, birds, mythical creatures and humans — depicted on either side of the shield in a coat of arms. They are, in short, symbols of eminence and are normally granted only to peers and knights of the first class of the orders of chivalry — although some baronets also have armorial supporters. Corporations may be granted these devices, but they are normally permitted only to counties, cities and councils of standing; and companies and institutions of an important national nature.

The significance of charges

Of considerable importance to the local historian are the representations of objects shown on shields. It has already been pointed out that family continuity, conjugal status, and marital affiliations can be determined by an informed examination of armorial achievements.

The objects (or designs) depicted on shields — the *charges* — can be anything the armiger wishes and the granting kings of arms deem fit. In the beginning, in the twelfth and thirteenth centuries, charges were chosen to appear on shields used in tournaments, and hence reflected this — lions, eagles, crosses, geometrical patterns — but with the passing of the Middle Ages and the emergence of a wealthy merchant class, charges were chosen to appeal to the armiger's interests or fancy. They could range from spurs to church bells, woolpacks, shuttles, rainbows, millrinds or staples, to sea-shells. Shakespeare's arms were charged with a tilting spear in allusion to his name; and the author's own arms are uniquely charged with Bristol nails, commemorating family associations with that ancient city.

A specific illustration may be given to show the value of the study of heraldic charges in the field of local studies. A Manchester family of Magnall, who also had business interests in London, had for many years borne arms without authority, and on 19 February 1765 Thomas Magnall was granted bearings blazoned *argent on a mount vert a swepe (or balista) azure* — a swepe/balista being a large siege catapult. The present author was much intrigued as to why a northern merchant family should choose what seemed to be a most inappropriate device (unless as indicative of their aggressive commercial practices). Reference to the actual grant of arms showed that it had a very strange limitations clause, for the arms were assigned to Thomas Magnall and his offspring and 'any such of the Descendants of his Father who shall write their Names Magnall and by no Others'! Further research revealed that the grantee's father had called himself *Mangnall*. This made the limitations clause even more interesting, for the older man (and no doubt his ancestral assumer) had quite obviously used not a swepe or balista as the charge, but an almost identical engine of war known as a *mangonel*, in witty and canting allusion to the family name as used by *them*. So here was an instance of the son of a local worthy insisting on recording his name differently from his father, making sure the charge was not described as a mangonel, and further trying to ensure that any of his father's descendants who sought to use the arms should spell their name Magnall, a form from which it is difficult if not impossible to divine the relevance and punning nature of the heraldic charge. This little study, when set in the appropriate context, was turned into a short piece for a local history magazine.

Locating coats of arms

Coats of arms are to be found in many places — churches, abbeys, town halls, stately homes, castles, police stations and public houses. They are never there without reason. In churches and places of worship they give clues to the identities of benefactors and, with a little skilled assistance, can be used to date important events. This is particularly true in the matter of monuments, chantry chapels, hatchments, memorial boards, ledger stones, floor tiles and misericords, but on the subject of stained glass a word of warning is necessary. Sometimes when the glass has been removed for cleaning and restoration it may have been reassembled back-to-front. In the main such errors are easy to detect because the charges face the heraldic sinister rather than the dexter, but occasionally, if the charges are non-directional and the arms are impaled, the historian can be misled as to which was the husband and which the wife, and hence infer the wrong family name.

A final word of caution concerns hatchments. These funerary items were nearly always painted by heraldic amateurs — signwriters, coachbuilders and so on — so although they provide useful clues they should not be regarded as authoritative, but of course the fact that they are *not* can also form part of the story the local historian has to tell.

On the outside of public buildings, particularly of the older sort, arms will give clues to the identity of previous owners, or if almshouses, benefactors. Sadly, arms on some modern buildings, though splendidly crafted, are occasionally inaccurate and may be misleading. Again this can be turned to the researcher's advantage.

Heraldic visitations

In the later Middle Ages as more and more families became armigerous, the abuse of arms by illegal assumption grew to the point where corrective action was necessary if the dignity of possessing a valid grant was not to be eroded beyond reclamation. Thus in the sixteenth century there began, by warrant of the king, systematic heraldic visitations with the mandate 'to put down or otherwise deface . . . plate, jewels, parchments, windows, gravestones and monuments . . . wheresoever they be set or placed' should those things bear unlawful arms. Moreover, the officer of arms making the visitation was directed to enquire into the lives of all those using a title of honour or dignity such as knight, esquire or gentleman, and if such a title or coat of arms had been falsely assumed or usurped, the offender was to be publicly denounced by proclamation.

Major visitations were conscientiously carried out by the heralds or their *deputes* — assisted by the sheriffs and their officers — for more than a hundred and forty years.

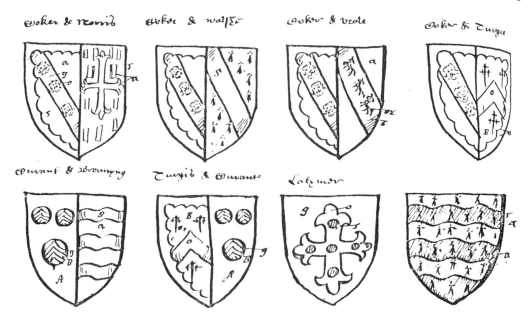

Part of a manuscript depicting arms once in a stained-glass window in a church. When the history of the church was being researched a footnote in an 18th century volume identified a drawing of some stained-glass panels which had long since fallen into disrepair and had been replaced by plain lights. The drawing was located in a British Museum collection, and showed not only the shields which had formerly adorned the window but identified the families whose arms they were, and in some cases gave the tinctures of the fields and charges. The principal family, Coker, were well-known Parliamentarians and several members were senior officers in the Cromwellian forces.

Records of their findings now comprise the Library of Visitation Books of the College of Arms, and a number have been published by the Harleian Society. This body was founded in 1869 for the purpose of publishing not only the manuscripts of the heraldic visitations but other 'inedited' documents of a related nature. Since its foundation it has issued 91 volumes of parish registers, 54 volumes of heraldic visitations and 65 drawn from other sources.

The visitation records have several values for the local historian. The first is that being spread over a period of time which began before the Armada, included the civil war and Commonwealth, and finished only after the accession of William of Orange, they are an unrivalled source of information on the changing status of many local families. The second is that they include not only pedigrees and arms but also, in many cases, ancillary material such as lists of persons to be summoned, correspondence, church notes and lists of disclaimers. Where they survive, 'tickets of summons' are occasionally found attached to paintings of family arms.

It is apparent from studies made that not all those summoned actually attended the heralds — a number ignored the college officers because they understood themselves too grand, of ancient family and proud lineage, and thus beyond any need to have their pedigrees recorded, much less authenticated. Not the least valuable to the local historian are the lists of names of *ignoble omnes* who falsely claimed arms and were publicly shamed.

Reference books

In addition to the books already mentioned, the following are among others of value: *Burke's General Armory*, published in 1842 and reissued in facsimile in London in 1984. It contains tens of thousands of blazons of arms held (or recorded as held) by English families, listed alphabetically by name. It is neither complete nor authoritative — the family of Forsey, to take just one small example, being listed separately as Forterishey, Fortersley, and Fortryshey without cross reference, attempt to verify a definitive spelling, or verification of blazon — but it is almost the only generally available starting point, and cannot be ignored. The counterpart to *Burke's General Armory* is *Papworth's Ordinary of British Armorials*, published in 1874 and reissued in London in 1985. The book comprises an alphabetical dictionary 'in which the arms are systematically divided throughout . . . so that the names of families whose shields are found on buildings, monuments, seals, paintings, plate, etc., whether mediaeval or modern can be readily ascertained.' And that statement, given that such a book can never be complete nor, when based as it is on Burke's volume, without error, is true. But the user of Papworth *must* be able to blazon.

The *Oxford Guide to Heraldry* (Oxford 1988), by Thomas Woodcock and John M. Robinson, is a welcome, lavishly illustrated, new text. *Anglo-Norman Armory* (Vols I & II) by Cecil Humphery-Smith (Canterbury 1978) is of value to the researcher needing assistance in identifying arms on early rolls. The volumes are not especially easy to use, however, and more detailed and accessible information is contained in two works published in 1950 and 1967 by the Society of Antiquaries of London: *A Catalogue of English Medieval Rolls of Arms* by Sir Anthony Wagner, and *Rolls of Arms - Henry III* edited by T.D. Tremlett and Hugh Stanford London, with additions by Wagner. *Honour and Arms* by J.F. Huxford (London 1984) is a quite sumptuous book covering augmentations from early, legendary, varieties up to the present century. Each coat of arms touched on is illustrated in full colour, and the augmentation is blazoned. A series of publications under the title *Hatchments of Britain* is in the process of appearing, edited by Peter Summers. So far the following have been released: Vol.I, 1974, *Northampton, Warwickshire and Worcestershire*; Vol.II, 1976, *Norfolk and Suffolk*; Vol.III, 1980, *Northern Counties*; Vol.IV, 1983, *Oxfordshire, Buckinghamshire, Bedfordshire, Berkshire and Wiltshire*; Vol.V, 1985, *Kent, Surrey and Sussex*; Vol.VI, 1987, *Cambridgeshire, Essex, Hertfordshire, Huntingdonshire and Middlesex*.

Seals are dealt with in the series issued by HMSO: *Catalogue of Seals in the Public Record Office* by R.E. Ellis (1978-81); and brasses by *A List of Monumental Brasses in the British Isles* by Stephenson Mill (1926, with an appendix, London 1938). *A Guide to Stained Glass in Britain* by P.A. Cowan (London 1985) is, in its field, most valuable for it contains a gazetteer. *Medieval Chantries and Chantry Chapels* by G.H. Cook (London 1968) has much to commend it, as has *English Misericords* by M. Laird (London 1986). Finally, the *New Dictionary of Heraldry* includes useful articles on churchyard monuments, tomb chests and medieval tiles.

Lincoln. The arch of a Roman gate to the colonia.

28 Buildings and architecture

For the purposes of this chapter the word 'architecture' — the art or science of building — is employed in the widest possible sense, from the construction of the circular huts of the Bronze Age peoples to the curtain-walled apartment blocks or 'space-age' experimental structures of the late twentieth century. Each succeeding system or style drew on the techniques of preceding systems or styles, and all are of interest to the local historian.

Ecclesiastical buildings

No extensive treatment will be accorded to ecclesiastical buildings, be they humble parish churches, cathedrals, abbeys, monasteries, friaries, nunneries, or any other such. Almost without exception these structures (past and present) are already well covered. Some, like St Paul's Cathedral in London, and the Metropolitan Cathedral of Christ the King in Liverpool, have handsome four-colour booklets devoted to them, and these publications are useful starting points for the serious student. Others, like the now all but vanished Saxon cathedral in North Elmham in Norfolk, are the subjects of academic papers by the staff of the Ancient Monuments and Historic Buildings division of the Department of the Environment. A third group, the humble parish churches, have their guide books. These too are obvious starting points but should be treated with caution, because the authors, conscientious as they may be, are almost always non-professional antiquaries, historians or architects, and errors or misapprehensions frequently creep into their work.

A vast number of religious buildings have been surveyed by competent authorities, and detailed descriptions (with photographs and plans) are available from the Royal Commission on Historical Monuments (see Addresses, Appendix III). Even where the buildings are described in the Commission's published series, *An Inventory of Historical Monuments in the County of . . .*, the researcher should write to (or, better still, visit) the Commission's London offices for more information than has appeared on the printed pages. The photographs which are available frequently include tombs, wall monuments, brasses, cartouches, and important exterior details such as grotesques, gargoyles and sundials, for which there was no space in the books.

Before embarking on detailed research on an individual, quite ancient, building it will be prudent to refer, in addition to the *Inventory* noted above, to the *Victoria County History*, for in many cases valuable data will be found. The *Monasticon Anglicanum* has already been mentioned in this book. It should be remembered that the title of this mammoth work is, essentially, *A History of the Abbies and other Monasteries, Hospitals, Frieries and Cathedral and Collegiate Churches . . . together with a particular account of their respective foundations . . . .* Being published, originally, in 1655-73 it is of the greatest importance in connection with ecclesiastical buildings up to that time. Also of prime relevance are the old county histories. A modern work of importance describing all the main monastic sites still surviving is *Medieval Monasteries of Great Britain* by L. Butler and C. Given-Wilson (London 1983).

As has been indicated for the parish church, it will be prudent to determine if a descriptive booklet is, or has ever been, available. Such a publication will be a pertinent reference aid. Indeed, if superbly well written, it may contain everything that is required. Experience has, however, shown that although many such works appear *prima facie* comprehensive, they frequently are not. The more ancient the building, the greater the problem. It must be remembered that what is described is, almost without exception, the church as it existed at the time of writing. It is of course true that in many cases it will be stated that the nave is, for example, twelfth-century, the chancel fifteenth (with nineteenth-century restorations), the north chapel twentieth, and so on, but it will not record the stained glass now gone or the wall monuments which have decayed (or, obviously, the changes wrought since the booklet was written). In the former of these circumstances the old county histories may be searched to considerable effect, for not only may they describe the church as it then was, but give further clues as to where data may be found. In a specific instance the author discovered a footnote in a county history (1774) describing how stained glass in a local church was falling into decay. There was no mention of any such glass in an early twentieth-century description, and it seemed to have disappeared before a restoration of 1869. However, by careful reading of the footnote, a manuscript was found in the Harleian Collection of the British Library which dated from 1599 and gave details of the armorial panels which at that date existed. These were of great value not only regarding the history of

This aerial view of Pevensey Castle shows the Roman fort together with the medieval keep and bailey in the southeast corner. The fort was built c.AD300, and the castle during the period AD1100-1300.

the architecture of the fabric and fitments, but also the matrimonial alliances of long-dead notables.

Regarding the changes made since the writing of the booklet, the researcher will gain pleasure from discovering them on site.

Castles and forts

There are dozens of castles, or sites of forts and castles, in England — from Corfe (Dorset) in the south to Ford (Northumberland) in the north, from Shrewsbury (Shropshire) in the west to Caister (Norfolk) in the east. They range from sites of long-gone timber motte and bailey structures, through ruined stone works to well-preserved extensive buildings still lived in and enjoyed by owners or tenants.

Every castle and site of consequence has its guide book, and many of these are well written if not actually comprehensive. The old county histories contain interesting material, sometimes with plans and drawings not easily obtainable elsewhere. The volumes in the *Victoria County History* and the *Inventories* of the Royal Commission on Historical Monuments are invaluable. There are also modern books on the subject. One which has much to commend it is *Great Medieval Castles of Britain* by James Forde-Johnston (London 1979), for it contains, in addition to many photographs and line drawings, a good bibliography, and provides historical perspectives — political, military and architectural.

Stately homes

Much of the generality of what has been said about important religious buildings and castles is true about stately homes. Many have guide books, the information in which can be augmented by diplomatic approaches to the owners or custodial bodies (such as the National Trust and English Heritage) — there may be estate papers showing details of constructional features, modifications, contractors' itemized bills for work done, and so on. Sometimes personal tours can be arranged in the company of a qualified member of staff, and these are of particular value for 'special subject' histories.

Industrial and special-purpose buildings

A moment's reflection will show there have, from very early times, been 'industrial' and other special-purpose buildings — 'henges', fogous, shrines, kilns, mints, abattoirs, amphitheatres, salthouses and many others. The first industrial revolution brought numerous new structures — textile mills, engine sheds, foundries, pumping stations — the second brought everything from telephone exchanges to towering office blocks, nuclear and photovoltaic power stations, vertical-axis wind turbines and multi-storey carparks. All are built *somewhere* and hence within the province of the local historian. The sources of information are countless: from the Archaeology Branch of the Ordnance Survey to the publicity departments of large civil engineering contractors and multi-national corporations, the Departments of the Environment and Energy, county halls, and museums. Each researcher must make a personal choice, in the multiplicity of circumstances which now exist.

Domestic buildings and architecture

It is fairly obvious to say there are two classes of buildings to be studied — those which still stand, and those which have been destroyed, fallen down, or otherwise disappeared. The disappearances may range in cause from the Roman invasion to the obliteration of a village for an aircraft runway, from sheer neglect to site redevelopment. To the local historian, all the architectural features on buildings past and present are of interest. The search for details of buildings now gone is as fascinating as that of the discovery of features of those that remain.

There are three (perhaps four) sources of information — archaeological, documentary, and new observation through personal research; the dubious fourth being the stories by third-parties who 'remember' things about buildings now gone, or changed.

312

19th century weavers cottages in Heptonstall. The wide windows provided light for the looms inside.

Archaeological sources

Hardly a week goes by without a report in the press of some find of archaeological importance. Excavation in a town centre or new rural development unearths traces of Bronze Age habitations, Roman foundations, sections of medieval walls, etc. It is, therefore, sometimes a little difficult to keep up-to-date, for although what is found may not be in the area being researched by the local historian concerned, it may, nonetheless, have a bearing, for the style of housing suggested for one place may be typical of that formerly existing in another, ten or even a hundred miles away.

The first places of research are, therefore, the local authority archaeological officer, the central reference library and the county or city museum. There will be found a wealth of information in all kinds of forms — from details of sites which have been excavated and studied, to actual examples of materials used, given that they have been sufficiently durable as to survive. Even when no substantial physical remains have been found, archaeologists, using bodies of knowledge gained over many years, may have been able to infer what kinds of buildings may have stood on particular spots which show foundation-traces, and have rendered 'artists impressions' of what the structures probably looked like. These may range from circular huts set in a farmyard, with small closes dating from the Ornamental Horizon of the Middle Bronze Age, through the hill-fort 'village' of the Iron Age, first-century Roman villa with out-buildings, to much later structures up to, and sometimes including, the twentieth century.

Documentary sources

Documentary sources vary widely over time and in quality. They may range from a brief mention of a thirteenth-century tithe barn near the manor house, to a fully

An engraving from the 18th century of the magnificent guild hall in Hereford. The timber-framed building dating from the late 16th century was demolished in the 19th century.

detailed true-to-scale plan of a building as it existed in earlier times, but which is now changed. Or they may be of a different kind. The farmhouse in which the author now lives was thought, locally, to be about 250 years old — its general style and construction seeming to indicate this. It was not, however, shown on the tithe map of 1838, and recent modifications to the structure revealed a stone set above the front doorway (and previously hidden by an Edwardian porch) which was 'documented' with the date 1880. The house was indeed of that later time, but in the style and materials which at first glance indicated a greater age.

It is unusual to find documentary evidence earlier than the fifteenth century, and extremely fortunate to find actual details of buildings. For example, the author discovered an early fifteenth-century 'survey' of a village (describing the sizes of fields and the uses to which they were put) which mentioned a *grange* close to the manor house. This led to a field study which at least seemed to locate not only the site but the probable outlines of the building. In another case, the name Cruckerne ('the house where the pottery was made') permitted the identification of a valuable site and foundation traces. Manorial court records sometimes give useful clues as to when a particular building existed (even when it was built), but seldom are there clues to the sizes or layout. Glebe terriers, cathedral records, borough records and tax returns can also be of value. So too can wills and probate inventories. Descriptions of houses and their environs can sometimes be reconstructed from such items as 'goods in the *hall*, in the *middle chamber*, in the *hall-chamber*, in the *kitchen*, in the *milkhouse*, in the *barn* and *another barn.*' With a little knowledge, ingenuity, and the help of local authority staff, these definitions (all taken from one inventory of 1717/18), and others of like kind, can be translated into probable floor plans.

One of the most useful sources of documentary evidence is that afforded by maps and plans, particularly if they are of large estates and augmented by written records. Some early maps of this type show, albeit crudely, the kinds of houses existing at the time of drafting, and it is possible to appreciate the difference between the houses of, say, the more well-to-do freeholder and the lowlier tenant. It may also be possible to compare these early drawings with a still existing building on the same site, to determine if it *is* the same structure, and, if so, if any general exterior modifications have been made.

There is an important official source of relevant information — the publications of the Royal Commission on the Historical Monuments of England. These fall into several categories. The first is the *Inventories*, mentioned several times already in this book, detailing architectural (and archaeological) treasures in many counties. The second category (called *Occasional Publications*) ranges over a wide area of subjects from *Peterborough New Town* (1964), *Industry and the Camera* (1985), to *English Vernacular Houses* (reprinted in paperback 1980). This last-named is a quite essential source of both information and ideas for the local researcher. A third category, termed *Supplementary Series,* deals mainly with working-class houses — *West Yorkshire - 1400-1830* and *1750-1920* are typical examples (1986). The *National Monuments Record Photographic Archive* is the fourth category, and *Buildings for the Age: New Building Types 1900-1939* (1982) and *Farms in England: Prehistoric to Present* (1983) are representative titles. The final category, *The Survey of London,* is made up of volumes describing the buildings in parishes, and books devoted to individual London structures such as Cromwell House, Highgate, and Trinity Hospital, Mile End. The Royal Commission publishes an *Annual Review* of its work (with maps and photographs) and this is a worthwhile document to seek out, for it gives not only the background to the work undertaken but keeps the publications record up-to-date. A useful paper, 'The Royal Commission on Historical Monuments', was published in *Antiquity* Vol.LV (1981) pp.106-14, and points to the way some present, and future, publications will be made.

Important as the foregoing publications are, the crucial thing for local historians to be aware of is the richness of the records maintained by the Commission, which have not been, and perhaps never will be, published. These are maintained in three sections: architectural records, air photography, and archaeology, and they contain millions of individual entries. For the time being enquiries should be made to the Commission (see Addresses, Appendix III). A guide to the records is currently being written by the Commission's staff.

A further official record is the *List of Buildings of Special Architectural Interest* compiled by the Department of the Environment (see Addresses, Appendix III). This series, with accompanying maps, was started in 1950 (and has been in revision since 1970). It is prepared within the authority of the Town and Country Planning Acts, and appropriate sections are available for inspection at county and district council offices.

Town and city guidebooks are further sources of information. These publications frequently contain pictures and other details of notable domestic buildings. More particularly, careful scrutiny of the 'Acknowledgements' sections will occasionally lead to other avenues to be explored — private collections of photographs being a notable instance.

Of more academic, secondary reference, works two in particular may be of special value. The first is *The English Medieval House* by Margaret Wood (London, reprint 1985) which, although dealing mainly with larger houses, is well organised into a series of chapters dealing with *features*, such as porches, fireplaces, staircases, windows, and so on. It is very well illustrated with innumerable photographs, line drawings and ground plans. The second book is *How Old is Your House?* by Pamela Cunnington (London, revised 1988), and is even more valuable. It quite belies its title for it deals with a very wide spectrum of architectural and building topics, has many pictures and plans, useful addresses and a pertinent bibliography. It deals with all historical periods from the medieval to Victorian, and is an essential aid to the study of vernacular buildings. Reference should also be made to the section entitled *Housing* in Chapter 31 of this present volume.

There is a surprising number of medieval houses still standing, sometimes quite unexpectedly awaiting discovery. For example, Miss Cunnington cites a small house at Pamphill, Dorset, which may have once been a fourteenth-century hunting lodge. When first surveyed, a few years ago, it had rendered outer walls and unprepossessing windows. On closer examination it proved to be a medieval first-floor hall house, with solar, garderobe, seventeenth-century overflooring, and to have spent part of its time as a farmhouse. It has now been handsomely restored. The book cites a number of further case histories and examples from later centuries, and others similar to those quoted may, of course, be repeated many times over, in all parts of the country.

Conclusion

There are, then, many avenues open to the local investigator wishing to research the history of the buildings in any geographical area. Perhaps more than in any other specialist area of study the means to do so are readily available. When the sources of the local authority archaeological office, reference library, county or city museum, Royal Commission publications and collections, *Victoria County History* volumes and the secondary texts quoted earlier have been exhausted, then the historic buildings officer may be consulted, together with the county or district planning departments.

For *very* modern buildings of all classes it will also be possible to contact the developers and architects concerned. In the case of ecclesiastical property this may be done through the church authorities; in the case of other buildings it will be possible to consult with the agents who handled the commercial matters concerned; these can be identified by consultation with the local authority.

An excellent example of the rewards of careful research. This small house in Pamphill, Dorset, presented until recently a very drab and rundown appearance. When all the rendering was removed and interior studies made, it proved to be a late medieval first-floor hall house, and its appearance is now as in the lower picture.

29

Chronology and some problems of dating

At some point or other the student of local history will encounter dates expressed in a variety of different ways with which he will have to become familiar. Each has its own terminology, logical basis and history, several are complex and worth exploring in some detail.

Regnal years

Most local historians are familiar with the term 'regnal year' and are used to seeing dates in printed texts and commentaries expressed in forms such as 11 Edward III, or 63 Victoria, meaning a time between 25 January 1337 and 24 January 1338, or between 20 June 1899 and 19 June 1900 respectively. It is quite usual to seek translation in tables of regnal years such as those printed in the more common reference books without, perhaps, recognising the historical significance of the system or the traps which lie within it for the unwary. Indeed, two of the most popular reference books contain errors in their tables of regnal years, their compilers having made the grievous mistake of assuming the method is a straightforward one, when in fact it is not.

It has been a common practice since ancient times to date official documents by the year of the rulers issuing them, or from within whose jurisdiction they emanated. In Roman times the law required that certain types of document carry the names of the consuls, and in AD537 the Emperor Justinian decreed that the year of the emperor's reign should be added. The system of dating by the regnal year was afterwards adopted by a variety of authorities including bishops, popes and kings, and it found its way into literary narratives as well as official documents. In a number of cases it ousted earlier conventions, such as the indiction or year of grace (see later).

The system is known to have been used in England in the first part of the eighth century, and continued to be employed by Anglo-Saxon kings until the tenth, when it fell into almost total disuse. From the beginning of the reign of King Richard I in 1189 the method was revived and, from that time onwards, has been the accepted way of expressing the year date in civil government and other documents; the form being, for example, that names of signatories are subscribed or the seal affixed 'this first day of July in the Thirtyseventh year of the Reign of Our Sovereign Lady Elizabeth the Second . . . and in the year of Our Lord One thousand and nine hundred and eighty eight.'

A reliable table of regnal years for English monarchs starts (popular reference books to the contrary) with the accession of King Henry II on 19 December 1154. There is no positive evidence as to how the regnal year was reckoned in periods before that time.

Edward the Confessor, for example, came to the throne sometime in June 1042, and was crowned on 3 April 1043, but did he become king as *soon* as Harthacnut died on 8 June 1042, or was he adjudged king only after his anointing? Problems of a somewhat similar kind occur up to the death of Stephen on 25 October 1154, and even after that date there are various kinds of complication; the first to be noted is that the reign of a monarch did not automatically start, or be deemed to start, on the day his or her predecessor died, or vacated the throne, as has been the custom since the death of William III on 8 March 1722. It is true that Edward V's one and only regnal year began on the day the previous sovereign expired, as did those of Henry VII and Henry VIII, Edward VI, Queens Jane, Mary I and Elizabeth I, James I, Charles I and James II. But Henry II died on 6 July 1189 and Richard I succeeded nearly two months later on 3 September. John followed Richard after a lapse of some six weeks, to be succeeded in turn by Henry III after a vacancy of a week, and Edward I succeeded *him* after a four-day interval. A number of kings assumed sovereignty the day after the demise of their predecessors — Edward II, Richard II, Henry IV, Henry V, Henry VI and Richard III. In other cases, circumstances of national moment prevailed.

In the case of Henry VI, he was deposed on 4 March 1461 (thus ending his 39th regnal year), to be succeeded on the same day by Edward IV. The new king fled the country on 29 September 1470 and Henry VI was restored very shortly afterwards, but deposed again on 11 April 1471. The duration of his restoration was deemed his 49th regnal year — in other words, the reign of Edward was ignored. But when Edward recaptured the throne he went on dating *his* regnal years as though the restoration of Henry had never happened.

Queen Jane (the former Lady Jane Grey) lost the throne on 19 July 1553 — having been sovereign for twelve days — to be succeeded by Mary whose first regnal year was dated from that day, but her second regnal year began on 6 July 1554, thus ignoring the 'reign' of Jane. When Mary I married Philip of Spain she decreed they ruled England jointly, and for the next few years until Elizabeth came to the throne the following strange convention was adopted for recording their regnal years:

Mary

	Regnal year			Regnal year
1	19 July 1553-5 July 1554		2	6* July 1554-24 July 1554

Philip and Mary

1&2	25 July 1554-5 July 1555	3&5	6 July 1557-24 July 1557
1&3	6 July 1555-24 July 1555	4&5	25 July 1557-5 July 1558
2&3	6 July 1556-24 July 1556	4&6	6 July 1558-24 July 1558
3&4	25 July 1556-5 July 1557	5&6	25 July 1558-17 Nov 1558

* Edward VI's reign ended on 6 July 1553, to be followed by that of (Queen) Lady Jane Grey who 'ruled' until 19 July 1553. Mary, for her second regnal year, adopted 6 July as the starting point, thus ignoring Jane's intrusion.

On 17 March 1649 the monarchy was abolished and during the period until parliamentary government was overtaken by the Restoration, English official documents were dated by the year of grace. Charles II was proclaimed king in May 1660 and, because parliament declared he had been *de jure* king since his father's death, his first year of actual kingship was designated his twelfth and a starting date of 29 May was adopted. Two minor points need to be noted — firstly that Charles himself was, in April 1660, already dating documents 'in the twelfth year of our reign', and secondly that although his father's sovereignty terminated on 30 January (1649), his own did not begin as though immediately following. After the flight of King James II on 11 December 1688 the legal fiction was adopted that this day was the last of his reign (thus 4 James II is 6 February 1688 to 11 December 1688), and there followed an interregnum until William III and Mary II were made king and queen for their joint and several lives on 13 February 1689. Their last regnal year (6 William and Mary) ended with the queen's death on 27 December 1694. The period from 28 December 1694 until 12 February 1695, is known as 6 William III, and from then on the normal conventions applied.

In the reign of George II, in 1752, eleven dates were omitted in September when the New Style calender was adopted (see below). Thus 25 George II ran from 11 June 1751 to 10 June 1752, 26 George II from 11 June 1752 to 21 June 1753, and 27 George II from 22 June 1753 to 21 June 1754, thus ensuring that the 26th regnal year contained 365 days.

There are two final peculiarities to be noted. The first concerns the reign of King John, whose monarchy dates from his coronation on Ascension Day 1199. Now Ascension Day is a movable feast in the Church calendar, and hence John's regnal years vary in length so that, for example, his eighth year contains both 12 May 1206 and 12 May 1207. The second is tantamount to the same thing in reverse. Easter is also a movable feast, and because of this there is no Easter in 10 or 37 Henry VIII, or in 3 or 14 Charles I. On the other hand, there are two such Pascal days in 11 Henry VIII and 13 Charles I.

The year of grace

The dating of years from the Incarnation of Jesus Christ — AD1 — started in England in the eighth century quite informally, and then spread throughout the countries of Western Europe with the exception of the Iberian peninsula, where a quite different system against a base of 1 January 38BC prevailed for a number of centuries. But this latter convention has no place in a volume about English local history, or at least none the author has ever discovered.

The practice of using the passage of years since the birth of Christ as a numbering system had its genesis in some work carried out by a monk, Dionysius Exiguus, in AD525. Dionysius, who lived in Rome, compiled a table for calculating the date of Easter, and in committing this to writing used as his datum not the regnal year of the pagan Emperor Diocletian, but the more appropriate Incarnation of Our Lord. In AD664 the Dionysian Easter Table (with its list of years) was accepted by the synod of Whitby for use in England. The eighth-century chronicler Bede adopted the year-numbering system in his historical works and its use spread, for in a Christian country it had much to commend it. The year of grace is found in Saxon documents of both a royal and civil nature at this time, in the term *ab incarnatione*, sometimes supplementing and sometimes replacing dating by indiction — of which more later. The royal chancery adopted the year of grace and by the Middle Ages it was in general use, and providing the chronological framework for English histories of all kinds.

The problem is that for many centuries there were a number of variant systems in which the year of grace began at different times — 1 January, Christmas Day, the Annunciation, Easter Day, and 1, 24 and 29 September.

The local historian should be aware of the systems and the difficulties they create. These range from determining exactly *where* in Europe the lord of an English medieval manor was at a certain date (for the more senior magnates were often crusaders, pilgrims, legates and diplomatists) to ascertaining precisely when an eighteenth-century trading agreement with a French merchant was concluded. The problem might even be confined to England itself, for it is not unusual, particularly in the twelfth century, to find two systems of reckoning in use at the same time for different classes of computation. The historical writer Gervase (a monk of Canterbury and contemporary of Becket), although sometimes using the Annunciation discipline which at that time was in more general use, preferred for the bulk of his work, *Chronica, Gesta Regum*, etc., the Christmas system — much to the irritation of later writers.

The historical year

The historical year, now in general use in England for all everyday purposes and many official and ecclesiastical, begins on 1 January, and thus coincides with the Roman civil year which was widely used until at least the seventh century. 1 January was also used as the octave of the Nativity (Christmas) in the first centuries of the Christian era, and later as marking the Feast of the Circumcision. However, during the Middle Ages 1 January lost favour against a start date of the feast of the Annunciation (25 March), the main reason no doubt being the Church's wish to underline its pre-eminence by using one of its own major festivals to mark the inauguration of each year. Even so, some medieval documents treat 1 January as the first day of the year of grace. In the sixteenth and seventeenth centuries continental Europe gradually changed to a 1 January system, but it was not adopted in England until 1751/2 when the day after 31 December 1751 became 1 January 1752, rather than remaining 1 January 1751. It should be noted in passing that in Scotland the change had been made in 1599/60.

It is a little difficult to explain why the 1 January method superseded 25 March as the start of the historical year, although it can be shown that it was in ordinary use early in the eighteenth century, as witness such as 'A True and Perfect Inventory of the Goods and Chattells of John Green Deceased the eight day of January 1713/14'. A number of partial explanations have been put forward — the persistence of the calculations of calendars based on a solar year starting 1 January, and the popular association of the date with 'New Year'. Samuel Pepys, the noted diarist who died in 1703, dated his journals on the basis of the Annunciation, but invariably noted 1 January as 'New Year'.

The Nativity

The convention of marking the beginning of years of grace by the Nativity (or Christmas Day) has a long history. It was used in the Roman Empire until early in the thirteenth century, and in most of Western Europe until the twelfth. The Anglo-Saxon and Norman kings employed the system, but during Plantagenet times it fell into desuetude. It was, however, retained by Benedictine writers, and local historians will do well to note this, for some confusion can be caused to the unwary or uninformed researcher. For example, Matthew Paris, the medieval author of *Historia Anglorum* and who used the Nativity reckoning, wrote in consequence that certain eminent people were born, or died, on certain dates which were at a variance of a full year with the Historical. It should also be noted that, in much the way that the period 25 December to 1 January is nowadays increasingly a 'holiday' but without religious content, so in medieval times the octave was an important festival and sometimes Christmas and Historical reckoning became uncertain in the dating of documents.

The Annunciation

The term 'annunciation' (announcement) is that given to the message presented by the angel Gabriel to the Blessed Virgin Mary that she would in due time be delivered of the Son of God, and the festival commemorating this — Lady Day — has the date 25 March.

This date was adopted by various countries as marking the beginning of the year. Here again two conflicting conventions grew up and were in use at one and the same time in the medieval England of the eleventh and twelfth centuries. The first system used 25 March *preceding* the Nativity as the start date, and the second system employed 25 March *following* the Nativity as its beginning. Thus there were two year dates running absolutely parallel with one another. The first method, which started on the continent in the ninth century, was used in the papal chancery from 1088 until 1145, and although little used in *English* documents nonetheless has a bearing on local ecclesiastical history for that period. The second method, the use of which became much more widespread, also began in Europe — in the eleventh century. It gained gradual acceptance in England, as witness certain entries in the *Anglo-Saxon Chronicle*, and had general application in the twelfth century, remaining in use until 1752 when the Historical year gained official approval.

From the middle of the sixteenth century there had, however, been some confusion in England, mainly because most continental countries had adopted 1 January as the beginning of their year, and had also assumed the same year number. Thus for official purposes the old reckoning of 25 March was used, but its employment for unofficial and private purposes was waning to the extent that many documents carried a double indicator for the period 1 January to 24 March, as was illustrated by the inventory quoted in the Historical Year section, above. If no double indicator is used the local historian may usually assume that seventeenth-century and eighteenth-century documents dated up to 1752 use the Annunciation method. Because of the now universal use in England of the Historical year system, it is normal for reference books to mark events of all kinds which happened between 1 January and 24 March in any one year with a double indicator — thus King Henry V may be judged to have come to the throne on 21 March 1412/13, that is 1412 by Annunciation reckoning, but 1413 by Historical (now conventional) reckoning.

The Easter Day system

This system has little impact on English local history, except in those cases where Anglo-Norman magnates retained interests in France which bore a relation to their holdings in England. It was a method which reckoned the year from the movable feast of Easter, and was introduced by the French king Philip Augustus (1180-1223). It did not last long because of its complexity in application.

September dating

There are several styles of year-dating which start with a day in the month of September. The oddest is that used in the fourteenth century by the English historian Adam of Murimuth. This writer, for no reason which is apparent, began his year on Michaelmas Day, 29 September, in advance of the Historical year. In Saxon times two other conventions were adopted, both based on Indiction (see next section). A September method was employed by Bede in his ecclesiastical history written in AD731, and he used either 1 September or 24 September as his year-start dates (the Greek and the Caesarian systems). The September method is also used in the late ninth century *Anglo-Saxon Chronicles*, before the Christmas style was re-introduced in the tenth century. The local historian should beware of placing too much credence on year-dates given in older volumes of Anglo-Saxon history, for these can be in error by twelve months; but it is unlikely that any modern scholar of repute has been led astray.

Indiction

The term 'indiction' has been used earlier in this chapter, and although the system is unlikely to be encountered in isolation by a local historian it is worth recording, if only for the sake of completeness. It was a method of year-dating of civil, as distinct from religious, application first adopted by Imperial Rome and then continued in both the papal and royal chanceries of Europe during the early Middle Ages. However, it gradually fell into disuse and was finally abandoned by its last users, the public notaries, in the sixteenth century.

The indiction was a cycle of fifteen years computed always from AD312, and in practice there were three ways to calculate the opening date. These were the Greek or Constantinopolitan which began on 1 September, the Caesarian or Imperial beginning on 24 September, and the Roman or Pontifical which commenced either on 25 December or 1 January. It is unlikely that the local history researcher will require the dating formula to compute an *indictio primo, secunda,* and so on, so the matter is not dealt with here. A full description appears in *A Handbook of Dates* by C.R. Cheney (London, corrected edition 1978).

323

Divisions of the year

The calendar in use today is known as the Gregorian or New Style, to distinguish it from the Julian or Old Style, and was introduced by Pope Gregory XIII in 1582. Its functioning, including leap years, is so familiar that it sometimes comes as a revelation to researchers into early English local history to learn that there were several calendars in use in the past, each somewhat different from the other, with quite distinct ways of referring to months and days, and with days whose hours varied in length according to the season of the year.

The Roman calendar

The Roman 'Julian' calendar was introduced in 45BC by Julius Caesar, and hence carries his name. It was in use until the sixteenth century, when small inaccuracies it contained had compounded to the point that minor revision was necessary. The Julian calendar established a year of 365 days with an extra one (24 February was repeated) every fourth year to rectify the difference between calendar and solar years, which contained 365¼ days. There were initial problems, and Augustus made certain small adjustments which need not be recounted here.

The Romans divided the year into twelve months, and each month into groups of days called respectively Kalends, Nones and Ides, with the days after Ides reckoned in relation to the Kalends of the next month following. The local historian unfamiliar with Roman practice may, therefore, have slight initial difficulty on finding, for example, Lady Day (25 March) expressed as VIII Kal April; or that although III Non June is indeed *3 June*, IV Non June is *2 June*, or equally that whilst XVI Kal July is *16 June* XVI Kal August is *17 July*. It is best, therefore, to use a conversion calendar rather than attempt to cast from Roman to Gregorian. Even here a word of caution is necessary, for although medieval writers employed the Roman calendar they sometimes reckoned the Kalend, None and Ide elements in reverse order; so that, for example, 14 January might appear not as XIX Kal Feb but as Pridi Kal Feb (*prima die kalendarum Feb*). Too much need not be made of this, and the Roman calendar will suffice for all but the quite rarest occasions.

In addition to dividing the months into days as just described, another Roman system was in use until the Middle Ages. This was the *custom of Bologna* and was employed in England by public notaries. In this, the month was divided into two parts, the first (of fifteen or sixteen days) being counted forwards, the second being reckoned backwards. It has little impact on local history studies, for gradually the system of numbering the days of the month as a continuous series was, with one outstanding exception, accepted. The exception was embodied in the ecclesiastical calendar.

The ecclesiastical calendar

From about AD500 the Christian Church introduced a practice of dating according to the nearest religious festival. To begin with the system was used by chroniclers, then for specifying the dates on which fairs were held or rent payments due, and finally, in the thirteenth century, it came into use for dating letters and other documents. Because the list of festivals included saints' days (of which there are a large number) the system became complex. Sunday was the first and chief day of the week, and saints' days always fell on the same date, as did some of the major festivals such as Christmas, which was celebrated on VIII Kal Jan (25 December). Easter, however, was not only a movable feast but its incidence was calculated on different dating systems by the Celtic and Roman churches. In due time the Latin Church decreed that Easter should be 'celebrated on the Sunday following the first full moon on or after 21 March', and although this simplified matters slightly Easter Day might still fall on any one of thirty-five days, starting with 22 March and ending with 25 April, and the whole of the calendar was controlled by this wide spectrum. Hence a series of tables is required by the researcher to determine the date of Easter in any given year, and then another set of tables is needed to establish the dates of the other major festivals. Such tables are provided in the book already mentioned, *A Handbook of Dates* by C.R. Cheney.

The subject of saints' days poses different questions altogether. In the first place there were many local and idiosyncratic variations: the uses of the bishopric of Sarum were different from those of Canterbury, the allegiance of certain chroniclers to some saints above others, and the preferences of certain abbeys for certain saints. Then there is the problem of two saints with the same name, such as Thomas (the Apostle, and à Becket), whose feasts, octaves and translations occur on different dates.

Faced with these considerations the researcher may be lucky, for if a secondary source is being used the editor may well have provided an interpretation (which should as far as possible be checked, for even the most eminent historians have been known to err). If a primary source is being accessed then the student must look to other indicators for confirmation — such as the regnal year, the indiction and the day of the month in Roman fashion, already covered, but also the golden number, the epact, the dominical letter and the concurrents.

The golden number This is a symbol assigned to each year in the series of one to nineteen, calculated from 1 January in the year 1BC. The figure nineteen is derived from the close approximation of lunar and solar cycles after a lapse of this number of solar years. The approximation was (and is) used as a basis for calculating the date of the paschal moon and hence determining when Easter occurs. The golden number was used as an auxiliary indication of dates in the Middle Ages (see Cheney *op cit*).

Epact and dominical letters These devices also appear as additional symbols and supporters of dates on documents penned in the Middle Ages; they are auxiliaries dependent on the computation of Easter dates and, if there is any doubt created by the main convention used, can be of value. Sources for the determination of the epact and dominical letter are given in the section *Reference books* at the end of this chapter.

Concurrents Concurrents is the term given to a number in the series 1 to 7 assigned to each year, and has close correspondence with the dominical letter. (It too is mentioned in Cheney — see *Reference books* below.)

Fractions of the day

In pre-Conquest and later medieval times the day was divided into two periods of twelve hours, one running from sunrise to sunset and one from sunset to sunrise. It followed that the periods varied in length from season to season and hence the duration of the hours fluctuated. The times appointed for church services (the canonical hours) of Matins, Prime, Terce, Sext, None, Vespers and Compline also varied.

With the gradual introduction of mechanical clocks around the fourteenth century, hours of standard length became general. These new measurements were counted in two series of twelve with their poles at noon and midnight, and to differentiate between them the terms *ante meridiem* and *post meridiem* ('am' and 'pm') were coined. Lately there has been a move towards counting the twenty-four hours in a single progression from 00.00, representing midnight, to 23.59, the figures on the left of the punctuating point being the hours and those to the right the minutes. Students of local history may *very* occasionally need to take into account the difference between Greenwich Mean Time and Summer Time, but those who are researching the histories of maritime ports from which merchant or royal naval vessels sailed will almost certainly have to pay regard to the system of reckoning found in ships' log-books, particularly between the seventeenth and nineteenth centuries. During this period mariners employed a day (of twenty-four hours) starting and ending at noon, with the *date* twelve hours in advance of the land calendar. Just to make matters more difficult, sailors used the normal calendar day in their journals.

The Gregorian calendar

The use of the New Style calendar (to distinguish it from the Old Style, or Julian, calendar) was ordered by Pope Gregory XIII on 24 February 1582. Its purpose was to rectify an accumulated error between the solar and calendar years since the modifications introduced by Augustus. The immediate difference was to cut ten dates out of the October of 1582, 4 October being followed by 15 October, and making a slight change to the incidence of leap years at the ends of centuries.

For various reasons of a nationalistic and religious nature the New Style calendar did not gain immediate acceptance except in those countries honouring the will of Rome. In England the change was not effected until the Earl of Chesterfield's Act of 24 George II which stipulated, in March 1751, that the first day of the January immediately following should be the start of 1752, and that 2 September 1752 should be followed by 14 September.

Many local historians will encounter the problem of the varying practices regarding the adoption of the Gregorian calendar — the dating of letters concerning a town's rope trade with Spain or the wool trade with Russia, to name but two. Spain, for instance, being under obedience to Rome paid prompt heed to the bull of Gregory III; but Russia, under the rule of the Orthodox Church, did not adopt the New Style until the early twentieth century. Frequently correspondents give two dates to their letters: '12/22 December 1635' or '16/29 August 1907', or indicate the convention being used by the addition of the letters 'OS' or 'NS' to the date. But sometimes there are no such identifiers and the student must make a personal judgement depending on the document being analysed.

Other considerations

There are a number of fairly minor conventions and devices used, especially in the legal profession — the 'limit of legal memory', for example, being 3 September 1189, the start of the reign of King Richard I — and the reader is referred to the list of printed works in the next section.

Reference books

The most valuable book is the one already mentioned, the full title of which is *Handbook of Dates for Students of English History* edited by C.R. Cheney. Published by the Royal Historical Society, London, in 1945, it has been frequently reprinted with minor corrections. In addition to the subjects discussed in this chapter it contains a list of rulers from the English settlement to 1154, a table of regnal years; exchequer years; a list of popes from Gregory I to Paul VI, and a tabulation of saints' days and other festivals. A large section deals with legal chronology — law terms, exchequer of pleas, chancery and star chamber, parliament and statutes, county court days, the Court of Arches, and other ecclesiastical and civilian courts. It includes the following calendars: Roman; all possible dates for Easter; for England in the year AD1752 (in which eleven dates were dropped); and a chronological table for Easter Days AD500-2000.

The *Handbook of British Chronology* edited by E.B. Fryde *et al* (London, 3rd edition 1986) is also published by the Royal Historical Society. It is a long book giving the dates and details of rulers, officers of state, archbishops and bishops, dukes and marquesses, parliaments and assemblies, and councils of the Church of England. There are minor infelicities and inconsistencies in typography which are irritating, and although purporting to be revised and updated there are imbalances and inaccuracies in the styles accorded to various officers of state. That said, the book is one which all local historians should own or to which they should have easy access. *The Oxford Dictionary of the English Church* (Oxford, reprint 1985) is a valuable aid, especially regarding details of church dignitaries and holders of high religious office. *The Penguin Dictionary of Saints* (London, reprint 1985) is also useful. Finally, the annual volumes of *Whitaker's Almanac* can be of great value regarding fractions of the day and other matters.

30

Vocabularies and orthography

The subjects of vocabularies (ranges of words used in languages) and orthography (correct or conventional spelling) are very much linked in the field of local history research.

Dealing first with vocabularies, there are, it is suggested, three general kinds. The first is that of the language itself: English, French and Latin. The second is the language related to the time in question: for example, Old English, Norman French and Medieval Latin. The third is possible changes in meaning which have occurred in certain words since the time when the writing was executed and the present day. In addition to the general vocabularies there are the special terms used in such things as parish records, manorial rolls, legal documents, and so on.

In the case of orthography it is only in comparatively recent times that spelling has been standardised into 'correct' forms, it being, in former centuries, very much at the whim of the writer as to how a word was spelt, and it was not unusual for several styles — 'king', 'kyng', 'kynge' are examples — to be used in the same document, or even sentence. A related point concerns calligraphy (in its everyday sense, handwriting) — in early manuscripts 'u', 'v' and 'n' are easily confused, for instance, and until the development of ascenders for letters such as 'b', 'd' and 'h ', and descenders for 'p', 'q', 'y' and 'z', other kinds of misreading are possible.

General vocabularies

In the next chapter is a section devoted to dictionaries — Anglo-Saxon, Middle English, Old French and so on, and these will not be detailed here. The purpose of this chapter is to provide several basic wordlists, to point to where more detailed lists (other than in dictionaries) may be found, and to comment on certain aspects of orthography. The comments will be confined to works of the type which have been transcribed and printed, not to holograph manuscripts, for in this instance all the uncertainties mentioned compound to produce results which will be beyond the skills of the vast majority of local historians to interpret.

Latin

The Latin used in medieval documents likely to be of interest to readers of this present volume was not the classical language of antiquity, nor were its standards universally high, and it varied from century to century as time advanced. Additionally, as needs changed, new words were coined for new situations and were 'Latinised' to fit more

328

easily into the documents being called for. There are literally thousands of Latin words occurring in texts of interest to the local historian — and these may date from the sixth or seventh centuries down to the seventeenth. Indeed, in the author's own village the parish register was being kept in Latin as late as 1657. Perhaps the most difficult problem to be coped with (apart from grammar and syntax which are quite outside the scope of this book) is that of semantic shift — the new meanings which Classical words acquired in medieval times, sometimes making them unintelligible to readers who remember only fragments of the language from their schooldays. Just a few examples may be cited to highlight this problem. *Miles* which in Classical times denoted an ordinary soldier had, by the eleventh century, come to mean 'knight' and led to such forms as *Miles Parliamentalis* = knight of the shire, and *miles agrarius* = holder of a knight's fee. The word *villa* = a mansion, came to mean both 'town' and 'village'. *Pacare*, originally meaning 'to appease', took on the interpretation 'to pay (a debt)'.

As long ago as May 1954 R.E. Latham (who went on to prepare the *Revised Medieval Latin Word List* for the British Academy) wrote in the *Amateur Historian* Vol.I, No.11, p.332: 'The student who strays from the beaten track in the realm of Medieval Latin may expect the trials and joys of the pioneer. He may easily find himself drawn into uncharted regions of medieval law and administration, agriculture and technology, ecclesiology and theology ... Printed texts, if he can find them, may be wildly inaccurate, and notes and glossaries either hesitant or misleading.'

Although much work has been done in the decades since those words were written, it is still true to say that many texts in printed form do not reflect the contents of the original manuscripts with complete accuracy, although more recent printed transcriptions tend to be reliable, not least because they have usually been scanned by a number of scholars before publication.

Any wordlist, short of a full-blown dictionary, must be highly selective and although the following must needs be short, it contains terms which over the years the author has found particularly useful.

Useful Latin terms

abatatio annulment
accredo to lend
acer steel
advocatio advowson
advoves to vow
aesnus unfree/poor
afferare to assess
agape eucharist/alms
agistare to assess pasture rights
allocare to credit
apportum profit/revenue
assartum clearing of woodland
assecutio pursuit
assisa assize/tax/regulate

astrictio restriction/obligation
attilium gear/equipment
averagium transport
avesagium pay for pasturage

baccalarius lad/young retainer
ballivus bailiff
balcus baulk/strip of land
bannum edict/penalty
baratator impostor/disturber
bercarius shepherd/tanner
bersator poacher
bertha city ward
blocca wooden block

bochelanda 'bookland' granted by charter
bordarius smallholder
bossus/buscus wood/thicket
brada broad field
brasium malt
breve letter
bubulcus oxherd/ploughman
burgus fortified town/borough
butimen swamp (marshy)
cambium change/transform
caminus road
campana bell
campus open field

capa cape/cloak

captagium payment on change of lord

carcana iron collar/pillory

carecta cart

caritas charity

catalum chattel

carta charter/deed/document

cassa house/village

case cheese

catabulum pigsty

caula sheepfold

cavitio avoidance

cementarius mason

cissore tailor

civera barrow/bier/stretcher

clerico clerk

cliva baulk in open field

cnipulus knife

coco cook

colibertus freed serf

conigeria rabbit warren

conquestio bill of complaint

curia court

curtallus small pig

custus cost

cuva tub/vat

cyrbes tables of the law

decen(n)a tithing (set of ten)

decertatio dispute

deductus game/hunting

delegiatus outlaw (person)

dominicum demesne

dominium lordship

domus room/workshop

donum bridal gift

dulia worship/service

ecclesia church

edes religious house

eirenarcha justice of the peace

electio deliberate choice

eleemosyna alms

elogium statement

encenium festival of dedication

essonium excuse for absence (essoin)

exitus issue/profit

expositio put up for sale

fabro smith/blacksmith

feodum fee

ferdellum yardland

feria festival/fair

finis fine (settlement)

firma farm/rent (also sometimes a banquet)

flecca arrow shaft

folkesmotum folkmoot

forcerium strongbox

forinsecus foreigner

forum trading/bargain

francus widow's dower

fritha woodland pasture

funiculus boundary line

fusio smelting

fyrderinga military service

gabella gavel/tax

galea helmet

garcio boy/servant

garnistura garrison

gaza wealth/treasure

gelamen gathering/assembly

genealogia offspring

gens people/followers

gersuma premium/fine

gleva field

gludum straw for thatching

gradus degree/rank/office

gravatio oppression

gymnasium military service

haia hedge/ploughbeam

halla market house

halva half acre

hamfara breach of peace

havota dairy farm

helvewecha customary payment

herestrata military road

hesa brushwood/thicket

heusira customary payment

homo man/follower/retainer

hospes villein/customary tenant

husbandus householder/crofter

husum house

hypodiaconus subdeacon

ides sheep

ignis fuel

imbarello store in barrels

inactorium pound/pinfold

incistato to put in a chest

infans minor in wardship

instanta practice/instance

insula aisle of a church

inwara military service

iter right of way, also eyre (circuit of judge)

judex lawman

jugeria jurisdiction

juramentum oath/swearing

jus right/due

keysetria serjeanty of the peace

kunda kinship

leuca league (distance)

liberata livery/allowance

libra pound (weight)

locus district/territory

lotura sheep dipping

lucarius woodward/forester

lucrum interest on money

maerdredum demesne vill

manuopus stolen goods

marescallus farrier/marshal

matricula register/list

meandri menial persons

mensa food/board/table money

mercatum market

miles knight/knight's fee

minister thegn/official/reeve/ serjeant/bailiff

molendinario miller

moralitas character/virtue

mortalitas plague

mulcator despoiler

municeps castellan/constable

naevitas villein status

nausa swampy pastureland

nemusculum underwood/scrub

nidus home of villein

nuge poor/helpless people

obulus halfpenny

obsecundatio compliance

obses guarantor of covenant

obsonium offering of food

obtentus protection

odor repute

offnama enclosure/intake

oppidani townsmen

ordura rubbish

ovttollum 'out-toll' paid on vacating burghal land

overlondum excess land

ovis sheep

panis pastry

pannus measure of cloth

paries side or branch of family

parochia diocese or province

pascua pasture land

pastio pannage

pastor visitor/inspector
pedale footpath/measure of length
perangaria additional burden of service
pergamenum parchment/document
perscrutator searcher/examiner
pesso boundary mark
pignus sacred relic
pistore baker
planum level/open country
plebs (pleps) parish/people of a diocese
polis city
pompla fodder
porcus wild boar
portegravius port reeve/mayor
posse power/dominion
posteritas inheritance
precaria boonwork
prepositus reeve
preco appraiser
prelatus ruler/secular official
preposito prior/abbot/reeve
preses alderman/sheriff
pretor reeve/provost
princeps alderman/bishop
putura (pultura) allowance of food/maintenance

qualitas rank
quo warranto name of a writ (1289)

redditus rent
refectio food maintenance
rentaria rented tenement
rescriptio written answer
restauratio restoration/reparation
rigiditas severity
rito to perform according to custom
rodefalla a measure of land
roga dole/alms
rusticus serf/villein
ruta route/road

scaccarium exchequer (chess board)

scatavena scotrent
scheda sheet of paper
schira shire/county parish/district
sedes site of building
semen sowing (of grain)
senescallus steward
silva timber
sletta level field
socius servant/reeve
solidus shilling
sors portion of land
spargitio spreading of hay
spissum thicket
splottum plot of land
stocgabulum a form of market due
strata alta highway
stroda marshy thicket
subaccasatus under-tenant
subballivus under-bailiff
substantia property/wealth
successio progeny
sulcus furlong
suus one's 'own man'

tallia tally/tax/entail/retail
talwoda firewood
tapenarius clothworker
tassatus rick/haycock
tectura roof/roofing
telligraphus land-book/charter/ deed
tempus period of office/season/ weather/fashion/style
tenesa maintenance/livery
tentio holding/possession
terminus term/fixed period of time
terra country/kingdom/piece of land/feudal holding/ tenement/courtyard
testamentum charter
textor thatcher
thalamus treasury/council/crop/ gizzard
theca moneybox/letterbag
tipulator ale or wine vendor
tiro squire

tolta writ
transitio crossing place in river
trenchera path through woodland
tripartior to work a three field system
truncus market stall (block of wood)
tuba pipe
tumba tomb/shrine
tutatio protection/maintenance

ulnata measure of length (of cloth)
uncea ounce
undecima tax of one eleventh
urbecula little town
utlaga outlaw
utlanda outland (not in common field)

vadium/wadium wages
vallum embankment
vannus winnowing fan
vavassor under-tenant
venatio place of hunting
venda toll on goods for sale
verbum right of speech
vernaculum custom/usage
vestis cloth/material
viola a kind of fish
voluptas sport/game animal

waino measure of weight
wandelardus rogue
wanga strip of land in open field
wapentacum wapentake, or its tenantry
wara/werra a measure of land
wica dairy farm/saltworking
wikenarius collector of amercements
wista measure of land

yomanus yeoman

zizania weed
zythicoctor brewer

Latin Christian names

At a somewhat different level from the terms listed in the previous section, the spelling of Christian names in Latin can sometimes pose a problem of interpretation to modern eyes. *Bartholomaeus* is obviously Bartholomew, but *Aluredus* is less apparently Alfred, and *Matilda* not self-evidently Maud. The following list contains names whose

331

later English forms are not readily apparent. It must be appreciated that the spelling of Latin names varied in much the way that today Catharine, Catherine, Katharine, Katherine, Kathryn and Catrina are, for example, versions of a single form, hence in the list only the more obscure renderings are given.

Adelheidis Adelaide	*Galterus* Walter	*Malculinus* Malcolm
Ademarus Aymer	*Garinus* Warren	*Mattacus* Matthew
Ægidius Giles	*Geva* Eve/Eva	*Mattilda* Maud
Aelizia Alice	*Gislebertus* Gilbert	*Meuricius* Maurice
Agna/Agneta Agnes	*Goisfridus* Geoffrey	*Milesanta* Millicent
Alberedus Alfred	*Gualterus* Walter	*Moyses* Moses
Albredus Albrey	*Guido* Guy	*Natalis* Noel
Aldrida Audrey	*Gulielmus* William	*Oeneus* Owen
Amabilia Mabel	*Hawisia* Avice/Hawyse	*Oliva* Olive
Andreas Andrew	*Hendricus* Henry	*Paganus* Pagan/Payn
Arcturus Arthur	*Hereweccus* Harvey	*Pero* Piers
Audoenus Owen	*Hieremais* Jeremiah	*Petronilla* Parnell
Auicia Avice	*Hieronymus* Jerome	*Petrus* Peter/Piers
Cæcilius Cecil	*Hoelus* Howell	*Quaspatricius* Gospatrick
Dermicius Dermot	*Imania* Emma	*Radulfus* Randolph/Ranulf/Ralph
Desiderata Desirée	*Ingelramus* Ingram	*Roesia* Rose
Dionysius Dennis	*Ismania* Emma	*Rohelendus* Roland
Drago/Droco/Drogo Drew	*Jacobus* James/Jacob	*Sescilia* Cicely
Dunechanus Duncan	*Joceus* Joyce	*Sibella* Sybil
Eadgitha Edith	*Junana* Jane	*Sidneus* Sydney
Egidius Giles	*Kenelmus* Kenelm	*Silvanus* Silas
Ennis Agnes	*Laetitia* Lettice	*Tedbaldus* Theobald
Ethelburga Aubrey	*Laurentius* Lawrence	*Teodoricus* Terence
Ethelreda Audrey	*Leonellus* Lionel	*Tobias* Toby
Fides Faith	*Lionhardus* Leonard	*Vadimus* Valentine
Fulqueyus Fulk	*Lucasius* Luke	*Wido (Guido)* Guy
Galfridus Geoffrey	*Ludovicus* Lewis	*Ylaria* Hillary

Old English (Anglo-Saxon) and Middle English

This is not the place to discuss the linguistic differences between Old English and Middle English. It is sufficient to say that in broad definition the former term applies to the language used up to the twelfth century, and the latter that given to the language between the twelfth and the fifteenth, when Modern English started to emerge. There cannot be a sharp dividing line, as there can be between one year and the next; the evolution of language is a gradual one, as witness the modern divergences between American, Australian and United Kingdom English, and the differences between the everyday languages of Cornwall and Northumberland.

In his book *Anglo-Saxon England* (Cambridge 1970) Peter Hunter Blair wrote (p.370): 'The novice should take his first steps ... with the aid of the *Anglo-Saxon Primer* by H. Sweet (9th edition, revised 1953) ... [then with] *An Introduction to Old English* by G.L. Brook (Manchester 1955) ... and for a dictionary *A Concise Anglo-Saxon Dictionary* by J.R.C. Hall.' He could have added 'the 4th edition, with supplement, 1960.' For most local history purposes a simple wordlist will suffice for both Old and Middle English — the dictionary for the latter being *Stratmann's Middle English Dictionary* (Oxford

1891) — and what now follows are words the author has found most useful in pursuing his studies. The letter ð is called 'thorn', and is pronounced 'th'.

abbod abbot

ac oak

acennend parent

ademan to judge

aebebod legal injunction

aecer field/cultivated land

aecerhege hedge (of a field)

aecerweorc field work

aefsweorc pasturage

aehhyp assault

aelmesaecer 'first fruits'/alms

aeppel fruit/apple

aern dwelling house/store/
   building/closet

aes food/meat/carrion

aescperend soldier

aeðelboren of noble birth

ambihtere servant

andheafod unploughed headland

and-leofen nourishment/food/
   money/wages

Angelcynn England/the English
   people

atleag oatfield

aðolware citizens

awoh wrongly/unjustly

bacca ridge

baecere baker

bearn child/son/offspring

bearu grove/wood

becan grant of charter

belacan to enclose

benrip compulsory service at
   harvest time

beodland glebe land

beorg mountain/hill

beran bear/carry/bring

bere barley

bewindla hedge/border

bōccaeceras 'book acres'/freehold
   land

bōcung conveyance by charter

bōnda freeman/householder/
   husband

brōm brushward

Brytenlond Britain/Wales

būr apartment/chamber/
   storehouse/cottage/dwelling/
   'bower'

(ge)būr peasant/farmer/freeholder
   of lowest class

burg dwelling(s)

burgfolc townspeople

burgscipe borough

burgweg road/street

burhgeðinhð town council

burhwealda burgess

burn brook/stream

būne cultivated/inhabited/
   occupied

byrele butler/steward

cafortun court/courtyard/hall/
   residence

castelmann townsman

cēap cattle

cēapstōw marketplace

ceorlfolc common people

ceorlman freeman

cīepa merchant

cniht boy/youth/servant

cornteoðung tithe of corn

cotlīf hamlet/village/manor/
   dwelling

cotsetla cottager

crocc crock/vessel

cuffer pigeon/dove

cyneham royal manor

cȳpend merchant

daeg day

dālland land owned jointly/
   common land divided into
   strips

denu valley/dale

dēor animal/beast/deer

dōmbōc code of laws/statute book/
   'doombook'

dūnland open country/'downland'

dyð fuel

eaht assembly/council

eald old

ealdor elder/parent

earningland land granted as
   freehold

efendenung supper

eorl brave man/warrior/leader

eorðe earth/soil

ēowd sheepfold/flock/herd

ēowu ewe

eðelstaðol settlement

etelond pasture

etenlaēs pasture

faeder father

faederland inheritance

faebēna peasant

fald fold/stall/stable/pen

fearhryðer bull

feld 'field'/open land

feoh cattle/herd/movable goods/
   money/riches/property

feorm food/meal/supper/feast

fisc fish

flaēscstraēt meat market

fōda food

folc people/tribe/nation

fofangfeoh reward for rescuing
   cattle

forierð headland

frēolaēta freedman

frumgewrit deed/document

furlang length of furrow/'furlong'

fyrdfor military service

gaers grass/young corn/herb/hay/
   plant

gaerstun meadow

gafol tribute/rent/duty/debt/due

gāt goat

geanbōc duplicate charter

glind hedge/fence

grīsta baker

grytta coarse meal

haefer he-goat

haēð heath/untilled land

haga hedge/enclosure

hām village/manor/hamlet/estate/
   'home'

heah high

hecg enclosure/hedge

hoerd herd/flock

heorð 'hearth'/house/home

hierde shepherd

hild war/combat

hīred household

hof enclosure/dwelling/building/
   house/court

hrīðer cattle/ox/bull/cow

hwīl 'while' (time)
Hymbre Northumbrians

infaer ingress/entrance
infangeneðeof right to judge local thieves
inheord demesne herd
inn dwelling/apartment/lodging/quarters
innefeoh household goods
inorf furniture
inwudu private woodland

Words beginning with the sound *k* are listed under *c*

lāeden 'Latin'/a foreign language
lagu law/ordinance/rule
landbōc written grant of land
landhlāford lord of a manor/landlord
landmearc boundary
lanu street/'lane'
lēah meadow/'lea'/piece of ground
lēodwita elder/chief/wise man
leowe league (distance)
līfneru food/sustenance
loca enclosure/stronghold
lȳtle female slave

māed meadow/pasture
maer boundary
maeðel council/meeting/assembly
massere merchant
mearc 'mark'/boundary/line of division
meolc milk
meox dung/dirt
mere lake/pond/pool/sea
mersc marsh/swamp
mixen dungheap
mōdor mother
mōrlāes marshy pasture
mōt 'moot'/society/court/council/synod
munuc monk
mynsterham monastery

nēah near/close
nēahceaster nearest town
nēahtun nearby village
nietenlic animal/brutish
nord north

ōdencole threshing floor
ofer over

oferwealdend overlord
oneardiend inhabitant
onrīptīd harvest time
onwealda ruler/sovereign/God
onwunung dwelling place
ōra border/bank/shore
orf cattle/livestock
orfcynn cattle
oxa ox
oxangang one-eighth of a hide or 'ploughland'

paeð 'path'/track
pear roc enclosed land
plaece open space/street
port town with market rights
portherpað main road to a town
prēostlagu ecclesiastical law
pull pool/creek
pundfald 'pinfold'/pound

rādcniht tenant holding subject to service on horseback, 'radknight'
rāed advice/counsel
rāew row/hedgerow
rēfmāed reeve's meadow
regol rule/regulation/law
resthūs chamber
riht right/equity/rule
ryt underwood

saeburg seaport town
saedian to sow grain
saeld dwelling/house
saeta holding of land
scēap sheep
scipe pay/wage
scipgyld ship tax/ship money
scir office/appointment
scīrmann sheriff/prefect
scōere shoemaker
scōmhylte brushwood/copse
sealtere saltworker
seleðegn retainer/attendant
smið handicraftsman/blacksmith/armourer/carpenter
sōð truth/justice
stān stone
stoc place/house/dwelling
strāet highroad/'street'
sunor herd of swine
sūð south
swāesende food/meal/dinner
swān swineherd/peasant
swaðu track/pathway
swīn wild boar/pig/hog/'swine'

sȳla ploughman
tannere tanner
tēam family/race/lineage
tēoðingdoeg tithingday
tilia workman/farmer/labourer
toft homestead/site of a house
trūs brushwood
tūn enclosure/garden/yard/field/farm/manor/house/mansion/village/'town'
tūnesman townsman
tūnscipe township
tȳnan to enclose/hedge in

ðegn servant/retainer/vassal/freeman/noble/warrior
ðēod people/nation/tribe
ðēowdōm slavery/servitude
ðiccet thicket
ðorp (ðrop) farm/village/'thorp'
ðriðing thirding/'riding' of a conty
ðuft thicket
ðȳfel shrub/bush/copse/thicket

underngeweore breakfast
undermete breakfast
unfrið breach of peace
unlagu abuse of law
unlandāgende not owning land
unrīm countless number
unsāwen unsown

ūtlāes out-pastures
waedelnes poverty
waepen(ge)taec subdivision of a riding/wapentake
waeterpytt well
waeterstrēam river
wanāeht want/poverty
wang plain/meadow/field
weardsteall watch tower
webba weaver
wēod 'weed'/herd/grass
West-Centingas people of West Kent
West Wēalas Cornishmen
weðer ram/wether sheep
wīc lodging/habitation
wīcgerēfa bailiff/reeve/tax gatherer
wīf 'wife'/woman/female
wīg strife/war/battle
witenagemōt meeting of wise men/national council
wōhdāed crime
worðig farm/street
writ letter/book/charter
wucweorc 'weekwork'

wudu wood/forest/grove
wudufeoh forest-tax
wuduweard forester/woodward
wyllen woollen
wyrhta wright/artist/worker

wyrðing fallow land

ýddisc furniture
ymbcyme assembly
ymbfaestnes enclosure

yrfeland inherited land
yrð ploughing/tilling/crop/
  produce/'earth'
yrðling farmer/ploughman

Old French, Anglo-Norman

Of the more ancient languages the local historian will encounter in the course of his studies, Old French (Anglo-Norman) will be the least important. It is true that the Anglo-Norman aristocracy spoke French among themselves and wrote to each other in that language, long after they came to regard themselves as Englishmen. As but one example, records of the famous case of Scrope versus Grosvenor before the Court of Chivalry 1385-1390 show testimony was given in French, and even today French phrases linger in the language of heraldry.

A selection of words from the Old French language will be of value:

acorder accept/agree to
adober arm/equip
afere rank/dignity
afiancer promise
amanantir provide with a dwelling
  or fief
ancele maidservant
ancessor ancestor
anor honour
arme weapon
armeüre armour
assembler join battle
ave grandfather
bacheler young warrior/squire
baille bailey (castle)
baillie power/possession
barnage assemblage of barons
berser hunt/shoot
blecier wound (injury)
bone boundary stone
borc town
boscheron woodcutter
brachet hunting dog
bregier shepherd
broigne hauberk
burel woollen cloth
cerge wax candle
chacier chase/hunt
chalengement claim/possession
chalongier contend for
chapleïs swordplay
char meat/flesh
chevalerie knightly deed
cité city/town/'ville'
cortoisement in courtly fashion
dangier prerogative/power
debonaire honourable/worthy/

defois fief/enclosure
deputaire lowborn/vile
disme tithe (tenth)
disner dine/principal meal
donjon main tower of castle
enorance respect/honour
envaïe attack/assault
escremir swordplay
escuir shield bearer/'esquire'
esplé spear/pike/lance
espois thicket/clump of trees
essart cleared land/burnt clearing/
  'assart'
estage dwelling/abode/rank/estate
estal dwelling/position
estor joust/combat/battle
estree road/way
eve water/stream
fermeté fortress
festu straw
fieffer enfeoff/grant/bestow
fiet fief/privilege
forfet misdeed/wrongdoing
forrer plunder/pillage/forage
franc freedman/noble
fuer price
fustoie clump of trees
gaaing booty/crop/harvest
gast deserted/waste land
geldon soldier
gent people/folk/race/army
giet bowshot
gué watering place/low-lying
  grassland/ford
guionage safe conduct
haiete hedge/enclosure
harnois armour/equipment

herber graze/herb brew/strew
  with grass/potion
herberge encampment/shelter
honor honour/fife/domain/
  distinction/wealth
hort garden/orchard
iglise church
ingal flat land
ive mare (horse)
jovent youth
justarme weapon like poleaxe
lande open country
laris moor/hillside/rough ground/
  waste
lices tilting ground/lists
  (tourney)/field of combat
lige 'liege'/vassal/free
loge upper room/bower/tent/lodge
longainge dunghill/anything foul
maille armour/'mail'
mainbrunie power/guardianship
manage house/apartment/family/
  furniture
marce border country/'march'
marois marsh/bog
meffet crime/wrong
merc boundary stone
moillier wife
mostier convent/monastery/church
naïf native/natural/foolish
nonne nun
noreture food/education/training
ore hour/now/then/soon
ost army/enemy/camp
oste landlord/host
ostel dwelling/guestroom/lodging/
  quarters

335

pastorel shepherd	*riviere* shore/bank/river	*tros* treestump
pastoure shepherdess	*roion* country district	*vissier* doorkeeper/'usher'
peon footsoldier	*routure* tenure/feudal due	*val* valley
per peer/equal	*saignor* master/lord/sire	*valee* valley
planche footbridge	*sale* hall/public rooms	*vaslet* squire/youth/servant
plesseïz enclosure	*seignier* place on a mark/sign	*vassal* 'vassal'/true knight/valliant
prael field/meadow	*sente* path	man
praerie field/meadow	*serjant* servant	*ver* wild boar
pré field/meadow	*soif* hedge/fence	*vergier* garden
pree field/meadow	*souper* have supper	*viande* food/flesh (meat)
pui hill/height	*tenant* dependant/vassal/supporter	*vilain* peasant/farmer
raie ridge/furrow	*terrier* ground/earthwork	*vilenie* base conduct
recoillir harvest/reap	*toiere* swamp/muddy pool	*voie* road
rere cut down/mow	*tornele* watch tower	*vuit* fallow land

Specialised vocabularies

In addition to the general vocabularies described and demonstrated in the previous section, there are many subjects associated with local history research which have their own special terms. These include architecture, church history, archaeology, legal documentation, and so on. Chapter 31, Personal Reference Libraries, identifies some of the many dictionaries now available to aid the researcher, and those listed are recommended as desirable if not downright essential. Space considerations dictate that detailed vocabularies are not possible in these present pages, but the following volumes contain wordlists which may be of value: *Anglo-Saxon England* by Sir Frank Stenton (Oxford, 3rd edition 1971) has, on pp.731-4, a 'Key to Anglo-Saxon Place Names'; *Historical Interpretation: I* by J.J. Bagley (Penguin Books 1965) has, on pp.265-73, a 'Glossary of Archaic and Technical Words', and this is useful for compound terms. In addition, *The Amateur Historian* published, in its early volumes, useful glossaries. These included 'Manorial Terms' by R.H. Hilton (Vol.I, No.3, January 1953), 'Terms from Parochial Records' by P.V. Harris (Vol.I, No.4, February/March 1953), 'Glossary of an Old Church' by Lawrence Maidbury (Vol.II, No.1, August/September 1954), 'Archaeological Terms' by P.W. Gathercale (Vol.II, No.5, April/May 1955), 'Legal Terms and Phrases' by G.D. Johnston (Vol.III, No.6, Winter 1957/58).

The most valuable of all the modern publications at the more general level of a local historian's vocabulary is *A Dictionary of British History* by a variety of editors. This was first published in hardback in 1981 and was reissued in 1982 by Pan Books; the editorial consultant being J.P. Kenyon. It covers everything from 'abjuration of the realm' to the 'Young England Movement', and has a lengthy chronology.

Orthography

In his book *The Parish Chest* (3rd edition, reprinted 1983) W.E. Tate says, on p.309, 'The orthography of 17th and 18th century parish officers is often eccentric in the extreme and the inquirer must be prepared to translate [such terms] as *arter david* into "affidavit" [and] *carvaers* into "surveyors" . . .'. There follows in Mr Tate's book an interesting list of examples. They can, however, be matched by almost any local historian: *plenty cut* = Pentecost, *poyentyng* = pointing (of tiles), *hollyear* = whole year, *sarples* and *seaplece* = surplice, *sparrs* = sparrows, *comen* = common, *comenen* = communion, *cute* = cut, and so on. Occasionally there may be bafflement. The author was, for example, frustrated for some time by a field name written in 1736 as *Abboxry Land*, and could come to no sensible conclusion as to what was meant. Fortunately, in 1749, it was recorded in the form *Abotsbery Land* and was shown subsequently to belong to the poor lands charity of *Abbotsbury*, a few miles from Weymouth in Dorset.

The foregoing examples are taken from documents written by uneducated men who committed to paper, as best they could, what they thought they had heard, or spellings they believed appropriate. Such difficulties of interpretation as the modern local historian may encounter are not, however, confined to this class of writing alone, as a single example taken from the sixteenth century will illustrate. The document, dated 1549, comprised the letters patent of privileges granted by 'Edwarde the Sixt' to his Officers of Arms. It was, presumably, drafted and engrossed by persons of reasonable educational standard, and the eccentricities (to modern eyes) in the orthography cannot be put down to illiteracy. In the course of a few hundred words the following occur: *catalles* = chattels, *Chrystean* = Christian, *peax* = peace, *freyle* = freely, *delyved* = delivered, *auctorytye* = authority, *mad* = made, *borow* = borough, *rome* = room, *jarretier* = garter, and *playnle* = plainly.

Little general guidance (or comfort) can be given in respect of the interpretation of words spelt in unfamiliar ways or the basis of phonetics. It will, without doubt, be useful to say a word aloud in a variety of stresses and vowel sound combinations, and if this does not work then to ask a native of the place being researched to say it —this is frequently a useful device if the document originated locally. A talent for crossword puzzles and acrostics will sometimes help!

Turning to the subject of handwriting, this has been touched on at the beginning of this chapter. No complete certainty is ever possible in the matter of 'u', 'n', 'v', 'i' and so on, particularly where names are concerned — Juliano could easily be Juliana, Pothe could be Poche, Tonn might be Toun. All the foregoing are drawn from documents employed by the author in various studies, and there are many more examples which could be quoted. In one fourteenth-century case a surname could have been Penerine, Penerive or even Penerme, and an interesting study on bynames and family names was thwarted. But success can be achieved. In a nineteenth-century printed version of a fourteenth-century document a family was called de Farbereshaye, a form which seemed reasonable and *could* conceivably have been a version of *Fabro* = Smith and *(ge)haeg* = enclosure. Further study, however, together with research of a parallel nature and an examination of the original membrane indicated that *o* had been read as *a*, and *t* as *b*, and that the name was de Fortereshaye = of/from the forester's enclosure (or holding). This later, correct reading enabled a complex study to be successfully continued, completed, and finally published in a journal of academic standing.

31

Personal reference libraries

It is fairly obvious that the size of any local historian's personal reference library will be controlled by two main things and several less important ones. The principal considerations are the interests being pursued and the depth of the personal pocket; the subsidiary ones are the ease with which a good public reference library can be accessed, the speed with which further volumes can be obtained via the public lending service, and the lengths of the permitted retention periods.

If the interests are restricted to the history of one particular place, or confined to one special area of study, then a private library of books and offprints is quite readily assembled. If, however, the studies are pursued more widely and the research becomes deeper, the need for ready-to-hand volumes and essays will increase geometrically.

In considering the topics of the works to be collected it may be useful to visualize the whole subject in the form of a large sheet of paper divided into columns and rows. The columns (and there may be twenty or more) represent chronological periods — pre-historic, pre-and post-Conquest, and up to the present day — and the numerous rows represent identified fields of study. Thus *Bond Men Made Free* by Rodney Hilton (London 1973), which deals with the peasants' revolt of 1381, would be classified in the column of the fourteenth century, and the row of, say, 'Social Structure'; and *The Hungry Mills* by Norman Longmate (London 1978) which describes the Lancashire cotton famine of 1861-65, would appear in the column for the nineteenth century and a row possibly designated 'Trade and Industry'. The bulk of this chapter is, therefore, written with the possibility in mind that the reader might use such a system to help identify gaps in any present personal library, or to lay the structure for a proposed collection of books. The headings used, by way of illustration, are: *general reference* publications applicable to a wide variety of subjects and periods, *social structure, local government, agriculture, trade and industry, personal prosperity, housing, religion,* and *education*.

General reference books

Language dictionaries and word lists

The complete text of the *Oxford English Dictionary* is available in micrographically reduced form at a price which is more readily in the reach of the local historian than that of the multi-volume set. It is bound in three volumes in the form of 'four-pages-to-view', and may be read with the aid of a low-powered magnifying glass. A wealthy researcher may, of course, wish to invest in the conventionally produced *OED*, the price of which runs into hundreds of pounds.

Apart from his native language, the British (or American) student of English local history will need a nodding acquaintance with, or at least dictionaries of, three other languages. These are the related sources of Modern English — Anglo-Saxon/Middle English, Medieval Latin, and Old French. *A Concise Anglo-Saxon Dictionary* by J.R. Clark Hall (4th edition, with a supplement by H.D. Meritt, Cambridge 1975), and *Stratmann's Middle English Dictionary* (rearranged by Henry Bradley, Oxford 1940), are two reference works of value for the first language group.

With respect to Latin, the essential text is the *Revised Medieval Latin Word List* by R.E. Latham (London 1983). This volume includes, in principle, all words found in British document sources insofar as they are non-Classical either in form or meaning. The local historian must judge quite separately any need for the large (and expensive) *Latin Dictionary* by Charton Lewis (Oxford 1879/1980).

So far as Old French, or Norman French, is concerned there is an admirable *Short Old French Dictionary for Students* by Kenneth Urwin (Oxford paperback 1985).

In addition to the foregoing there are numerous dialect dictionaries, each devoted to the colloquial (or traditional) speech of a particular region. Typical of these is *A Glossary of the Dorset Dialect* by William Barnes, first published in 1886 and later reprinted, in Guernsey, in 1980. Valuable support to the dictionaries of these early languages or dialects are three books in lexicon form, published by Cambridge University Press for the English Place Names Society. The first two, by A.H. Smith, comprise *English Place Name Elements* which appeared in 1970, and *Cornish Place Name Elements* by O.J. Padel in the same series, published in 1985.

Biographical reference books and dictionaries

An important work relevant to many fields of study is *The Dictionary of National Biography*. This, like the *OED*, is also available in a compact form produced in two volumes by micrography at twelve-pages-to-view (Oxford 1975). It contains short biographies of many thousands of distinguished British and English people from the earliest of recorded times down to 1960. Although not specifically termed 'dictionaries', two related works of a similar kind are *The Complete Peerage* and *The Complete Baronetage*. Both are photoreduced at four-pages-to-view, and can be read without the aid of a magnifying glass. The former is now available in paperback, and is of special value to local historians for it is, in effect, a genealogical dictionary of every person who has held a 'peerage' from the period of the very first post-Conquest earldoms. Equally importantly, its many appendices are of great interest and benefit to the historical researcher. Vol.II, Appendix B, for example, is devoted to 'The Great Offices of State' and covers 45 pages; Vol.IV, Appendix H, names peers whose late nineteenth-century estates were in excess of 100,000 acres each; Vol.XII, Appendix B, describes portraits appearing in the *Town and Country Magazine*.

Special subject dictionaries

Every year the number of special subject dictionaries increases, and today they range from popular interests such as Christian names to works with more limited appeal, such as *A Dictionary of Fairies* by Katharine Briggs (London 1976). The following works are among the more important to the local historian: *Archaeology* by Warwick Bray and

David Trump (Penguin Books 1970); *Architecture* by John Fleming and others (Penguin Books 1966); *Field Names* by John Field (London 1972); *British Folk Customs* by Christina Hale (London 1978) — a related book, *British Folk Tales and Legends* by Katharine Briggs, London 1977, is not in dictionary format but is valuable; *Genealogy* by Terrick FitzHugh (Sherborne, new edition 1988); *Heraldry* by Stephen Friar (Sherborne 1987); *Burke's General Armory* (London, reprint 1984); *Historical Slang* (London 1972); *Nursery Rhymes* by Iona and Peter Opie (Oxford, revised 1977); *English Place Names* by Eilert Ekwall (Oxford, 4th edition 1960); *English Plant Names* by Geoffrey Grigson (London 1974); *Religions* by J.R. Hinnells (Penguin Books 1984); *The Christian Church* by F.L. Cross and E.A. Livingstone (Oxford, corrected edition 1983); *Ecclesiastical Terms* by J.S. Purvis (1962); *Saints* by Donald Attwater (Penguin Books, revised 1983); *British Surnames* by P.H. Reaney (London, revised 1977); *English Weights and Measures* by R.E. Zupko (1968).

A most useful dictionary (although not called such) for the country historian, a copy of which has an honoured place in the author's library, is *Old Country and Farming Words* by James Britten (The English Dialect Society, London 1880). This book contains words collected from many sources, ranging from the *Dictionarium Rusticum* (1681) to the *Cyclopaedia of Agriculture* (1863), and runs to some 220 pages. A number of local societies publish booklets which may be classified as mini-dictionaries. Typical of these is *A Glossary of Household, Farming and Trade Terms from Probate Inventories* by Rosemary Milward (Chesterfield 1982). Finally, *The Local Historian's Encyclopaedia* by John Richardson (New Barnet, 2nd edition 1986) is a worthwhile volume, containing many hundreds of definitions of words and terms of value to the researcher, and the *Dictionary of British History* (Pan Books 1982) is essential.

Other works of a general nature

One of the best guides to works currently in print, and which deals with publications on local history and the associated fields of genealogy and the material heritage, is the annual catalogue issued by the well known specialist booksellers and publishers, Phillimore. These catalogues, which are now issued in sections, provide a quick ready-reference to the hundreds of volumes available. A second useful source of information is the periodic booklist issued by another specialist company, *Heraldry Today*, and includes sections on family history, history and biography, genealogy and topography, as well as the expected subjects of heraldry and the peerage.

That said, the following books are of quite fundamental value and should be possessed by every student of local matters: *Local History in England* by W.G. Hoskins (London, 2nd edition 1972), which remains possibly the best overall introduction to the subject; *The Parish Chest* by W.E. Tate (Chichester, 3rd edition 1983), which, for all its apparently limiting title is, in fact, 'a study of the records of parochial administration in England'; *Town Records* (Chichester 1983) and *Village Records* (Chichester 1982), both by John West, are further important works of a basic kind, as is *How to Write a Parish History* by R.B. Pugh (1954).

County and local histories

Reference has been made elsewhere to the early county histories written in the seventeenth, eighteenth and nineteenth centuries, sometimes by gentlemen in the priesthood. If the researcher's interest is sufficiently wide and his pocket sufficiently deep it is advisable to obtain a copy of the appropriate work even if a catalogue does describe the volumes on offer as 'disbound', 'shaken', with 'weak hinges' or some other euphemism for falling apart. Precisely the same comments may be made about the pertinent books in the *Victoria County History* series. The point may be stressed, for experience has shown how important it is to have these volumes always on hand for cross-referencing with later works, or providing new ideas for lines of investigation.

In the decade of the 1950s a new series of county histories was initiated under the heading *The Darwen Series*, after its founder Lord Darwen. The books are quite short (about 40,000 words, less than a quarter of the text of this present volume), but each has about 150 drawings and pictures. As concise synopses of the history of each county they represent good value. In the case of Kent, for example, the Darwen *History* may be acquired in conjunction with *The Kingdom of Kent* by K.P. Witney (1982), *Domesday Book: Kent* (1986), *Medieval Kentish Society* by F.R.H. du Bouley (1964), the *Victoria County History* and Edward Hasted's *History of Kent* (1797/1801) to form a powerful basic collection. A further series of 'county' books is that devoted to 'The Making of the English Landscape', of which more than a dozen have appeared under the Hodder & Stoughton imprint.

On the subject of local histories — especially town histories — it is very possible that the ground will have already been explored by a previous researcher and the results of the study published. It is always sound to add any such volumes to personal collections, for however well or badly done, they will always be a source of inspiration — if only on how to approach certain topics.

Atlases and maps

The latest Ordnance Survey maps are of great value and, when related to those of earlier editions, tithe apportionment, commutation and estate maps of past centuries assist in the unravelling of the development of tenurial holdings, field boundaries, land usage, road layouts, the development of town and city centres, the linking of suburbs and all manner of things covered, in later years, by the umbrella term 'town and country planning'. It is of benefit to compare all the very early maps one with another, as each will show something different, and there may be anomalies which lead to interesting studies and, quite possibly, new discoveries. The Ordnance Survey maps of the Iron Age, Roman and other historical periods, are necessary references, and the specialist atlases — Anglo-Saxon England, Historical Atlas of Britain, etc., mentioned elsewhere in this book — may be considered essential.

For the dedicated, long-term researcher *An Agricultural Atlas of England and Wales* by J.T. Coppock (London, reprint 1982) is useful, and a further basic work is the *Phillimore Atlas and Index of Parish Registers* by Cecil Humphery-Smith (Chichester 1984), composed mainly of 'genealogical maps' of the pre-1832 parishes on a county-by-county basis, topographical maps from Bell's *Gazetteer* of 1834, and a 283-page index of deposited registers at county and public record offices, plus copies noted in Boyd's marriage, Pallot's marriage, and other lists. There is also a useful booklet *Maps and Plans in the Public Record Office* (PRO 1967).

Social structure

A good general introduction to the subject is *A Social History of England* by Asa Briggs (Pelican Books 1987), which also contains an excellent forty-page bibliography. *The Common People* by J.F.C. Harrison (London 1984) is also relevant. It covers the period from the Norman Conquest to the present day, and has a long section on suggestions for further reading. Also useful in this area is *An Introduction to English Demography*, edited by E.W. Wrigley (1966).

As has been shown earlier, the records of social structure (and population) may conveniently be divided into three. Those before 1538 (the point when Thomas Cromwell legislated for parish registers), those after 1801 (when official censuses began), and those between the two dates mentioned.

For the first period, local historical societies or historians with local interests are increasingly publishing lay subsidy and other early records, which permit a (sometimes incomplete) picture to be built up of local populations and the relative prosperity of individual heads of family. The information contained in the Domesday folios is, when used cautiously, also of value to the pre-plague period. The following volumes are relevant: *Rural England 1066-1348* by R.E. Hallam (London 1981), *Lay Subsidies and Poll Taxes* by M.W. Beresford (1963), *Parliamentary Taxes on Personal Property 1290-1344* by J.F. Willard (1934). A valuable work, covering many aspects of social structure and population distribution, is that edited by R.E. Glasscock, *The Lay Subsidy of 1334* (1975). Two articles of interest are 'The Pre-Plague Population of England' by J.C. Russell, which appeared in the *Journal of British Studies* vi(2) 1966, and 'The Population of an English Village –1086-1801' by W.G. Hoskins, which was printed in his volume *Provincial England* (1963).

For the second of the historical periods mentioned (1538-1801) the following books (all available in paperback) are most useful background texts: *Sixteenth Century England* by Joyce Youings (London 1984), *English Society in the Seventeenth Century* by Margaret Spufford (1985), and *English Society in the Eighteenth Century* by Roy Porter (London 1982). These are works in the *Pelican Social History* series, other volumes of which will be mentioned later. Two valuable books on the seventeenth century (apart from the *Oxford History* mentioned in an earlier chapter) are those published as Open University set texts, *Seventeenth-Century England – A Changing Culture* (London 1980). The first volume is edited by Ann Hughes and devoted to primary sources, and the second is edited by W.R. Owens and comprises a series of modern studies. *The Family, Sex and Marriage in England 1500-1800* by Lawrence Stone (Penguin Books, reprinted 1984) is a well illustrated book, particularly useful on matters of the changing relationships between family members. *Life and Labour in England 1700-1780* by R.W. Malcolmson (London 1981) and *The Rural World 1780-1850* by Pamela Horn (London 1980) are two volumes in Hutchinson's *Social History of England* series, containing, in addition to the principal text, a number of pages of academic commentary and reference.

In recent years local societies have been active in publishing transcripts of, and commentaries on, a number of primary sources. These include Tudor lay subsidies, muster rolls, protestation returns, and so on. They are useful documents, not only for insights into such things as parish organisations, but also (when used cautiously) population movements, family prosperity and Christian and surname patterns. Copies of these publications are well worth obtaining as permanent additions to personal libraries, and may be supported by such articles as :'The Population of Elizabethan England' by E.E. Rich, published in *Economic History Review* 2nd series ii (1950); 'English Country Towns in the 1520s' by J.C.K. Cornwall, which appeared in the same publication, 2nd series xv (1962); 'English Provincial Towns in the Sixteenth Century' by W.G. Hoskins, which appeared as a chapter in his book *Provincial England* (1963); and 'The Village Population in the Tudor Lay Subsidy Rolls' by S.A. Payton, in *English Historical Review* xxx (1915).

For the third period of history (1801 onwards) a useful volume is *British Population Growth 1700-1850* by M.W. Flinn (London 1970). Although this book covers just the first half-century of the period, it is a valuable contribution to the subject, as are the further volumes in the *Pelican Social History* series: *Britain 1800-1870* by V.A.C. Gatrell (London 1985); *Britain 1870-1914* by José Harris (London 1985); *Britain 1914-1945* by John Stevenson (London 1983); and *British Society Since 1945* by Arthur Marwick (London 1984).

As for previous periods, searches should be made of the contents of the proceedings of local historical societies, *Notes and Queries*, the *Victoria County History* volumes, and the *Amateur* (later *Local*) *Historian*. *Sources for English Local History* by W.B. Stephens pp.45-71 is valuable as an indicator of local publications of wider significance.

Local government

Today, the administration of local government is variously in the hands of the county, the borough, the district and the parish. But these bodies are of comparatively recent origin. County councils were established in 1888 and replaced the organisation of the lieutenants and the Justices of the Peace, which had operated since Tudor times. Parish councils were set up in 1894 and superseded parish vestries, which had in turn supplanted manor courts. District councils came into being as a result of the 1974 legislation which, *inter alia*, abolished rural district councils. It is best to start at the beginning.

For the centuries up to the Tudor times the main instrument of local government outside the boroughs was the manor court, and the best introduction to the whole subject remains *Life on the English Manor* by H.S. Bennett. First published in 1937, the book is still in print. A good overall view also appears in *English Local Administration in the Middle Ages* by H.M. Jewell (1972), but for the researcher who intends to carry out sustained and long-term work in the field the ten-volume *English Local Government* by S. & B. Webb (reprinted 1963) may be necessary. It comprises: (i) The Parish and County; (ii) and (iii) The Manor and The Borough; (iv) Statutory Authorities for Special Purposes; (v) The Story of the King's Highway; (vi) English Prisons under Local Government; (vii) (viii) and (ix) English Poor Law History; (x) English Poor Law Policy.

Other works of general interest are *Archives and Local History* by F.G. Emmison, *Local Records* by L.J. Redstone and F.W. Steer (1953), and, of course, books by R.B. Pugh and John West mentioned earlier. *The Early History of English Poor Law Relief* by E.M. Leonard (1900) is worth seeking, as are the following: *The Manor and Manorial Records* by N.J. Hone (3rd edition, 1925), *A History of the Boroughs and Municipal Corporations* by

H.A. Merewether and A.J. Stephens (originally published in 1835, but reprinted in 1972), *British Borough Charters 1042-1216* by A. Ballard (1913), *1216-1307* by A. Ballard and J. Tait (1923), and *1307-1660* by M. Weinbaum (1943), *A History of English Assizes from 1558-1714* by J.S. Cockburn (1972). *Sources for English Local History* by W.B. Stephens has many further references to published volumes.

Agriculture

Some slight insight into early local agricultural practices may be obtained from such things as Anglo-Saxon charters, details of which have been published (from 1961 onwards) in a series of volumes called *The Early Charters of . . .*, and commentaries on land usage such as in *The Domesday Geography of . . .*, each volume of which deals with a particular region. Reference may also be made to the relevant Domesday texts and the published volumes of the *curia regis* and other rolls, some of which make useful contributions to local knowledge. The appropriate publication in the *Victoria County History* series will also be of value.

To a substantial degree agricultural history and social history are inextricably bound up with one another — demesne and common land practices, copyhold and other tenures, enclosures — and many of the books already mentioned include sections and passages which will enlighten.

A recent series of volumes under the general title of *The Agrarian History of England and Wales*, each edited by a distinguished scholar, is basic to the study of the subject. There are dozens of specialist works on the subject of agricultural history, and many more dealing with purely local matters. The following are merely typical examples of books worthy of collection: *English Field Systems* by H.L. Gray (republished London 1969), *History of the Farmstead* by J. Weller (London 1982, with over 200 illustrations, a glossary and a bibliography), *Old Farm Implements* by Philip Wright (Gloucester 1983), *The Agricultural Revolution in South Lincolnshire* by David Grigg (Cambridge 1966), and *Bound to the Soil: A Social History of Dorset 1750-1918* by B. Kerr (London 1968). *The Village Labourer* by J.L. & B. Hammond was originally published in 1911 and has since been republished in paperback (London 1978). It has been edited by G.E. Mingay and now contains important bibliographic notes on open fields, the process of enclosure, the economic consequences of enclosure, the social consequences, the poor law, and agrarian unrest.

Trade and industry

There are few 'basic' books on the subject of trade or industry which the local historian will regard as essential to his personal library. The 'natural' industries of metal and mineral mining, forestry and fisheries have always been localised, for obvious reasons, as have the associated processes of conversion such as the smelting of ore, the dressing of stone and the manufacture of coke and charcoal. The holding of markets and fairs for the trading of livestock, agricultural produce and the output of craft industries has been widely spread, but the institutions themselves have been diverse. With the growth of towns, the coming of the Industrial Revolution, and the improvements in surface transportation, the pattern in all but the staple industries changed and the whole industrial and commercial structure grew (and grows) increasingly more diverse and complex, to the extent that it moves ever more out of the realms of the local researcher into those of the economic or social historian working at national, or even international, level.

For each locality the records of first resort remain the early county histories, the relevant volumes in the *Victoria County History* series, and the proceedings of the county, or similar, historical or record society; and no doubt local historians will wish to obtain some of these or, subject to the laws of copyright, obtain photocopies of selected sections. There is a valuable chapter, 'Industry, Trade and Communications', in Stephens' *Sources for English Local History* which points, particularly, to references in the public records. Beyond this, the local studies collection in the public reference library will be a source of essential information. There are, however, a number of books, now mostly out of print, which are worth seeking: *Fairs Past and Present* by C. Walford (1883), and *The English Craft Guilds* by S. Kramer (1927) both deal with early institutions of wide application. The Phillimore annual catalogue will also serve to identify books of individual interest.

For the local researcher concerned with studies of bygone industries the following are useful: *Industrial Archaeology* by M. Rix (1967), *The Techniques of Industrial Archaeology* by J.P.M. Pannell (1974), and *Fieldwork in Industrial Archaeology* by J.K. Major (1975).

Personal prosperity

The subject of the prosperity of individuals and families is very closely connected with social structure, agriculture, and trade and industry. To some degree aspects of local (and national) government also bear on the topic — be they methods of charitable distribution of the eighteenth century, poor relief of the nineteenth, or welfare benefits of the twentieth. A great deal of information is contained in the numerous books already cited in this chapter as worthy of forming part of a personal library, and the local researcher should not lose sight of the early comparative data obtainable from the published Domesday folios, and the later in such things as the hearth tax assessments, all of which volumes are well worth places on private shelves. The author is not aware of any book dealing with the totality of this field, indeed it is so wide that generalisations can be misleading. However, a search in town and country reference libraries (and local studies collections) will reveal titles of books which are worth acquiring, especially on the subjects of the impact of indigenous trade, industry, and agriculture on the well-being of local populations. The chapter 'Poor relief, charities, prices and wages' in *Sources for English Local History* (Stephens) contains numerous references of local and sometimes more general value.

Housing

A key reference book is *Sources for the History of Houses* by John Harvey (London 1974), and to this may be added *The Illustrated Handbook of Vernacular Architecture* by R.W. Brunskill (London, 3rd edition 1986), and *Traditional Buildings of Britain* by the same author (London 1985). *The Timber-Framed House in England* by Trudy West (London 1971) and *English Stone Buildings* by Alec Clifton Taylor and A.S. Ireson (London 1983) may be useful for the periods and styles they cover. Further works which may be deemed desirable acquisitions are: *The English House* by James Chambers (London 1985), *English Vernacular Houses* by E. Mercer, and *The English Medieval House* by Margaret Wood (London, reprint 1985). Reference to *British Books in Print* and the trade catalogues of specialist publishers will show many titles of works dealing not only with houses, but also with the broadly related field of what has been called 'national prosperity'. These may be referred to, and selected works obtained, from public lending libraries, before any decision to purchase is taken.

Religion

The history of religion in England has been a complex one — Monasticism, the Dissolution, the Reformation, Nonconformity, and other events and disciplines have also played their part. The study of religion in the context of local history will be influenced by such things as 'Was the area dominated by a religious institution in medieval times?' 'Did the Tudor period have a recorded local impact?' 'Were the philosophies of Commonwealth times — Puritanism, the Levellers — of dominant concern?' 'When did Methodism, Unitarianism, the Baptist Church (or whatever) come first to the area?' The answers to these questions will determine which books the local researcher will purchase and retain.

A useful starting point is the reference sections appearing at the end of each major entry in *The Oxford Dictionary of the Christian Church* already mentioned. Under 'Baptists', for example, there are dozens of works, starting with *A History of the Baptists ... to the year 1886* by T. Armitage (London 1888). Under the heading 'Methodist Churches' there are many works regarding all branches of this faith. Similar extensive bibliographies appear for the Church of England, all the monastic orders, Roman Catholicism, Spiritual Healing, Judaism, Islam and all other religious denominations and orders of, or relating to, Christianity.

Education

The field of education is as wide as that of religion, and it would be futile to attempt to particularise over such a vast subject. The starting point must again be *British Books in Print*, and the card index of the nearest large public reference or lending library.

A further useful beginning to identifying needs is the long article on the History of Education in the *Encyclopaedia Britannica*; whilst much of this is not relevant directly to the study of local history, it is good background to the history of the English national systems of the nineteenth and twentieth centuries. Many useful references are given, but it must be recognised that both juvenile and adult education has changed very considerably indeed in the last decade — and more changes are due. This makes the identification of basic texts very important — and the enlistment of expert help from the town or county hall most desirable

32

Specialist archives and collections

The importance of the great national repositories of original documents was stressed in Chapter 5, and subsequent chapters have indicated many ways in which their resources may be used by local researchers. Attention has also been paid to the importance of collections maintained in museums, reference libraries, universities, and by corporations. These collections, in addition to having work of a distinctly 'local', that is to say geographical, concentration have, in many cases, manuscripts and printed works of much wider significance in the fields of social development, religious beliefs, technological innovation, the functioning of particular industries, and so on.

The purpose of this chapter is to identify the places where specialist collections of more than local importance may be found, as well as indicating the kind of local material that is so freely accessible. The locations of the various collections will be found in Appendix III, Addresses.

Local authority record offices

These provincial centres, set up at different periods in the past, vary in the sizes of the archives they maintain. In general terms they house the expected local authority records, but also frequently hold large numbers of estate, manorial, business and family papers, enclosure and tithe awards. Often they have custody of borough archives, Quarter Session records, and the registers of baptisms, marriages and burials deposited by ancient parishes, some of whose records go back to Elizabethan times. Other material of wide interest dates from as early as the Saxon period.

What now follows is a listing of important, more general, archives in the keeping of these local depositories, some of which have been considerably reorganised subsequent to the county boundary changes of 1974.

Cambridge Papers of a number of women's rights organisations from 1885 onwards. The Huntingdon office has manuscripts from the muniments of the earls and dukes of Manchester.
Chester Archives of city gilds are held. These are of general value, as well as illuminating the history of the local organisations.
Cumbria (Carlisle) Records relating to the suffragist and pacifist movements, from 1880 onwards.

Derbyshire (Matlock) Three groups of records of general interest are held: papers on the Titus Oates plot, papers relating to the Civil War, and the pre-vesting date archives of the National Coal Board.

Devon Papers, dating from the nineteenth century, of the geologist William Buckland and the naturalist Frank Buckland.

Durham Records relating to coal mining and coal interests have been deposited. These include not only National Coal Board records but also pre-nationalisation documents.

East Sussex (Lewes) The collections include papers of J. Baker-Holroyd, first earl of Sheffield (1735-1821), an authority on agricultural topics.

Leeds An important group is the papers of Samuel Smiles (1812-1904), the political reformer, biographer of Josiah Wedgwood and others, and the author of *Self-Help* (1859), *Character, Thrift* and *Duty.*

London The Corporation of London office holds the official archives from the eleventh century to the present, and many documents are of wide interest, for they deal with jurisdiction and property interests in many countries, including the estates granted in 1628 for sale by the Crown to settle national debts. The Greater London Record office has the papers of a number of hospitals and medical institutions, the most important of which are: St Thomas' (1556-1948), including the Nightingale School (1860 onwards); Guy's (1860-1948), and the personal records of Thomas Guy. Also held are the records of the Westminster Hospital Group (1715 onwards), and the Foundling Hospital (1793 onwards).

Manchester The city archive has the two following collections likely to be of wide interest: the first deals with women's suffrage in the north, and the second comprises the documents and papers of William Farmer, an editor of the *Victoria County History: Lancashire*. The Greater Manchester Record Office has many canal records, including those of the Manchester Ship Canal and the Rochdale canal enterprises.

Merseyside There is considerable material on docks and shipping, plus correspondence regarding the American Civil War, the slave trade, and other commercial ventures. An archive of special social interest is that of the Society for the Relief of Sick and Distressed Needlewomen (1864-1927).

Surrey The Guildford office holds records of the Office of the King's Tents (1542-58), and the Lieutenancy of the Tower of London (1615-17). The Surrey office at Kingston-on-Thames has the records for the Royal Philanthropic Society's School for the reform of juveniles, from 1788 onwards.

West Yorkshire The collections include the records of the British Waterways Board from the year 1652 and thereafter.

University and college archives

Several universities and institutions of higher education have departments of local history in which the subject may be studied to the end of achieving a recognised qualification, and hence have well-stocked reference libraries. Others, being anciently established, also have manuscript materials going back to the days of their foundation in the Middle Ages or the Tudor period. A third group has, in addition, deliberately created specialist collections of both manuscript and printed works.

It is probably true to say that, with the exception of the more recently founded universities and colleges, all higher educational establishments have archival collections of varying sizes which they have generated, been given, or have purchased. The larger collections are usually estate papers or the personal libraries of people with direct connections, as witness, say, the Thomas Arnold manuscripts at Rugby School, the Montefiore collection of Jews' College, or the Conan Doyle correspondence in the University of London Library. Some of the archives, however, are not only of substantial national or international repute, but are of paramount relevance to local history research. Among the more notable are, by classification:

Agricultural history The Sheffield University Library contains several specialist collections, one of the more important being the Hartlib MSS, a seventeenth-century group devoted to describing methods of agricultural improvement.

Cultural activity The Library of Contemporary Culture Records was founded in 1970 and is now in the custody of the University of East Anglia. It holds a vast collection of manuscripts dating from 1965 onwards. The items are drawn from all parts of the country, and cover such things as local festivals, art associations, poetry circles, and so on.

Cultural tradition The Centre for English Cultural Tradition and Language of the University of Sheffield houses the Russell Wortly collection of folk dance and song. There is an extensive index. The centre also has a wide-ranging collection of artifacts relating to folklore and craft industries.

Ecclesiastical history The Borthwick Institute (University of York) was established in 1953 and specialises in the study of ecclesiastical history — particularly the administrative and legal history of ecclesiastical institutions. These include the Community of the Resurrection and the Society of Friends. The Gurney Library of some 15,000 books concerns, mainly, ecclesiastical history.

Genealogical studies The John Rylands Library of Manchester University has many collections. In the Charter Rooms are deeds, genealogical and family papers for the twelfth to twentieth centuries, from the counties of Cheshire, Derbyshire, Warwickshire and Yorkshire.

Gypsy lore The Sydney Jones Library of the University of Liverpool houses the records of the Gypsy Lore Society (1895-1974) and the Scott Macfie collection of gypsy and Romany material.

Labour history Within the University of Hull is the Brynmor Jones library, which specialises in labour and socialist history. The collections are extensive.

Local history Large collections of local history books, pamphlets, manuscripts and the proceedings of interested bodies are held in the Department of Local History of the University of Leicester and the Bodleian Library, Oxford. This latter institution also has a vast assemblage of deeds, rolls, family papers and ecclesiastical records of importance to local history research.

Palatinate of Durham Within the Department of Palaeography of the University of Durham, established in 1948 for the promotion of the study of manuscript material mainly from the northern counties, there are major collections dating from the eleventh to the nineteenth centuries.

Power generation The University of Bath is a technological institution, and has custody of the Watkins Collection of photographs and written material on the evolution of steam power generation and the part it played in Britain in the years 1850-1914.

Rural life There are two important resources in the University of Reading. The first, within the Institute of Agricultural History and the Museum of Rural Life, has over 250,000 photographs, and many major collections of documents illustrating farming methods over the centuries, as well as thousands of tools, items of equipment and implements. The second resource is in the Department of Archives and Manuscripts, and consists of thousands of farm records, from every English county from the sixteenth century to the present.

Social studies The Tom Harrisson Mass-Observation Archive is housed in the University of Sussex. The records are those of a unique social science research organisation set up in 1937 to record the anthropology of everyday life in a wide variety of places. Volunteers kept diaries, answered regular questionnaires, and generally responded to points put to them by the directors of the study, Tom Harrisson and Charles Madge. The work continued into the 1950s and the Mass-Observation Archive is complete.

Topography The Department of Geography of the University of Keele has a collection of air photographs, which are the property of the Public Record Office. There are more than 5,000,000 vertical air-photographs (not all of places in Britain), which may be accessed subject only to the provisions of the Official Secrets, and Public Record Acts.

Town planning Liverpool University archives contain two bodies of documents of interest to researchers in local history: the first is Lord Holford's papers on town planning, and the second is Sir Charles Reilly's documents on architecture.

Local studies collections in public libraries

There is hardly a public library in the country which does not have, under one heading or another, a 'local studies' section, and these are vital sources to the student of local history. The contents of the sections vary a great deal in both quality and quantity — depending very much on the space available, the interests of past librarians and local historians, the cash resources of the competent authority, and any transient idiosyncrasies of fashion.

The paragraphs which now follow single out some of the more important, more specialised, local collections, and particularly those which are likely to be of value to researchers working over a fairly wide geographical area, or concentrating on a single subject.

Avon County Reference Library (Bristol) A collection relates to slavery and the slave trade, and there is, in the Emanuel Green Library, a host of publications on the history of Somerset.

Birmingham Reference Library Among the many collections housed (including the famous Shakespeare Library) are business archives — the Boulton and Watt archive is a major source of reference for the history of the Industrial Revolution; the Assay Office Collection relates to the Mint and the Midlands toy and silver trades — and the more general local studies department has a fine collection of maps and seals.

Derbyshire Library (Chesterfield) Contents of general value are the Wyatt Collection concerning lead mining in the nineteenth century; records of the Derby Canal Company; and the Duesbury Collection on china and porcelain manufacture.

Devon Library Services (Exeter) The library has a large number of books dealing with the south-west of England. There are more than 2,500 volumes of pre-1800 imprint, and an extensive assemblage of maps, illustrations and ephemera.

Doncaster Central Library A substantial archive is devoted to the history of horse racing, and another to railways.

Dudley Local History Department Included in these archives are the muniments of the lords Dudley, fifteenth to twentieth centuries. It will be recalled that the Dudley (or Sutton) family was prominent in the history of England especially in late Tudor times, and held many estates and titles including, for a short time, the dukedom of Northumberland.

Gateshead Library The local history collection includes estate papers from the seventeenth and eighteenth centuries, of particular relevance to the early history of coal mining in the Palatinate of Durham.

Kidderminster Library Useful papers of eighteenth-century Ironmasters are stored.

Liverpool City Library The local studies group has manorial and estate papers of the widely spread holdings of the earldom (later, marquessate) of Salisbury.

Westminster City Library This archive contains the important Grosvenor estate papers. The Grosvenor family (now holders of the dukedom of Westminster) is of ancient lineage (the Scrope versus Grosvenor controversy of the late fourteenth century is a pertinent study), and, over the ages, members have held estates in a number of counties and participated in governmental matters in many localities.

Specialist archives

There are hundreds of specialist archives around the country. Some, like the British Telecom Museum, deal with technology; others, like the Library of Political and Economic Science, with ideology; a third group, such as the Bethlem Hospital (Bedlam), with an institution; a fourth, as represented by the Hatfield House Collection, with a great family; another, as witness the Huguenot Library, with a cultural and religious group. The list is not exhaustive, but what this present section sets out to do is give a very substantial selection illustrating the range of material which can be drawn on by the researcher.

Army Ogilby Trust (Aldershot) Established in 1954 with the purpose of collecting papers, books, journals and lists dealing with British regiments and their uniforms.

Baptist Union Library (London) Includes the Baptist Historical Library, and many histories of Baptist churches from the seventeenth century onwards. Much of the material is unpublished.

Bethlem Royal Hospital (Beckenham, Kent) Bedlam, as it was called, was founded in 1247 as the Priory of St Mary of Bethlehem. By 1400 it was a hospital for the insane. As an archive it is recognised by the Public Records Act 1958. It has the collected papers of a number of hospitals, some medieval records, and a library devoted to the history of insane asylums and hospitals. It has hundreds of drawings, engravings and photographs.

British Architectural Library (London) has more than 400 metres of shelving of manuscript works from the seventeenth century onwards, on all manner of architectural topics; there are more than 250,000 drawings and 50,000 photographs on architecture and topography.

British Library of Political and Economic Science (London) The library specialises in modern British political, economic and social history, social anthropology, and has a vast collection of books. The Charles Booth Survey of London (1885-1905) fills 426 volumes. The term 'modern' is interpreted widely, for some works date from as early as the sixteenth century.

British Steel Record Services (London) The Corporation maintains a central archive, and also regional collections. Given the nature of the corporation —it was formed in 1967 — its major collections are devoted to the history of the many companies from all the great steel-producing centres, which constitute the corporate body. Its regional archives are in Wellingborough, Middlesborough and Deeside (plus, for Wales and Scotland, Cardiff and Glasgow).

British Telecom Museum (London) This museum contains, in addition to the important displays of equipment from the earliest electro-mechanical to the latest digital fibre-optic, the Historical Telephone Directory Library containing London directories 1800 onwards, and provincial directories 1900 onwards.

Charity Commission (London and Liverpool) The Commission was established in 1853 under the Charitable Trust Act. Its principal archival collection comprises records relating to some 140,000 charities. The London office covers national charities and those in England south of the River Severn to the Wash, and the Liverpool office has responsibility for those north of that line.

Chetham's Library (Manchester) The policy of this library is to collect works of all kinds dealing with the local histories and topography of places in north-west England.

Christ's Hospital (Abingdon) Records of the Fraternity of the Holy Cross and the Guild of Our Lady, 1165-1547, the records of benefactors and charities administered by the Governors, and the records of the hospital 1533-1918 are the principal collections.

College of Arms (London) The college was granted its charter by King Richard III in 1484, but some of its papers date from before that time, to the very earliest days of heraldry in the thirteenth century. The official records include heralds' visitations, grants of arms, and pedigrees. Semi-official and unofficial collections include rolls of arms, armorials, ordinaries, work books and papers relating to orders of chivalry. There are some 50 private archives created by past heralds, miscellaneous family papers, as well as seals and bookplate collections.

Duchy of Cornwall Office (London) All records of the duchy are maintained. They include parchment and paper rolls prepared by receivers, manorial court officials and other functionaries.

Council for the Care of Churches (London) Established in 1921, the principal collection is the National Survey of Churches, including photographs and guide books on almost all the 17,000 parish churches and associated chapels of the Church of England. There are extensive records on nineteenth-century stained glass.

Customs and Excise (London) HM Customs & Excise library dates from 1671, the time at which the Board of Customs was founded. An important collection concerns taxation on goods and smuggling, and there are eighteenth-century maps and charts of British coastal areas.

Dean and Chapter Library (Durham) The library has developed from the one founded by the Benedictine house of the tenth century. It comprises an extensive accumulation of medieval manuscripts, and a number of antiquarian collections.

Devonshire Collection (Derbyshire) The archive is that of the Cavendish family, earls and dukes of Devonshire. It includes estate papers (from 1618 to the present) and numerous books of household accounts.

Exeter Cathedral Library The library was founded in the eleventh century, and the Exon Domesday and several other documents survive *in situ* from that date. There are many important collections of charters, leases and other capitular works, maps, cartularies, deeds, manorial records and so on, of pre-Reformation properties. There is an archive of Vicars Choral thirteenth-twentieth centuries.

Fawcett Library (London) Originally the library of the London Society for Women's Suffrage (1867), it is now named after Millicent Garrett Fawcett, its founder. The collections include suffrage, equal status, the feminist controversy of 1863-86, and the records of the Association for Moral and Social Hygiene.

Folklore Society (London) Founded in 1878, the society has more than 50 major collections, but at the time of writing these have not been catalogued.

Gloucester Collection (Gloucester) In addition to numerous estate records, the collection includes the Dancey Gift of works relating to the county (225 volumes, more than 300 pamphlets, almost the same number of prints and paintings). There are some fine manuscripts illustrating the histories of the county's Saxon churches.

Guildhall Library (London) The library holds thousands of records of the trading history of the City of London and it is, in effect, the county record office for the City. It also houses the records of most of the city livery companies.

Harrow School (Middlesex) In addition to school and estate records, the collections include Harrow manor court rolls.

Hatfield House (Hertfordshire) Papers include those of Lord Burghley (1520-98), Secretary of State to Queen Elizabeth I, and other distinguished members of the Cecil family down to those of the 3rd marquess (1830-1903), Prime Minister of Great Britain.

Hereford Cathedral Manuscripts survive from the eighth century, and the earliest deed is dated *c*.840. There is a chained library of 1500 books and many works of more than local interest.

Huguenot Library (London) Further to the papers of philanthropic institutions founded or supported by the Huguenots, there is a fine collection of pedigrees and other genealogical works.

Institute of Geological Studies (London) The collection of some 30,000 items is, in effect, a national geological archive, and includes the Geological Survey and the Palaeontographical Society records (1847-1950).

Institute of Heraldic and Genealogical Studies (Canterbury) Many thousands of unpublished manuscripts relating to family histories; manorial papers thirteenth-twentieth centuries, records of armorial bearings in all Sussex churches, Canterbury Cathedral and elsewhere; an extensive index of British arms; transcripts of rolls of arms and heraldic treatises; heralds' original note books; and hundreds of genealogical documents are held at the Institute.

Lambeth Palace Library (London) The library holds registers of the archbishops of

Canterbury from the thirteenth century onwards, and the archives of many societies connected with the Church of England, together with those of bishops and statesmen. There are more than 150,000 printed books, many being of historical importance within the Church.

Leeds Diocesan Library (Leeds) The archive includes papers of the Roman Catholic Church in the north of England after the year 1688.

Methodist Archives and Research Centre (Manchester) The collections are housed in the John Rylands Library and comprise documents and books devoted to the religious history of the denomination. In addition there are thousands of letters, diaries and journals which were the property of prominent Methodists.

Middlesex Polytechnic (London) The Silver Studio Collection is maintained by this institution. The Silver family were wallpaper manufacturers and textile designers in London, and the collection includes many thousands of photographs, designs, samples and related ephemera.

Modern Records Centre (Coventry) The centre is maintained within the University of Warwick, and has the objects of collecting and preserving written and printed material of special interest to labour history, industrial relations and kindred subjects. The papers of many trade unions are housed at the Centre.

National Meteorological Archive (Bracknell) Climatological data covering the British Isles have been gathered, some as early as 1900.

National Monuments Record (London) There are records of The Royal Commission on Historical Monuments, 1908 to the present, 400,000 Ordnance Survey record cards of sites of archaeological importance; 2 million photographs, drawings and reports on historical buildings and archaeological sites; and numerous reference books.

Duke of Norfolk's Archive (Arundel) This extensive collection is valuable for many reasons. Firstly, it is a family archive covering the period since the thirteenth century; secondly, the dukes of Norfolk have been Earls Marshal and Hereditary Marshals of England for many centuries; and finally, as the family has adhered to the old religion, many documents have an important bearing on English (Roman) Catholic history.

Duke of Northumberland's Archive (Alnwick and Middlesex) The Percy family and its successors have been prominent in English history since the thirteenth century, firstly as earls, and later as dukes, of Northumberland. Members have always owned vast estates and, through important heiress alliances, acquired (and sometimes disposed of) property in many counties as far south as Dorset and Kent. Their archives reflect this.

Office of Population Censuses and Surveys (The General Register Office in St Catherine's House, London) A central register of births, deaths and the solemnization and registration of marriages, was begun on 1 July 1837 and was called The General Register Office. In 1970 it was amalgamated with the Government Social Survey to form the Office of Population Censuses and Surveys. The collections are an essential reference source, especially for the Victorian period. The decennial census data which have so far been published in accordance with the 100-year closure rule provide unique information on social patterns and mores.

Order of St John Library (London) The Sovereign and Military Order of St John of Jerusalem was founded *c*.1100, and the collection includes a number of manuscripts dating from the early centuries. The (English) priory of the medieval order was dissolved in 1540 and the archive consists mainly of records of post-1831 date, when the Venerable Order of St John was founded. There are fine collections of books, pamphlets and coins.

Port of London Authority Records of London Dock and Thames Navigation authorities and companies dating from 1770 onwards.

Post Office Archives (London) Although the collections mainly concern the work of the General Post Office, there are significant holdings of records from the late seventeenth century which are of importance to local historians researching the evolution of communication methods. The National Postal Museum is also of potential value in this field.

Queen Mary College (London) This college of the University of London, developed from the People's Palace in the East End (1884), by way of the East End Technical College. The archive of The People's Palace (1884-1920) is voluminous.

Royal Geographical Society (London) The Society was founded in 1830 with the object of sponsoring geographical research and exploration. It has a large accumulation of books, manuscripts, maps and pictures.

St George's Chapel (Windsor Castle) The College of St George was founded in 1348, the probable date of the creation of the Order of the Garter. There are many manuscripts dating from that time, and a few from the earlier period, starting 1140. There are many property deeds and papers referring to the knights of the order, some of whom were powerful land-holding magnates, close to the throne.

Society of Antiquaries (London) The Society (founded in 1701) has nearly a thousand manuscripts dating from 1100 onwards, representing every branch of antiquarian studies. It has some 20,000 prints and drawings of a topographical nature, and about 3000 broadsheets, some as old as 600 years. There is a large collection of material about the civil war, and 10,000 casts of seals.

Society of Friends Library (London) The archive, founded in 1673, has large resources, with indexes and search lists, of documents of importance to the Quaker movement. Many family papers are stored and there is an extensive picture library.

Society of Jesus Archive (London) The Jesuit mission to England began in 1580 and some of the archive material dates from that time. The main sources of acquisition are the Jesuit houses, and there are quantities of letters from the central and provincial curia.

Spalding Gentlemen's Society This body was founded in 1710. It has a fine collection of manorial and local government records, and its archive of fens drainage papers is unique.

Thames Water Authority (London) The Authority's territory covers 5000 square miles. It has records of the older companies and boards, plus plans and letter books dating from the eighteenth century and onwards. There is a valuable library of works concerning the River Thames.

United Reform Church History Society (London) The main sections of the archive house the papers of the Presbyterian Historical Society, the Congregational Churches of Christ and the United Reform Church. There is a library of seventeenth-century pamphlets and tracts.

Westminster Diocesan Archive (London) The collections date from after the Elizabethan Reformation settlement of 1559. Records of Catholics in the Home Counties in the sixteenth-nineteenth centuries are held, and there are leaflets, scrap-books and correspondence.

Dr Williams's Library (London) Daniel Williams was a Presbyterian Minister who died in 1716, and his personal library is the foundation of the present collection, which specialises in English Nonconformity of the Protestant type. There are nearly 140,000 printed books now held.

Wiltshire Library and Museum Service (Trowbridge) The importance of this establishment is its use of a computer data base for recording archaeological sites and historic monuments. Work is also being carried out (on a wider than county basis) on transferring information regarding charities onto computer-based storage media.

Winchester College Archives The College was founded in 1382 and there are extensive records of its estates in, mainly, Hampshire, Wiltshire and Dorset. These papers include maps, plans and architectural drawings.

York Minster Archives There is much material from the Middle Ages to the present (1150 onwards). The archive contains documents of a non-ecclesiastical nature, not only relative to the city itself, but also the county and, indeed, the properties of the Minster elsewhere in England.

Museum archives and collections

Every local historian will be familiar with his own county, town or privately-run district museum, and of its importance in the field of historical studies. Many such institutions also have substantial libraries, not only about local places, people and conditions, but works *by* local authors, all of which can be of value in building a picture of a place, its people, and their social preoccupations. The closest attention should also be given to the contents of such national museums as the British, Ashmolean, Science, Victoria & Albert, London, and the Fitzwilliam, all of which have incomparable collections of artifacts, documents, books, and all manner of relevant material.

What now follows is a list of museums (many with archives) which specialise in material of general as well as narrowly local moment.

Costume and Fashion Centre (Bath) The centre was opened in 1974 and the collections deal with fashionable dress for men, women and children of the sixteenth to twentieth centuries.

Ironbridge Gorge Museum Trust (Telford) Established in 1968, the Museum Trust conserves the unique industrial remains of the area, which comprise coke-smelting furnaces, the world's first iron bridge, china factories and much more. The work of the Trust is of wide significance — it includes, for instance, the Berkeley and Gloucester Canal archives, and the Elton Collection of material relating to the Industrial Revolution.

National Maritime Museum (London) Public records including Admiralty, Navy Board and dockyard muniments for seventeenth-nineteenth centuries are maintained. The personal papers of a number of distinguished sailors are held, and there are thousands of historic photographs.

National Museum of Labour History (London) The extensive collections of exhibits, records and papers cover radical movements from the Industrial Revolution onwards: Labour Party, Independent Labour Party, and the archives of many trade unions. There is also a well stocked reference library of books, newspapers, posters and ephemera. There is a collection of photographs (and projector slides).

National Railway Museum (York) Set up in 1975, as a part of the Science Museum, London, the Yorkshire body houses the contents of the old British Museum of Transport. There are several collections, including many records of minor railways in the West Midlands and the Welsh Borders, and the Lancashire and Yorkshire Railway. There are official glass negative collections of a number of major companies, 1880-1950.

North Western Museum of Science and Industry (Manchester) Opened in 1969, the displays cover the industries representative of the north-west of England. Of special interest are books on papermaking, photography and heavy electrical engineering.

Guides and reference books

Without exception the bodies, institutions and archives mentioned in this chapter have catalogues, guides, indexes or lists to help the researcher determine what is relevant and where to find it. Copies of the more important volumes are held in the larger reference libraries, or may be borrowed from the lending division of the British Library.

In support of these publications there are several general reference books of value. *British Archives* by Janet Foster and Julia Sheppard (London 1982) is a work of more than 500 pages and is described as 'guide to the archive resources in the United Kingdom'. Its particular merit is the brief descriptions of the contents of many of the archives. *Record Repositories in Great Britain* (HMSO 1982) is a useful handlist, as is *Materials for Theses in Local Record Offices and Libraries* by F.G. Emmison and W.J. Smith (London 1973). This latter publication lists, by county, important archives (and suggests ways in which they may be used). *Record Offices* (how to find them) by J. Gibson and P. Peskett (Birmingham 1981) complements the last-named booklet by providing maps showing where most public record offices are located.

Turning now to commentaries, the following are relevant: *Archives and Local History* by F.G. Emmison (London 1978), and *Enjoying Archives* by David Iredale (London 1985). Finally, *Sources for English Local History* by W.B. Stephens (Cambridge 1981) is a quite indispensable guide, for not only does it refer to archives and collections, but suggests ways in which they may be used, and does so by major subject categories: population and social structure; local government and politics; poor relief; charities, prices and wages; industry, trade and communications; agriculture; education; religion; and houses, housing and health.

Section V WRITING A LOCAL HISTORY
33
The story of Combsburgh
— an imaginary place

Writing a good parish history is not a task to be undertaken lightly. If the work is to be comprehensive, thoroughly researched and well constructed it will take many years. The present author, working almost full-time, spent just over five years on a single village; the result was a book of A4 format (11½ x 8 inches) containing 436 pages of printed text and 62 pages of illustrations — photographs, maps and diagrams. The village itself was in Dorset, but visits were needed to Alnwick in Northumberland, Seal in Kent, Syon in Middlesex, Southampton in Hampshire, Slapton in Devon and Salisbury in Wiltshire to examine original manuscripts and take photographs. At least a dozen visits were necessary to the Public Record Office, the British Library, the National Monuments Record and the Institute of Historical Research in London. Many letters were exchanged with people in America, France and the Antipodes, as well as in Britain. Thus material about the specific parish and its people was gathered.

But no parish is a closed community — it is bounded by other communities (and sometimes by the sea) and all these have helped to shape its boundaries, layout, population and activities. National events and policies have played their part, from the arrival of a new overlord in 1066, through the effects of the civil wars of the seventeenth century, to the present-day activities of the Department of the Environment. All these things must be considered.

To end this book a chapter will, therefore, be devoted to the history of a fictitious place called Combsburgh, with the objects of demonstrating ways in which data obtained by careful research may subsequently be incorporated into a narrative. The story opens with a brief scene-setting introduction, followed by a much fuller treatment of the social history of Combsburgh during the years 1820-60.

Combsburgh — setting the scene

Combsburgh is the name of an ecclesiastical parish of great antiquity and a civil parish whose latest status was established by the local government legislation of 1972/4. The parish contains a small market town (also called Combsburgh) and several outlying hamlets and farms. It covers about 3630 acres, traversed by the River Holbeck and drained by several small tributaries, mainly Fitlock Brook. The land undulates between 200 and 250 feet above sea level, except in the south-east where the altitude nears 300 feet. A broad band of Corallian Limestone and Sand crosses the central part —northeast to south-west — and this is bounded on each side by Oxford Clay. The small market town area (see map) is to the east of the parish, and this, together with the

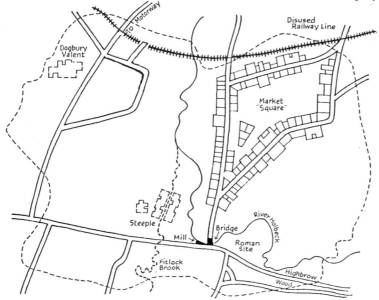

high ground south of the river and the tiny hamlets of Steeple and Dogbury Valent, all appear to have been the sites of pre-Conquest settlement. Combsburgh has evolved into a pleasant shire parish containing the little market town mentioned, to which local farmers, traders and visitors come with pleasure and occasional profit.

It was the site of a Roman estate in the first-third centuries, the Saxons established farm clusters, two of its settlements were mentioned in Domesday, and King John used it as a hunting base (and purchased his wines there). By late Tudor times it had become a prosperous wool-producing centre, and had a thriving tannery, but after the civil wars, during which it housed a small Parliamentary garrison, it gradually declined in activity and status. After the First World War the town thrived briefly, but in later decades achieved a near-dormitory state, having been discovered by couples wishing to retire from the frenetic life in the larger urban conurbations. Then, in the late 1970s, a new motorway thrust through the county and a junction was constructed just six miles to the west. The land speculators and property developers moved in, and the parish has been given a priority status within the County Structure Plan.

Today the social life of Combsburgh has many facets. The parish is fortunate in having a spacious and well-appointed parish hall (erected and administered by the Combsburgh Recreational and General Trust, with a generous gift from the Carradine-Haye family), and a fairly well-stocked branch library. Organisations range from Brownies, Cub-Scouts, Scouts and Guides to the Silver Lining Club for the 'Senile Citizens', as they tend to be called locally. There is a Women's Institute branch (the W.I. — known, inevitably, as the Witches International by the habitués of the Smoke Room of the Red Lion), a Choral Group, and an Amateur Dramatic Society. The Combsburgh High School stages a Christmas pantomime in which every young Jack and Jill (or Wayne and Tracy as they are all called today) has at least a walk-on part. Football and cricket clubs flourish. A well-written, well-produced parish magazine appears monthly (with the exception of July); edited by the rector, the Reverend

Leonard Gaines, this publication includes a calendar of forthcoming events — those of general interest as well as those connected with the churches.

The River Holbeck has much to offer. It follows a winding course through low-lying water meadows, between the piers which supported the old railway arch (unused in the wake of Dr Beeching), down through attractive wooded slopes to Steeple Mill. The banks of the river are accessible to walkers, and are much appreciated by anglers anxious for coarse fishing — chub, perch, roach, tench and pike are plentiful. In the summer, the parish children and others delight in the hens, ducks, geese and cattle living the traditional rural life. The mill-house, with its white-painted cast iron foot-bridge over the river below the weir, forms a seductive spot for photographers, painters, picnickers and what used to be called courting couples, but are now gender-opposite persons endeavouring to establish meaningful relationships by pair-bonding and role-playing.

Friday is market day and it must be admitted that even in these times of high-speed travel, mini-breaks, and the lure of the larger towns, Combsburgh comes alive. It is the day when gossip is exchanged, slander is perpetuated, goods are bought and sold, refrigerators, deep freezes and wine cellars are replenished, bubblegum stuck to the more inviting parts of old ladies' dresses, and money transferred from the coffers of the DHSS to the tills of the Red Lion in joyous cacophony. Combsburgh is, then, a typical English rural parish.

A social history of Combsburgh 1820-1860

In the early nineteenth century Combsburgh, in common with the areas surrounding it, was in straitened circumstances. In 1820 Sir Frederick Adam published his *Survey of the State of the Poor*, in which he showed that throughout the shires rates of pay for labourers of all types were low, and that many families lived on small quantities of wheaten or barley bread, skimmed milk, cheese, potatoes and legumes, meat hardly ever figuring in their diet. On as little as 8/6d (42 new pence) a week a working-class family might have to pay 3 shillings (15p) for bread, 1 penny (3p) for cheese, 2 pence for tea, 4 pence for milk, 1½ pence for salt. In addition, their tenancy had to be paid for, fuel, clothes and thread provided. Cakes baked on the gridiron were regarded as a luxury, and sometimes a substitute for tea was made by pouring boiling water over burnt crusts of bread. Sanitation was primitive and the poorhouses in regular use. As a twentieth-century writer has said, 'Parish destitution had passed beyond any solution: repressions, palliatives, exhortations and sermons were of no avail.' The workers began to organise.

The lush farmlands of Combsburgh and the main trade of the little town had come into the hands of just a few landlords. An attempt had been made to offset recent enclosures by letting out a few five-acre plots, rent and tithe free, to deserving poor, but the newer legislation continued to make things difficult. The Game Law of 1816 was especially overbearing by rendering a man suspected, much less convicted, of poaching liable to transportation. Attempts to snare even rabbits became dangerous forays. There had, in 1814, been six convictions at the Quarter Sessions for these and other offences, such as deer stalking and assaults on keepers. By 1821 the number had risen to 43, four men being from Combsburgh.

In 1822 there came to the parish as rector, the great Walter Henry, a graduate of King's College, Cambridge, and a Fellow of the Royal Society. He did everything within his power to assist his parishioners, including letting out twenty acres of glebe land at £2 an acre rather than the £8 normally charged for potato ground. But unrest continued, not only in Combsburgh but in the rest of the county, and sporadic riots occurred. The accession of the new king, William IV, in June 1830 brought some slight relief, mainly because it was widely believed that His Majesty favoured the destruction of machinery and the payment of 2 shillings a day to men of the labouring classes. But discontent rose again; the fine autumn, plentiful harvest and good potato crop did not lessen the murmurings of the poor. As winter drew near, the folk of Combsburgh and the surrounding parishes became more restive. Talk in the Red Lion became increasingly spirited as the season wore on, and the rumours passed from farm cottage to town hovel. There remained talk that the new king would pay for the destruction of the threshing machines which the agricultural workers believed lay at the root of their misery, and there were stories that the new police — the 'Peelers' — had been armed with 6000 cutlasses from the Tower.

On 26 November 1830, hungry, cold, sickly and tied to their parish by the restrictions of the Poor Removals Act, the destitute of Combsburgh rose in an outbreak of physical violence. From the tranquility of the first decade of the twentieth century, the *Victoria County History* recorded: 'Farmers and petty employers [in Combsburgh] would not engage the best labour, but preferred the inferior hands at low wages . . . it was, therefore, scarcely surprising there were riots . . .'.

Walter Henry, as might be expected of a man of his background, calling and intellect, was much concerned with the well-being of his people and campaigned actively on their behalf. A remarkable and long letter from this gentleman has survived. It was addressed to Mr G.E. Bateman, the acting magistrate for the county who was conducting inquiries into the operation of the Poor Laws. A Mr Ashton had given evidence to the Inquiry and quoted a third party, who appeared to criticise its works. From the bench Bateman had said: 'I here beg leave, not merely in my own name but in the name of the whole bench, to require from Mr Ashton the name of the individual on whose statements he has thus presumed to impugn our magisterial conduct.' Henry replied, in an open letter, 'It is I', and over the course of no fewer than 63 pages drew a factual, logical and haunting picture of the plight of his beloved Combsburgh, as he perceived it in the winter of 1830/31. He pointed out to the magistrates that the people of the parish had previously been law-abiding, that riotous demonstrations and the destruction of property were rare, and even now were believed by many of the farmers and traders (and the poor themselves) to have been the work of gypsies. Henry continued, 'The riots here followed those in neighbouring counties, of which our people had heard rumours, as if those rioters had been able to overpower the gentry and as if large masses of men were moving on from London, to aid them in forcing their masters to give higher wages. The population of this district had not been previously deeply dissatisfied; but it was natural that they should wish well to people of their own class, supposed to be fighting for higher wages; and they presently heard with truth that several employers hereabouts had begun to promise higher payments under the dread of seeing the population armed against them.'

Henry went on to point out the evils of sweated labour and the pay make-up system, how it fostered a disinclination to work and how it encouraged landless men to marry just so that their income would be augmented 'in proportion to the number of their children', and how it led to degradation of the character: 'The weak, the indolent, and worthless worker is now secure of the maximum payment settled by the standards you have determined from parish funds, and the industrious, skilful and honest workman can expect no more ... the pernicious and demoralising practice of paying wages out of rates ... ought to be suppressed and prohibited.' He went on: 'I feel that, as a minister of a parish having no other resident gentleman, I ought to act as a guardian of my own poor; and if I should neglect any opportunity, which the Lord may place within my reach ... I shall be deserting a plain duty.' The Rector implored the inquiry to consider the case for living wages to be paid, as was the case in more enlightened parts of the county. In contradistinction to the indolent paupers who sponged off the Poor Rate and exploited pay make-up, and the hard-working landless town dweller who also suffered, he further cited the most respectable portion of the peasantry who were prevented from rising above the nominal low price of hire, so that the wage level 'must soon fall too low to allow the most abstemious worker to maintain himself. The cottager is, therefore, first entangled with debts for food and clothing, and then constrained to raise money by mortgaging his loved little tenement . . .'.

This was heady and powerful stuff, written by a passionate, articulate, sincere and devout man. The result was little enough, and the days of the Combsburgh riots passed. As the *Victoria County History* puts it, somewhat laconically, 'The chief result appears to have been an order given to the overseers to relieve ten more able-bodied families.' There were other personal repercussions, as the calendar and register of prisoners in the county gaol shows. Combsburgh got off fairly lightly — Aaron Howes aged 22 and John Foot aged 34 were transported, and William Dole aged 23 was sentenced to one year of hard labour — but adjoining parishes were not so lucky.

The rioters had done but small things. Under the apparent leadership of John Foot, 'as honest and quiet a man as any in the kingdom', to quote the court records, they had smashed a threshing machine and burned a hayrick. They had been vociferous to the effect that the 'tithes should come down' and the men should 'have higher wages'. There were other incidents of a minor nature, but in their wake the county was roused. Special constables were enrolled, the 9th Lancers were called in, and the 3rd Dragoons. The rioters took refuge in Highbrow Woods, but on 4 December moved into open country and were quietly taken. The Crown and Nisi Prius courts sat, the men were tried and sentenced. All petitions for leniency failed and the transportees were loaded onto the prison hulk *York* on 4 February 1831. In Van Dieman's Land, to which the men from Combsburgh were sent, some of their fellow rioters died of despair and others were permanently 'stupefied with care and grief.'

Things did not improve in the county for a long time to come. The wandering poor got short shrift — a burial is recorded in the Combsburgh register of an unknown man the neighbouring overseers had refused to receive when dying of cold. The number of paupers continued to increase from 18,600 in the county in 1840 to 22,700 in 1845.

Over the many years preceding the period now being described the ownership of properties and land in Combsburgh had changed hands many times. On occasion, distinguished local people such as Lord Brooks were landlords, at other times the owners were quite remote and took little interest in their holdings. As a national newspaper reported in June 1851: 'Some of the cottages in the parish, from continual neglect and the total absence of repair, are rendered insecure to that degree, that the inmates must be in a continual state of "fear and trembling". One of these tenements, the property of the lord of the manor and situated in the little town, deserves particular attention. A labourer and his family — in all eight persons — are the occupiers of this hovel, in which there is but one bedroom for their accommodation. There is a small opening, about a foot square, in this apartment, which is unglazed and serves the purpose of a window. The numerous cracks and fissures in the walls, which on every side present themselves, denote that at no very distant period this disgrace to the parish in which it stands will effectively remove itself. The furniture in the lower room, which in every respect corresponds to the upper one, consists of one chair, of most antique and unsafe appearance; two tables, which may be referred to an equally remote period; and a rude wooden bench, about four feet long. The rents of most of the houses in Combsburgh vary from 1/- to 1/6d per week.'

It is now, perhaps, fitting to turn away from stories of poverty and squalor, for although sickness and misery abounded and early death a commonplace of everyday existence, there were, in fact, social developments of a positive nature in the parish.

One of the most significant was in the increase in formal schooling, particularly of the young. If we examine the parish registers from 1763 onwards (from which date the principals and witnesses were required to 'sign' their names) it will be apparent that up to 1830 more than half the bridegrooms could not write and nearly three-quarters of the brides were devoid of the skill. Much the same went for the witnesses. In 1832 Walter Henry built a Sunday School near the church, and in 1839 founded a day-school for boys while his wife began to teach young girls in the rectory. Notes by the Rector about his establishments survive and we learn that in the first year of the new Sunday School there were 45 male and 32 female attendees. The master was paid 2 pence per week and he had four unpaid helpers. The day-school at its inception catered for 19 males and 13 females. The figures were low enough, for other records (baptisms and deaths) suggest there were nearly 90 boys of school age in the parish and more than 100 girls. As may be expected, most of the children attending school were the offspring of the more well-to-do traders and farmers, although exceptionally one or two daughters and sons of the labouring poor attended. The remainder of these unfortunates were already contributing to family incomes as labourers, shop boys, glovers, house-servants, rag collectors and so on. The notes kept by Walter Henry recorded in 1842 that, 'Each child pays a penny a week [when attending school] to which the Rector adds a penny. The Rector also pays the rates. All the children learn to read, 22 to write, 23 arithmetic, 12 geography. Four boys learn to knit, 13 girls learn to sew or make buttons.'

The Rector, his wife and their helpers were not the only folk in Combsburgh ministering to the spiritual and educational needs of the population, for Methodism was, by 1848, beginning to be a force in the parish. Indeed, there is in the fabric of the present chapel a stone perpetuating the memory of Myles Emsworth, a local haberdasher, who in that year qualified as a lay preacher.

To begin with, the local followers of the Methodist creed met in each others homes, then, in the 'hungry forties' when their members numbered about a score, they undertook the building of a chapel to seat 120. This lean-to structure lasted until about 1858, when the construction of the present chapel was put in hand, to be opened on Good Friday 1860. The Methodist Sabbath School had been founded ten years before, and just one year after that date the 'collections were liberal'. A record shows, 'The inhabitants of the place said we never saw it in this fashion before; we were left to wander and none cared for our souls; but now a brighter day has dawned for us.' This is a pleasantly worded and, no doubt, sincere statement, but must be balanced by the fact that Walter Henry was recording attendances in excess of 250 each Sunday in the parish church. The Methodists *were* nonetheless going from strength to strength, and noting that they listened to 'hearty, racy, cutting and unctuous speeches which surely would never be forgotten.' By 1861 there were 13 Sabbath school teachers and they taught 51 children.

In previous chapters we have seen how the ancient manor of Combsburgh had been partially enclosed as early as the fourteenth century, especially in the areas close to the market town, and how the bulk of the field structure had been established by the late sixteenth century. However, there remained in the 1850s several hundred acres of open land, particularly in the north of the parish near Dogbury Valent. A number of Acts permitting enclosure were passed by parliament in the eighteenth and nineteenth centuries, and the Combsburgh Enclosure Award (the granting of fields to be enclosed by people who, up to that time, had common grazing rights) was, in 1858, based on an Act of 1836. This legislation provided for the enclosure of certain types of open fields *without* private legislation, provided two-thirds of the interested parties agreed. The Combsburgh award was recorded in a document of 16 April 1858, engrossed on parchment and now in the keeping of the county archivist. All the folk having grazing rights according to the poor rate assessment of 1833 received their apportioned share of the fields, 'due consideration being given to the public carriage roads, drift ways and public halter paths or bridle ways through and over the [land] divided and enclosed.'

So it thus came about that the fields, meadows, pastures and arable acres of Combsburgh were finally taken in from the waste which had existed for millenia. The parish geographical and morphological infrastructure was complete. The changes which have since occurred have at worst been cosmetic, and at best commercial.

The year 1860 was, in effect, the end of a difficult time for Combsburgh. The years covered by this present chapter were broadly sad ones, so it is, for this author, a pleasure to be able to end on something of a light-hearted note. A recently discovered 'memoir' of an old bedridden resident has, for December 1860, the following: 'In an old house that was next to Mr Wagoner's shop near the Red Lion there lived a man by the name of C. . . . . ., who had been a gentleman's servant, but had lost his character and situation and was very lazy. One day he stole a sheep from a stall in the market. The constable traced the sheep to his house and found it hung up and dressed in his stable. He got five or seven years in gaol. Also one T. . . . . R. . . . . stole a cow and drove it to a distant market for sale. From this, Combsburgh men of that generation got a bad name for sheep stealing and cattle lifting and men from the next parish retaliated on them by nicknaming them Baa-Lambs.' The next parish was, in fact, Higher Piddle, and we may wonder what *their* men were called.

Appendix I
Publications of the Royal Commission on the Historical Monuments of England

Unless otherwise stated, all the publications listed are issued by Her Majesty's Stationery Office, Nine Elms Lane, London SW8 5DR. All inventories published up to the end of 1975 are available separately on microfiche from Chadwyck-Healey Limited, 20 Newmarket Road, Cambridge CB2 8DT.

Inventories	Date
Buckinghamshire	
I South	1912*
II North	1913*
Cambridgeshire	
City of Cambridge	1959*
I West	1968
II North-East	1972
Dorset	
I West	1952*
reprint with addendum	1974
II South-East	1970
III Central	1970
IV North	1972
V East	1975
Essex	
I North-West	1916*
II Central and South-West	1921*
III North-East	1922*
IV South-East	1923*
Gloucestershire	
Iron-Age and Romano-British Cotswolds	1977
Herefordshire	
I South-West	1931*
II East	1932*
III North-West	1934*

* = out of print

Hertfordshire			1910*
Huntingdonshire			1926*
Lincolnshire			
Town of Stamford			1977
London			
I	Westminster Abbey		1924*
II	West		1925*
III	Roman		1928*
IV	City		1929*
V	East		1930*
Middlesex			1937*
Northamptonshire			
I	North-East Archaeological Sites		1976
II	Central Archaeological Sites		1979
III	North-West Archaeological Sites		1981
IV	South-West Archaeological Sites		1982
V	Archaeological Sites and Churches in Northampton		1985
VI	North Architectural Monuments		1984
Oxfordshire			
City of Oxford			1939*
reprint			1967*
Westmorland			1936*
Wiltshire			
City of Salisbury I			1981
Yorkshire			
City of York	I	Roman	1962*
		reprint with addendum	1977
	II	Defences	1972
	III	South-West	1972
	IV	East	1975
	V	Central	1981

Occasional publications

Hampton Court Palace	1938*
St Albans Cathedral Guide	1952*
revised edition	1982

A Matter of Time: archaeological survey	1960*
Monuments Threatened or Destroyed	1963*
Monuments Threatened or Destroyed (1963-74),	1975*
interim report only	
Newark on Trent: Civil War Siegeworks	1964*
Peterborough New Town	1969*
Shielings and Bastles	1970*
York Minster Central Tower sculpture	1972*
reprint	1981
York Minster Chapter House	1974*
reprint	1981
York Castle (offprint from City of York II)	1973*
reprint	1981
Sherborne Abbey (addendum to Dorset I)	1975*
English Vernacular Houses	1975*
reprint	1980
Long Barrows in Hampshire and the Isle of Wight	1979
Survey of Surveys	1979*
Survey of Bedfordshire: Brickmaking	1979
(published by Bedfordshire County Council)	
Survey of Bedfordshire: Roman Period	1984
(published by Bedfordshire County Council)	
Stonehenge and its Environs	1979
(published by Edinburgh University Press)	
York: Historic Buildings in the Central Area	1981
Excavation of Garton and Wetwang Slack	1981
(published by RCHME) microfiche only	
Photographing Historic Buildings	1983
Rockbourne Roman Villa	1983*
(offprint from *Archaeological Journal* 140)	
Industry and the Camera	1985
Excavations at York Minster II:	1985
Cathedral of Archbishop Thomas of Bayeux	
Nonconformist Chapels and Meeting-houses in Central England	1986
Nonconformist Chapels and Meeting-houses — Inventory fascicules:	
Buckinghamshire	1986
Derbyshire	1986
Gloucestershire	1986
Hereford, Worcestershire & Warwickshire	1986
Leicestershire, Nottinghamshire & Rutland	1986
Northamptonshire & Oxfordshire	1986
Shropshire & Staffordshire	1986
The Archaeology of the Uplands: A Rapid Assessment of	1986
Archaeological Knowledge and Practice	
(published by RCHME & CBA)	
Churches of South-East Wiltshire	1987

Houses of the North York Moors	1987
Stained Glass in England 1180-1540	1987
Roman and Anglian York: historical map and guide (published by RCHME, Ordnance Survey & York Archaeological Trust)	1988
Viking and Medieval York: historical map and guide (published by RCHME, Ordnance Survey & York Archaeological Trust)	1988
Wilton House and English Palladianism	

Supplementary series

1	Liverpool Road Station, Manchester (published by Manchester University Press)	1980
2	Northamptonshire: Archaeological Atlas (published by RCHME)	1980
3	Early Industrial Housing: the Trinity Area of Frome	1981
4	Beverley: an archaeological and architectural study	1982
5	The Pottery Kilns of Roman Britain	1984
6	Danebury: An Iron Age Hillfort in Hampshire (published by RCHME)	1984
7	Liverpool's Historic Waterfront	1984
8	Rural Houses of West Yorkshire 1400-1830	1986
9	Workers' Housing in West Yorkshire 1750-1920	1986
10	Rural Houses of the Lancashire Pennines 1560-1760	1985

National Monuments Record Photographic Archives

Hotels and Restaurants: 1830 to the present day	1981
Buildings for the Age: New Building Types 1900-1939	1982
The Garden Room	1982
Farms in England: Prehistoric to Present	1983
Yesterday's Gardens	1983
London's Bridges	1983

OPPOSITE *The History does not cover Wales and Monmouthshire. Material collected for Northumberland was transferred to the County History Committee, who subsequently published a history of the county. A volume on the city of York has been published, in addition to the county volumes. Of the uncompleted counties the following have had general volumes published: Cheshire, Cornwall, Cumberland, Derbyshire, Devon, Dorset, Kent, Lincolnshire, Norfolk, Nottinghamshire, Suffolk, and Yorkshire (West Riding). In addition, some topographical volumes have been published for Cambridgeshire, Durham, Essex, Gloucester, Leicestershire, Northamptonshire, Oxfordshire, Shropshire, Somerset, Staffordshire, Sussex, Wiltshire, and Yorkshire (East Riding). In the following counties more than half the parish histories have been published: Cambridgeshire, Middlesex, Oxfordshire, and Sussex. It should be noted that Middlesex has, broadly speaking, been completed, the exception being the 'inner' portion of that county.*

Appendix II

The status of the Victoria County History programme

The map below shows the current status of the *Victoria History of the Counties of England* (based on the county boundaries prior to the legislation of 1972).

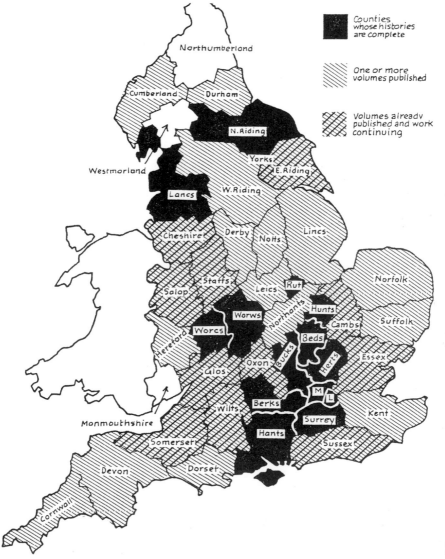

Counties whose histories are complete

One or more volumes published

Volumes already published and work continuing

Appendix III
Addresses

This appendix contains the addresses of the specialist archives described in Chapter 32, and the addresses of organisations and societies mentioned in the other chapters. In addition, it identifies further bodies which may be of use to the local historian. It does not give the addresses of local authority record offices (other than those housing special collections), for these are readily available on enquiry through the town or county hall, or from British Telecom.

Ancient Monuments Society, St Andrew-by-the-Wardrobe, Queen Victoria Street, London EC4
Antiquarian Booksellers Association, 31 Great Ormond Street, London WC1
Arkwright Society (industrial history), Tawney House, Matlock Green, Matlock, Derbyshire
Arms and Armour Society, 30 Alderney Street, London SW1
Army Ogilby Trust, Connaught Barracks, Duke of Connaught Road, Aldershot, Hampshire GU11 2LR
Ashmolean Museum, Beaumont Street, Oxford
Association for Industrial Archaeology, The Wharfage, Ironbridge, Telford, Shropshire
Avon County Reference Library, College Green, Bristol, Avon BS1 5TL

Baptist Historical Society, 4 Southampton Row, London WC1
Baptist Union Library, at the Angus Library, Regents Park College, Oxford
Bethlem Royal Hospital, Monks Orchard Road, Beckenham, Kent BR3 3BX
Birmingham Reference Library, Chamberlain Square, Birmingham, B3 3HQ
Bodleian Library, Oxford OX1 3BG

Borthwick Institute of Historical Research, University of York, St Anthonys Hall, Peasholme Green, York YO1 2PW

Brewery History Society, 10 Ringstead Court, Sutton, Surrey

British Agricultural History Society, Museum of Rural Life, Whiteknights, University of Reading, Berkshire

British Archaeological Association, 61 Old Park Ridings, Winchmore Hill, London N21

British Archaeological Trust (rescue archaeology), 304 Eddison House, Grove End Road, London NW8

British Architectural Library, 66 Portland Place, London W1N 4AD

British Association for Local History, Shopwyke Hall, Chichester, West Sussex PO20 6BQ

British Library, Great Russell Street, London WC1B 3DG

British Library of Political & Economic Science, University of London, 10 Portugal Street, London WC2A 2HD

British Museum, Bloomsbury, London WC1B 3DG

British Record Society, Department of History, The University, Keele, Staffordshire ST5 5BG

British Records Association, Master's Court, The Charterhouse, Charterhouse Square, London EC1M 6AU

British Steel Corporation, Record Services Section, 33 Grosvenor Place, London SW1

British Telecom Museum, Baynard House, 135 Queen Victoria St, London EC4V 4AT

Brynmor Jones Library, University of Hull, Cottingham Rd, Hull, Humberside HU6 7RX

Burke's Peerage, Eden Street, Kingston-upon-Thames, Surrey

Business Archives Council, 185 Tower Bridge Road, London SE1

Cambridge Record Office, Shire Hall, Castle Hill, Cambridge CB3 0AP

Canterbury & York Society, 79 Whitewell Way, Cambridge CB3 7PW

Catholic Archives Society, 4a Polstead Road, Oxford

Catholic Record Society, 114 Mount Street, London WC2Y 6AH

Centre for English Cultural Tradition & Language, University of Sheffield, Sheffield

Charity Commission, 14 Ryder Street, London SW1Y 6AH

Charity Commission (Liverpool), Graeme House, Derby Square, Liverpool L2 7SB

Chester City Record Office, The Town Hall, Chester CH1 2HJ

Chetham's Library, Long Millgate, Manchester M3 1SB

Christ's Hospital, 33 Bath Street, Abingdon, Oxfordshire

Church Monuments Society, c/o Royal Armories, H.M. Tower of London, London EC3N 4AB

City of Manchester Archives Department, Manchester Central Library, St Peter's Square, Manchester M2 5PD

Close Society (map study), The Map Library, British Library, Great Russell Street, London WC1B 3DG

College of Arms, Queen Victoria Street, London EC4V 4BT

Corporation of London Records Office, Guildhall, London EC2P 2EJ

Costume Society, c/o Court Dress Collection, Kensington Palace, London W8 4PX

Costume Society, 251 Popes Lane, London W5

Costume & Fashion Research Centre, Bath Museums Service, 4 The Circus, Bath, Avon BA1 2EW
Council for British Archaeology, 112 Kennington Road, London SE11
Council for the Care of Churches, 83 London Wall, London EC2M 5NA
Countryside Commission, John Dower House, Crescent Place, Cheltenham, Gloucester
Cumbria Record Office, The Castle, Carlisle, Cumbria CA3 8UR
Customs & Excise *see* Her Majesty's Customs & Excise

Dean & Chapter Library, Durham College, Durham DH1 3EH
Debrett's Peerage, 56 Walton Street, London W3
Department of Palaeography *see* Durham University
Department of the Environment, 2 Marsham Street, London SW1
Derbyshire Library Service, Corporation Street, Chesterfield, Derbyshire S41 7TY
Derbyshire Record Office, Matlock, Derbyshire DE4 3AG
Devon Library Services, Exeter Central Library, Castle St, Exeter, Devon EX4 3PQ
Devon Record Office, Castle Street, Exeter, Devon EX4 3PQ
Devonshire Collection, Chatsworth, Bakewell, Derbyshire DE4 1PP
Doncaster Central Library, Waterdale, Doncaster, South Yorkshire DN1 3JE
Dr Williams's Library, 14 Gordon Square, London WC1H 0AG
Duchy of Cornwall Office, 10 Buckingham Gate, London SW1E 6LA
Dudley Local History Department, St James's Rd, Dudley, West Midlands DY1 1HR
Duke of Norfolk's Archive, Arundel Castle, Arundel, West Sussex BN18 9AB
Duke of Northumberland's Archive, The Estate Office, Alnwick Castle, Alnwick, Northumberland
Durham Record Office, County Hall, Durham DH1 5UL
Durham University (Dept of Palaeography), 5 The College, Durham DH1 3EQ

Early English Text Society, Lady Margaret Hall, Oxford
East Sussex Record Office, Pelham House, St Andrews Lane, Lewes, E Sussex BN7 1UN
Ecclesiastical History Society, Dept of History, Birkbeck College, Malet St, London WC1
Economic History Society, London School of Economics, Houghton St, London WC2
English Folk Dance & Song Society, Cecil Sharp House, 2 Regents Park Rd, London NW1
English Heritage, Fortress House, 23 Savile Row, London W1
English Place Names Society, University College, Gower Street, London WC1
English Surnames Series, Department of Local History, University of Leicester, Leicester
Exeter Cathedral Library, Bishop's Palace, Exeter, Devon EX1 1HX

Fawcett Library, Old Castle Street, London E1 7NT
Fitzwilliam Museum, Trumpington Street, Cambridge CB2 1RB
Folklore Society, University College, Gower Street, London WC1E 6BT
Friends Historical Society, Friends House, Euston Road, London NW1
Friends of Fashion *see*, Museum of London
Furniture History Society, Victoria & Albert Museum, London SW7

Garden History Society, 12 Charlbury Road, Oxford

Gateshead Central Library, Prince Consort Road, Gateshead, Tyne & Wear
General Register Office *see* Office of Population Censuses
Geological Society, Burlington House, Piccadilly, London W1V 0JU
Gloucester Collection, Gloucester Library, Brunswick Road, Gloucester GL1 1HT
Greater Manchester Record Office, 56 Marshall Street, New Cross, Ancoats, Manchester M4 5FU
Guildhall Library, Aldermanbury, London EC2P 2EJ

Harleian Society *see* The College of Arms
Harrow School Library, 5 High Street, Harrow-on-the-Hill, Middlesex HA1 3HP
Hatfield House Library, Hatfield House, Hatfield, Hertfordshire
Heraldry Society, 44/45 Museum Street, London WC1
Heralds' Museum, H.M. Tower of London, London EC3N 4AB
Hereford Cathedral Library, The Cathedral, Hereford, HR1 2NG
Her Majesty's Customs & Excise, The Library, King's Beam House, Mark Lane, London EC3R 7HE
Her Majesty's Stationery Office (HMSO), 49 High Holborn, London WC1V 6HB
Historical Association, 59a Kennington Park Road, London SE11 4JH
Historic Churches Preservation Trust, Fulham Palace, London SW6
Historic Houses Association, 38 Ebury Street, London SW1
History of Education Society, University of London, Institute of Education, 20 Bedford Way, London WC1
House of Lords Record Office, Westminster, London SW1A 0PW
Huguenot Library, University College, Gower Street, London WC1E 6BT
Huguenot Society, 67 Victoria Road, London W8

Independent Methodist Churches Historical Society, Providence Independent Methodist Church, Albert Road, Colne, Lancashire
Institute of Agricultural History *see* University of Reading
Institute of Archaeology (conservation of historic buildings), 31-34 Gordon Square, London WC1
Institute of Dialect & English Folk Life Studies, School of English, University of Leeds, Leeds
Institute of Geological Studies, Exhibition Road, London SW7 2DE
Institute of Heraldic & Genealogical Studies, 80 Northgate, Canterbury, Kent CT1 1RB
Institute of Historical Research (*Victoria County History*), University of London, Senate House, London WC1
Insurance History Society, c/o Chartered Insurance Institute, 20 Aldermanbury, London EC2
Ironbridge Gorge Museum, The Wharfage, Iron Bridge, Telford, Shropshire TF8 7AW

Jewish Historical Society, University College, Gower Street, London WC1
Jews' College London, 44a Albert Road, London NW4
John Rylands Library, University of Manchester, Deansgate, Manchester M3 3EH

Keele University Library, Keele, Staffordshire ST5 5BG

Kidderminster Library, Market St, Kidderminster, Hereford & Worcester DY10 1AD

Lambeth Palace Library, Lambeth Palace Road, London SE1 7JU
Leeds Archives Department, Chapeltown Road, Sheepscar, Leeds LS7 3AP
Leeds Diocesan Library, Diocesan Curia, 13 North Grange Road, Leeds LS6 2BR
List & Index Society, Public Record Office, Ruskin Avenue, Kew, Surrey TW9 4DU
Liverpool City Libraries, William Brown Street, Liverpool L3 8EW
Local Population Studies Centre, 17 Rosebery Square, Rosebery Av, London EC1
Local Population Studies Society, Department of Anthropology, University of Durham,
    43 Old Elvet, Durham
Lord Chamberlain's Office, St James's Palace, London SW1A 1BG

Merseyside County Archive Service, Merseyside County Museums, RCA Building,
    64-66 Islington, Liverpool L3 8LG
Methodist Archives & Research Centre *see* John Rylands Library
Middlesex Polytechnic Collection, Bounds Green Road, London N11 2NQ
Military History Society, Duke of York's Headquarters, London SW3
Modern Records Centre, University of Warwick Library, Coventry, West Midlands
    CV4 7AL
Monumental Brass Society, The Society of Antiquaries, Burlington House, Piccadilly,
    London W1V 0HS
Museum of London, 150 London Wall, London EC2

National Association of Decorative & Fine Arts Societies (NADFAS), 38 Ebury Street,
    London SW1W 0LU
National Association of Mining History Organisations, 30 Main Street, Sutton via
    Keighley, Yorkshire
National Maritime Museum, Romney Road, Greenwich, London SE10 9NF
National Meteorological Archive, Meteorological Office Met 0 18e, Eastern Road,
    Bracknell, Berkshire RG12 2UR
National Monuments Record *see* Royal Commission on Historical Monuments
National Museum of Labour History, Limehouse Town Hall, Commercial Road,
    London E14
National Railway Museum Library, Leeman Road, York YO2 4XJ
National Register of Archives, Quality Court, London WC2A 1HP
National Trust, 36 Queen Anne's Gate, London SW1
Navy Records Society, Royal Naval College, Greenwich, London SE10
North Western Museum of Science & Industry, 97 Grosvenor St Manchester M1 7HF

Office of Population Censuses & Surveys, General Register Office, St Catherine's
    House, 10 Kingsway, London WC2B 6JP
Oral History Society, Department of Sociology, University of Essex, Wivenhoe Park,
    Colchester, Essex
Order of St John Library & Museum, St John's Gate, Clerkenwell, London EC1M
    4DA
Ordnance Survey (all branches), Romsey Road, Maybush, Southampton SO9 4DH

Phillimore & Co.Ltd (specialists in local history publications), Shopwyke Hall, Chichester, Sussex

Pipe Roll Society, c/o Public Record Office, Chancery Lane, London WC2 1AH

Police History Society, c/o Norfolk Constabulary, Martineall Lane, Norwich, Norfolk

Port of London Authority, London Dock House, 1 Thomas More St, London E1 9AZ

Post Office Archives, P.O. Headquarters Building, St Martin's-le-Grand, London EC1A 1HQ

Postal History Society, Lower Street Farmhouse, Hildenborough, Tonbridge, Kent

Prehistoric Society, Department of Prehistoric & Romano-British Antiquities, British Museum, London WC1B 3DG

Principal Registry of the Family Division, Somerset House, Strand, London WC2R 1LP

Printing Historical Society, St Bride's Institute, Bride Lane, Fleet Street, London EC4

Public Record Office, Chancery Lane, London WC2 1AH

Public Record Office, Kew, Richmond, Surrey TW9 4DU

Public Record Office, Portugal Street, London WC2

Queen Mary College, University of London, Mile End Road, London E1 4NS

Railway & Canal Historical Society, 64 Grove Avenue, London W7

Roman Military Research Society, Midfield Court, Thorplands, Northampton

Royal Commission on Historical Manuscripts, Quality House, Quality Court, Chancery Lane, London WC2A 1HP

Royal Commission on Historical Monuments (National Monuments Record), Fortress House, 23 Savile Row, London W1X 2HE

Royal Geographical Society, 1 Kensington Gore, London SW7 2AR

Royal Historical Society, University College, Gower Street, London WC1

Rugby School Temple Reading Room, Barby Road, Rugby

St George's Chapel, Dean's Cloister, Windsor Castle, Windsor, Berkshire SL4 1NJ

Science Museum, Exhibition Road, London SW7

Sheffield University Library, Western Bank, Sheffield S10 2TN

Sidney Jones Library, University of Liverpool, P.O. Box 123, Liverpool L69 3DA

Society for Army Historical Research, National Army Museum, Royal Hospital Road, London SW3

Society for Medieval Archaeology, University College, Gower Street, London WC1

Society for Post-Medieval Archaeology, The Museum of London, London Wall, London EC2

Society for the Social History of Medicine, 47 Banbury Road, Oxford

Society for Study of Labour History, Department of Social & Economic History, University of Sheffield, Sheffield

Society for the Promotion of Roman Studies, 31-34 Gordon Square, London WC1

Society of Antiquaries of London, Burlington House, Piccadilly, London W1V 0HS

Society of Architectural Historians, 2nd Floor Chesham House, 30 Warwick Street, London W1

Society of Friends Library, Friends House, Euston Road, London NW1 2BJ

Society of Genealogists, 14 Charterhouse Buildings, London EC1M 7BA
Society of Jesus Archive and Library, 114 Mount Street, London W1Y 6AH
Spalding Gentlemen's Society, The Museum, Broad Street, Spalding, Lincolnshire
Strict Baptist Historical Society, 26 Denmark Street, Bedford
Surrey Record Office, Guildford Muniment Room, Guildford, Surrey GU1 3SX
Surrey Record Office, County Hall, Penrhyn Rd, Kingston-on-Thames, Surrey KT1 2DN

Thames Water Authority, New River Head, Rosebery Avenue, Clerkenwell, London EC1R 4TP
Thirties Society, 3 Park Street West, London NW1
Tramway Museum Society, National Tramway Museum, Crich, Matlock, Derbyshire
Transport Trust, Marylebone Station Offices, London NW1

Unitarian Historical Society, 8 Tavistock Place, London WC1
United Reform Church History Society, 84 Tavistock Place, London WC1H 9RT
University of Bath Library, Claverton Down, Bath, Avon BA2 7AY
University of East Anglia Library, Norwich, Norfolk NR4 7TJ
University of London Library, Senate House, Malet Street, London WC1
University of Reading (Museum of Rural Life), Whiteknights, Reading, Berkshire RG6 2AG
University of Sussex Library, Falmer, Brighton, East Sussex BN1 9QL

Veterinary History Society, 32 Belgrave Square, London SW1
Victoria & Albert Museum, Cromwell Road, South Kensington, London SW7 2RL
Victorian Society, 1 Priory Gardens, London W4

Wellcome Institute for the History of Medicine, 183 Euston Road, London NW1
Wesley Historical Society, 34 Spicelands Road, Northfield, Birmingham
Westminster City Libraries, Victoria Library, Buckingham Palace Rd, London SW1W 9UD
Westminster Diocesan Archive, Archbishop's House, Ambrosden Avenue, London SW1P 1QJ
West Yorkshire Record Office, Registry of Deeds, Wakefield, W Yorkshire WF1 2DE
Wiltshire Library & Museum Service, Bythesea Rd, Trowbridge, Wiltshire BA14 8BS
Winchester College Archives, Winchester College, Winchester, Hampshire SO23 9NA

York Minster Archives, York Minster Library, Deans Park, York YO1 2JD

Index

Numbers in italics refer to illustrations.